ON THE POETRY OF ALLEN GINSBERG

UNDER DISCUSSION
David Lehman, General Editor
Donald Hall, Founding Editor

Volumes in the Under Discussion series collect reviews and essays about individual poets. The series is concerned with contemporary American and English poets about whom the consensus has not yet been formed and the final vote has not been taken. Titles in the series include:

On the Poetry of
Allen Ginsberg

Edited by Lewis Hyde

Ann Arbor

THE UNIVERSITY OF MICHIGAN PRESS

Copyright © by the University of Michigan 1984
All rights reserved
Published in the United States of America by
The University of Michigan Press
Manufactured in the United States of America
⊛ Printed on acid-free paper

2002   2001   2000   1999   6 5 4 3

Photo credits: p. 9—Harry Redl; p. 181—Ettore Sottsass;
p. 317—Steve Groer (courtesy *Rocky Mountain News*);
p. 365—Marc Trivier.

Library of Congress Cataloging in Publication Data
Main entry under title:

On the poetry of Allen Ginsberg.

   (Under discussion)
   Bibliography: p.
   1. Ginsberg, Allen, 1926–   —Criticism and interpretation—Addresses,
essays, lectures. I. Ginsberg, Allen, 1926–   . II. Hyde, Lewis, 1945–   .
III. Series.
PS3513.I74Z82   1984   811'.54   84-13000
ISBN 0-472-09353-3
ISBN 0-472-06353-7 (pbk.)

Contents

Introduction

To introduce a collection of responses to a poet's work is to come only a few syllables shy of the twilight of American letters as prophesied by H. L. Mencken, "criticism of criticism of criticism." But I want, at least, to offer the readers and browsers of this volume a map of its high points and a sense of its omissions, of the work that remains to be done.

When *Howl and Other Poems* appeared in 1956 it must have seemed to many to have sprung without background, the spontaneous utterance of an unlettered young Bohemian. But Allen Ginsberg was thirty years old at the time; he had earned a bachelor's degree from Columbia University, had studied and fought with and troubled its dons (Lionel Trilling and Mark Van Doren in particular), had sought out teachers of his own beyond the walls of the academy (most notably William Carlos Williams), and had read until he found a usable past, a literary tradition to inform his sensibility (Smart, Melville, Blake, and others). Ginsberg had been dedicated to his calling for over a decade when *Howl* appeared, and though it was the first to be published, it was his third collection of poems, each written in a style distinct from that of its predecessor.

"I greet you at the beginning of a great career, which yet must have had a long foreground somewhere, for such a start." Thus, Emerson to Whitman 101 years before *Howl*. A good portion of the most useful work we have on Ginsberg's poetry has come from those who have charted *his* long foreground. In the summer of 1948, lying on his bed in Spanish Harlem, Ginsberg heard what he took to be the voice of William Blake speak a series of poems to him. In *The Visionary Poetics of Allen Ginsberg* (parts of which are excerpted here), Paul Portugés demonstrates how the progression of styles in Ginsberg's first three collections reflects an extended search for a "poetics of vision," for a way of writing which would allow him to communicate states of awareness such as he had known during his Blake experience.

Ginsberg once spoke of "Howl" as a "homage to Cézanne's method," and in a separate essay here Portugés shows us the path that led from Blake to Cézanne, indicating which commentaries on Cézanne's work and which of his paintings and letters find their homage finally in the method of "Howl." Bruce Hunsberger has done a similar piece of work on Christopher Smart. Smart's "madness" and especially his long poem *Jubilate Agno* also find obeisance in the early Ginsberg, and, by the simple act of placing side by side lines from Smart and lines from "Howl," Hunsberger highlights the similarities in both their form and purpose.

Our view of the tradition out of which Ginsberg's work emerges has been given depth by several essays which touch on how he *differs* from his progenitors. As Louis Simpson makes clear, for example, Ginsberg was hardly a slavish student of Williams. "Williams was a pragmatist," writes Simpson, "and nowhere admits of any visionary or hallucinated speech," which of course is exactly the kind of speech that Ginsberg grafted onto the good doctor's wheelbarrows and newspaper clippings. And as both Allen Grossman and Czeslaw Milosz point out, Ginsberg may have gone back to Whitman for the long line, and he may share Whitman's longing for a collective marked by tenderness, but his temperament and his vision are distinct from Whitman's. He is much more melancholy, for one thing, and in the American city or (to put it generally) in the creations of the collective which Whitman loved for their expansiveness and bustle, Ginsberg discerns as often the grotesque face of a devouring god.

The context out of which Ginsberg's work emerged is reflected in two different sorts of materials collected here. Scattered among the traditional commentaries on the biographical, political, cultural, and spiritual setting of the work, readers will find documents that are not so much reflections of that setting as evidences of it. A number of reviews are reprinted here more because they recall the flavor of the times than because they offer any insight into the work. Two reports—one early and one late—from *Time* magazine, and a selection of documents culled from Ginsberg's massive government files serve to show that at least some of Ginsberg's obsessions have adequate bases in fact. (In 1956 he worries that *Time* will lecture him about responsibility and two years later they dutifully deliver the lecture; like his mother before him he worries that the FBI will plot the repression of his joy, and they, dutifully, acquire and place in a "locked sealed envelope" [!] a photograph of him "in an indecent pose.") Diana Trilling's motherly report ("I was curiously pleased for him") of the reading that Ginsberg and his friends gave at Columbia in 1959 is reprinted here not for its attempt to place a poet in his times but as a sample of the prevailing sensibility to which a young man might turn for counsel when he thought he had been summoned to poetry by the voices of the dead. And Timothy Leary's memoir of the day he gave Ginsberg hallucinogenic mushrooms manages to bring back the simple enthusiasm, the shared messianic hopes, of the early sixties.

As for those essays that comment directly on the context of Ginsberg's poetry, many are best seen as attempts to differentiate and describe the relationship between the public and private portions of his voice. Does his "Kaddish" bespeak a son's grief at his mother's death, or is it a Jew's grief after the Second World War, or is it both? M. L. Rosenthal, comparing Ginsberg to Robert Lowell, writes that each man's family life "strikes us as unique, yet leaves us with the uneasy sense that far more misery is endemic to our contemporary existence than we usually allow ourselves to acknowledge. Implicit in the work of both poets is the idea of liberation through perfect candor. . . ." The work is a private lyric which strikes a public chord. And yet Charles Molesworth, taking up the same comparison, finds that both Lowell and Ginsberg come to their fullest voices when the public events that trouble them turn into "private musings." The work is a political poetry enriched by its roots in the private.

George Dennison cites an observation about Gandhi which breaks up this polarity:

Nothing can make a man feel so much at home in the world as to realize that not only the role he has created for himself has value for his time, but that his very being, his whole underground, unconscious, instinctual life also belongs, in its most private aspect, without shame, to the universe of man. There is bound to be joy in this, and an end to the usual loneliness.

Allen Ginsberg's poetry has been both important and enduring in part because it moves back and forth so effectively between the public and the private. Any number of essays here may be taken as meditations on that fact: James Breslin's excellent evocation of the biographical origins of "Howl" and "Kaddish," Allen Grossman's reflections on Ginsberg as a post-Holocaust Jewish poet, Louis Simpson's meditation on the post-Modernist writer in the bureaucratic state, and Warren Tallman's essay on what might be called the "geography of self-acceptance" (in a nation settled from the east, a poet with a censorious father will write his "Sunflower Sutra" on the west coast).

Ginsberg has always been interested in politics. His mother took her child to political meetings as other mothers might take theirs to the seashore or the park. At age thirty-two, as Paul Berman remarks, he traveled to India on a spiritual quest, "only to find himself on shipboard daydreaming about forming a new political party to oppose Adlai Stevenson." He has been the object of surveillance by the government in this country and of actual harrassment in others. (In Cuba, among other mistakes, he unfortunately asked about a rumor that Raúl Castro was gay and offered the opinion that Che Guevara was "cute." The authorities flew him out of the country. One spring in Prague the students elected him King of the May. And the authorities. . . .) His politics is not exactly party politics, as these anecdotes indicate. The first time he took part in a demonstration—a 1963 picket protesting a visit to this country by Madame Nhu—the sign he carried did not say "Death to Madame Nhu," or even "Free Vietnam," it said, "I am here saying seek mutual surrender tears / That there be no more hell in Vietnam / That I not be in hell here in the street / War is black magic. . . ." Such politics, as Floyce Alexander suggests, is Norman O. Brown's "metapolitics," or, as James Heffernan has it, it is the politics of Blake in which psychological freedom is the only sure warrant of political freedom. (Shepherd Bliss's memoir of being a soldier

4

stationed in Kansas and hearing Ginsberg read his poems may be the best testimony here that poetry is the appropriate vehicle of such politics.)

We have as yet no full account of Ginsberg as a political poet, these essays notwithstanding, and if our response to this portion of his work has been spotty it is probably because his politics takes its shape from his spiritual concerns, and it is in this last that we shall find its meaning. Kenneth Rexroth was the first to name publically the tradition within which Ginsberg's early writing lies. During the 1957 obscenity trial of *Howl* the defense attorney asked Rexroth to identify the "nature" of the book under indictment, and he replied:

> The simplest term for such writing is prophetic; it is easier to call it that than anything else because we have a large body of prophetic writing to refer to. These are the prophets of the Bible, which it greatly resembles in purpose and in language and in subject matter.

One detail of Ginsberg's initial interpretation of his Blake experience deserves attention in this regard. All cultures provide their citizens with mythologies by which to organize even their deepest experiences; Ginsberg's response to his calling was Western and traditional to the core:

> This was the moment I was born for, this initiation . . . , this consciousness of being alive unto myself, alive myself unto the Creator. As the son of the Creator—who loved me, I realized, or who responded to my desire. . . .

There is a God, Creator of the universe, whose Son, a messiah, a prophet, has been born on earth. To write prophetic poetry, as Ginsberg himself has explained, does not mean to announce that a bomb is going to explode next Tuesday; it means to speak of what will be true in the future because it is true in eternity, in all time. It is entirely possible therefore to write a nontheistic prophetic poetry, but Ginsberg's early work is not prophetic in that spare sense. The epithets by which his critics speak of that work—a vatic poetry, the messianic tradition, and so forth—

refer not only to the style of the work but to its motive. To overstate the case only a little, Ginsberg put himself in the service of God and His angels. At the time of the Blake visions, he says, he felt "an inner / anterior image / of divinity / beckoning [him] out / to pilgrimage." He spoke of a "future, unimaginable God" and undertook to reimagine that deity for his people.

This phase of Ginsberg's work has been well discussed. Fred Moramarco has given us a close reading of the poem from which these lines are taken, "Siesta in Xbalba," and from several others (Paul Portugés and John Tytell most notably) we have readings of the texture of Ginsberg's labors in the "messianic tradition." Paul Carroll noticed early on that what others took to be "drug poems" at the end of *Kaddish*—"Lysergic Acid" and the aya-huasca series—were in fact "pentecostal." "Ginsberg wrestles with the Godhead—the first American writer to do so since Melville."

What we are missing, unfortunately, is the second half of this story. During a 1963 trip to Israel, India, and Japan, Ginsberg slowly abandoned his gods and their adjunct devils and angels. Commenting recently on the poems in *Howl,* he tells us that "at the time I believed in some sort of God and thus Angels, and religiousness—at present as Buddhist I see an awakened emptiness (*Śūnyatā*) as the crucial term. No God, no Self, not even great Whitman's universal Self. . . ." Ginsberg's critics have tended either to pass over his Buddhism or to dismiss it. (Reed Whittemore, for example, belittles Ginsberg's interest in the East as a "kind of cheaply acquired religious experience—hop the plane, get the drugs. . . .") But to ignore the shift from a Judeo-Christian theism to a Buddhist atheism is to miss the most important distinctions between Ginsberg's early and recent work.

Because the system of belief catalyzed by the Blake experience included much besides God and His angels. It included a premonition of impending apocalypse both private and public, a wrestling with death as if death might be overcome, a sense of obligation to break down ordinary consciousness, and an attachment to drugs as the means to that end. It included also the subtle lack of self-acceptance which lies hidden in a belief in exterior powers from whom acceptance might be won, and a subtle rejection of the body made evident by years spent "wandering in various alternative possible metaphysical universes," as Ginsberg once put it, rather than sitting at home, an ordinary mind in a mortal body in a human universe.

The shift away from this complex of ideas and attitudes (a slow shift over many years but marked by "The Change," written in July of 1963) includes, therefore, Ginsberg's abandoning his interpretation of and attachment to his vision, a lessening of his programmatic interest in drugs, a return to the "human universe" and the body, and above all a move toward that Buddhism which asks the student to cling to neither the good nor the bad, to pay attention and learn from fears of death, and to abandon the struggle for self-acceptance for there is no Self.

We have, as I say, a fairly full account of the first half of this story but little has been said of the second. Several writers here touch on it—in a retrospective occasioned by the publication of Ginsberg's early journals, for example, Paul Berman muses on the dilemmas this shift has injected into Ginsberg's career (how does a public figure step away from "his persona as a visionary seer with a proven record?"). But on the whole we have little on Ginsberg's Buddhism, which means we have little sense of his maturation and little framework within which to appreciate the differences between, say, the politics of "Plutonian Ode" and those of the Moloch section of "Howl," or between the salutory stubbornness ("I refuse to give up my obsession") of the early poems and the salutory detachment of the recent work ("Which country is real, mine or the teacher's?"), between the frenzied sorrow of "Kaddish" and the melancholy quietude of the poems on the death of Ginsberg's father.

In sum, our response to Allen Ginsberg's work is remarkably full and quite unfinished. That we have such scant accounts of him as a political poet and as a practicing Buddhist seem to me the main omissions, but there are others. There is more to be done on the tradition out of which he comes (on his relationship to Pound, for example, or on his early interest in Plotinus). I have searched but found no really good essay on Ginsberg as a gay writer (though Charley Shively's reviews, included here, are a good beginning). To my surprise there has been little discussion or explication of Ginsberg's ideas on prosody. *Allen Ver-*

batim and *Composed on the Tongue,* his two books on method, have gone essentially unreviewed. His "spontaneous bop prosody" cannot be dismissed as a "simple inability to express anything in words," as Norman Podhoretz did in 1958. Ginsberg's prosody derives from specific and diverse sources (e.g., Gertrude Stein and jazz musicians) and is embedded in his philosophical and spiritual outlook (his sense of appropriate and inappropriate discipline—of the mind, of the body, and in the body politic—for example).

But perhaps such omissions are to be expected. Allen Ginsberg is still very much with us, as a poet and a teacher and a public figure, and he will be for years to come, we hope. His collected poems are only just being published. In five or ten years, when it comes time for another volume such as this one, I am sure that many of the gaps will have been filled in our response to this enduring and valuable voice.

Acknowledgments

Donald Hall kindly offered me the opportunity to assemble this collection. Bill Clark gave me access to valuable research materials. The staff of the Manuscript Reading Room in Butler Library, Columbia University, were patient and helpful as I sifted through the papers that Allen Ginsberg has deposited with them. Linda Howe not only copyedited the manuscript, but in so doing saved me from several grievous errors. Bob Rosenthal, Allen Ginsberg's secretary, gave me hours of his time. And Allen Ginsberg himself responded to all my queries, opened his library and his files, and then left me alone.

I wish to thank all authors, publishers, and institutions who have permitted me to reprint previously published material. Every effort has been made to secure permission for all copyrighted items in this volume.

My gratitude to all.

"I got high on Peyote . . . , wandered down Powell Street muttering 'Moloch Moloch' all night, and wrote 'Howl II' nearly intact in cafeteria at foot of Drake Hotel. . . ."

LETTERS OF INTRODUCTION

WILLIAM CARLOS WILLIAMS

A Letter to Marianne Moore

May 24, 1952

Dear Marianne:

Would you not or will you not see Allen Ginsberg. I'm instinctively drawn to him—I can't tell exactly why other than he has a clean, rigorously unrelenting mind that would do outstanding work if only the man can survive. I have a strange feeling of exceptional sensitivity that is almost lost. Well, see him if you can.

About being lost, there is much to be said from many many sources.

Best Luck,

Bill

MARIANNE MOORE

A Letter to Allen Ginsberg

July 4, 1952

Dear Mr. Ginsberg:

I have been thinking about this manuscript [*Empty Mirror*] which you left me. I am sad to find that it reflects hardship. You have ability, and that means responsibility, does it not? There are in writing, a few technicalities to think about; but the thing that matters is our sense of awareness; this comes first. What are we to do about it? I am not satisfied with your solution of the problem.

. . . In the opening piece . . . you say, "I wandered off in search of a toilet." And I go with you, remember. Do I have to? I do if you take me with you in your book. . . .

PATERSON: slobs and dumbells hardly sustain the Cru-cifixion metaphor.

THE TREMBLING OF THE VEIL: The suggestion of the moon makes this penetrating; brings it to life. (Though as with my own work, I am not so sure about taking others' words and titles.) . . .

"holding the dog with a frayed rope" [a line from "A Crazy Spiritual"]. I like this.

THE ARCHETYPE POEM: Are you for this? Is there any "universal principle" to be deduced?

"sweat, skin, feces, sperm, saliva, odor" [line from "The Night-Apple"]. My comment here is the same as for the first poem.

Previously unpublished.

13

THE NIGHT-APPLE: "Last night I dreamed / of one I loved." Why could you not go on with this in the way in which it starts? You betray us with a taunt; with an "I fooled you." This is wit with nothing spoiling it:

> I learned a world from each
> one whom I loved;
> so many worlds without
> a Zodiac.

The brick-layers' lunch hour is fine work, accurate, contagious—even if it is William C. Williams instead of (or as well as) Allen Ginsberg. . . .

Now you see, Mr. Ginsberg, that I am speaking to myself as well as to you, in the above comments. Let me, though I seem topheavy in doing it, try to think why the book as a whole dejected me. Patient or impatient repudiating of life, just repudiates itself. There is no point to it. What can be exciting to others is one's struggle with what is too hard. Unless one is improved by what hurts one, it can't be of interest to others. What makes us read a gruesome thing like Tolstoi's THE POWER OF DARKNESS or Gogol's A LODGING FOR A NIGHT or the Book of Job? We read it and thank it because it puts a weapon in our hands; we are the better able to deal with injustice and with a sense of "God's injustice." An understanding eye penetrated the dispiriting and called it dispiriting. If we share in the conspiracy against ourselves and call existence an insult, who cares what we write?

Your disgust worries me and I can't make clear what I mean without being objectionable. . . . EMPTY MIRROR is too literal, you don't get behind it. You don't see that it is? It is "treatment." It is your taste. . . . Something is wrong. What is it? The old hackneyed truism; affirm or die. If I feel negative, why can't I say I am? Why feign what I don't feel? I am not grateful. What would make me grateful? Soliloquize in this way over and over; people will not listen.* What can you do about it,

---

*Written in the margin: "Self-pity is bad, friend."—ED.

I don't know. As D. H. Lawrence said: "To hold on or to let go?" You see and feel with interest. Can't you be grateful for *that*? If not, not. *But try*.

Why do I say all this? Because your trials, your own realness, and capacity affect me. . . .

M. M.

MARIANNE MOORE

A Letter to Louis Ginsberg

July 11, 1952

I am grateful to you, Mr. Ginsberg, for your reassuring letter. It pained me to run the risk of perhaps estranging your son from wholesome pertinacity and humility by possibly ill-adjudged resistance to his manuscript. If I have persuaded him even somewhat toward "gratitude"—toward confidence in God or humanity—I am glad. . . .

Your son, from what you tell me, has reason for being tempted to melancholy. I had not known this. I have had experience, myself—have experienced the mystery of others' disability. As for William Carlos Williams, loyal though I feel to him personally, I wish he could perceive the folly of a doctrinaire attitude to degredation and unhope. We are here to transcend and help others transcend what impairs us. . . .

Sincerely yours,

Marianne Moore

Previously unpublished.

WILLIAM CARLOS WILLIAMS

From the Introduction to
Empty Mirror

. . . This young Jewish boy, already not so young any more, has recognized something that has escaped most of the modern age, he has found that man is lost in the world of his own head. And that the rhythms of the past have become like an old field long left unploughed and fallen into disuse. In fact they are excavating there for a new industrial plant.

There the new inferno will soon be under construction.

A new sort of line, omitting memories of trees and watercourses and clouds and pleasant glades—as empty of them as Dante Alighieri's *Inferno* is empty of them—exists today. It is measured by the passage of time without accent, monotonous, useless—unless you are drawn as Dante was to see the truth, undressed, and to sway to a beat that is far removed from the beat of dancing feet but rather finds in the shuffling of human beings in all the stages of their day, the trip to the bathroom, to the stairs of the subway, the steps of the office or factory routine the mystical measure of their passions.

It is indeed a human pilgrimage, like Geoffrey Chaucer's; poets had better be aware of it and speak of it—and speak of it in plain terms, such as men will recognize. In the mystical beat of newspapers that no one recognizes, their life is given back to them in plain terms. Not one recognizes Dante there fully deployed. It is not recondite but plain.

Written 1952. First published in *Black Mountain Review,* no. 7 (Fall 1957).

And when the poet in his writing would scream of the crowd, like Jeremiah, that their life is beset, what can he do, in the end, but speak to them in their own language, that of the daily press?

At the same time, out of his love for them—a poet as Dante was a poet—he must use his art, as Dante used his art, to please. He must measure, he must so disguise his lines, that his style appear prosaic (so that it shall not offend) to go in a cloud.

With this, if it be possible, the hidden sweetness of the poem may alone survive and one day rouse the sleeping world. . . .

LOUIS SIMPSON

Going Beyond Williams

. . . Some of the poems in *Empty Mirror* are close imitations of
Williams:

> When I sit before a paper
>   writing my mind turns
> in a kind of feminine
>   madness of chatter . . .[1]

This might have been written by the old man himself. So might
the poem on a painting by Cézanne and the poem about trees:

> . . . I saw
> the scarlet-and-pink shoot-tips
> of budding leaves wave
>
> delicately in the sunlight,
> blown by the breeze,
> all the arms of the trees
> bending and straining downward
>
> at once when the wind
> pushed them.[2]

Ginsberg's poem about ". . . the girl / who proposed love to
me in the neon / light of the Park Avenue Drugstore," and who
died a few months later of "an unforeseen / brain malignancy,"
might have come from the typewriter Doc Williams kept in his
office, on which he wrote poetry between appointments.[3]

Reprinted with permission of Macmillan Publishing Co., Inc., from *A Revolution in Taste* (1978) by Louis Simpson.

19

Monotonous, Williams called these early poems by Ginsberg, and they are. *Empty Mirror* is an in-between book: Ginsberg has got rid of English conventions, is trying to be "objective" in the manner of Williams—"no ideas but in things." On the whole the effect is a drab, depressing realism.

Two poems, however, go beyond this. From his reading of Artaud and other Surrealists, Ginsberg saw that you could admit anything into the poem, however crazy it seemed. There was even a precedent for this in English literature, the psalms of Christopher Smart. Smart had included everything he knew in his locality together with the City of God; there was no dividing line of here and there, life and vision—everything that lives is holy.

Ginsberg tried writing like Smart. The poem, titled "Hymn," stands out from the drabness of *Empty Mirror:*

> No hyacinthine imagination can express this clock of
> meat bleakly pining for its sweet immaterial
> paradise which I have celebrated in one gone
> dithyramb after another and have elevated to
> that highest place in the mind's angelical empyrean
> which shall in the course of hot centuries to
> come come to be known as the clock of light . . . [4]

It is only a step from this to a poem that is absolutely Ginsberg's—the title, "Paterson"; the date, 1949:

> What do I want in these rooms papered with visions of money?
> How much can I make by cutting my hair? If I put new heels
> on my shoes
> bathe my body reeking of masturbation and sweat, layer upon
> layer of excrement
> dried in employment bureaus, magazine hallways, statistical
> cubicles, factory stairways,
> cloakrooms of the smiling gods of psychiatry;
> if in antechambers I face the presumption of department store
> supervisory employees,
> old clerks in their asylums of fat, the slobs and dumbbells of
> the ego with money and power

to hire and fire and make and break and fart and justify their
    reality of wrath
and rumor of wrath to wrath-weary man,
what war I enter and for what a prize! the dead prick of
    commonplace obsession,
harridan vision of electricity at night and daylight misery of
    thumb-sucking rage . . . [5]

With "Paterson" Ginsberg discovered his own voice. Though he would go on to write more impressive poems, "Paterson" signaled his emergence. Though he would play many variations, "Paterson" remains the touchstone of his style.

He has gone beyond Williams, the short line that Williams preferred, being a cautious man. The rhythms of Ginsberg's poem are a chant; the long, rushing lines overwhelm the listener and make him share the poet's emotion. Unlike Williams, too, is the language, ranging from mention of factory stairways to Golgotha. Williams was a pragmatist and nowhere in his writing admits any visionary or hallucinated speech. . . .

NOTES

1. Allen Ginsberg, *Empty Mirror* (New York: Corinth, 1961), p. 13.
2. Ibid., p. 15.
3. Ibid., p. 47.
4. Ibid., p. 32.
5. Ibid., p. 51.

HOWL IN THE 1950s

"What living and buried speech is always vibrating here, what howls restrain'd by decorum. . . ."

—*Walt Whitman*

RICHARD EBERHART

West Coast Rhythms

The West Coast is the liveliest spot in the country in poetry today. It is only here that there is a radical group movement of young poets. San Francisco teems with young poets. . . .

Part of the activity of the young group has been inspired by Kenneth Rexroth, whose presence in San Francisco over a long period of time, embodying his force and convictions, creates a rallying point of ideas, interest and informal occasions. The influence of Kenneth Patchen is also felt by this group. Robinson Jeffers looms as a timeless figure down the Coast. . . .

In the Bay region there are several poetry readings each week. They may be called at the drop of a hat. A card may read "Celebrated Good Time Poetry Night. Either you go home bugged or completely enlightened. Allen Ginsberg blowing hot; Gary Snyder blowing cool; Philip Whalen puffing the laconic tuba; Mike McClure his hip highnotes; Rexroth on the big brass drum. Small collection for wine and postcards . . . abandon, noise, strange pictures on walls, oriental music, lurid poetry. Extremely serious. Town Hall theatre. One and only final appearance of this apocalypse. Admission free."

Hundreds from about sixteen to thirty may show up and engage in an enthusiastic, freewheeling celebration of poetry, an analogue of which was jazz thirty years ago. The audience participates, shouting and stamping, interrupting and applauding. Poetry here has become a tangible social force, moving and unifying its auditors, releasing the energies of the audience through spoken, even shouted verse, in a way at present unique to this region.

From the *New York Times Book Review*, 2 September 1956. © 1956 by The New York Times Company. Reprinted by permission. Reprinted with background material in *To Eberhart from Ginsberg* (Lincoln, Mass.: Penmaen Press, 1976).

The Bay region group, by and large, is antiuniversity. Its members make a living at odd jobs. Ambiguity is despised, irony is considered weakness, the poem as a system of connotations is thrown out in favor of long-line denotative statements. Explicit cognition is enjoined. Rhyme is outlawed. Whitman is the only god worthy of emulation. These generalizations would probably not be allowed by all members of the group. They may serve, however, as indicators.

The most remarkable poem of the young group, written during the past year, is *Howl,* by Allen Ginsberg, a twenty-nine-year-old poet who is the son of Louis Ginsberg, a poet known to newspaper readers in the East. Ginsberg comes from Brooklyn; he studied at Columbia; after years of apprenticeship to usual forms, he developed his brave new medium. This poem has created a furor of praise or abuse whenever read or heard. It is a powerful work, cutting through to dynamic meaning. Ginsberg thinks he is going forward by going back to the methods of Whitman.

My first reaction was that it is based on destructive violence. It is profoundly Jewish in temper. It is Biblical in its repetitive grammatical buildup. It is a howl against everything in our mechanistic civilization which kills the spirit, assuming that the louder you shout the more likely you are to be heard. It lays bare the nerves of suffering and spiritual struggle. Its positive force and energy come from a redemptive quality of love, although it destructively catalogues evils of our time from physical deprivation to madness.

In other poems, Ginsberg shows a crucial sense of humor. It shows up principally in his poem "America," which has lines "Asia is rising against me. / I haven't got a chinaman's chance." Humor is also present in "Supermarket in California." His "Sunflower Sutra" is a lyric poem marked by pathos. . . .

JOHN HOLLANDER

Review of *Howl and Other Poems*

It is only fair to Allen Ginsberg . . . to remark on the utter lack
of decorum of any kind in his dreadful little volume. I believe
that the title of his long poem, "Howl," is meant to be a noun,
but I can't help taking it as an imperative. The poem itself is a
confession of the poet's faith, done into some 112 paragraphlike
lines, in the ravings of a lunatic friend (to whom it is dedicated),
and in the irregularities in the lives of those of his friends who
populate his rather disturbed pantheon. Here is the poem's
beginning:

I saw the best minds of my generation destroyed by madness,
    starving hysterical naked,
dragging themselves through the negro streets at dawn looking for
    an angry fix,
angelheaded hipsters burning for the ancient heavenly connection to
    the starry dynamo in the machinery of night,
who poverty and tatters and hollow-eyed and high sat up smoking
    in the supernatural darkness of cold-water flats floating
    across the tops of cities contemplating jazz,
who bared their brains to Heaven under the El and saw
    Mohammedan angels staggering on tenement roofs illuminated,
who passed through universities with radiant cool eyes hallucinating
    Arkansas and Blake-light tragedy among the scholars of war,
who were expelled from the academies for crazy publishing obscene
    odes on the windows of the skull . . .

This continues, sponging on one's toleration, for pages and
pages. A kind of climax was reached for me, in a long section of

From *Partisan Review* (Spring 1957). Reprinted with permission.

screams about "Moloch!", at a rare point of self-referential lucidity: "Dreams! adorations! illuminations! religions! the whole boatload of sensitive bullshit!" *Howl* seems to have emerged under the influence of a kind of literary *Festspiel* held at frequent intervals on the West Coast, in the course of which various poets, "with radiant cool eyes," undoubtedly, read their works before audiences of writhing and adoring youths. "Howl" and the other longer poems in this book, including "America," "Sunflower Sutra," "In the Baggage Room at Greyhound" and some dismal pastiches of William Carlos Williams (who wrote a brief reminiscence of the poet to introduce this volume), all proclaim, in a hopped-up and improvised tone, that nothing seems to be worth saying save in a hopped-up and improvised tone. There are also avowed post-Poundian pacts with Walt Whitman and Apollinaire, and perhaps an unacknowledged one with Lautréamont. I don't know; Mr. Ginsberg prefaces *Howl* with a long dedication to some of his fellow-writers that reads just like his poems ("To . . . William Seward Burroughs, author of *Naked Lunch,* an endless novel which will drive everybody mad"), and in the book he alludes to a "spontaneous bop prosody." Perhaps this is as good a characterization of his work as any.

I have spent this much time on a very short and very tiresome book for two reasons. The first of these is involved with the fact that Mr. Ginsberg and his circle are being given a certain amount of touting by those who disapprove of what Horace Gregory, writing in these pages last fall, christened "The Poetry of Suburbia." If it turns out to be to anybody's profit, I shouldn't be a bit surprised if *Howl* and its eventual progeny were accorded some milder version of the celebration Colin Wilson has received in England. This may not be a real danger, however. If it suddenly appeared that there were no possible worlds between suburbia and subterranea, I expect most of us would go underground. But this is not quite yet the case, and the publicity seems regrettable, in view of the fact (my second reason for dealing with him here) that Allen Ginsberg has a real talent and a marvelous ear. It shows up in some of the funniest and most grotesque lines of "Howl," and even without knowing his profound and carefully organized earlier writing (unpublished in book form), one might suspect a good poet lurking behind the modish façade of a frantic and *talentlos* avant-garde.

[When contacted for permission to reprint, John Hollander expressed reluctance to see the "tone" of this review perpetuated. He has allowed us to use it on condition that we include the addendum which follows.]

Addendum (February 1984)

This review was written in my youth and in a sort of worked-up high dudgeon which echoed the high-camp-prophetic mode of *Howl*'s front matter, and which may have masked some of my disappointment in a turn I saw an old friend and poetic mentor to have taken. I only regret now that I hadn't given "America" and "In a Supermarket in California" time to register; I should have certainly commended them. As for not foreseeing that Allen Ginsberg would provide so much hymnody and doctrine to the counterculture which was soon to emerge, I have no regrets, having no stake in prophecy.

M. L. ROSENTHAL

Poet of the New Violence

The two most striking pieces in Allen Ginsberg's pamphlet *Howl and Other Poems*—the long title-piece itself and "America"—are sustained shrieks of frantic defiance. The themes are struck off clearly in the opening lines of each:

> I saw the best minds of my generation destroyed by madness,
> starving hysterical naked . . .

and

> America I've given you all and now I'm nothing.

Isolated quotation, however, will not convey the real tone of these poems, though their drift is not hard to define. We have had smoking attacks on the civilization before, ironic or murderous or suicidal. We have *not* had this particular variety of anguished anathema-hurling in which the poet's revulsion is expressed with the single-minded frenzy of a raving madwoman.

Ginsberg hurls, not only curses, but *everything*—his own paranoid memories of a confused, squalid, humiliating existence in the "underground" of American life and culture, mock political and sexual "confessions" (together with the childishly aggressive vocabulary of obscenity which in this country is being increasingly substituted for anti-Semitism as the "socialism of fools"), literary allusions and echoes, and the folk-idiom of impatience and disgust. The "best minds" of his generation as Ginsberg, age thirty, remembers them "howled on their knees in the subway and were dragged off the roof waving genitals and

Review of *Howl and Other Poems,* from the *Nation,* 23 February 1957. Reprinted with permission.

manuscripts." They "scribbled all night rocking and rolling over lofty incantations which in the yellow morning were stanzas of gibberish."

Would you inquire? discuss? rebuke? "I don't feel good don't bother me."

That is to say, this poetry is not "rational discourse," such as we find in almost all other American literature of dissidence. Nor is it that flaccid sort of negation, too easy and too glib, that so often reduces the charge in the writing of Patchen and others, though it does occasionally lapse into mere rant and scabrous exhibitionism. It is the fury of the soul-injured lover or child, and its dynamic lies in the way it spews up undigested the elementary need for freedom of sympathy, for generous exploration of thought, for the open response of man to man so long repressed by the smooth machinery of intellectual distortion. It is further evidence, the most telling yet, perhaps, of the Céline-ization of nonconformist attitudes in America, or should we say their Metesky-ization? Homogenize the dominant culture enough, destroy the channels of communication blandly enough, and you will have little Mad Bombers everywhere.

Though his style is effectively, sometimes brilliantly, his own, Ginsberg shows the impact of such poets as Whitman, Williams and Fearing in his adaptations of cadence to rhetorical and colloquial rhythms; once in a while he falls entirely into the cadence and voice of one or another of these writers, on occasion—as in "A Supermarket in California"—deliberately. But he does break through as these poets, who are among the men who have most earnestly sought to be true native voices in their several ways, have prepared him to do. Is Ginsberg of the same calibre? Despite his many faults and despite the danger that he will screech himself mute any moment now, is he the real thing?

What we can say, I think, is that he has brought a terrible psychological reality to the surface with enough originality to blast American verse a hairsbreadth forward in the process. And he has sent up a rocket-flare to locate for his readers the particular inferno of his "lost battalion of platonic conversationalists jumping down the stoops off fire escapes off windowsills off Empire State out of the moon," all of them "yacketayackking screaming vomiting whispering facts and memories and anecdotes and eyeball kicks and shocks of hospitals and jails and wars."

And very simply, this is poetry of genuine suffering. The "early" pieces at the back of the little book have a heavy Yiddish melancholy—

> The weight of the world
>   is love.
> Under the burden
>   of solitude
> under the burden
>   of dissatisfaction
>
>   the weight
> the weight we carry
>   is love.

The more recent poems, as Williams writes, present "our own country, our own fondest purlieus," as a "Golgotha," a "charnel house, similar in every way to that of the Jews in the past war." Seen from above the water, Ginsberg may be wrong; his writing may certainly have many false notes and postures. For the sake of self-respect and of hope let us take the position that this is all too destructive and therefore mistaken, and that a total assault may be even worse than mere acquiescence. But that is all beside the point. The agony, in any case, is real; so are the threats for the future that it signals.

KENNETH REXROTH

San Francisco Letter

Allen Ginsberg's *Howl* is much more than the most sensational book of poetry of 1957. Nothing goes to show how square the squares are so much as the *favorable* reviews they've given it. "Sustained shrieks of frantic defiance," "single-minded frenzy of a raving madwoman," "paranoid memories," "childish obscenity"—they think it's all *so* negative. Also—which is much more important—they think there is something unusual about it. Listen you—do you *really* think your kids act like the bobby soxers in those wholesome Coca-Cola ads? Don't you know that across the table from you at dinner sits somebody who looks on you as an enemy who is planning to kill him in the immediate future in an extremely disagreeable way? Don't you know that if you were to say to your English class, "It is raining," they would take it for granted you were a liar? Don't you know that they never tell you nothing? That they can't? That faced with the system of values which coats you like the insulating rompers of an aircraft carrier's "hot papa"—they simply can't get through, can't, and won't even try any more to communicate? Don't you know this, really? If you don't, you're headed for a terrible awakening. *Howl* is the confession of faith of the generation that is going to be running the world in 1965 and 1975—if it's still there to run. "The Poetry of the New Violence"? It isn't at all violent. It is *your* violence it is talking about. It is Hollywood or the censors who are obscene. It is Dulles and Khrushchev who are childishly defiant. It is the "media" that talk with the single-minded frenzy of a raving madwoman. Once Allen is through telling you what you have done

From "San Francisco Letter," *Evergreen Review* (Summer 1957). Copyright ©
1957. Used by permission of Bradford Morrow for The Kenneth Rexroth Trust.

to him and his friends, he concerns himself with the unfulfilled promises of *Song of Myself* and *Huckleberry Finn,* and writes a sutra about the sunflower that rises from the junk heap of civilization . . . your civilization. Negative? "We must love one another or die." It's the "message" of practically every utterance of importance since the Neolithic Revolution. What's so negative about it? The fact that we now live in the time when we must either mind it or take the final consequences? Curiously, the reviewers never noticed—all they saw was "total assault." All this aside, purely technically, Ginsberg is one of the most remarkable versifiers in American. He is almost alone in his generation in his ability to make powerful poetry of the inherent rhythms of our speech, to push forward the conquests of a few of the earliest poems of Sandburg and of William Carlos Williams. This is more skillful verse than all the cornbelt Donnes laid end to end. It is my modest prophecy, that, if he keeps going, Ginsberg will be the first genuinely popular, genuine poet in over a generation—and he is already considerably the superior of predecessors like Lindsay and Sandburg.

NORMAN PODHORETZ

A Howl of Protest in San Francisco

During the past few months, the godfather of the San Francisco Renaissance, Kenneth Rexroth, has been swashbuckling his way through the paperback periodicals with a series of lively, if intellectually irresponsible, essays on the young poets, novelists, and painters of what he calls the "Beat Generation" (as distinguished from its more respectable contemporaries, the "Silent Generation"). . . .

It turns out on close inspection that the San Francisco group is composed of two or three good writers, a half dozen mediocre talents, and several worthless fellow-travelers. What they all have in common is the conviction that any form of rebellion against American culture (which for them includes everything from suburbia and supermarkets to highbrow literary magazines like *Partisan Review*) is admirable, and they seem to regard homosexuality, jazz, dope-addiction, and vagrancy as outstanding examples of such rebellion. Most of them like using bop-language, and though they are all highly sophisticated, they fancy themselves to be in close touch with the primitive and the rugged. They talk endlessly about love; they are fond of Christian imagery, and especially fond of appealing to St. Francis in support of some of their ideas.

Occasionally, the rebelliousness in these poems and stories can descend to the level of puerile sniveling and self-righteous braggadocio. The worst offender is Michael Rumaker, author of a long story called "The Desert" in which the coldness, superficiality, and stupidity of two ladies driving a snow-white Jaguar convertible is mechanically contrasted with the vitality and spontaneity of a small gang of bums lolling in the California desert. . . .

What appears to be operating in Rumaker's story is the fantastic notion that homosexuality can be dressed up in a religious image or two and then offered without further ado as an adequate protest against the vulgarity and cruelty of American life. Allen Ginsberg's remarkable poem, "Howl" (currently banned in San Francisco) is not above throwing out the same suggestion, but Ginsberg gets away with it because he is frankly justifying himself in the poem, because his assault on America is a personal cry that rings true, because his hysteria is tempered with humor, and because the dope-addicts, perverts, and maniacs he celebrates are not finally glamorized. There are also two other good poets represented in the *Evergreen Review*—Robert Duncan, who is responsible for some of the loveliest lyric verse being written today, and the Dominican Brother Antoninus (William Everson), who can sound like Hopkins while remaining very much himself.

Judging from the *Evergreen Review,* then, I would say that the avant-garde "renaissance" in San Francisco is a product of Rexroth's publicistic impulses. No new territory is being staked out by these writers—Ginsberg's return to Whitman is a shift in fashion, not the mark of a revolutionary sensibility, and Duncan's lyric talent can easily be matched by the "square" Silent-Generation man, Louis Simpson. The fact is that it takes more than a feeling of "disengagement" from the contemporary world to provide the materials for a genuine avant-garde revolt.

MICHAEL RUMAKER

Allen Ginsberg's "Howl"

The language of "Howl" is curiously "materialistic." I mean it is quantitative (a quantity of verbiage) without reference to quality. I speak later of fever in this poem and I think it's that: the feelings are not precise (are an onrush of emotional bulk) and therefore the words, the language, cannot be precise. The abstractions of adjective and noun don't help to name the thing—to lock in the lines, precisely, what the poet means.

It's a "bad" poem—it's not *said* right. It should be said so that the impact of the anger slams in every line—a fury to lift the reader from his chair, force him to get up and walk about to read the thing. The disappointment is that Mr. Ginsberg fails in this when he seems to have the thing so close in hand, and instead, corrupts it with sentimentality, bathos, Buddha and hollow talk of eternity. But there are qualities of the writer that come through in spite of this. One is certainly made cognizant that he *needs,* desperately, and that there is tremendous love and desire in him, a care and compassion—however hidden beneath the cumbrous and hysterical language. A poem like this, the anger of it, is too valuable to disperse itself in hysteria. The hysteria distorts, preventing emergences of images.

The onrush of the lines is vigorous, has energy. The focus, where the poem gets off, is anger. Which supplies the force and is maintained on a pretty even pitch throughout. But the anger, as such, is not enough to make the poem. The grasping of words (in lieu of welding the word to the feeling) is too literary (circa Dos Passos)—the anger, fine as it is, bears the strain of a descriptive and nonexact vocabulary to define it.

The poem does not contain itself.

From *Black Mountain Review,* no. 7 (Fall 1957). Reprinted with permission.

A listing of horrors described with inaccurate adjectives sheared would have produced greater shock—the cumulative adjectives exhaust whatever fine tension of feeling the poet may have had in the concept—but it is reduced to hysteria and the force of the poem loses by waywardness, thrashing about. The right words (found, culled) and not overloaded with adjectives for fear the point will be missed if too spare. It's spareness that's needed here, to let the poem emerge from its adjectival obfuscation.

The poem builds to hysteria. The last section (Footnote) is chaos, the logical conclusion to the buildup. The poem scatters itself, finally, on its own pitiful frenzy. A way has not been found. The poet has not broken through, the poem remains unsaid. Everything is "holy." Which is not so. This confusion, this gibberish, is Satan. But by listening one hears protestations of love, of an actual need for revivification of the spirit, of a genuine need for a way out, of loyalty and, truly, love for a broken friend—this one "gets" but as echoes amidst the din.

It is, ultimately, the inability to find *anything* holy. The poem is a shriek on this from beginning to close.

There are a few fine things: "flips and crucifixions!" ". . . shuddering cloud and lightning in the mind . . ."

". . . Who digs Los Angeles IS Los Angeles!" (Straight from the hipster's mouth.)

who walked all night with their shoes full of blood on the snowbank
    docks waiting for a door in the East River to open to a room
    full of steamheat and opium . . .

and who were given instead the concrete void of insulin metrasol
    electricity hydrotherapy psychotherapy occupational therapy
    pingpong & amnesia . . . (The flip of "pingpong" amidst the
    "erapies" and other psycho-scientific nirvanas.)

with mother finally . . . , and the last fantastic book flung out of the
    tenement window, and the last door closed at 4 AM and the last
    telephone slammed at the wall in reply and the last furnished
    room emptied down to the last piece of mental furniture, a
    yellow paper rose twisted on a wire hanger in the closet, and

even that imaginary, nothing but a hopeful little bit of
hallucination—

and:

who broke down crying in white gymnasiums naked and trembling
   before the machinery of other skeletons . . .

(In the same collection, in "An Asphodel," the surprise of the
word "treat," the use of it, its placement, puts the poem there.)
   But those phrases like "angelheaded hipsters" when
"hipsters" alone would suffice. Hipsters are not "angelheaded,"
are anything but. The adjective sentimentalizes, implies a mushed
"goodness," "innocence," that no hipster, worthy the name,
would tolerate. (Unless the poet was trying to be ironic—it
would work well then—but from the context that's dubious.)
The flipness and glibness, naiveté, of the Dedication, of the men
named therein (save perhaps for Mr. Carr), does not arouse
sympathy. That is, one's ears close. For instance, Mr. Kerouac's
attempt to graft Buddhism on America: America is yet to be
discovered, by each of us—hyphenating Buddha to it simply
throws another layer of trash on the already overly littered
scene. Buddha is for the Indians. It is not our way. We have our
own redskinned terrors to come to grips with, spectres tho they
be, and confined now largely to dream and scattered passages in
a very few good books.
   Mr. Kerouac's work demands another paper. It's pertinence
here is that it adds to the confusion. Which is: you cannot have
religion *and* art. Art is enough, more than enough, to demand
your absolute attention and energy. That is, you can't pine for
eternity and Buddhistic visions and hope also to make good
poems. It has to be one way or the other. The eye must be kept
in focus. Art does not concern itself with systems of religion—
or systems of any kind.
   The strain of the poem "Howl," its failure to make itself, is
precisely this laceration—a falling into ineffectual halves for
failure to see that if you yearn for *that* Soul you sacrifice the surer
one under your very nose. And you lose both.
   The anger of the poet is not only directed at the horrors of

contemporary existence, but also at the unobtainability of the impossible vision. The language sweats to conjure forth the vision. He calls it Eternity, he calls it Holy, he calls it the Internationale, he calls it many an inadequate noun. He *wants* the vision because it is only the vision which will restore him, which will heal him—feed him "the ancient connection." The poem is a scream for that. But eternity is beyond the encompassing of man's mind. We try to describe it in poor metaphors. Man cannot *experience* eternity. Buddhism is of no use because, like Christianity, it has become a system and has lost whatever force and meaning it had in its original conception.

One is forced to turn one's back and to take what is under the nose, what one can see and hear, to take what is within hands' grasp. Otherwise, there will be no peace, the laceration will grow and whatever qualities of spirit, mind and body that were once there will dissolve in the inrush of emptiness. A great void settles within, the body slumps lethargic, the eyes go dreamless and undesiring. A chance touch of such flesh, of anonymous hands in an elevator, a crowded bus, and there is a shock, a recoil, as of touching something dead and vacant of life.

This is a certain type of man, Ginsberg. I see him in varying likenesses everywhere. On the loose they don't know what to do, can't take care of themselves. Something monastic about them. Frail is the seed of grace. Must be protected in its growth. Some asylum needed, where the handful possessing such capabilities gather, to be private, each to himself, to let this frail thing germinate. Black Mountain College closed its doors— everything there, equipped, ready, *willing*—no money. Nobody who had it interested enough, daring, aware enough, generous. Shows regard for education in America: i.e., the inquisitive, the curious, the experimental and adventurous spirit, *not* wanted. Jump in, but don't make a ripple.

Universities out of the question. The other asylums (state: nuthouse, reform school, psycho wards—gray hand of care) won't do—not the necessary atmosphere: different men joined together to make art, let blossom their own frail flower, to talk about things, to sometimes get *at* the thing. (One can only talk non-sense in the boobyhatch—which is not the whole matter.) Stoney Point too artsy-craftsy—"Awareness, restful and fake . . ." In isolate cases, very *few* can make it on their own. Of course those who have it, will, regardless—anywhere, anyhow. I am speaking of those who need a group thing, and haven't yet reached that point of being able to go it alone, or who perhaps won't ever, but who may, in time, write a story or poem worth keeping, or maybe several. With things rare as they are—no possibilities should be let to escape—or, re "Howl," flattened in the contemporary mangle. . . .

[Upon rereading this review in June 1983, Michael Rumaker wrote the following postscript:]

Later Thoughts on "Howl"

"Howl" literally moved a generation, unblocking energy in wavy rhythm rippling direct from Whitman. It's easier to recognize that now, 1983, than when this strange, yowling beast first came lumbering up out of the bowels of subterranean America. The startling roughness of its imagery and beat was enough to make a whole generation tremble in its collective Eisenhower water closet, either in excitement or fear. Often both. I trembled too, reading it, San Francisco ca. 1956, then writing a critique of it for the *Black Mountain Review,* writing largely out of resistance to this new, shrill and unknown voice howling outloud what I, and many others of the time, only mentioned in oblique and cynical whispers. The review is really more about my own stance then, largely muzzled and buried (gagging vapors from the cerements of Poe), but also exhilarated and striving in the reawakened energy in the San Francisco of the day—including the vitality discharged by Ginsberg and his poem, although I, like so many others, couldn't admit or recognize it, how much it blasted open all our artistic and sexual closet doors, anywhere from a chink to totally off the hinges.

"Howl" is a great purgative poem—still. And Ginsberg one of the prime movers of the day.

Remarks

(by various hands)

How meet it is for Dr. Williams, pediatrician, to introduce *Howl* to the world!
—Donald Justice in *Western Review* (Iowa City), Spring 1958

Among contemporary poets, Ginsberg is the perfect inhabitant, if not the very founder of Babel, where conditions do not so much make tongues incomprehensible, but render their utterances, as poetry, meaningless. *Howl* is the skin of Rimbaud's *Une Saison en Enfer* thrown over the conventional maunderings of one American adolescent, who has discovered that machine civilization has no interest in his having read Blake.
          —James Dickey in *Sewanee Review,* Summer 1957

It is a very shaggy book, the shaggiest I've ever seen.
          —Frederick Eckman, in his review of *Howl* in *Poetry,*
                                        September 1957

"Howl" is a wild, volcanic, troubled, extravagant, turbulent, boisterous, unbridled outpouring, intermingling gems and flashes of picturesque insight with slag and debris of scoriac matter. It has violence; it has life; it has *vitality*. In my opinion, it is a one-sided neurotic view of life; it has not enough glad, Whitmanian affirmations.
—Louis Ginsberg in a letter to Allen Ginsberg, 27 May 1956

LAWRENCE FERLINGHETTI

Horn on *Howl*

Fahrenheit 451, the temperature at which books burn, has finally
been determined not to be the prevailing temperature at San
Francisco, though the police still would be all too happy to make
it hot for you. On October 3 last, Judge Clayton Horn of Mu-
nicipal Court brought in a thirty-nine-page opinion finding
Shigeyoshi Murao and myself not guilty of publishing or selling
obscene writings, to wit Allen Ginsberg's *Howl and Other Poems*
and issue 11 & 12 of *The Miscellaneous Man.*

Thus ended one of the most irresponsible and callous police
actions to be perpetrated west of the Rockies, not counting the
treatment accorded Indians and Japanese.

When William Carlos Williams, in his Introduction to *Howl,*
said that Ginsberg had come up with "an arresting poem" he
hardly knew what he was saying. The first edition of *Howl,*
Number Four in the Pocket Poets Series, was printed in England
by Villiers, passed thru Customs without incident, and was pub-
lished at the City Lights bookstore here in the fall of 1956. Part
of a second printing was stopped by customs on March 25, 1957,
not long after an earlier issue of *The Miscellaneous Man* (pub-
lished in Berkeley by William Margolis) had been seized coming
from the same printer. Section 305 of the Tariff Act of 1930 was
cited. The San Francisco *Chronicle* (which alone among the local
press put up a real howl about censorship) reported, in part:

> Collector of Customs Chester MacPhee continued his cam-
> paign yesterday to keep what he considers obscene literature
> away from the children of the Bay Area. He confiscated 520
> copies of a paperbound volume of poetry entitled *Howl and*

Notes on the obscenity trial of *Howl,* from *Evergreen Review* (Winter 1957).
Copyright © 1957 by Lawrence Ferlinghetti. Reprinted by permission of City
Lights Books.

Other Poems. . . . "The words and the sense of the writing is obscene," MacPhee declared. "You wouldn't want your children to come across it."

On April 3 the American Civil Liberties Union (to which I had submitted the manuscript of *Howl* before it went to the printer) informed Mr. MacPhee that it would contest the legality of the seizure, since it did not consider the book obscene. We announced in the meantime that an entirely new edition of *Howl* was being printed within the United States, thereby removing it from customs jurisdiction. No changes were made in the original text, and a photo-offset edition was placed on sale at City Lights bookstore and distributed nationally while the customs continued to sit on the copies from Britain.

On May 19, book editor William Hogan of the San Francisco *Chronicle* gave his Sunday column to an article by myself, defending *Howl* (I recommended a medal be made for Collector MacPhee, since his action was already rendering the book famous. But the police were soon to take over this advertising account and do a much better job—10,000 copies of *Howl* were in print by the time they finished with it.) In defense of "Howl" I said I thought it to be "the most significant single long poem to be published in this country since World War II, perhaps since T. S. Eliot's *Four Quartets.*" To which many added "Alas." Fair enough, considering the barren, polished poetry and well-mannered verse which had dominated many of the major poetry publications during the past decade or so, not to mention some of the "fashionable incoherence" which has passed for poetry in many of the smaller, avant-garde magazines and little presses. "Howl" commits many poetic sins; but it was time. And it would be very interesting to hear from critics who can name another single long poem published in this country since the war which is as significant of its time and place and generation. (A reviewer in the *Atlantic Monthy* recently wrote that *Howl* may well turn out to be *The Waste Land* of the younger generation.) The central part of my article said:

> . . . It is not the poet but what he observes which is revealed as obscene. The great obscene wastes of "Howl" are the sad

wastes of the mechanized world, lost among atom bombs and insane nationalisms. . . . Ginsberg chooses to walk on the wild side of this world, along with Nelson Algren, Henry Miller, Kenneth Rexroth, Kenneth Patchen, not to mention some great American dead, mostly in the tradition of philosophical anarchism. . . . Ginsberg wrote his own best defense of "Howl" in another poem called "America." Here he asks:

What sphinx of cement and aluminum bashed open their skulls and
  ate up their brains and imagination?
Moloch! Solitude! Filth! Ugliness! Ashcans and unobtainable dollars!
  Children screaming under the stairways! Boys sobbing in
  armies! Old men weeping in the parks!*

A world, in short, you wouldn't want your children to come across. . . . Thus was Goya obscene in depicting the Disasters of War, thus Whitman an exhibitionist, exhibiting man in his own strange skin.

On May 29 customs released the books it had been holding, since the United States Attorney at San Francisco refused to institute condemnation proceedings against *Howl*.

Then the police took over and arrested us, Captain William Hanrahan of the juvenile department (well named, in this case) reporting that the books were not fit for children to read. Thus during the first week in June I found myself being booked and fingerprinted in San Francisco's Hall of Justice. The city jail occupies the upper floors of it, and a charming sight it is, a picturesque return to the early Middle Ages. And my enforced tour of it was a dandy way for the city officially to recognize the flowering of poetry in San Francisco. As one paper reported, "The Cops Don't Allow No Renaissance Here."

The ACLU posted bail. Our trial went on all summer, with a couple of weeks between each day in court. The prosecution soon admitted it had no case against either Shig Murao or myself as far as *The Miscellaneous Man* was concerned, since we were

---

*The lines are taken from the second part of "Howl," not from "America."—
ED.

not the publisher of it, in which case there was no proof we knew what was inside the magazine when it was sold at our store. And, under the California Penal Code, the willful and lewd *intent* of the accused had to be established. Thus the trial was narrowed down to *Howl*.

The so-called People's Case (I say so-called, since the People seemed mostly on our side) was presented by Deputy District Attorney Ralph McIntosh whose heart seemed not in it nor his mind on it. He was opposed by some of the most formidable legal talent to be found, in the persons of Mr. Jake ("Never Plead Guilty") Ehrlich, Lawrence Speiser (former counsel for the ACLU), and Albert Bendich (present counsel for the ACLU)—all of whom defended us without expense to us.

The critical support for *Howl* (or the protest against censorship on principle) was enormous. Here is some of what some said:

Henry Rago, editor of *Poetry* (Chicago):

> . . . I wish only to say that the book is a thoroughly serious work of literary art. . . . There is absolutely no question in my mind or in that of any poet or critic with whom I have discussed the book that it is a work of the legitimacy and validity contemplated by existing American law, as we know it in the statement of Justice Woolsey in the classic *Ulysses* case, and as we have seen it reaffirmed just recently by the Supreme Court in the Butler case. . . . I would be unworthy of the tradition of this magazine or simply of my place as a poet in the republic of letters . . . if I did not speak for the right of this book to free circulation, and against this affront not only to Allen Ginsberg and his publishers, but to the possibilities of the art of poetry in America. . . .

> . . . *Howl and Other Poems,* according to accepted, serious contemporary American literary standards, is a dignified, sincere and admirable work of art. . . .

Robert Duncan and Director Ruth Witt-Diamant of the San Francisco (State College) Poetry Center:

. . . *Howl* is a significant work in American poetry, deriving both a spirit and form from Walt Whitman's *Leaves of Grass*, from Jewish religious writings. . . . It is rhapsodic, highly idealistic and inspired in cause and purpose. Like other inspired poets, Ginsberg strives to include all of life, especially the elements of suffering and dismay from which the voice of desire rises. Only by misunderstanding might these tortured outcryings for sexual and spiritual understanding be taken as salacious. The poet gives us the most painful details; he moves us toward a statement of experience that is challenging and finally noble.

Thomas Parkinson (University of California):

. . . *Howl* is one of the most important books of poetry published in the last ten years. Its power and eloquence are obvious, and the talent of Mr. Ginsberg is of the highest order. Even people who do not like the book are compelled to testify to its force and brilliance. . . .

James Laughlin (New Directions):

I have read the book carefully and do not myself consider it offensive to good taste, likely to lead youth astray, or be injurious to public morals. I feel, furthermore, that the book has considerable distinction as literature, being a powerful and artistic expression of a meaningful philosophical attitude. . . .

Kenneth Patchen:

The issue here—as in every like case—is not the merit or lack of it of a book but of a Society which traditionally holds the human being to be by its very functional nature a creature of shameful, outrageous, and obscene habits. . . .

Eugene Burdick (novelist and critic):

The poem "Howl" strikes me as an impressionistic, broadly gauged, almost surrealistic attempt to catch the movement, color, drama, and inevitable disappointments of life in a complex, modern society. "Howl" is a pessimistic, and indeed, almost a tragic view of life. . . . It is my impression that the total impact of the poem is far from lascivious or obscene. It is depressing, but not licentious or extravagant in its use of harsh words. . . .

Northern California Booksellers Association:

It may or may not be literature but it does have literary merit. . . . The proposition that adult literature must meet the standards of suitability for children is manifestly absurd. . . . To quote Supreme Court Justice Frankfurter in a similar case—". . . the effect of this is to reduce the adult population to reading only what is fit for children . . . surely this is to burn the house down to roast the pig."

Barney Rosset and Donald Allen, editors of the *Evergreen Review* (in which "Howl" was reprinted during the trial):

The second issue of *Evergreen Review,* which was devoted to the work of writers in the San Francisco Bay Area, attempted in large part to show the kinds of serious writing being done by the postwar generation. We published Allen Ginsberg's poem "Howl" in that issue because we believe that it is a significant modern poem, and that Allen Ginsberg's intention was to sincerely and honestly present a portion of his own experience of the life of his generation. . . . Our final considered opinion was that Allen Ginsberg's "Howl" is an achieved poem and that it deserves to be considered as such. . . .

At the trial itself, nine expert witnesses testified in behalf of *Howl.* They were eloquent witnesses, together furnishing as good a one-sided critical survey of *Howl* as could possibly be got up in any literary magazine. These witnesses were: Mark Schorer and Leo Lowenthal (of the University of California faculty), Walter Van Tilburg Clark, Herbert Blau, Arthur Foff, and Mark Linenthal (all of the San Francisco State College faculty), Kenneth Rexroth, Vincent McHugh (poet and novelist), and

Luther Nichols (book editor of the San Francisco *Examiner*). A few excerpts from the trial transcript:

DR. MARK SCHORER: The theme of the poem is announced very clearly in the opening line, "I saw the best minds of my generation destroyed by madness, starving hysterical naked." Then the following lines that make up the first part attempt to create the impression of a kind of nightmare world in which people representing "the best minds of my generation," in the author's view, are wandering like damned souls in hell. That is done through a kind of series of what one might call surrealistic images, a kind of state of hallucinations. Then in the second section the mood of the poem changes and it becomes an indictment of those elements in modern society that, in the author's view, are destructive of the best qualities in human nature and of the best minds. Those elements are, I would say, predominantly materialism, conformity and mechanization leading toward war. And then the third part is a personal address to a friend, real or fictional, of the poet or of the person who is speaking in the poet's voice—those are not always the same thing—who is mad and in a madhouse, and is the specific representative of what the author regards as a general condition, and with that final statement the poem ends. . . .

MR. MCINTOSH: (*later in cross-examination*): I didn't quite follow your explanation to page 21, "Footnote to Howl." Do you call that the second phase?

MARK SCHORER: I didn't speak about "Footnote to Howl." I regard that as a separate poem.

MR. MCINTOSH: Oh, I'm—

MARK SCHORER: It is not one of the three parts that make up the first poem. It's a comment on, I take it, the attitude expressed in "Howl" proper, and I think what it says—if you would like my understanding of it—is that in spite of all of the depravity that "Howl" has shown, all of the despair, all of the defeat, life is essentially holy and should be so lived. In other words, the footnote gives us this state in contradistinction to the state that the poem proper has tried to present.

MR. McINTOSH (*later*): Did you read the one in the back called "America"? . . . What's the essence of that piece of poetry?

MARK SCHORER: I think that what the poem says is that the "I," the speaker, feels that he has given a piece of himself to America and has been given nothing in return, and the poem laments certain people who have suffered at the hands of—well, specifically, the United States Government, men like Tom Mooney, the Spanish Loyalists, Sacco and Vanzetti, the Scottsboro boys and so on.

MR. McINTOSH: Is that in there?

MARK SCHORER: That's on page 33. In other words, that is the speaker associating himself with those figures in American history whom he regards as having been martyred. He feels that way about himself.

MR. McINTOSH: Well, "America" is a little bit easier to understand than "Howl," isn't it? . . . Now [*referring to shorter poems in the back of the book*]—you read those two? You think they are similar, in a similar vein?

MARK SCHORER: They are very different. Those are what one would call lyric poems and the earlier ones are hortatory poems.

MR. McINTOSH: What?

MARK SCHORER: Poems of diatribe and indictment, the mood is very different, hortatory.

MR. McINTOSH: That's all.

DR. LEO LOWENTHAL: In my opinion this is a genuine work of literature, which is very characteristic for a period of unrest and tension such as the one we have been living through the last decade. I was reminded by reading "Howl" of many other literary works as they have been written after times of great upheavals, particularly after World War I, and I found this work very much in line with similar literary works. With regard to the specific merits of the poem "Howl," I would say that it is structured very well. As I see it, it consists of three parts, the first of which is the craving of the poet for self-identification, where he roams all over the field and tries to find allies in similar search for self-identification. He then indicts, in the second part, the villain, so to say, which does not permit him to find it, the Moloch of society, of the world as it is today. And in the third part he indicates the potentiality of fulfillment by friendship and love, although it ends on a sad and melancholic note actually indicating that he is in search for fulfillment he cannot find.

KENNETH REXROTH: . . . The simplest term for such writing is prophetic, it is easier to call it that than anything else because we have a large body of prophetic writing to refer to. There are the prophets of the Bible, which it greatly resembles in purpose and in language and in subject matter. . . . The theme is the denunciation of evil and a pointing out of the way out, so to speak. That is prophetic literature. "Woe! Woe! Woe! The City of Jerusalem! The Syrian is about to come down or has already and you are to do such and such a thing and you must repent and do thus and so." And "Howl," the four parts of the poem—that is including the "Footnote to Howl" as one additional part— do this very specifically. They take up these various specifics seriatim, one after the other. . . . And "Footnote to Howl," of course, again, is Biblical in reference. The reference is to the Benedicite, which says over and over again, "Blessed is the fire, Blessed is the light, Blessed are the trees, and Blessed is this and Blessed is that," and he is saying, "Everything that is human is Holy to me," and that the possibility of salvation in this terrible situation which he reveals is through love and through the love of everything Holy in man. So that I would say, that this just about covers the field of typically prophetic poetry. . . .

HERBERT BLAU: The thing that strikes me most forcefully about "Howl" is that it is worded in what appears to be a contemporary tradition, one that did not cause me any particular consternation in reading, a tradition most evident in the modern period following the First World War, a tradition that resembles European literary tradition and is defined as "Dada," a kind of art of furious negation. By the intensity of its negation it seems to be both resurrective in quality and ultimately a sort of paean of possible hope. I wouldn't say that the chances for redemption or chances for salvation in a work of this kind are deemed to be very extensively possible but, nonetheless, the vision is not a total vision of despair. It is a vision that by the salvation of despair, by the salvation of what would appear to be perversity, by the salvation of what would appear to be obscene, by the salvation of what would appear to be illicit, is ultimately a kind of redemption of the illicit, the obscene, the disillusioned and the despairing. . . .

VINCENT McHUGH: In this case . . . we have a vision of a modern hell. Now, we have certain precedents for that, for example, the book that it makes me think of, or the work of literature that it makes me think of offhand, the work of literature which is ferociously sincere in the same way, is Mr. Pound's—some of Mr. Pound's *Cantos,* especially Canto XIV and Canto XV. These, for example, in turn derive certainly from Dante and from the famous so-called cantos in Dante, and Dante, in turn, derives from the *Odyssey,* and so on into all the mythologies of the world. . . .

The prosecution put only two "expert witnesses" on the stand—both very lame samples of academia—one from the Catholic University of San Francisco and one a private elocution teacher, a beautiful woman, who said, "You feel like you are going through the gutter when you have to read that stuff. I didn't linger on it too long, I assure you." The University of San Francisco instructor said: "The literary value of this poem is negligible. . . . This poem is apparently dedicated to a long-dead movement, Dadaism, and some late followers of Dadaism. And, therefore, the opportunity is long past for any significant literary contribution of this poem." The critically devastating things the prosecution's witnesses could have said, but didn't, remain one of the great Catholic silences of the day.

So much for the literary criticism inspired by the trial. Cross-examination by the prosecutor was generally brilliant, as in the following bit:

MR. McINTOSH: Does Mr. Ferlinghetti attend your poetry
   writing workshop?
DR. MARK LINENTHAL: He does not.
MR. McINTOSH: Do you attend his?
DR. LINENTHAL: I do not.
MR. McINTOSH: You haven't been over there hearing him
   read poetry?
DR. LINENTHAL: No, I haven't.
(etc.)

Legally, a layman could see that an important principle was
certainly in the line drawn between "hard core pornography"
and writing judged to be "social speech." But more important
still was the court's acceptance of the principle that if a work is
determined to be "social speech" the question of obscenity may
not even be raised. Or, in the words of Counsel Bendich's
argument:

> The first amendment to the Constitution of the United States
> protecting the fundamental freedoms of speech and press pro-
> hibits the suppression of literature by the application of
> obscenity formulae unless the trial court first determines that
> the literature in question is utterly without social impor-
> tance." (*Roth* v. *U.S.*)
>
>   . . . What is being urged here is that the majority opinion
> in *Roth* requires a trial court to make the constitutional deter-
> mination; to decide in the first instance whether a work is
> utterly without redeeming social importance, *before* it permits
> the test of obscenity to be applied. . . .
>
>   . . . The record is clear that all of the experts for the de-
> fense identified the main theme of *Howl* as social criticism.
> And the prosecution concedes that it does not understand the
> work, much less what its dominant theme is.

Judge Horn agreed, in his opinion:

> I do not believe that *Howl* is without even 'the slightest re-
> deeming social importance.' The first part of "Howl" pre-
> sents a picture of a nightmare world; the second part is an

indictment of those elements in modern society destructive of the best qualities of human nature; such elements are predominantly identified as materialism, conformity, and mechanization leading toward war. The third part presents a picture of an individual who is a specific representation of what the author conceives as a general condition. . . . "Footnote to Howl" seems to be a declamation that everything in the world is holy, including parts of the body by name. It ends in a plea for holy living. . . .

And the judge went on to set forth certain rules for the guidance of authorities in the future, [including] . . . :

In considering material claimed to be obscene it is well to remember the motto: *Honi soit qui mal y pense* (Evil to him who thinks evil).

At which the Prosecution was reliably reported to have blushed.

Under banner headlines, the *Chronicle* reported that "the Judge's decision was hailed with applause and cheers from a packed audience that offered the most fantastic collection of beards, turtlenecked shirts and Italian hairdos ever to grace the grimy precincts of the Hall of Justice." The decision was hailed editorially as a "landmark of law." Judge Horn has since been reelected to office, which I like to think means that the People agree it was the police who here committed an obscene action.

The Disorganization Man

(from Time *magazine)*

. . . The central Beat character that unintentionally emerges is a
model psychopath. The hipster has a horror of family life and
sustained relationships. In a brilliant, poignant story, "Sunday
Dinner in Brooklyn," Anatole Broyard recounts the ordeal of a
highbrow Greenwich Village bohemian returning for an hour or
two of strained parental nuzzling. Says the hero plaintively: "I
realized that I loved them very much. But what was I going to
do with them?" The hipster is also estranged from nature. In
George Mandel's "The Beckoning Sea," the suicide-bent hero
runs screaming along a beach, and "with a roar the ocean came
up and bit at him with its foam-teeth."

Even when he is not being bitten by foam-teeth, the hipster is
a chronic manic-depressive ("Crazy, man!"; "Everything drags
me now"). A kind of urban waif in the asphalt jungle, he regu-
larly tastes despair, or what Kerouac calls "the pit and prune-
juice of poor beat life itself in the god-awful streets of man."
Sometimes he "flips," i.e., goes mad. Allen Ginsberg, thirty-
two, the discount-house Whitman of the Beat Generation, be-
gins his dithyrambic poem "Howl" (which the New York
Times's critic J. Donald Adams has suggested should be retitled
"Bleat") with the lines: "I saw the best minds of my generation
destroyed by madness, starving hysterical naked, / dragging
themselves through the negro streets at dawn looking for an
angry fix . . ."

A good mind is hard to find among the Beats, but the leading
theoreticians of hipdom are probably Jack Kerouac and Clellon
(*Go*) Holmes. Each insists that the Beat Generation is on a my-

A review of *The Beat Generation and the Angry Young Men,* edited by Gene
Feldman and Max Gartenberg, from *Time* magazine, 9 June 1958. Copyright
1958 Time Inc. Reprinted by permission from *Time.*

stic search for God. To be beat, argues Holmes in a recent *Esquire,* is to be "at the bottom of your personality looking up." Says Kerouac: "I want God to show me His face." This might be more convincing if Kerouac's novels did not play devil's advocate by preaching, in effect, "Seek ye first the Kingdom of kicks," e.g., drink, drugs, jazz and chicks.

The Angry Young Men are scarcely beat; yet British reserve merely muffles several striking similarities in theme and attitude. When Kingsley Amis (*Lucky Jim*) virtually dismisses politics as a "mug's game," any hipster would reply "Yes, man, yes!" When one of John Wain's characters in *Hurry on Down* tries to avoid introducing his parents to a friend because he is ashamed of their working-class manner and appearance, there is more than an echo of "Sunday Dinner in Brooklyn." When Colin Wilson proclaims that the Outsider "is the one man who knows he is sick in a civilization that doesn't know it is sick," he echoes the basic charge of the hipster against the square.

There is also a central difference between the Beats and the Angries. Where the hipster is asocial—society's Underground Man—the Angry Young Man is eager to belong, feeling as he does that the welfare state has given him the credentials of a gentleman without the cash to be one.

. . . The Angry Young Man is a rebel with a cause, a disorganization man in transition who will eventually make his peace with a society in which he means to make good.

The case of the hipster is not so hopeful. He is a rebel without a cause who shirks responsibility on the ground that he has the H-bomb jitters. His disengagement from society is so complete that he treats self as the only reality and cultivates sensation as the only goal. But the self-revolving life is a bore, a kind of life-in-death that requires ever intenser stimulants to create even the illusion of feeling. Stepping up the tempo, "go, go, go" becomes the rhythm of madness and self-destruction. The future of the Beat Generation can be read in its past—the James Deans and Dylan Thomases and Charlie "Yardbird" Parkers—and the morbid speed with which its romantic heroes become its martyred legends.

DIANA TRILLING

The Other Night at Columbia
A Report from the Academy

The "Beats" were to read their poetry at Columbia on Thursday
evening and on the spur of the moment three wives from the
English department had decided to go to hear them. But for me,
one of the three, the spur of the moment was not where the
story had begun. It had begun much farther back, some twelve
or fourteen years ago, when Allen Ginsberg had been a student
of my husband's and I had heard about him much more than I
usually hear of students for the simple reason that he got into a
great deal of trouble which involved his instructors, and had to
be rescued and revived and restored; eventually he had even to
be kept out of jail. Of course there was always the question,
should this young man be rescued, should he be restored? There
was even the question, shouldn't he go to jail? We argued about
it some at home but the discussion, I'm afraid, was academic,
despite my old resistance to the idea that people like Ginsberg
had the right to ask and receive preferential treatment just be-
cause they read Rimbaud and Gide and undertook to be writers
themselves. Nor was my principle, if one may call it that, of
equal responsibility for poets and shoe clerks so firm that I didn't
need to protect it by refusing to confront Ginsberg as an indi-
vidual or a potential acquaintance. I don't mean that I was
aware, at the time, of my motive for disappearing on the two or
three occasions when he came to the house to deliver a new
batch of poems and report on his latest adventures in sensation-
seeking. If I'd been asked to explain, then, my wish not to meet

From *Claremont Essays* (New York: Harcourt Brace, 1964). Originally published
in *Partisan Review* (Spring 1959). Reprinted with permission.

and talk with this disturbing young man who had managed to break through the barrier of student anonymity, I suppose I'd have rested with the proposition that he made life too messy, although then I'd have had to defend myself against the charge, made in the name of art, of a strictness of judgment which was too little tolerant of deviation from more usual and respectable standards of behavior. But ten, twelve, fourteen years ago, there was still something of a challenge in the "conventional" position; I still enjoyed defending the properties and proprieties of the middle class against friends who persisted in scorning them. Of course, once upon a time—that was in the thirties—one had had to defend even having a comfortable chair to sit in, or a rug on the floor. But by the forties things had changed; one's most intransigent literary friends had capitulated by then, everybody had a well-upholstered sofa and I was reduced to such marginal causes as the Metropolitan Museum and the expectation that visitors would put their ashes in the ashtrays and go home by 2:00 A.M. Then why should I not also defend the expectation that a student at Columbia, even a poet, would do his work, submit it to his teachers through the normal channels of classroom communication, stay out of jail, and, if things went right, graduate, start publishing, be reviewed, and see what developed, whether he was a success or failure?

Well, for Ginsberg, things didn't go right for quite a while. The time came when he was graduated from Columbia and published his poems, but first he got into considerable difficulty, beginning with his suspension from college and the requirement that he submit to psychiatric treatment, and terminating—but this was quite a few years later—in an encounter with the police from which he was extricated by some of his old teachers who knew he needed a hospital more than a prison. The suspension had been for a year, when Ginsberg had been a senior; the situation was not without its grim humor. It seems that Ginsberg had traced an obscenity in the dust of a dormitory window; the words were too shocking for the Dean of Students to speak, so he had written them on a piece of paper which he pushed across the desk to my husband: "Fuck the Jews." Even the part of Lionel that wanted to laugh couldn't; it was too hard for the Dean to have to transmit this message to a Jewish professor—

this was still in the forties when being a Jew in the university was not yet what it is today. "But he's a Jew himself," said the Dean. "Can you understand his writing a thing like that?" Yes, Lionel could understand; but he couldn't explain it to the Dean. And anyway, he knew that to appreciate why Ginsberg had traced this particular legend on the window required more than an understanding of Jewish self-hatred, and also that it was not the sole cause for administrative uneasiness about Ginsberg and his cronies. It was ordinary good sense for the college to take protective measures with Ginsberg and for him.

I now realize that even at this early point in his career I had already accumulated a fund of information about young Ginsberg which accurately forecast his later talent for self-promotion although it was surely disproportionate to the place he commanded in his teacher's mind and quite failed to jibe with the physical impression I had caught in opening the door to him when he came to the apartment. He was middling tall, slight, dark, sallow; his dress suggested shabby gentility, poor brown tweed gone threadbare and yellow. The description would have fitted any number of undergraduates of his or any Columbia generation; it was only the personal story that set him acutely apart. He came from New Jersey, where his father was a school-teacher, or perhaps a principal, who wrote poetry too—I think for the *Saturday Review,* which would be as good a way as any of defining the separation between father and son. His mother was in a mental institution, and she had been there, off and on, for a long time. This was the central and utterly persuasive fact of the young man's life; I knew this before I was told it in poetry at Columbia the other night, and doubtless it was this knowledge that at least in some part accounted for the edginess with which I responded to so much as the mention of Ginsberg's name. Here was a boy on whom an outrageous unfairness had been perpetrated: his mother had fled from him into madness and now whoever crossed his path became somehow responsible, caught in the impossibility of rectifying what she had done. It was an unjust burden for Ginsberg to put, as he so subtly did, on those who were only the later accidents of his history and it made me defensive instead of charitable with him. No boy, after all, could ask anyone to help him build a career on the terrible but gratuitous circumstance of a mad mother; it was a justification for neither poetry nor prose nor yet for "philosophy" of the kind young Ginsberg liked to expound to his teacher. In the question period which followed the poetry reading the other night at Columbia, this matter of a rationale for the behavior of Ginsberg and his friends came up: someone asked Ginsberg to state his philosophy. It was a moment I had been awaiting and I thought: "Here we go; he'll tell us how he's crazy like a daisy and how his friend Orlovsky is crazy like a butterfly." I had been reading *Time;* who hadn't? But, instead of repeating the formulations of earlier interviews, Ginsberg answered that he had no philosophy; he spoke of inspiration, or perhaps it was illumination, ecstatic illumination, as the source of his poetry, and I was more than surprised; I was curiously pleased for him because I took it as a considerable advance in self-control that he could operate with this much shrewdness and leave it, if only for this occasion, to his audience to abstract a "position" from his and his friends' antics while he himself moved wild, mild, and innocent through the jungle of speculation. Back in the older days, it had always been my feeling that so far as his relationship with his teacher was concerned, this trying to formulate a philosophy must reveal its falseness even to himself; his recourse to it was somehow beneath his intelligence. Apart from the need to force a recognition of his personal suffering upon certain figures who, in his mind, stood for society, two motives, it seemed to me, impelled him then: the wish to shock his teacher, and the wish to meet the teacher on equal ground. The first of these motives was complicated enough, involving as it did the gratifications of self-incrimination and disapproval, and then forgiveness: but the second was more tangled still. To talk with one's English professor who was also a writer, a critic, and one who made no bones about his solid connection with literary tradition, about one's descent from Rimbaud, Baudelaire or Dostoevsky was clearly to demonstrate a good-sized rationality and order in what was apparently an otherwise undisciplined life. Even more, or so I fancied, it was to propose an alliance between the views of the academic and the poet-rebel, the unity of a deep discriminating commitment to literature which must certainly one day wipe out the fortuitous distance between boy and man, pupil and teacher. Thus, Ginsberg standing on the platform at Columbia and refusing the philosophy gambit might well be announcing a new and sounder impulse toward self-definition for which one could be grateful.

But I remind myself: Ginsberg at Columbia on Thursday night was not Ginsberg at Chicago—according to *Time,* at any rate—or Ginsberg at Hunter either, where Kerouac ran the show, and a dismal show it must have been, with Kerouac drinking on the platform and clapping James Wechsler's hat on his head in a grand parade of contempt—they were two of four panelists gathered to discuss "Is there such a thing as a Beat Generation?"—and leading Ginsberg out from the wings like a circus donkey. For whatever reason—rumor had it he was in a personal crisis—Kerouac didn't appear on Thursday night, and Ginsberg at Columbia was Ginsberg his own man, dealing with his own history, and intent, it seemed to me, on showing up the past for the poor inaccurate thing it so often is: it's a chance we all dream of but mostly it works the other way around, like the long-ago perhaps-apocryphal story of the successful theater director coming back to Yale and sitting on the fence weeping for a youth he could never rewrite no matter how many plays of Chekhov he brought to Broadway, no matter how much money he made. I suppose I have no right to say now, and on such early and little evidence, that Ginsberg had always desperately wanted to be respectable, or respected, like his instructors at Columbia, it is so likely that this is a hindsight which suits my needs. It struck me, though, that this was the most unmistakable and touching message from platform to audience the other night, and as I received it, I felt I had known something like it all along. Not that Ginsberg had ever shown himself as a potential future colleague in the university; anything but that. Even the implied literary comradeship had had reference, not to any possibility of Ginsberg's assimilation into the community of professors, but to the professor's capacity for association in the community of rebellious young poets. Still, it was not just anyone on the campus to whom Ginsberg had come with his lurid boasts which were also his confession; it was Lionel, it was Mark Van Doren; if there was anyone else it would very likely be of the same respectable species, and I remember saying, "He wants you to forbid him to behave like that. He wants you to take him out of it, or why does he choose people like you and Mark Van Doren to tell these stories to?" To which I received always the same answer: "I'm not his father," a response that of course allowed no argument.

And yet, even granting the accuracy of this reconstruction of the past, it would be wrong to conclude that any consideration of motive on Ginsberg's part was sufficiently strong to alter one's first and most forceful image of Ginsberg as a "case"—a gifted and sad case, a guilt-provoking and nuisance case, but, above all, a case. Nor was it a help that my husband had recently published a story about a crazy student and a supposedly normal student in which the author's affection was so plainly directed to the former; we never became used to the calls, often in the middle of the night, asking whether it wasn't the crazy character who was really sane. Allen Ginsberg, with his poems in which there was never quite enough talent or hard work, and with his ambiguous need to tell his teacher exactly what new flagrancy had opened to his imagination as he talked about Gide with his friends at the West End Café, had at any rate the distinction of being more crudely justified in his emotional disturbance than most. He also had the distinction of carrying mental unbalance in the direction of criminality, a territory one preferred to leave unclaimed by student or friend.

Gide and the West End Café in all its upper-Broadway dreariness: what could the two conceivably have in common except those lost boys of the forties? How different it might have been for Ginsberg and his friends if they had come of age ten or fifteen years sooner was one of the particular sadnesses of the other evening; it virtually stood on the platform with them as the poets read their poems, whose chief virtue, it seemed to me, was their "racial-minority" funniness, their "depressed-classes" funniness of a kind which has never had so sure and live a place as it did in the thirties, the embittered fond funniness which has to do with one's own impossible origins, funniness plain and poetical, always aware of itself, of a kind which would seem now to have all but disappeared among intellectuals except as an eclecticism or a device of self-pity. It's a real loss; I hadn't quite realized how much I missed it until Thursday night when Ginsberg read his poem "The Ignu," and Corso read his poem "Marriage" (a compulsive poem, he called it, about a compulsive subject), and they were still funny in that old racial-depressed way but not nearly as funny and authentic as they would have been had they been written before the Jews and the Italians and the Negroes, but especially the Jews, had been awarded a place as Americans-like-everyone-else instead of remaining outsiders raised in the Bronx or on Ninth Avenue or even in Georgia. The Jew in particular is a loss to literature and life—I mean the Jew out of which was bred the Jewish intellectual of the thirties. For a few short years in the thirties, as not before or since, the Jew was at his funniest, shrewdest best; he perfectly well knew the advantage he could count on in the Gentile world, and that there was no ascendancy or pride the Gentile comrades could muster against a roomful of Jewish sympathizers singing at the tops of their voices, "A SOCialist union is a NO good union, is a COM-pan-y union of the bosses," or against Michael Gold's mother, who wanted to know did her boy have to write books the whole world should know she had bedbugs. If Ginsberg had been born in an earlier generation it would surely have been the Stewart Cafeteria in the Village that he and his friends would have frequented instead of the West End, that dim waystation of undergraduate debauchery on Morningside Heights—and the Stewart Cafeteria was a well-lighted place and one of the funniest places in New York; at least, at every other table it was funny, and where it was decadent or even conspiratorial, that had its humor too, or at least its robustness. As for Gide—the Gide of the thirties was the "betrayer of the Revolution," not the Gide of the *acte gratuite* and homosexuality in North Africa. One didn't use pathology in those days to explain or excuse or exhibit oneself and one never had to be lonely; there was never a less lonely time for intellectuals than the Depression, or a less depressed time—unless, of course, one was recalcitrant, like Fitzgerald, and simply refused to be radicalized, in which stubborn case it couldn't have been lonelier. Intellectuals talk now about how, in the thirties, there was an "idea" in life, not the emptiness we live in. Actually, it was a time of generally weak intellection—or so it seems to me now—but of very strong feeling. Everyone judged everyone else; it was a time of incessant cruel moral judgment; today's friend was tomorrow's enemy; whoever disagreed with oneself had sold out, God knows to or for what; there was little of the generosity among intellectuals which nowadays dictates the automatic "Gee, that's great" at any news of someone else's good fortune. But it was surely a time of quicker, truer feeling than is now conjured up with marijuana or the infantile camaraderie of Kerouac's *On the Road*. And there was paradox but no contradiction in this double truth, just as there was no contradiction in the fact that it was a time in which the neurotic determination of the intellectual was being so universally acted out and yet a time in which, whatever his dedication to historical or economic determinism, personally he had a unique sense of free will. In the thirties one's clinical vocabulary was limited to two words, escapism and subjectivism, and both of them applied only to other people's wrong political choices.

Well, the "Beats" weren't lucky enough to be born except when they were born. Ginsberg says he lives in Harlem, but it's not the Harlem of the Scottsboro boys and W. C. Handy and the benign insanity of trying to proletarianize Striver's Row; their comrades are not the comrades of the Stewart Cafeteria nor yet of the road, as Kerouac would disingenuously have it, but pickups on dark morning streets. But they have their connection with us who were young in the thirties, their intimate political connection, which we deny at risk of missing what it is that makes the "Beat" phenomenon something to think about. As they used to say on Fourteenth Street, it is no accident, comrades, it is decidedly no accident that today in the fifties our single overt manifestation of protest takes the wholly nonpolitical form of a group of panic-stricken kids in blue jeans, many of them publicly homosexual, talking about or taking drugs, assuring us that they are out of their minds, not responsible, while the liberal intellectual is convinced that he has no power to control the political future, the future of the free world, and that therefore he must submit to what he defines as political necessity. Though of course the various aspects of a culture must be granted their own autonomous source and character, the connection between "Beat" and respectable liberal intellectual exists and is not hard to locate: the common need to deny free will, divest oneself of responsibility and yet stay alive. The typical liberal intellectual of the fifties, whether he is a writer or a sociologist or a law-school professor, explains his evolution over the last two decades—specifically, his current attitudes in foreign affairs—by telling us that he has been forced to accept the unhappy reality of Soviet strength in an atomic world, and that there is no alternative to capitulation—not that he calls it that—except the extinction of nuclear war. Even the diplomacy he invokes is not so much flexible, which he would like to think it is, as disarmed, an instrument of his impulse to surrender rather than of any wish to win or even hold the line. Similarly docile to culture, the "Beat" also contrives a fate by predicating a fate. Like the respectable established intellectual—or the organization man, or the suburban matron—against whom he makes his play of protest, he conceives of himself as incapable of exerting any substantive influence against the forces that condition him. He is made by society, he cannot make society. He can only stay alive as best he can for as long as is permitted him. Is it any wonder, then, that *Time* and *Life* write as they do about the "Beats"—with such a conspicuous show of superiority, and no hint of fear? These periodicals know what genuine, dangerous protest looks like, and it doesn't look like Ginsberg and Kerouac. Clearly, there is no more menace in "Howl" or *On the Road* than there is in the Scarsdale P-TA. In the common assumption of effectlessness, in the apparent will to rest with a social determination over which the individual spirit and intelligence cannot and perhaps even should not try to triumph, there merge any number of the disparate elements of our present culture—from the liberal intellectual journals to Luce to the Harvard Law School, from Ginsberg to the suburban matron.

But then why, one ponders, do one's most relaxed and non-square friends, alongside of whom one can oneself be made to look like the original object with four sides of equal length, why do one's most politically "flexible" friends, alongside of whom one's own divergence from dominant liberal opinion is regularly made to look so ungraceful, so like a latter-day sectarianism, feel constrained to dispute Columbia's judgment in giving the "Beats" a hearing on the campus and my own wish to attend their poetry reading? Why, for instance, the dissent of Dwight

MacDonald, whom I happened to see that afternoon; or of W. H. Auden, who, when I afterward said I had been moved by the performance, gently chided me, "I'm ashamed of you"; or of the editor of *Partisan Review,* who, while he consents to my going ahead with this article for his magazine, can't hide his editorial puzzlement, even worry, because I want to give the "Beats" so much attention? In strict logic, it would seem to me that things should go in quite the other direction and that I, who insist upon at least the assumption of free will in our political choices, who insist upon what I call political responsibility, should be the one to protest a university forum for the irresponsibles whereas my friends whose politics are what I think of as finally a politics of passivity and fatedness, should be able to shrug off the "Beats" as merely another inevitable, if tasteless, expression of a *Zeitgeist* with which I believe them to be far more in tune than I am. I do not mean, of course, to rule out taste, or style, as a valid criterion of moral judgment. A sense of social overwhelmment which announces itself in terms of disreputableness or even criminality no doubt asks for a different kind of moral assessment than the same emotion kept within the bounds of a generally recognized propriety. But I would simply point to the similarities which are masked by the real differences between the "Beats" and those intellectuals who most overtly scorn them. Taste or style dictates that most intellectuals behave decorously, earn a regular living, disguise instead of flaunt any private digressions from the conduct society considers desirable; when they seek support for the poetical impulse or ask for light on their self-doubt and fears, they don't make the naked boast that they are crazy like daisies but they elaborate a new belief in the indispensability of neurosis to art, or beat the bushes for some new deviant psychoanalysis which will generalize their despair though of course without curing it. And these differences of style are undeniably important, at least for the moment. It is from the long-range view of our present-day cultural situation, which bears so closely upon our continuing national crisis, that the moral difference between a respectable and a disreputable acceptance of defeat seems to me to constitute little more than a cultural footnote to history.

But perhaps I wander too far from the other night at Columbia. There was enough in the evening that was humanly immediate to divert one from this kind of ultimate concern.

It was not an official university occasion. The "Beats" appeared at Columbia on the invitation of a student club—interestingly enough, the John Dewey Society. Whether the club first approached Ginsberg or Ginsberg initiated the proceedings, I don't know, but what had happened was that Ginsberg in his undergraduate days had taken a loan from the university—$200? $250?—and recently the Bursar's office had caught up with him in his new incarnation of successful literary itinerant, to demand repayment. Nothing if not ingenious, Ginsberg now proposed to pay off his debt by reading his poetry at Columbia without fee. It was at this point that various members of the English department, solicited as sponsors for the operation, had announced their rejection of the whole deal, literary as well as financial, and the performance was arranged without financial benefit to Ginsberg and without official cover; we three wives, however, decided to attend on our own. We would meet at 7:45 at the door of the theater; no, we would meet at 7:40 at the door of the theater; no, we would meet no later than 7:30 across the street from the theater: the telephoning back and forth among the three women was stupendous as word spread of vast barbarian hordes converging on Columbia's poor dull McMillin Theater from all the dark recesses of the city, howling for their leader. The advance warnings turned out to be exaggerated. It was nevertheless disconcerting that Fred Dupee of the English Department had consented, at the request of the John Dewey Society, to be moderator, chairman, introducer of Ginsberg and his fellow-poets, for while it provided the wives of his colleagues with the assurance of seats in a section of the hall reserved for faculty, it was not without its uncomfortable reminder that Ginsberg had, in a sense, got his way; he was appearing on the same Columbia platform from which T. S. Eliot had last year read his poetry; he was being presented by, and was thus bound to be thought under the sponsorship of, a distinguished member of the academic and literary community who was also one's long-time friend. And indeed it was as Dupee's friend that one took a first canvass of the scene: the line of

66

policemen before the entrance to the theater; the air of suppressed excitement in the lobbies and one's own rather contemptible self-consciousness about being a participant in the much-publicized occasion; the shoddiness of an audience in which it was virtually impossible to distinguish between student and camp-follower; the always-new shock of so many young girls, so few of them pretty, and so many blackest black stockings; so many young men, so few of them—despite the many black beards—with any promise of masculinity. It was distressing to think that Dupee was going to be "faculty" to such an incoherent assembly, that at this moment he was backstage with Ginsberg's group, formulating a deportment which would check the excess of which one knew it to be capable, even or especially in public, without doing violence to his own large tolerance.

For me, it was of some note that the auditorium smelled fresh. The place was already full when we arrived; I took one look at the crowd and was certain that it would smell bad. But I was mistaken. These people may think they're dirty inside and dress up to it. But the audience was clean and Ginsberg was clean and Corso was clean and Orlovsky was clean. Maybe Ginsberg says he doesn't bathe or shave; Corso, I know, declares that he has never combed his hair; Orlovsky has a line in one of the two poems he read—he's not yet written his third, the chairman explained—"If I should shave, I know the bugs would go away." But for this occasion, at any rate, Ginsberg, Corso and Orlovsky were all beautifully clean and shaven; Kerouac, in crisis, didn't appear, but if he had come he would have been clean and shaven too—he was entirely clean the night at Hunter; I've inquired about that. Certainly there's nothing dirty about a checked shirt or a lumberjacket and blue jeans; they're standard uniform in the best nursery schools. Ginsberg has his pride, as do his friends, however much they may dissemble.

And how do I look to the "Beats," I ask myself after that experience with the seats, and not only I but the other wives I was with? We had pulled aside the tattered old velvet rope which marked off the section held for faculty, actually it was trailing on the floor, and moved into the seats Dupee's wife had saved for us by strewing coats on them; there was a big gray overcoat she couldn't identify: she stood holding it up in the air murmuring wistfully, "Whose is this?"—until the young people in the row in back of us took account of us and answered sternly, "*Those* seats are reserved for faculty." If I have trouble unraveling undergraduates from "Beats," neither do the wives of the Columbia English department wear their proper manners with any certainty.

But Dupee's proper manners, that's something else again: what could I have been worrying about, when had Dupee ever failed to meet an occasion, or missed the right style? I don't suppose one could witness a better performance than his on Thursday evening: its rightness was apparent the moment he walked onto the stage, his troupe in tow and himself just close enough and yet enough removed to indicate the balance in which he held the situation. Had there been a hint of betrayal in his deportment, of either himself or his guests—naturally, he had made them his guests—the whole evening might have been different: for instance, a few minutes later when the overflow attendance outside the door began to bang and shout for admission, might not the audience have caught the contagion and become unruly too? Or would Ginsberg have stayed with his picture of himself as poet serious and triumphant instead of succumbing to what must have been the greatest temptation to spoil his opportunity? "The last time I was in this theater," Dupee began quietly, "it was also to hear a poet read his works. That was T. S. Eliot." A slight alteration of inflection, from irony to mockery, from wit to condescension, and it might well have been a signal for near-riot, boos and catcalls and whistlings; the evening would have been lost to the "Beats," Dupee and Columbia would have been defeated. Dupee transformed a circus into a classroom. He himself, he said, welcomed the chance to hear these poets read their works—he never once in his remarks gave them their name of "Beats" nor alluded even to San Francisco—because in all poetry it was important to study the spoken accent; he himself didn't happen especially to admire those of their works that he knew; still, he would draw our attention to their skillful use of a certain kind of American imagery which, deriving from Whitman, yet passed Whitman's use of it or even Hart Crane's. . . . It was Dupee speaking for the Academy, claiming for it its place in life, and the performers were inevitably captive to his dignity and self-assurance. Rather than Ginsberg and his friends, it was a photographer from *Life,* exploding his flashbulbs in everybody's face, mounting a ladder at the back of the stage the more effectively to shoot his angles, who came to represent vulgarity and disruption and disrespect; when a student in the audience disconnected a wire which had something to do with the picture-taking, one might guess that Ginsberg was none too happy that his mass-circulation "story" was being spoilt but it was the photographer's face that became ugly, the only real ugliness of the evening. One could feel nothing but pity for Ginsberg and his friends that their front of disreputableness and rebellion should be this vulnerable to the seductions of a clever host. With Dupee's introduction, the whole of their armor had been penetrated at the very outset.

Pity is not the easiest of our emotions today; now it's "understanding" that is easy, and more and more—or so I find it for myself—real pity moves hand in hand with real terror; it's an emotion one avoids because it's so hard; one "understands" the crippled, the delinquent, the unhappy so as not to have to pity them. But Thursday night was an occasion of pity so direct and inescapable that it left little to the understanding that wasn't mere afterthought—and pity not only for the observed, the performers, but for us who had come to observe them and reassure ourselves that we were not implicated. One might as readily persuade oneself one was not implicated in one's children! For this was it: these *were* children, miserable children trying desperately to manage, asking desperately to be taken out of it all, so that I kept asking myself, where had I had just such an experience before, and later it came to me: I had gone to see O'Neill's *Long Day's Journey into Night,* and the play had echoed with just such a child's cry for help; at intermission time all the mothers in the audience were so tormented and anxious that they rushed in a body to phone home: was the baby really all right, was he really well and warm in his bed; one couldn't get near the telephone booths. A dozen years ago, when Ginsberg had been a student and I had taxed Lionel with the duty to forbid him to misbehave, he had answered me that he wasn't the boy's father, and of course he was right. Neither was Mark Van Doren the boy's father; a teacher is not a father to his students and he must never try to be. Besides, Ginsberg had a father of his own who couldn't be replaced at will: he was in the audience the other night. One of the things Ginsberg read was part of a long poem to his mother, who, he told us, had died three years ago, and as he read it, he choked and cried; but no one in the auditorium tittered or showed embarrassment at this public display of emotion, and I doubt whether there was a young existentialist in the audience who thought, "See he has existence: he can cry, he can feel." Nor did anyone seem very curious when he went on to explain, later in the evening, that the reason he had cried was because his father was in the theater. I have no way of knowing what Ginsberg's father felt the other night about his son being up there on the stage at Columbia (it rather obsesses me), but I should guess he was proud; it's what I'd conclude from his expression at the end of the performance when Ginsberg pressed through the admirers who surrounded him to get to his father as quickly as he could: surely that's nice for a father. And I should suppose a father was bound to be pleased that his son was reading his poems in a university auditorium: it would mean the boy's success, and this would be better than a vulgarity; it would necessarily include the chairman's critical gravity and the fact, however bizarre, that T. S. Eliot had been the last poet in this place before him. In a sense, Orlovsky and Corso were more orphans than Ginsberg the other night, but this was not necessarily because they were without fathers of their own in the audience; I should think it would go back much farther than this, to whatever it was that made them look so much more masked, less openly eager for approval; although they were essentially as innocent and childlike as Ginsberg, they couldn't begin to match his appeal; it was on Ginsberg that one's eye rested, it was to the sweetness in his face and to his sweet smile that one responded; it was to him that one gave one's pity and for him one felt one's terror. Clearly, I am no judge of his poem "Lion in the Room," which he announced was dedicated to Lionel Trilling; I heard it through too much sympathy, and also self-consciousness. The poem was addressed as well as dedicated to Lionel; it was about a lion in the room with the poet, a lion who was hungry but refused to eat him; I heard it as a passionate love-poem; I really can't say whether it was a good or bad poem, but I was much moved by it, in some part unaccountably. It was also a decent poem, and I am willing to admit this surprised me; there were no obscenities in it as there had been in much of the poetry the "Beats" read. Here was something else one noted about the other evening: most of the audience was very young, and Ginsberg must have realized this because when he read the poem about his mother and came to the place where he referred to the YPSLs of her girlhood, he interposed his only textual exegesis of the evening: in an aside he explained, "Young People's Socialist League"—he was very earnest about wanting his poetry to be understood. And it wasn't only his gentility that distinguished Ginsberg's father from the rest of the audience; as far as I could see, he was the only man in the hall who looked old enough to be the father of a grown son; the audience was crazily young, there were virtually no faculty present: I suppose they didn't want to give this much sanction to the "Beats." For this young audience the obscenities read from the stage seemed to have no force whatsoever; there was not even the shock of silence, and when Ginsberg forgot himself in the question period and said that something or other was bullshit, I think he was more upset than his listeners; I can't imagine anything more detached and scientific outside a psychoanalyst's office, or perhaps a nursery school, than this young audience at Columbia. And even of Corso himself one had the sense that he mouthed the bad word only with considerable personal difficulty: this hurts me more than it hurts you.

Obviously, the whole performance had been carefully planned as to who would read first and what, then who next, and just how much an audience could take without becoming bored and overcritical: it would be my opinion we could have taken a bit more before the question period, which must have been an anticlimax for anyone who had come to the reading as a fellow-traveler. I've already reported how Ginsberg dealt with the philosophy question. There remains, of the question period, only to report his views on verse forms.

I don't remember how the question was put to Ginsberg—but I'm sure it was put neutrally: no one was inclined to embarrass the guests—which led him into a discussion of prosody; perhaps it was the question about what Ginsberg as a poet had learned at Columbia; but anyway, here, at last, Ginsberg had a real classroom subject: he could be a teacher who wed outrageousness to authority in the time-honored way of the young and lively, no-pedant-he performer of the classroom, and suddenly Ginsberg announced firmly that no one at Columbia knew anything about prosody; the English department was stuck in the nineteenth century, sensible of no meter other than the old iambic pentameter, whereas the thing about him and his friends was their concern with a poetic line which moved in the rhythm of ordinary speech; they were poetic innovators, carrying things forward the logical next step from William Carlos Williams. And now all at once the thing about Ginsberg and his friends was not their social protest and existentialism, their whackiness and beat-upness: suddenly it had become their energy of poetic impulse that earned them their right to be heard in the university, their studious devotion to their art: Ginsberg was seeing to that. Orlovsky had made his contribution to the evening; he had read his two whacky uproarious poems, the entire canon of his work, and had won his acclaim. Corso had similarly given his best, and been approved. The question period, the period of instruction, belonged to Ginsberg alone, and his friends might be slightly puzzled by the turn the evening had taken, the decorousness of which they suddenly found themselves a part—Corso, for instance, began to look like a chastened small boy who was still determined, though his heart was no longer in it, to bull his way through against all these damned grown-ups—but they had no choice except to permit their companion his deviation into high-mindedness. And thus did one measure, finally, the full tug of something close to respectability in Ginsberg's life, by this division in the ranks; and thus, too, was the soundness of Dupee's reminder, that there is always something to learn from hearing a poet read his poems aloud, borne in on one. For the fact was that Ginsberg, reading his verse, had naturally given it the iambic beat: after all, it is the traditional beat of English poetry where it deals with serious subjects, as Ginsberg's poems so often do. A poet, one thought—and it was a poignant thought because it came so immediately and humanly rather than as an abstraction—may choose to walk whatever zany path in his life as a man; but when it comes to mourning and mothers and such, he will be drawn into the line of tradition; at least in this far he is always drawn toward "respectability."

The evening was over, we were dismissed to return to our homes. A crowd formed around Ginsberg; he extricated himself and came to his father a few rows ahead of us. I resisted the temptation to overhear their greeting. In some part of me I wanted to speak to Ginsberg, tell him I had liked the poem he had written to my husband, but I didn't dare: I couldn't be sure that Ginsberg wouldn't take my meaning wrong. Outside, it had blown up a bit—or was it just the chill of unreality against which we hurried to find shelter?

There was a meeting going on at home of the pleasant professional sort which, like the comfortable living room in which it usually takes place, at a certain point in a successful modern literary career confirms the writer in his sense of disciplined achievement and well-earned reward. It is of course a sense that all writers long for quite as much as they fear it; certainly it is not to be made too conscious, not ever to be spoken of except with elaborate irony, lest it propose a life without risk and therefore without virtue. I had found myself hurrying as if I were needed, but there was really no reason for my haste; my entrance was an interruption, even a disturbance of the orderly scene, not the smallest part of whose point for me lay, now, in the troubling contrast it made with the world I had just come from. Auden, alone of the eight men in the room not dressed in a proper suit but wearing a battered old brown leather jacket, was first to inquire about my experience. I told him I had been moved; he answered gently that he was ashamed of me. In a dim suffocated effort of necessary correction, I said, "It's different when it's human beings and not just a sociological phenomenon," and I can only guess, and hope, he took what I meant. Yet as I prepared to get out of the room so that the men could sit down again with their drinks, I felt there was something more I had to add—it was so far from enough to leave the "Beats" as no more than human beings—and so I said, "Allen Ginsberg read a love-poem to you, Lionel. I liked it very much." It was an awkward thing to say in the circumstances, perhaps even a little foolish as an attempt to bridge the unfathomable gap that was all so quickly and meaningfully opening up between the evening that had been and the evening that was now so surely reclaiming me. But I'm certain that Ginsberg's old teacher knew what I was saying, and why I was impelled to say it.

ROBERT BLY

The Other Night in Heaven

My name is Diana Tilling and I am very important. My husband is Lionel Tilling, and he is also very important. Between the two of us, we are so important that everything we do, think, or say deserves a lot of space in the *Partisan Review*.

The other night the "Beats" were to read their poetry at Columbia, and we three wives of the English Department decided to go. Ginsberg was an old student of my husband's years ago. Ginsberg wanted terribly to be like the teachers at Columbia; I saw that even then. He always wanted to serve perfect martinis, and eat dinner on East Indian plates, and have famous friends like us. It is a shame that Ginsberg didn't turn out to be more like Lionel, when he had such a perfect model!

How different it might have been for Ginsberg and his friends if they had been born ten or fifteen years sooner! That was one of the particular sadnesses of the other evening. That they weren't born before the thirties was a real loss; they should at least have tried to. If they had, they could have sung union songs, played Mah-Jongg, and been great rebels like us! They could have criticized Freud, and ended up running the *Partisan Review*, like Lionel and me. They could even have looked down on Frost! All their poems would have been much better if they had been written in our generation. In those days, in the wonderful thirties, one never had to be lonely. The intellectuals were never depressed in the Depression. But these Beats were good boys, even if they were lonely.

If these boys were good, why did Jimmy Hoffa, whom I met on the street that afternoon, tell me he was ashamed that I was

A parody of the preceding essay by Diana Trilling, from *The Fifties*, Third Issue (1959). Reprinted with permission.

attending that night? Why did Prince Rainier chide me, and why did Herman Hesse and Charlie Chaplin and W. H. Auden try to dissuade me? All these people, my friends, were wearing new clothes. All intellectuals do this. It is one of the rewards of being a successful writer in America.

Perhaps I wander. It was all a matter of finance that brought Ginsberg to Columbia that Thursday night. Just before we left, the maid had cleaned our house. Our house is always comfortable and clean. (That is the reward of being a successful writer in America.) For me, it was of some note that the auditorium smelled fresh when I arrived. I took one look at the crowd and was certain that it would smell bad. Columbia students are all so dirty. Nevertheless, they smelled all right. The audience was clean and Ginsberg was clean and Corso was clean and Orlovsky was clean, and the kitchen was clean and the politics were clean and we were all good clean Americans. All intellectuals are clean.

My next great worry was, how did *I* look to the Beats? I mean, can they see that I am important, that I am a wife to the English Department, in fact that I *am* the English Department? Did I look like a Faculty Wife? The students didn't even recognize me! Lionel will flunk them all. I looked around, and luckily saw dear Norman. (Norman Podhoretz, born 1930, critic for the *Partisan Review,* and an old student of Lionel's. He is not in our generation, but a darling boy anyway.)

The poets were to be introduced by Fred Dupee, a very close friend of my husband's, and his wife Andy was with me. And how about Dupee, whom I have made an ass of by dragging him into this article—how would Dupee fare? What was he doing back there with all those terrible people?

Pity is very hard for most people, especially those born after the thirties. When the poets came out, I discovered something. All these poets are children! They wanted their bottles! I know that what I wanted to do was to go up on the stage, bundle Allen up, take him home, and feed him warm milk.

The biggest thrill of the evening came when Ginsberg read a poem for my Lionel. It was entitled "Go Home, Lionel," and it nearly moved me to tears. The poem had all the passion, goodness, sympathy, thankfulness, the wonderfulness, the hopefulness, the thirties-quality, of any decent poem. The others then read, and then the question period came. Now at last Ginsberg was able to be a real teacher, like the professors at Columbia.

The evening over, we returned to our homes. When I got home, I found in our comfortably-furnished living room a comfortable professional meeting going on. I found there Pope John, Charlie Chaplin, Boris Pasternak, Daddy Warbucks, William Phillips, Randall Jarrell, Smiling Jack, W. H. Auden, Henry Ford, Picasso, The Dean of Canterbury, Mao Tse Tung, The Wright Brothers, The Hathaway Man, Jacques Barzun, Stephen Markmus, Robert Hall, and Henry Luce. To find your living-room so full is the reward of being a successful writer in America. (Stephen Markmus, born 1932. Old student of Lionel's. He reviews for the *Partisan Review*.) I said to Lionel, "Allen Ginsberg read a love-poem to you, Lionel. I liked it very much." It was a strange thing to say in the circumstances, perhaps even a little foolish. But I'm sure that Ginsberg's old teacher knew what I, as a wife of the English Department, was saying, and why I was impelled to write this ridiculous article.

"It's a Vast Trap!"

All these people [Kerouac, Corso, Olson, Creeley, Snyder, Whalen, Levertov, Zukofsky, Blackburn, Burroughs, McClure, Wieners, Duncan, and other writers whose work Ginsberg discussed in a long section of the letter not included here] should have long ago been having books out in NY & reviewed seriously everywhere & the lack of their material has left the atmosphere poisoned by bad poetry and bad people and bad criticism—and the criticism! incredible after 2 decades of new criticism & the complete incompetence to evaluate & recognise anything new—nothing but lame sociological bullshit in response to Jack's prose or my poetry—or total amnesia with Gregory's or Creeley's & Olson's etc. All the universities been fucking dead horse for decades and this is *Culture*!? Yet prosidy & conceptions of poetry been changing for half a century already and what a columbia instructor can recognise in Pound he can't see in Olson's method, what he can see in Lorca or Apollinaire he can't see in Howl—it's fantastic. You call this education? I call it absolute brainwashed bullshit. Not saying that either Olson or Howl are Lorca or Pound—I'm saying there's a recognizable continuity of method—yet I have to listen to people giving me doublethink gobbledygook about why don't I write poems with form, construction, something charming and carefully made. O Lawrence thou should be living at this hour! and diana trilling in public correspondence with that eminent representative of the younger generation Podhoritz about Lawrence! It's a vast Trap. and god save the poor young students who

From a letter to John Hollander written in the fall of 1958. The letter was in part a reply to Hollander's review, reprinted on pages 26–28 in this collection. For a fuller version of this letter, see Jane Kramer's book, *Allen Ginsberg in America*, pp. 163–77. Reprinted with permission.

know nothing but that mad incestuous atmosphere. I could go on all night. What else what else? Some jerk named Brustein who TEACHES at columbia writing in a new money money money magazine Horizon attacking the Cult of Unthink, grand-scale vicious attack on Stanislavsky Method, abstract painting (bedfellows!) & beat writing drooling on about how I express every degradation but the one humane one Loneliness—I mean some completely inaccurate irrelevant piece of journalism!—ignoring big queer lonely lyrics about Whitman & Moloch in whom I sit lonely cocksucking—just goes on and says this here vicious incoherent Ginsberg refuses to admit he's lonely. He TEACHES! is such a shit allowed on this earth? The whore of Babylon's befallen us! Run for your life! and in Highclass Partisan, Podhoretz (I keep coming back to him it seems he has collected all the garbage in one mind, archetype) quoting me about Jack's "spontaneous bop prosody" proceeds to attack it instead of trying to figure what i mean—because I put it there as a tip, a helpful hint to criticism, a kindly extraverted gesture—and winds up all balled up confusing jack's *diction* & use of the mind's hiptalk to itself with the *rhythm* of the consequent sentences—This sort of ignorant Babel in partisan Review—and they tell me he'll be editor someday? Could that be true? Well they deserve it if they put up with that Yahoo type creepy mentality. I'm sick of the creeps bugging the scene, my scene, America's scene, we only live once, why put up with that grubby type ambitious vanity. Ugh. It's too ignoble. Take it away. I'll take a sick junky any day to this hoarde of half educated deathly academicians. Not *one* yet, not ONE in all the colleges, magazines, book pages has said anything real, has got the point, either of spirit or prosody (what a camp word—I'm sorry I keep using it—it really is that—but *another* way) NOT ONE. And this is the product of the schools of the richest nation of the earth, this is the Intelligentsia that's supposed to run the world, inc. moon? It's a monster shambles.

Complaints, complaints, you hear them on a summers day. Pound is absolutely right . . . With Usura. The whole problem is these types want money & security and not ART.

Notes Written on
Finally Recording "Howl"

By 1955 I wrote poetry adapted from prose seeds, journals, scratchings, arranged by phrasing or breath groups into little short-line patterns according to ideas of measure of American speech I'd picked up from W. C. Williams's imagist preoccupations. I suddenly turned aside in San Francisco, unemployment compensation leisure, to follow my romantic inspiration— Hebraic-Melvillian bardic breath, I thought I wouldn't write a *poem,* but just write what I wanted to without fear, let my imagination go, open secrecy, and scribble magic lines from my real mind—sum up my life—something I wouldn't be able to show anybody, writ for my own soul's ear and a few other golden ears. So the first line of "Howl," "I saw the best minds etc.," the whole first section typed out madly in one afternoon, a huge sad comedy of wild phrasing, meaningless images for the beauty of abstract poetry of mind running along making awkward combinations like Charlie Chaplin's walk, long saxophone-like chorus lines I knew Kerouac would hear *sound* of—taking off from his own inspired prose line really a new poetry.

I depended on the word "who" to keep the beat, a base to keep measure, return to and take off again onto another streak of invention: "who lit cigarettes in boxcars boxcars boxcars," continuing to prophesy what I really knew despite the drear consciousness of the world: "who were visionary indian angels." Have I really been attacked for this sort of joy? So the poem got serious, I went on to what my imagination believed true to Eternity (for I'd had a beatific illumination years before during

From the record jacket of *Allen Ginsberg Reads* Howl and Other Poems, Fantasy Records 7005 (1959). Reprinted with permission.

which I'd heard Blake's ancient voice and saw the universe unfold in my brain) and what my memory could reconstitute of the data of celestial experience.

But how sustain a long line in poetry (lest it lapse into prosaic?). It's natural inspiration of the moment that keeps it moving, disparate thinks put down together, shorthand notations of visual imagery, juxtapositions of hydrogen jukebox—abstract *haikus* sustain the mystery and put iron poetry back into the line: the last line of "Sunflower Sutra" is the extreme, one stream of single word associations, summing up. Mind is shapely, Art is shapely. Meaning Mind practiced in spontaneity invents forms in its own image—gets to Last Thoughts. Loose ghosts wailing for body try to invade the bodies of living men. I hear ghostly Academies in Limbo screeching about Form.

Ideally each line of "Howl" is a single breath unit. . . . My breath is long—that's the Measure, one physical and mental inspiration of thought contained in the elastic of a breath. It probably bugs Williams now, but it's a natural consequence, my own heightened conversation, not cooler average-dailytalk short breath. I get to mouthe more madly this way.

So these poems are a series of experiments with the formal organization of the long line. Explanations follow. I realized at the time that Whitman's form had rarely been further explored (improved on even) in the U.S. Whitman always a mountain too vast to be seen. Everybody assumes (with Pound?) (except Jeffers) that his line is a big freakish uncontrollable necessary prosaic goof. No attempt's been made to use it in the light of early XX Century organization of new speech-rhythm prosody to *build up* large organic structures.

I had an apt. on Nob Hill, got high on Peyote, and saw an image of the robot skullface of Moloch in the upper stories of a big hotel glaring into my window; got high weeks later again, the Visage was still there in red smokey downtown Metropolis, I wandered down Powell street muttering "Moloch Moloch" all night and wrote "Howl II" nearly intact in cafeteria at foot of Drake Hotel, deep in the hellish vale. Here the long line is used as a stanza form broken within into exclamatory units punctuated by a base repetition, Moloch.

The rhythmic paradigm for Part III was conceived and half-written same day as the beginning of "Howl," I went back later and filled it out. Part I, a lament for the Lamb in America with instances of remarkable lamblike youths; Part II names the monster of mental consciousness that preys on the Lamb; Part III a litany of affirmation of the Lamb in its glory: "O starry-spangled shock of Mercy." The structure of Part III, pyramidal, with a graduated longer response to the fixed base.

I remembered the archetypal rhythm of Holy Holy Holy weeping in a bus on Kearney Street, and wrote most of it down in notebook there. That exhausted this set of experiments with a fixed base. I set it as "Footnote to Howl" because it was an extra variation of the form of Part II. (Several variations on these forms, including stanzas of graduated litanies followed by fugues, will be seen in other parts of "Kaddish" to be published by City Lights.)

A lot of these forms developed out of an extreme rhapsodic wail I once heard in a madhouse. Later I wondered if short quiet lyrical poems could be written using the long line. "Cottage in Berkeley" and "Supermarket in California" (written same day) fell in place later that year. Not purposely, I simply followed my Angel in the course of compositions.

What if I just simply wrote, in long units and broken short lines, spontaneously noting prosaic realities mixed with emotional upsurges, solitaries? "Transcription of Organ Music" (sensual data), strange writing which passes from prose to poetry and back, like the mind.

What about poem with rhythmic buildup power equal to "Howl" without use of repeated base to sustain it? "The Sunflower Sutra" (composition time 20 minutes, me at desk scribbling, Kerouac at cottage door waiting for me to finish so we could go off somewhere party) did that, it surprised me, one long Who.

Next what happens if you mix long and short lines, single breath remaining the rule of measure? I didn't trust free flight yet, so went back to fixed base to sustain the flow, *America*. After that, a regular formal type long poem in parts, short and long breaths mixed at random, no fixed base, sum of earlier experiments—"Baggage Room at Greyhound," not on this record. *In Back of the Real* shows what I was doing with short lines (see sentence 1 above) before I accidentally wrote "Howl."

The next two poems (in later book, *Kaddish,* City Lights 1959): First, a strong rhythm built up using free short syncopated lines, "Europe! Europe!" a prophecy written in Paris.

Last, the Proem to "Kaddish" (NY 1959 work)—finally, completely free composition, the long line breaking up within itself into short staccato breath units—notations of one spontaneous phrase after another linked within the line by dashes mostly: the long line now perhaps a variable stanzaic unit, measuring groups of related ideas, marking them—a method of notation. Ending with a hymn in rhythm similar to the synagogue death lament. Passing into dactyllic? says Williams? Perhaps not: at least the ear hears itself in Promethian natural measure, not in mechanical count of accent. . . .

A word on the Academies: poetry has been attacked by an ignorant and frightened bunch of bores who don't understand how it's made, and the trouble with these creeps is they wouldn't know poetry if it came up and buggered them in broad daylight.

A word on the Politicians: my poetry is Angelical Ravings, and has nothing to do with dull materialistic vagaries about who should shoot who. The secrets of individual imagination—which are transconceptual and non-verbal—I mean Unconditional Spirit—are not for sale to this consciousness, are no use to this world, except perhaps to make it shut its trap and listen to the music of the Spheres. Who denies the music of the spheres denies poetry, denies man, and spits on Blake, Shelley, Christ and Buddha. Meanwhile have a ball. The universe is a new flower. America will be discovered. Who wants a war against roses will have it. Fate tells big lies, and the gay Creator dances on his own body in Eternity.

LOUIS GINSBERG

To Allen Ginsberg

Almost like Theseus, you grope
Through dank, subterranean passageways
Of your different selves.
Through neon nights and dead-end days,
You fumble at and explore
Many a bewildering corridor.
You are your own labyrinthine maze.
May you soon see
The Ariadne-thread
Of your true identity
To find the sun-burst opening ahead.

From *Prairie Schooner* (Summer 1959). Reprinted with permission.

KADDISH AND OTHER POEMS

Exalted Lament

"Exalted and hallowed be God's great name in this world of His Creation," which is Allen Ginsberg's intent. The world of Creation, the part of it that is the world of Ginsberg's "Kaddish," is the world of insanity, the miserable streets we walk every day of our lives, dead Jews, some of our time. He has given us some of our time and a good piece of his own life fashioned into a long death anthem for his mother, Naomi. Few poets, I think, would want to summon that death, though the joy of release is in every line.

"Kaddish" (the title poem) is a breakthrough for Ginsberg, and part of the joy in reading it comes from the recognition that a contemporary has faced up to an incredible task successfully. I don't mean only that Ginsberg has been able to cut through and summon the dead, to recreate his insane mother, to make his peace with her, more than that to make a muse of her—the most bizarre muse in English Lit. It would be achievement enough. But he has been able to capture a story and a period of American-Jewish life, a fat novel-full, in verse that never slides under the material it has to carry while it keeps the long breath that is his signature and the pure impulse that is his gift.

Why speak of joy in commenting on a harrowing poem? Because there is joy and faith in the composition itself, in the actual process of composition, that comes across to the reader through the long, open lines, flung out in space and then quickly caught up, and through the poet's ability to make his imagination soar over the details of the remembered life when the poet and the poem need that relief:

From *Midstream* (Autumn 1961). Reprinted with permission.

Communist beauty, sit here married in the summer among
daisies, promised happiness at hand—

holy mother, now you smile on your love, your world is
born anew, children run naked in the field spotted with
dandelions,

they eat in the plum tree grove at the end of the meadow
and find a cabin where a white-haired negro teaches the mystery
of his rainbarrel—

That joy, which comes from having worked through problems
(personal and technical) so that the imagination is buoyed up and
free to play, sets Ginsberg apart from the great majority of his
contemporaries.

"Kaddish" begins as a meditation—a familiar mood, an emo-
tion recollected in (almost) tranquility. Three years after his
mother's death in an asylum, the poet walks the streets of Green-
wich Village into the lower East Side: Orchard Street "where
you walked 50 years ago, little girl—from Russia, eating the
first poisonous tomatoes of America." (Still another work of our
time that takes off from a walk through the city streets.) But the
drive of the poem is quickly established in this first section,
getting its initial emotive power, I think, from the direct address
to the dead. Much of the story of Naomi Ginsberg's life and her
son's reaction to it is collapsed here and the key images intro-
duced.

The section concludes with a lyric based on echoes of the
sound of the Hebrew prayer ("Magnificent, mourned no more,
marred of heart . . .") in which the exaltation of God's name
and the exaltation of the woman's insane life and death are
fused—the essential strategy of the poem.

Early in this first section the rhythm is set going in long end-
stopped lines that are in fact verse paragraphs.

the rhythm the rhythm—and your memory in my head three
years after—And read Adonais' last triumphant stanzas
aloud—wept, realizing how we suffer—
And how Death is that remedy all singers dream of, sing,

remember, prophesy as in the Hebrew Anthem, or the
Buddhist Book of Answers—and my own imagination
of a withered leaf—at dawn—

(From Ginsberg's own remarks about his habits of composition
in the end papers of *The New American Poetry* it would seem that
finding the basic beat is his way of getting into a work.)
Ginsberg accelerates the rhythm when he has to by breaking the
length of the individual units within the verse paragraphs—as in
the narrative that follows section I—and finally by fracturing the
paragraphs themselves.

Section II, the telling of Naomi Ginsberg's story ("re-
membrance of electrical shocks") is the heart of the poem. It
obviously posed the most difficulties and received the most
work. Ginsberg handles the narration in an ungrammatical
shorthand that appears to be swift notation of basic fact but does
in reality give you much side detail, characterization, descrip-
tion, affect, literary play ('On what wards—I walked there later,
oft—old catatonic ladies"), mimicry ("Roosevelt should know
her case, she told me"). His ability to recall and re-create this
story of breakdowns, hallucinations, and great scandalous scenes
is astounding.

The last scene in the narration is an account of the poet's final
interview with his mother two years before her death:

One hand stiff—heaviness of forties & menopause reduced by
one heart stroke, lame now—wrinkles—a scar on her head,
the lobotomy—ruin, the hand dipping downwards to death—

The section concludes with a "Hymmnn" summing up the hor-
ror ("Blessed be He in homosexuality! Blessed be He in Para-
noia!").

Sections III and IV, short passages, are echoes of the great
explosion of the narrative rather than attempts to restate it or
make abstract sense of it. Their key phrases—"Only to have not
forgotten" and "What have I left out"—mingle in the final sec-
tion with the sound of the crows over Naomi Ginsberg's grave
and the repeated naming of God.

It occurs to me that I have been treating Ginsberg's "Kaddish" as if it were a literary work—indeed, a literary work of some distinction. This approach may obscure the brutal, obscene story and the poem's desperate and at times consciously illiterate cry. The narrative itself is a splattering of phrases as if the poet were afraid that reflection or literary considerations might get in the way of what took a good deal of honesty to face, and give him an excuse to back off.

My view of Ginsberg's achievement is that he has said what he wanted to say with all the force of his original impulse, and with nothing left out. And that, as much as he had to fight literature to do this, he was able to do it through the use of the literary techniques of our day. Maybe that is true to some extent of most of our successful work. I don't know what is gained by calling "Kaddish" "antiliterature." It has shape, coherence, force; it is a complex mixture of realistic narrative (real people, places, things, happenings) and visionary arias, managed with skill. Moreover, it was written by a man very sure of his literary tradition and quick to name literary fathers.

Naturally, none of the other poems in the volume stand up to "Kaddish." They are mostly weak, wandering pieces with no place to go—some of them evidences of Ginsberg's growing preoccupation with his public self. (I would except "At Apollinaire's Grave," "The Lion for Real," and the little piece of realism, "To Aunt Rose.") Occasionally in these poems Ginsberg sweetens his observations. Then even his rhetoric seems false and borrowed: "no woman in house / loves husband in flower unity." Or the sentimentality that often threatens to show in a Ginsberg poem—but never in "Kaddish"—flashes belly upward. So in "At Apollinaire's Grave," after stating his wish to lay a copy of "Howl" on that dead poet, Ginsberg writes: "I hope some wild kidmonk lay his pamphlet on my grave for God to read me on cold winter nights in heaven."

Maybe that isn't any more sentimental than "So may some gentle muse / With lucky words favor my destined urn / And as he passes turn / And bid fair piece be to my sable shroud." But the earlier version has the saving grace of "lucky." Anyway, the conception of the poet as "wild kidmonk" is the dead-end, the winking anus of Beat Romanticism.

There's no point in belaboring these faults. The achievement of "Kaddish" is enough to ponder. Its power is such that when Ginsberg says in one of his political poems, "History will make this poem prophetic and its awful silliness a hideous spiritual music," I almost believe him.

Ginsberg has become such a public issue that it's difficult now to read him naturally; you ask yourself after every line, am I for him or against him. And by and large that's the kind of criticism he has gotten—votes on a public issue. (I see this has been one of those reviews.)

At a party some months ago—a gathering of poets, most of an unalloyed bohemianism, despite the sufferance granted me— I mentioned his work and found no one there who respected it or would even acknowledge it existed. Such a response to Ginsberg is an act of will, of willful blindness, I think, because his talent is self-evident—of a quick brilliance and all of it up on the wide, wide screen. (Corso's talent strikes me as similarly undeniable. As for Ferlinghetti, I read him as an agile, soft-shoe man.) How can you come away from the opening pages of "Howl" without seeing that a young poet has had a vision of the City, has bared his brains to heaven and caught the fire straight, as no one has since Blake?

Why the blindness? Resentment of the fact that Ginsberg has captured the only audience most poets want—the young, the college kids, the Village girls and boys? Resentment of the public relations pimps among the Beats? Resentment of the claims a boy from Newark makes for himself in his verse? ("And 'tis most wicked in a Christian Nation / For any man to pretend to Inspiration." Of course, if he's a Welsh import flown in on the blessings of a Sitwell, that's different.)

Maybe the major reason for the resistance to Ginsberg is that he opens questions many poets and critics have an interest in considering closed. When I first went to school to the quarterlies there was little doubt about the way American poetry was to go. Blackmur summed it up in an essay in *Kenyon Review* in 1952 ("Lord Tennyson's Scissors: 1912–1950"). The Apocalyptic and Violent school (Lindsay, Jeffers) and the other school of anti-intelligence (writers in *transition* who copied French poets like Apollinaire) were finished. The dominant school was to be the "school of Donne" (described at one point as writers of "a Court poetry, learned at its fingertips and full of a decorous willfulness called ambiguity"). Now, largely because of Ginsberg's work, we are not so sure. It will all have to be fought out again. An upsetting prospect.

A. ALVAREZ

Ginsberg and the Herd Instinct

The Beats have been remarkably faithful to each other. Where the Angry Young Men, at the first whiff of fame, turned their guns savagely on their own troops, the Beat writers have solemnly gone on dedicating poems, novels and lovers to fellow Beats. No doubt they have crowded together for warmth defensively; they wouldn't have done so had their work stood square—to use the wrong word—on its own feet. After all, to speak at large for a generation is, as every politician knows, a good deal easier than to speak precisely for oneself.

True to form, Allen Ginsberg's *Kaddish and Other Poems* is dedicated to Orlovsky,* quotes Corso, mentions other pals and includes a series of pieces on a Beat's best friend, his drugs. Also true to form, these group pieces are conceited and pretentious in that shouting surrealist style the Beats have reclaimed from the Dadaists and, with their flair for advertising, so efficiently popularized. "Were they listening to my ravings in the locker rooms of Bickfords Employment Offices?" asks Mr. Ginsberg. Well, they may not have been once but, oddly enough, they are now.

"Kaddish" itself, however, is of quite a different order from the other poems. This funeral lament for Ginsberg's mother is at once much more and much less a formal poem than anything he has so far produced. It is more a poem in that the poet is not, for once, concerned with peddling the public image of himself. Instead, he is simply trying to record in full his mother's madness and death in a lunatic asylum. And because he lets the appalling

---

Review of *Kaddish and Other Poems,* from the London *Observer,* 14 May 1961. Reprinted with permission.

Kaddish, the book, bears no dedication. "Kaddish," the poem, is dedicated to Naomi Ginsberg.—ED.

story speak for itself, the poem is at once moving and curiously detached; the sufferings of his mother were so overwhelming they leave him no time for his own; so everything goes into poetic accuracy. Yet it is also less a poem because Ginsberg's verse paragraphs—one can't call them lines any more—no longer retain even the ghost of the Whitmanesque thump which once sustained them. His work is now neither verse nor prose; it is the violent emotional shorthand of the analyst's couch, held together by a strong narrative thread:

> Opened the door to the ward—she went thru without a glance back, quiet suddenly—I stared out—she looked old—the verge of the grave—"All the Horror!"

"Kaddish" is by far the most impressive poem Ginsberg has yet produced and it may, like all good psychotherapy, have cleared the way for more adult work; indeed, already there are signs of this—a short poem on Vachel Lindsay and a longer piece called "The Lion for Real" which even shows traces of wit. But I suppose his future as a poet depends on how much he is chivvied by the literary P.R.O.s to keep up his frenetic act. Next to "Kaddish," a habitually hepped-up piece such as "Death to Van Gogh's Ear!" sounds merely like a faint echo of the paranoic ravings he had re-created and judged in the poem on his mother.

PAUL CARROLL

The Pentecostal Poems of *Kaddish*

. . . Allen Ginsberg's real accomplishments as a poet do not come from his public image or his political and social poems. The great Ginsberg poems are private. ("Howl"—that labyrinth of personal sorrow—is a very private poem.) The earlier ones were elegiac. In them Ginsberg mourned his own miseries and the insanity of his friend Carl Solomon, the death of his mother, the decay of his own body. The more recent poems are pentecostal. Tongues of fire flicker through them as Ginsberg wrestles with the Godhead—the first American writer to do so since Melville. . . .

There are four [such poems in *Kaddish*], "Lysergic Acid," the fierce, great "Magic Psalm," "The Reply," and "The End." (The last three were, according to the poet, "visions experienced after drinking ayahuasca, an Amazon spiritual potion.")

For the first time in our poetry we have a poet who celebrates the ancient ritual—Invoking of the God. These poems are both invocation and confrontation. In them Ginsberg asks and gives no quarter. One must take them as literal, experienced visions, or not at all. What is hard to bear is the shock of seeing a modern American poet struggling like a Hebrew prophet with his God. The God whom Ginsberg invokes, hates, loves, mocks, copulates with, and weeps on his knees in front of, is terribly present. The God of Eliot, for contrast, is a God honed from the tomes of the Fathers and Divines (which is not to say he is any the less real). The God of Ginsberg is the one who exists before the civilized sensibility. He is the barbarous, beautiful God who speaks from the Burning Bush.

From "Death is a Letter that was Never Sent," in *Evergreen Review* (July–August 1961). Reprinted with permission.

The title of this review is a line from the poem "Mescaline."* It seems to embody the best of Ginsberg: his elegiac powers that can resurrect the dead; his stubborn refusal to circumscribe experience to this empirical world of trees, offices, Richard M. Nixon, income tax returns, and taxis; his insistence, that is, on trafficking with the eternal things. If there is a Heaven, Allen Ginsberg will get into it—even if he has to break down the Gates of Pearl. He is one of the violent lovers. "From the days of John the Baptist until now, the kingdom of heaven suffereth violence, and the violent bear it away."

*"Death is a Letter that was Never Sent" is a line from "Ignu," not from "Mescaline."—Ed.

ROBERT ANTON WILSON

The Poet as Radar System

Forty years ago, Ezra Pound made his celebrated boast of the social function of art: "The artist is the antenna of the race, the barometer and voltmeter." Allen Ginsberg is nothing if not contemporary. He brings the boast up to date with a stunning effectiveness:

> I am the Defense Early Warning Radar System
> I see nothing but bombs

These lines are typical of Ginsberg's unpolished-looking verse. He seems to work in poetry the way Rouault worked in paint: hacking his way savagely, with crude and sweeping strokes, toward an image of maximum ferocity. Look at Rouault's "Three Judges," those faces of moronic evil plastered on the canvas as if in rage and colored with the darkest, smeariest blacks and browns this side of downtown Passaic; this is the typical "feel" of a Ginsberg poem. Actually, of course, neither Rouault nor Ginsberg work in a frothing frenzy. Ginsberg in particular probably spends as much effort sounding "uncivilized" as Henry James ever spent in sounding "civilized."

There has been little technical analysis of Ginsberg's verse thus far; the job requires an ear delicate as Pound's and the patience of an elephant. It generally takes me three or four readings aloud to feel my way toward Ginsberg's music; his great bass, as Pound would call it, is strong as a Watusi drum, but, like a Watusi drum, full of surprising polyrhythms and unexpected variations. I have heard that the poetry reviews in the *Saturday Review,* New York *Times,* etc. are actually written by

Review of *Kaddish,* from *Liberation* (November 1962). Reprinted with permission.

machines; and, from the reviews Ginsberg has gotten in those and similar publications, I would gather that the machines in question, like most university poetry teachers, are not yet capable of following a meter more challenging than the traditional *umpty-umpty-umpty* (followed occasionally by *umpty-umpty-UMty*.)

Let's take a closer look at one of Ginsberg's oral constructions. A poem is a statue in sound, or "frozen architecture," or anyway you slice it it's basically a *structure,* a form *manufactured* by a man. The chief thing about Allen Ginsberg as a poet is that he always shows you his form emerging, the way it builds up, a thing created out of ordinary speech but suddenly, by the height of its emotion, transcending ordinary speech. *Kaddish* begins with words you or I might speak:

> Strange now to think of you, gone without corsets & eyes, while
> I walk on the sunny pavement of Greenwich Village.

Like most modern poetry, this cannot be broken down into a traditional meter, but has to be considered in terms of Pound's Second Law of Imagism: "to write in the sequence of the musical phrase." There are three phrases above, the second syncopating slightly with the first, and the third a prolonged complication on both of the first two. It's rather like Charlie Parker taking off and searching for his theme. In a few lines Ginsberg finds his basic beat:

> . . . and I've been up all night, talking, talking, reading the
> Kaddish aloud, listening to Ray Charles blues shout blind
> on the phonograph
> the rhythm the rhythm

We are still in the area of normal American speech, but Ginsberg is beginning to pick out of it his own building blocks. "And I've been up all night, talking, talking . . . Ray Charles blues shout blind on the phonograph / the rhythm the rhythm": these lines syncopate beautifully, and the internal phrase, "reading the Kaddish aloud" picks up on the initial "Strange now to think of you." Allen Ginsberg sifts through the resources of American

97

English like a placer miner going through his dust, carefully lifting out a nugget at a time.

Once he has found what he's looking for, he hammers it out with the remorseless monotony of Beethoven, or perhaps I should say of Bizet in the *Arlesienne Suite*. "Kaddish" moves towards its close through a hymn to the God who allowed the poet's mother to go mad:

> In the house in Newark Blessed is He! In the madhouse Blessed is He! In the house of Death blessed is He!

Even the tragedy of the poor old woman is blessed:

> Blessed be you Naomi in Hospitals! Blessed be you Naomi in solitude! Blest be your triumph! Blest be your bars! Blest be your last years' loneliness!

But an even stronger rhythm breaks in to mourn the all-too-true truth that there is nothing blessed, only pain, in the story of Naomi Ginsberg:

> only to have seen her weeping on gray tables in long wards of her universe
> only to have known the weird ideas of Hitler at the door
> . . . .
> only to have seen the time-jumps, memory lapse, the crash of wars, the roar and silence of a vast electric shock

and the reality, the lack of blessing and triumph, is thereupon hammered like Pound's rock-drill till it almost bursts the reader's brain:

> with your eyes running naked out of the apartment screaming into the hall
> with your eyes being led away by policemen to an ambulance
> with your eyes strapped down on the operating table
> with your eyes of the pancreas removed
> with your eyes of appendix operation
> with your eyes of abortion

        with your eyes of ovaries removed
        with your eyes of shock
        with your eyes of lobotomy

The theme beats into the soul like a drum:

    with your eyes
    with your eyes

—and then suddenly turns around on itself and bursts forth into
a line of sheer genius:

    with your Death full of Flowers

    From "Strange now to think" through "the rhythm the
rhythm" the poem has gradually created, just through the integr-
ity of its own emotion, the justification from the drum-beat and
thunder of "only to have, only to have" and "with her eyes,
with her eyes." If anybody else repeated the "formula," it
would only be a trick, because the emotion is in the words and
the discovery of the words is the discovery of the emotion. It is
Ginsberg's personal Golgotha that we meet here, and if you or I
were to tell our own stories we would have to find our own
words and emotions. That is why a great work of poetry is
always so original as to seem "formless" at first glance. It ap-
pears to have no form because it is a new form, manufactured in
heart's agony, a shape cut in the air as a sculptor cuts.
    The last movement opens with a bird call:

    Caw caw caw crows shriek in the white sun over grave stones in
        Long Island

The crows seem to burst onto the page with the vividness of real
life; we actually hear them before we see them. But Ginsberg,
with the audacity of genius, has another trick for us in the next
line:

    Lord Lord Lord Naomi underneath this grass my halflife and my
        own as hers

The tom-tom is back again, this time in a half-rhymed fugue with "Caw caw caw" chasing "Lord Lord Lord" down the page. It is "only to have" and "with your eyes" picked up into greater urgency than before:

Lord Lord great Eye that stares on All and moves in a black cloud
caw caw strange cry of Beings sung up into sky over the waving
trees

The ending is pure fugue, pure as Bach:

Lord Lord Lord caw caw caw Lord Lord Lord caw caw caw Lord

The harsh monosyllables of American speech have dominated the poem from "Strange now to think" right through to "caw caw caw Lord." Pound showed us how to do this forty years ago, with his "Blue jade cups well set" etc., but he has had no student to apply him half so well as Allen Ginsberg. And the economy and magnificence of using "Lord Lord Lord" against "caw caw caw"—an implied identification picked up in the montagelike shift from God as "black cloud" to the black cloud of crows—this is balancing a poem as skillfully as Roebling balanced the Brooklyn Bridge.

Among the shorter poems in this volume, particularly good are "Poem Rocket," "Death to Van Gogh's Ear!," "The Lion for Real," and "Ignu." "Poem Rocket" contains a line that evokes extraterrestrial beauty better than the best of the science-fiction writers: "Which way will the sunflower turn surrounded by millions of suns?" And "The Lion for Real" brings the Spirits of Terror to the page in a way that makes one think of Dante; you can't laugh off Ginsberg's Lion anymore than you can smile at Dante's hell, or Blake's Tyger, or Melville's Whale. Ginsberg has *seen* the Lion, and, by God, he makes you see it, too. Naturally, *Life* magazine describes his vision as "sick" and "warped"; the System which is willing to create twenty thousand abnormal babies everytime it sets off a nuclear bomb cannot afford to listen to the reports of this extremely delicate instrument, the "Defense Early Warning Radar System" that is the soul of the poet today.

Remarks

(from reviews of "Kaddish")

Despite the use by Ginsberg . . . of Jewish references, we have a queazy feeling that [he is] pouring into Tradition values that are not there and that are not genuine and legitimate. There is a kind of illegitimate use of Jewish Tradition that is exceedingly exasperating.

. . . Speak the word Kaddish to any Jew—of high or low degree on the intellectual scale—and it bears a definite meaning. It is the hymn of praise to God for the gift of life; it is the assertion of faith in God as a God of love and justice; and all this despite Death in whose presence all man and his works seem so futile and transient. . . .

But in Ginsberg's "Kaddish"—powerful as the poem is and deeply moving as its many passages are—there is a total absence of any spiritual quality that in the slightest way warrants the use of the word Kaddish.

—Mortimer J. Cohen, in *Jewish Exponent,*
10 November 1961

It is not just for his mother that he says "Kaddish," . . . nor for himself alone; but for America, as he sees it, the America of "Money! Money! Money! shrieking mad celestial money of illusion! Money made of nothing, starvation, suicide! Money of failure! Money of death!"

Here is the nightmare that has driven The Beat to such excess. . . . Read "Kaddish" and see if you do not better understand why the writing of The Beat has become so influential among today's youth.

—Mike Newberry, in *The Worker,* 7 November 1961

ALLEN GROSSMAN

Allen Ginsberg

The Jew as an American Poet

The Jew, like the Irishman, presents himself as a type of the sufferer in history. At a mysterious moment near the end of the nineteenth century the Irish produced a literature of international importance without having previously contributed a single significant poem in English. The Jewish poet in America today resembles the Irishman in England during the 1890s. From a literary point of view, he is emerging from parochialism into the mainstream of writing in English, and he is bringing with him a cultural mystery arising out of his centrality in history as a sufferer, and also out of his relation to a vast body of literature in another language. The Irish at the end of the nineteenth century discovered rather suddenly that their political experience had a symbolic relation to modern history as a whole, and that their ancient literature provided an inexhaustible resource of mythology by which to interpret that history. The Jewish poet in America at this time is engaged in the attempt to express the meaning of his own historical centrality, and he too possesses a vast body of literature in another language—the *Zohar,* for example—which constitutes a symbolic resource as yet unworked in terms of English literature.

None of the Anglo-Irish poets of the Celtic Renaissance began as celebrants of the Irish subject matter, or practitioners of a style which might be called peculiarly Irish. They, all of them, "went Irish" when it became professionally useful for them to do so. Similarly, there is a tendency at the present for Jewish

From *Judaism* (Fall 1962). Reprinted with permission.

poets, whose work appeared at first under culturally neutral auspices, to present their work again (Karl Shapiro is the most obvious example) as *Poems of a Jew.* In the case of Allen Ginsberg, the development is quite clear. His earliest poems (reprinted as *Empty Mirror,* Totem Press, 1961) are culturally anonymous. His first published volume of poems (*Howl,* the Pocket Poets Series, 1955) draws its title from Blake, and presents itself as part of a completely formed artificial subculture called "Beat" which takes the place of the lost real ethnic and political subcultures which in the past succored and gave identity to the outcast by forming a community of outcasts. Ginsberg's most recent volume, *Kaddish,* is presented under an aggressively Jewish title despite the fact that it is in no simple sense a Jewish book.

The Beat movement, which is now more or less done with, is antinomian and predominantly mystic in substance, and Ginsberg, though still from a position within the movement, is quite clearly invoking the Jewish cultural mystery as a new ground for poetic identity beyond the disintegrating coterie which first gave him notoriety and a language.

Ginsberg's poetry belongs to that strange and almost posthumous poetic literature which began to be produced in America after World War II, and in which the greatest figure is the spoiled Calvinist (Catholic), Robert Lowell. The characteristic literary posture of the postwar poet in America is that of the survivor—a man who is not quite certain that he is not in fact dead. It is here that the Jew as a symbolic figure takes on his true centrality. The position can be stated hypothetically from the point of view of a European survivor who has made the Stygian crossing to America: "Since so many like me died, and since my survival is an unaccountable accident, how can I be certain that I did not myself die and that America is not in fact Hell, as indeed all the social critics say it is?" Ginsberg's poetry is the poetry of a terminal cultural situation. It is a Jewish poetry because the Jew is the prime symbolic representative of man overthrown by history.

It must be remembered that the image of the Jew in America as it underlies the poetry of Ginsberg is not in any sense the same as the image of the Jew in Europe, such as we find, for example, in the poetry of Eliot. Eliot's Jew is a familiar figure resembling Shylock and the Ugly American. Eliot's Jew is the phantom of a dead cultural situation. Ginsberg's Jewish protagonist is the apotheosis of the young radical Jewish intellectual, born out of his time and place, possessing now neither social nor political status. Having exhausted all the stratagems of personal identity, sexual and ethnic, he is nonetheless determined to celebrate his state of being and his moment in history.

From a general point of view, what Ginsberg says in "Kaddish" is that there is no longer any wisdom in experience. In a conversation not long ago with another poet of the "Beat scene," I was astonished to learn that Ginsberg is regarded as a "Dionysian" writer. One must hope that the Dionysian man has more joy in his ecstasy. Certainly the opposite is the case. "Howl," Ginsberg's only major poem, is a lament for the passing of experience as a resource for wisdom. In Ginsberg and the Beat writers generally the word "wisdom" is an important technical term. If there are two traditions of wisdom-education, the first proposing that the greatest wisdom arises from the most intense transaction with experience, as exemplified, for instance, in the career of Oedipus; and the second, that wisdom arises from the least transaction with experience, Socrates and Jesus being the examples—then Ginsberg represents a culture that has exhausted the first of these resources and that has turned, with hardly more certitude than the mere assertion, to the second. Ginsberg represents himself as the last wise child in a secular culture, whose mission it is to reconstitute the relation of the world and its soul.

The symbol of the ultimate transaction with experience for Ginsberg, as for Sophocles, is possession of the mother. Nothing, needless to say, could be more predictable from the point of view of the popular sociology of the Jewish family. But what represents Ginsberg's point of view as so entirely desolating is that he documents the death of the mother, and therefore of the ground of experience itself, as a source of value. At the end of the great sentence which constitutes the first 150 lines of "Howl," the speaker has reproduced the crime of Oedipus, and found guilt without transformation. The New York of Ginsberg is a kind of Thebes through which the poet wanders like a king become prophet by some terrible and inappropriate transformation: but beyond Thebes there is no Colonus where the prophet becomes a king once again outside of life. In "Kaddish" Ginsberg laments the death of the mother herself, the ground of all being both physical and ethnic. In "Kaddish" the archetypal female is a mutilated and paranoid old woman ("scars of operations, pancreas, belly wounds, abortions, appendix, stitching of incisions pulling down in the fat like hideous thick zippers . . .") haunted by the image of Hitler and dying, obscene and abandoned, in a sanatorium.

This is Ginsberg's version of the Jewish mother and, simultaneously, of the *shechina,* the wandering soul of Israel herself. Ginsberg is the last dutiful son of Israel reciting *kaddish* at the grave of his mother and of the symbolic image of his people. The mysticism of Ginsberg is peculiarly Jewish in the same sense that the *Zohar* is Jewish. As Gershom Scholem has recently shown, the origins of Zoharistic mysticism lie deeply embedded in Christian gnosticism. For Ginsberg, as for the Jewish mystic in general, the gnostic attitude represents the attempt of the Jewish mind to reconstitute itself outside of history. The Jewish mother in "Kaddish" phantasies herself hunted by friend and enemy alike, by her own mother, by her husband, by Roosevelt, Hitler, by Doctor Isaac, by history itself. She possesses an insane idealism of which her son is heir, and in the end she dies in a fashion so ignominious as to be obscene. Ginsberg erects on her grave an image which is no longer ethnic and which therefore is no longer obsessed by the mystery of the Jewish people in history. To Naomi dead he cries out:

O glorious muse that bore me from the womb, gave suck first mystic life & taught me talk and music, from whose pained head I first took Vision—

Tortured and beaten in the skull—What mad hallucinations of the damned that drive me out of my own skull to seek Eternity till I find Peace for Thee, O Poetry—and for all humankind call on the Origin

Death which is the mother of the universe!—Now wear your nakedness forever, white flowers in your hair, your marriage sealed behind the sky—no revolution might destroy that maidenhood—

O beautiful Garbo of my Karma—

In his poetry Ginsberg attempts simultaneously to document the death of history itself, of which the Jewish people personified by his mother Naomi is the symbol, and to erect a new ground of being beyond history of which his own poetry is the type and of which the symbol is the mother, or Israel, transformed as Muse.

Curiously enough, Ginsberg finds a tradition for his peculiar form of Jewish gnosticism in the history of American stylistics. Ginsberg, and to some extent the Beat movement in general, regards himself as the heir of the American transcendentalist rhetoric. He himself refers to his style as "Hebraic-Melvillian." The transcendentalism of Emerson, founded as it is on the *Metaphysics* of Leibnitz rather than on the *Ethics* of Spinoza, provides a national strain upon which Ginsberg, who is at once casual and profoundly serious about his references to history, attempts to graft his "Angelical Ravings." This mixture of nationalism and ethnicism represents the peculiar position of the American Jewish poet who regards himself as simultaneously native and, in the special sense which always pertains to the Jew, alien.

Significantly, Ginsberg's attempt to trace his particular form of transcendental ambition to Whitman is, in all but the grossest sense, absurd. The Whitmanian style is founded upon the celebration of the secular world as an inexhaustible resource of sensation and identity. The world of Ginsberg, on the other hand, is the world of the ruined mind presiding over the death of its physical being and attempting to refound itself in a new reality. The culture of Ginsberg's poems, despite its attempt to naturalize itself, is fundamentally an international culture, as the mind of the Jew is fundamentally an international or extranational phenomenon. "Kaddish" opens with a neo-Platonic reference to Shelley's *Adonais,* a prophetic memory of the Hebrew anthem, and echoes of Christian apocalypse. His style recalls successively Yeats, Hart Crane, William Blake, the Jacobean prose of the Authorized Version, the ecstatic prose of *Moby Dick,* the translations from the thirties of the Chinese wisdom literatures. Whereas the national image in Whitman is a stable symbol of an ideal form of the self, Ginsberg's reference to America is an effort to naturalize a fundamentally alien consciousness. For Ginsberg the poetic identity must supersede the ethnic identity if the poet is to survive.

Ginsberg's poetry, insofar as it is American poetry, represents an attempt to refound moral culture from a point of view outside any given tradition. The form of his poetry—that of the enormous unifying syntax of the single sentence—is proposed as a model or archetype of some new language of personal being. Like the Jewish Kabbalist, Ginsberg regards his words and indeed the letters of which they are composed as living things which in their form represent the recreation of "the syntax and measure of poor human prose." The ideal of unity in the self, which represents a legitimization of both the body and the soul in terms of one another, finds its source in the English poetic tradition in William Blake. Blake himself drew on Swedenborg, Law's translations of Boehme, Milton and other sources many of which are themselves identical with the culture out of which Jewish mysticism arises. Ginsberg gathers together in his peculiar way all these ancient cries of ecstatic being, and lays them down on the page as a kind of epitome of failed hopefulness.

The enemy in Ginsberg is Moloch, who is quite simply the image of the objective world of which the economic culture of America is the demiurgic creator. Moloch, or Capitalism, destroys the soul and drives the "angel" to a frenzied search for new worlds. Similarly, in the Jewish mystical tradition the neophyte attempts to uncreate himself and to return back along the developmental continuum to the womb and primal substance in which he had his origin. Curiously, the symbols which Ginsberg employs to identify the moral enemy are in part the symbols by which the Jewish role in culture is traditionally defined. Throughout Ginsberg's writing there is an ambivalence towards Jewishness which should be recognized, as it seems to be an emphatic part of his public statement.

The death of the Jewish mother in Ginsberg's "Kaddish," and the succession of cultural generations implied in the burden of identity laid by the mother on the son, is unquestionably the most momentous record in English of the problem of the passing of the older sociology and meaning of the Jewish family-centered culture in America. But the mysticism with which Ginsberg faces the problem of the death of Israel is, perhaps, less momentous than the poetry which he makes the vehicle of that problem. There is, as I stated at the outset, no major tradition of

Jewish poetry in America, as there was before Robert Lowell no major tradition of Catholic poetry, or as there was before Yeats no major tradition of Irish poetry in England. On the one hand Ginsberg uses his Jewishness as a way of representing the general condition of the culture of value in America without relying on meaninglessly familiar symbols.[1] On the other hand he represents himself as the only surviving son of a Jewish universe which died with the death of his mother. We may note that the Jewish symbology becomes available in American poetry just at the point at which the Jewish poet finds it necessary to document the death of the Jewish cultural fact.

The earlier poetry of Ginsberg, that represented primarily by the volume entitled *Howl,* is a great deal more buoyant than the poetry which we are here considering. Between *Howl* and *Kaddish* Ginsberg has lost his humor and gained a kind of horror which even he cannot accommodate to the necessary reticence of the poetic mode. Ginsberg's chief artistic contribution in *Kaddish* is a virtually psychotic candor which effects the mind less like poetry than like some real experience which is so terrible that it cannot be understood. In America, which did not experience the Second World War on its own soil, the Jew may indeed be the proper interpreter of horror.

Allen Ginsberg himself was too young to experience the Second World War either as a soldier or civilian. For him, as for other American poets in this decade, the extreme situation, the American analogy of the bombed city and the concentration camp, is mental illness and the horrors of private life. In this sense the Jewish family, as Ginsberg represents it, becomes the type of the private suffering of the American soul. The tendency of recent American poetry to represent the terrors of history in terms of purely mental agony is almost universal. This is the subject of Snodgrass's *Heart's Needle,* Sexton's *To Bedlam,* and, most recently, Dugan's *Poems.* Ginsberg's image, however, is more extreme than any of these, and I am inclined to think that it is the Jewish mystery which makes that stern agony possible.

Now I should like to return to the general problem of Jewish poetry in America with which I began. It is clear that Ginsberg uses Jewishness as a way out of the cultural *cul-de-sac* of the Beat style, and as a way into the soul of the American intellectual. It is clear also that Ginsberg can entertain the Jewish subject matter only as it is in the process of being transformed into something else. Quite possibly the documentation of the death of Judaism is, and will always be, the characteristic Jewish subject. However that may be, Ginsberg has had the sense to perceive that the only significant Jewish poetry will also be a significant American poetry in the sense that its style will be dictated by the universe of recognition formed by the discourse of American poetry as a whole, and not by the universe of recognition constituted by the parochial concern to which the typical Yiddish-American writer addresses himself.

The basic criterion for an American poetry which is also Jewish is an intimate commitment to the stylistic canons of the English and American literary community. It is only under the stylistic auspices of the great literary tradition of the English-speaking peoples that Jewish symbols and Jewish historical attitudes will become significant poetic subjects in America. The fact that Ginsberg seems to be a Jewish poet less by design than by the habitual candor of his nature is the sanction for such Jewish meaning as truly exists in his verse. What is happening in Ginsberg is that a sense of the disintegration of past cultural identities has led to a return to even more ancient symbols of moral being, such as those embedded in the matrix of medieval Jewish mysticism. The death of the mother in "Kaddish" represents the death of parochial culture, and the poem emerges at the point when it is necessary to lament that loss and to refound the sense of identity on more essential and less time-limited images.

Judaism is an ahistorical religion and the entry of its symbols into the English and American literary community at large has been prevented by a perverse commitment to history which is represented by cultural and linguistic parochialism. There is more essentially Jewish mystical symbolism in the use of Kabbalah by Yeats and the French Symbolists than there is in the current Jewish poetry which is presently appearing in the periodicals. Ginsberg represents a brilliant though uncertain invasion of the American literary community by the Jewish sensibility in the process of transcending parochial definitions. It is an irony, though not necessarily an unproductive one, that the *kaddish* which is recited for the death of the archetypal Jewish mother should be embedded in the language of Yeats and Whitman.

NOTE

1. In America, the idea that the European culture of symbolism is exhausted has been common enough. In this sense, Ginsberg's notion that Whitman is his master has a certain rectitude. The following is the second stanza of Whitman's "Song of the Exposition":

Come, Muse, migrate from Greece and Ionia,
Cross out please those immensely overpaid accounts,
That matter of Troy and Achilles' wrath, and Aeneas', Odysseus'
    wanderings,
Placard "Removed" and "To Let" on the rocks of your snowy
    Parnassus,
Repeat at Jerusalem, place the notice high on Jaffa's gate and on
    Mount Moriah,
The same on the walls of your German, French and Spanish castles,
    and Italian collections,
For know a better, fresher, busier sphere, a wide, untried domain
    awaits, demands you.

It will be observed, however, that Whitman rejects even the Semitic background as symbolic possibility. Whitman is striking beneath all historical symbolism, whereas Ginsberg, against the sensibility of his master, is the prophet of a non-European symbolic context which is nonetheless historical. Whitman is attempting to return to the non-cultural pieties of nature, Ginsberg to the purely cultural ecstasies of God and his angels.

M. L. ROSENTHAL

The Refusal to Repress

. . .The story [of Naomi Ginsberg, as it is told in "Kaddish," assumes . . .] the Communist political ambience as a simple condition of life, rather than as an abstraction of tendentious public debate. "Kaddish" tells us that the time of Naomi's first nervous breakdown "was 1919—she stayed home from school," where she taught retarded children, "and lay in a dark room for three weeks—something bad—never said what—every noise hurt. . . ." Whatever that first reason was, the paranoia progressed and, under the influence of the rise of Hitler and the internal, passionate struggles within the Communist movement, took the form of a suspicion that she was surrounded by spies and poisoners in the image of the obvious Russian models: "The enemies approach—what poisons? Tape recorders? FBI? Zhdanov hiding behind the counter? Trotsky mixing rat bacteria in the back of the store? . . ." Clearly, Naomi's unstable personality found the pressures of the 1930s unbearable. Acutely conscious of the Hitler terror and of the ravages of fascism in Europe generally—far more so than the majority of Americans, who were not sensitive to these developments until late in the game—she lived under tensions that were alien to far more sophisticated people. In addition, there were the hysterical obsessions with "Trotskyism" and with the Russian spy trials of the Communist movement. Superimposed on the early sexual and other causes that Ginsberg hints at knowingly, and that were doubtless the true ultimate source of her difficulties, these political pressures had a reality that should not be discounted.

Ginsberg's success as a confessional poet in this instance lies

From a chapter on "Confessional Poets" in *The New Poets: American and British Poetry Since World War II* (New York: Oxford University Press, 1967). Copyright © 1967 by M. L. Rosenthal. Reprinted with permission from M. L. Rosenthal.

partly in his refusal to repress this reality, which is so important to his experience. The refusal clarifies, too, the connection between the allusions to his mother in "Howl" and the series of outcries against modern civilization in that poem conceived as a speech by an extraordinarily imaginative and sardonic political orator. In *Life Studies,* the "disgrace" [Robert] Lowell confesses to, mainly, is his father's failure (and the failure of the culture to save him as a man and his son from breakdown). In "Kaddish," the "disgrace" Ginsberg confesses to is not alone his mother's madness and the pathetic condition to which it reduced every other member of the family. It is also the slightly exotic and generally despised Communist background, which he refuses to apologize for. In the earlier "America," indeed, the poet mocks the makers of repressive stereotypes in this country with his sentimental memories of this background, just as he does, in another context, with his homosexual attitudes when he speaks, for instance, of how he is "putting my queer shoulder to the wheel." One line especially of "America" is quite explicit:

America when I was seven momma took me to Communist Cell
    meetings they sold us garbanzos a handful per ticket a ticket
    costs a nickel and the speeches were free everybody was angelic
    and sentimental about the workers it was all so sincere you have
    no idea what a good thing the party was in 1835 Scott Nearing
    was a grand old man a real mensch Mother Bloor made me cry
    I once saw Israel Amter plain. Everybody must have been a spy.

A good deal of the emotional strength of Ginsberg's poetry lies in its springlike recoil against the repression of radical thought and organization in the United States after the Second World War, the repression generally associated with the word "McCarthyism." The virtual sealing off of any legitimacy for revolutionary debate and organization, in the wake of a war that had already—whatever we may say about its inevitability and justification—done immense damage to private personality throughout the Western world, wrought even more psychic than political havoc. The story of Naomi Ginsberg is to some degree a doughty effort to establish the human validity of a retroactively outlawed type of experience. For example, in the line from "Kaddish," "Then quiet for months that winter—walks, alone, nearby on Broadway, read Daily Worker—Broke her arm, fell on icy street," the important fact is not that the woman read the Communist newspaper but that in the midst of a period of quiet recovery and contemplation she suffered an unfortunate accident that interrupted the convalescence, perhaps catastrophically. In another sense, Naomi's story brings out in every possible way the psychopathology of the violence done by modern existence to the most vulnerable among us. The homosexuality of the poet, his use of drugs, and his rejection of squeamishness to the point where he has cultivated a positive addiction to the revolting are familiar motifs of recent literature, but Ginsberg understands, and shows, that they are not the result of spontaneous combustion but highly relevant to the current predicament of sensibility. The barriers of fastidiousness once broken down, the sophisticated intelligence must learn (with Whitman and Blake, to accept sympathetically Ginsberg's identification with these figures) entirely new perspectives of human acceptance and value. That is one important aim, at least, of the revolutionary movement in poetry as it exists today. . . .

LOUIS SIMPSON

Souls in Sympathy with
One Another

> *Naomi, Naomi—sweating, bulge-eyed, fat, the dress unbuttoned*
> *at one side—hair over brow, her stocking hanging evilly on her*
> *legs—screaming for a blood transfusion—one righteous hand*
> *upraised—a shoe in it—barefoot in the Pharmacy—*[1]

. . . "Kaddish" gives the impression of lives being revealed for
the first time—not only the lives of Naomi, Louis, Allen, and
Eugene, but many others who have never spoken of their shame
and grief and humiliation. Before "Kaddish" no one would have
thought that these things could be said in a poem.[2]

In the nineteenth century, Romantic authors praised nature
and celebrated the individual. The artist with his unusual powers
of feeling was regarded as a hero. But by the middle of the
century disillusionment had set in: that is, artists were disillu-
sioned. Science and industry were making great advances, and
people seemed to think little of art, only of making money.

Zola and the naturalists felt that the claims of art might be
revived by adopting the methods of scientific enquiry; the nov-
elist, by showing the principles of human behavior, could serve
a moral purpose. There was a catch, however: when the day
came that human passions were understood and regulated, there
would no longer be any need of art.

There was another point of view: art should not cleave to life
but suggest a higher reality. Flaubert said: "What seems beau-
tiful to me, what I should like to write, is a book about nothing,
a book dependent on nothing external, which would be held
together by the strength of its style, just as the earth, suspended
in the void, depends on nothing external for its support; a book
which would have almost no subject, or at least in which the
subject is almost invisible, if such a thing is possible. . . ."[3]

Reprinted with permission from Macmillan Publishing Co., Inc., from *A Revolu-
tion in Taste* (1978) by Louis Simpson.

Writers such as Flaubert concentrated on the internal organization of their poems and stories. This could not be maintained absolutely—their works have discernible points of connection with life—nevertheless, this way of working made a difference. Writers who believed in the impersonality and independent reality of the work of art produced a number of masterpieces, among them James Joyce's *Ulysses* and T. S. Eliot's *The Waste Land*.

There was a reaction: Henry Miller, for example, describes his impatience: "There were plenty of writers who could drag a thing out to the end without letting go the reins; what we needed was a man, like myself for instance, who didn't give a fuck what happened. Dostoievsky hadn't gone quite far enough. I was for straight gibberish. One should go cuckoo! People have had enough of plot and character. Life isn't in the upper story: life is here and now, any time you say the word, any time you let rip."[4]

The assumption here is that life determines art, and other writers after World War II would agree. The war may have helped, making them impatient with the laborious construction of art objects that might vanish overnight. In the world of concentration camps and atom bombs it had become impossible to believe in the permanence of art. There was a shift to a different way of thinking: the self was the only thing you could be sure of. You could know your own feelings—for the moment.

Talk of art was beside the point. "I'm not concerned," Ginsberg said, "with creating a work of art . . . And I don't want to predefine it . . . what I do is try to forget entirely about the whole world of art, and just get directly to the . . . fastest and most direct expression of what it is I got in heart-mind. Trusting that if my heart-mind is shapely, the objects or words, the word sequences, the sentences, the lines, the song, will also be shapely."[5]

This was the opposite of T. S. Eliot's idea of poetry. Eliot once remarked: "Poetry is not a turning loose of emotion, but an escape from emotion; it is not the expression of personality, but an escape from personality."[6] For thirty years Eliot's ideas had dominated the writing and teaching of poetry, but now, in a new generation, personality came back with a vengeance.

"Kaddish" is a work of art in the Modernist sense, with characters and a plot; "Howl" is post-Modernist, a direct expression of the writer's personality. Moreover, Ginsberg sees himself as a bard and prophet. "All you have to know is what you actually think & feel & every sentence will be a revelation."[7] So that besides expressing Ginsberg's personality, "Howl" reveals eternal truth.

Dickstein is probably right: it would be a mistake to regard Ginsberg as a merely "confessional" writer like Anne Sexton. Through his poems Ginsberg aimed to render an account of his spiritual development and to be speaking for the multitudes. . . .[8]

If one considers the impersonality of the modern bureaucratic state it is likely that, more and more, poetry will be written to express the life of an individual.

In order to do so it will narrow its scope. Personal writing cannot have the epic dimension, the grandeur of a Trojan war or a fall from Paradise. The personal voice does not speak for society at large or a belief held in common. Here and there a poet may subscribe to some form of mysticism, but in general the poet who writes about his experiences must be content to be a naturalist, believing, in Wordsworth's terrible phrase, that this world is where we find our happiness or not at all.

To most people living in the West, poetry has become almost exclusively a means of self-expression. This is bound to continue until the aim of education is changed, and this must wait on changes in society as a whole. Only then will what poets write and what the people think come together.

For the time being we do not have that poetry—we are stuck with our sweating selves, and worse. By the worse I mean "confessional" writing. One hears the author speaking of the most intimate details of his life, one sees the figure weeping, and then one remembers that this is all taking place before the camera. As a novelist said at the beginning of the century, "I have always suspected, in the effort to bring into play the extremities of emotions, the debasing touch of insincerity."[9] The confessional writer is at all times aware of the profit to be made from exhibiting his soul; there is nothing that he or she will not trot out for your inspection. Everything is for sale: furniture, rags, bundles of personal letters, everything.

In contrast to this, what I have called the personal voice is an expression of character. And character is something made. The self that appears in the novel or poem has been constructed according to certain aesthetic principles. This version of the self is not intended to direct attention upon the author but to serve the work of art. The purpose is to create a symbolic life, a portrait of the artist that will have meaning for others and so create a feeling of community, if only among a few thousand.

Until the birth of the larger community it appears that the best we can do is to live as individuals as happily as we can. Poetry that describes the effort may bind a few thousand souls in sympathy with one another. The books of poets create sub-societies of people bound together by something much closer to their heart's desire than the noise of the world.

In the absence of vision we gather around the lives of men and women who have lived to some purpose.

NOTES

1. Allen Ginsberg, *Kaddish and Other Poems* (San Francisco: City Lights Books, 1961), p. 18.

2. Delmore Schwartz, however, in his prose tale, "In Dreams Begin Responsibilities," had anticipated the tone and even the characters of "Kaddish."

3. Gustave Flaubert, *Selected Letters,* trans. Francis Steegmuller (New York: Farrar, Straus and Giroux, 1954), pp. 127–28.

4. Henry Miller, *The Rosy Crucifixion, Book One: Sextus* (New York: Grove Press, 1965), pp. 47–48.

5. Allen Ginsberg, *Allen Verbatim,* ed. George Ball (New York: McGraw-Hill, 1974), p. 107.

6. T. S. Eliot, *The Sacred Wood* (London: Methuen, 1966 reprint), p. 58.

7. Jane Kramer, *Allen Ginsberg in America* (New York: Random House, 1970), p. 174.

8. Morris Dickstein, *Gates of Eden* (New York: Basic Books, 1977), p. 16.

9. Joseph Conrad, *A Personal Record* (New York: Harper and Brothers, 1912), [no page given].

THE LONG FOREGROUND

ALLEN GINSBERG

A Blake Experience

Interviewer: What was the Blake experience you speak of ?

Ginsberg: About 1945 I got interested in Supreme Reality with a capital S and R, and I wrote big long poems about a last voyage looking for Supreme Reality. Which was like a Dostoevskian or Thomas Wolfeian idealization or like Rimbaud—what was Rimbaud's term, new vision, was that it? Or Kerouac was talking about a new vision, verbally, and intuitively out of longing, but also out of a funny kind of tolerance of this universe. In 1948 in East Harlem in the summer I was living—this is like the Ancient Mariner, I've said this so many times: "stoppeth one of three. / 'By thy long grey beard . . .'" Hang an albatross around your neck. . . . The one thing I felt at the time was that it would be a terrible horror, that in one or two decades I would be trying to explain to people that one day something like this happened to me! I even wrote a long poem saying, "I will grow old, a grey and groaning man, / and with each hour the same thought, and with each thought the same denial. / Will I spend my life in praise of the *idea* of God? / Time leaves no hope. We creep and wait. We wait and go alone." Psalm II—which I never published. So anyway—there I was in my bed in Harlem . . . jacking off. With my pants open, lying around on a bed by the window sill, looking out into the cornices of Harlem and the sky above. And I had just come. And had perhaps hardly even wiped the come off my thighs, my trousers, or whatever it was. As I often do, I had been jacking off while reading—I think it's probably a common phenomenon to be noticed among ado-

From an interview with Thomas Clark, recorded in June 1965 and published in the *Paris Review* (Spring 1966). Reprinted with permission.

lescents. Though I was a little older than an adolescent at the time. About twenty-two. There's a kind of interesting thing about, you know, distracting your attention while you jack off—that is, you know, reading a book or looking out of a window, or doing something else with the conscious mind which kind of makes it sexier.

So anyway, what I had been doing that week—I'd been in a very lonely solitary state, dark night of the soul sort of, reading Saint John of the Cross, maybe on account of that everybody'd gone away that I knew, Burroughs was in Mexico, Jack was out in Long Island and relatively isolated, we didn't see each other, and I had been very close with them for several years. Huncke I think was in jail, or something. Anyway, there was nobody I knew. Mainly the thing was that I'd been making it with N.C., and finally I think I got a letter from him saying it was all off, no more, we shouldn't consider ourselves lovers any more on account of it just wouldn't work out. But previously we'd had an understanding that we—Neal Cassady, I said "N.C." but I suppose you can use his name—we'd had a big tender lovers' understanding. But I guess it got too much for him, partly because he was three thousand miles away and he had six thousand girl friends on the other side of the continent, who were keeping him busy, and then here was my lone cry of despair from New York. So. I got a letter from him saying, Now, Allen, we gotta move on to *new* territory. So I felt this is like a great mortal blow to all of my tenderest hopes. And I figured I'd never find any sort of psychospiritual sexo-cock jewel fulfillment in my existence! So, I went into . . . like I felt cut off from what I'd idealized romantically. And I was also graduating from school and had nowhere to go and the difficulty of getting a job. So finally there was nothing for me to do except to eat vegetables and live in Harlem. In an apartment I'd rented from someone. Sublet.

So, in that state therefore, of hopelessness, or dead-end, change of phase, you know—growing up—and in an equilibrium in any case, a psychic, a mental equilibrium of a kind, like of having no New Vision and no Supreme Reality and nothing but the world in front of me, and of not knowing what to do with *that* . . . there was a funny balance of tension, in every direction. And just after I came, on this occasion, with a

Blake book on my lap—I wasn't even reading, my eye was idling over the page of "Ah, Sun-flower," and it suddenly appeared—the poem I'd read a lot of times before, overfamiliar to the point where it didn't make any particular meaning except some sweet thing about flowers—and suddenly I realized that the poem was talking about *me*. "Ah, Sun-flower! weary of time, / Who countest the steps of the sun; / Seeking after that sweet golden clime, / Where the traveller's journey is done." Now, I began understanding it, the poem while looking at it, and suddenly, simultaneously with understanding it, heard a very deep earthen grave voice in the room, which I immediately assumed, I didn't think twice, was Blake's voice; it wasn't any voice that I knew, though I had previously had a conception of a voice of rock, in a poem, some image like that—or maybe that came after this experience.

And my eye on the page, simultaneously the auditory hallucination, or whatever terminology here used, the apparitional voice, in the room, woke me further deep in my understanding of the poem, because the voice was so completely tender and beautifully . . . ancient. Like the voice of the Ancient of Days. But the peculiar quality of the voice was something unforgettable because it was like God had a human voice, with all the infinite tenderness and anciency and mortal gravity of a living Creator speaking to his son. "Where the Youth pined away with desire, / And the pale Virgin shrouded in snow, / Arise from their graves, and aspire / Where my Sun-flower wishes to go." Meaning that there *was* a *place,* there was a sweet golden clime, and the *sweet golden,* what was that . . . and simultaneous to the voice there was also an emotion, risen in my soul in response to the voice, and a sudden *visual* realization of the same awesome phenomena. That is to say, looking out at the window, through the window at the sky, suddenly it seemed that I saw into the depths of the universe, by looking simply into the ancient sky. The sky suddenly seemed very *ancient*. And this was the very ancient place that he was talking about, the sweet golden clime, I suddenly realized that *this* existence was *it*! And, that I was born in order to experience up to this very moment that I was having this experience, to realize what this was all about—in other words that this was the moment that I was born for. This initiation. Or this vision or this consciousness, of being alive unto myself, alive myself unto the Creator. As the son of the Creator—who loved me, I realized, or who responded to my desire, say. It was the same desire both ways.

Anyway, my first thought was this was what I was born for, and second thought, never forget—never forget, never renege, never deny. Never deny the voice—no, never *forget* it, don't get lost mentally wandering in other spirit worlds or American or job worlds or advertising worlds or war worlds or earth worlds. But the spirit of the universe was what I was born to realize. What I was speaking about visually was, immediately, that the cornices in the old tenement building in Harlem across the backyard court had been carved very finely in 1890 or 1910. And were like the solidification of a great deal of intelligence and care and love also. So that I began noticing in every corner where I looked evidences of a living hand, even in the bricks, in the arrangement of each brick. Some hand placed them there—that some hand had placed the whole universe in front of me. That some hand had placed the sky. No, that's exaggerating—not that some hand had placed the sky but that the sky was the living blue hand itself. Or that God was in front of my eyes—existence itself was God. Well, the formulations are like that—I didn't formulate it in exactly those terms; what I was seeing was a visionary thing, it was a lightness in my body . . . my body suddenly felt *light,* and a sense of cosmic consciousness, vibrations, understanding, awe, and wonder and surprise. And it was a sudden awakening into a totally deeper real universe than I'd been existing in. So, I'm trying to avoid generalizations about that sudden deeper real universe and keep it strictly to observations of phenomenal data, or a voice with a certain sound, the appearance of cornices, the appearance of the sky, say, of the great blue hand, the living hand—to keep to images.

But anyway—the same . . . *petite sensation* recurred several minutes later, with the same voice, while reading the poem "The Sick Rose." This time it was a slightly different sense-depth-mystic impression. Because "The Sick Rose"—you know I can't interpret the poem now, but it had a meaning—I mean I can interpret it on a verbal level, the sick rose is my self, or self, or the living body, sick because the mind, which is the worm "That flies in the night, / In the howling storm," or Urizen, reason; Blake's character might be the one that's entered the body and is destroying it, or let us say death, the worm as being death, the natural process of death, some kind of mystical being of its own trying to come in and devour the body, the rose. Blake's drawing for it is complicated, it's a big drooping rose, drooping because it's dying, and there's a worm in it, and the worm is wrapped around a little sprite that's trying to get out of the mouth of the rose.

But anyway, I experienced "The Sick Rose," with the voice of Blake reading it, as something that applied to the whole universe, like hearing the doom of the whole universe, and at the same time the inevitable beauty of doom. I can't remember now, except it was very beautiful and very awesome. But a little of it slightly scary, having to do with the knowledge of death— my death and also the death of being itself, and that was the great pain. So, like a prophecy, not only in human terms but a prophecy as if Blake had penetrated the very secret core of the *entire* universe and had come forth with some little magic formula statement in rhyme and rhythm that, if properly heard in the inner inner ear, would deliver you beyond the universe.

So then, the other poem that brought this on in the same day was "The Little Girl Lost," where there was a repeated refrain,

> Do father, mother, *weep*—?
> "Where can Lyca *sleep*?"
>
> How can Lyca *sleep*
> If her mother *weep*?
>
> If her heart does *ache*,
> Then let Lyca *wake*;
> If my mother *sleep*,
> Lyca shall not *weep*.

It's that hypnotic thing—and I suddenly realized that Lyca was me, or Lyca was the self; father, mother seeking Lyca, was God seeking, Father, the Creator; and " 'If her heart does ache / Then let Lyca wake' "—wake to what? *Wake* meaning wake to the same awakeness I was just talking about—of existence in the entire universe. The total consciousness then, of the complete universe. Which is what Blake was talking about. In other words a breakthrough from ordinary habitual quotidian consciousness into consciousness that was really seeing all of heaven in a flower. Or what was it—eternity in a flower . . . heaven in a grain of sand? As I was seeing heaven in the cornice of the building. By heaven here I mean this imprint or concretization or living form, of an intelligent hand—the work of an intelligent hand, which still had the intelligence molded into it. The gargoyles on the Harlem cornices. What was interesting about the cornice was that there's cornices like that on every building, but I never noticed them before. And I never realized that they meant spiritual labor, to anyone—that somebody had labored to make a curve in a piece of tin—to make a cornucopia out of a piece of industrial tin. Not only that man, the workman, the artisan, but the architect had thought of it, the builder had paid for it, the smelter had *smelt* it, the miner had dug it up out of the earth, the earth had gone through aeons preparing it. So the little molecules had slumbered for . . . for Kalpas. So out of *all* of these Kalpas it all got together in a great succession of impulses, to be frozen finally in that one form of a cornucopia cornice on the building front. And God knows how many people made the moon. Or what spirits labored . . . to set fire to the sun. As Blake says, "When I look in the sun I don't see the rising sun, I see a band of angels singing holy, holy, holy." Well, his perception of the field of the sun is different from that of a man who just sees the sun sun, without any emotional relationship to it.

But then, there was a point later in the week when the intermittent flashes of the same . . . bliss—because the experience was quite blissful—came back. In a sense all this is described in "The Lion for Real" by anecdotes of different experiences—actually it was a very difficult time, which I won't go into here. Because suddenly I thought, also simultaneously, Ooh, I'm going *mad*! That's described in the line in "Howl," "who thought they were *only* mad when Baltimore gleamed in supernatural ecstasy"—"who thought they were *only* mad. . . ." If it were only that easy! In other words it'd be a lot easier if you just were crazy, instead of—then you could chalk it up, "Well, I'm nutty"—but on the other hand what if it's all true and you're *born* into this great cosmic universe in which you're a spirit angel—terrible fucking situation to be confronted with. It's like being woken up one morning by Joseph K's captors. Actually what I think I did was there was a couple of girls living next door and I crawled out on the fire escape and tapped on their window and said, "I've seen God!" and they *banged* the window shut. Oh, what tales I could have told them if they'd let me in! Because I was in a very exalted state of mind and the consciousness was still with me—I remember I immediately rushed to Plato and read some great image in the *Phaedrus* about horses flying through the sky, and rushed over to Saint John and started reading fragments of *con un no saber sabiendo . . . que me quede balbuciendo,* and rushed to the other part of the bookshelf and picked up Plotinus about The Alone—the Plotinus I found more difficult to interpret.

But I *immediately* doubled my thinking process, quadrupled, and I was able to read almost any text and see all sorts of divine significance in it. And I think that week or that month I had to take an examination in John Stuart Mill. And instead of writing about his ideas I got completely hung up on his experience of reading—was it Wordsworth? Apparently the thing that got him back was an experience of nature that he received keyed off by reading Wordsworth, on "sense sublime" or something. That's a very good description, that sense sublime of something far more deeply interfused, whose dwelling is the light of setting suns, and the round ocean, and the . . . the *living* air, did he say? The living air—see just that hand again—*and* in the heart of man. So I think this experience is characteristic of all high poetry. I mean that's the way I began seeing poetry as the communication of the particular experience—not just any experience but *this* experience.

Interviewer: Have you had anything like this experience again?

Ginsberg: Yeah. I'm not finished with this period. Then, in my room, I didn't know what to do. But I wanted to bring it up, so I began experimenting with it, without Blake. And I think it was one day in my kitchen—I had an old-fashioned kitchen with a sink with a tub in it with a board over the top—I started moving around and sort of shaking with my body and dancing up and down on the floor and saying, "Dance! dance! dance! dance! spirit! spirit! spirit! dance!" and suddenly I felt like Faust, calling up the devil. And then it started coming over me, this big . . . creepy feeling, cryptozoid or monozoidal, so I got all scared and quit.

Then, I was walking around Columbia and I went in the Columbia bookstore and was reading Blake again, leafing over a book of Blake, I think it was "The Human Abstract": "Pity would be no more. . . ." And suddenly it came over me in the bookstore again, and I was in the eternal place *once more,* and I looked around at everybody's faces, and I saw all these wild animals! Because there was a bookstore clerk there who I hadn't paid much attention to, he was just a familiar fixture in the bookstore scene and everybody went in the bookstore every day like me, because downstairs there was a café and upstairs there were all these clerks that we were all familiar with—this guy had a very *long* face, you know some people look like giraffes. So he looked kind of giraffish. He had a kind of a long face with a long nose. I don't know what kind of sex life he had, but he must have had something. But anyway, I looked in his face and I suddenly saw like a great tormented soul—and he had just been somebody whom I'd regarded as perhaps a not particularly beautiful or sexy character, or lovely face, but you know someone familiar, and perhaps a pleading cousin in the universe. But all of a sudden I realized that *he* knew also, just like I knew. And that everybody in the bookstore knew, and that they were all hiding it! They all had the consciousness, it was like a great *un*conscious that was running between all of us that everybody *was* completely conscious, but that the fixed expressions that people have, the habitual expressions, the manners, the mode of talk, are all masks hiding this consciousness. Because almost at that moment it seemed that it would be too terrible if we communicated to each other on a level of total consciousness and awareness each of the other—like it would be too terrible, it would be the end of the bookstore, it would be the end of civ— . . . not civilization, but in other words the position that everybody was in was *ridiculous,* everybody running around peddling books to each other. Here in the universe! Passing money over the counter, wrapping books in bags and guarding the door, you know, stealing books, and the people sitting up making accountings on the upper floor there, and people worrying about their exams walking through the bookstore, and all the millions of thoughts the people had—you know, that I'm worrying about—whether they're going to get laid or whether anybody loves them, about their mothers dying of cancer or, you know, the complete death awareness that everybody has continuously with them all the time—all of a sudden revealed to me at once in the faces of the people, and they all looked like horrible grotesque masks, grotesque because *hiding* the knowledge from each other. Having a habitual conduct and forms to prescribe, forms to fulfill. Roles to play. But the main insight I had at that time was that everybody knew. Everybody knew completely everything. Knew completely everything in the terms which I was talking about.

Interviewer: Do you still think they know?

Ginsberg: I'm more sure of it now. Sure. All you have to do is try and make somebody. You realize that they knew all along you were trying to make them. But until that moment you never break through to communication on the subject.

Interviewer: Why not?

Ginsberg: Well, fear of rejection. The twisted faces of all those people, the faces were twisted by rejection. And hatred of self, finally. The internalization of that rejection. And finally disbelief in that shining self. Disbelief in that infinite self. Partly because the particular . . . partly because the *awareness* that we all carry is too often painful, because the experience of rejection and lack-love and cold war—I mean the whole cold war is the imposition of a vast mental barrier on everybody, a vast antinatural psyche. A hardening, a shutting off of the perception of desire and tenderness which everybody *knows* and which is the very structure of . . . the atom! Structure of the human body and organism. That desire built in. Blocked. "Where the Youth pined away with desire, / And the pale Virgin shrouded in snow." Or as

Blake says, "On every face I see, I meet / Marks of weakness, marks of woe." So what I was thinking in the bookstore was the marks of weakness, marks of woe. Which you can just look around and look at anybody's face right next to you now always—you can see it in the way the mouth is pursed, you can see it in the way the eyes blink, you can see it in the way the gaze is fixed down at the matches. It's the self-consciousness which is a substitute for communication with the outside. This consciousness pushed back into the self and thinking of how it will hold its face and eyes and hands in order to make a mask to hide the flow that is going on. Which it's aware of, which everybody is aware of really! So let's say, shyness. Fear. Fear of like total feeling, really, total being is what it is.

So the problem then was, having attained realization, how to safely manifest it and communicate it. Of course there was the old Zen thing, when the sixth patriarch handed down the little symbolic oddments and ornaments and books and bowls, stained bowls too . . . when the *fifth* patriarch handed them down to the sixth patriarch he told him to hide them and don't tell anybody you're patriarch because it's dangerous, they'll kill you. So there was that immediate danger. It's taken me all these years to manifest it and work it out in a way that's materially communicable to people. Without scaring them or me. Also movements of history and breaking down the civilization. To break down everybody's masks and roles sufficiently so that everybody has to face the universe *and* the possibility of the sick rose coming true and the atom bomb. So it was an immediate messianic thing. Which seems to be becoming more and more justified. And more and more reasonable in terms of the existence that we're living.

So. Next time it happened was about a week later walking along in the evening on a circular path around what's now I guess the garden or field in the middle of Columbia University, by the library. I started invoking the spirit, consciously trying to get another depth perception of cosmos. And suddenly it began occurring again, like a sort of breakthrough again, but this time—this was the last time in that period—it was the same depth of consciousness or the same cosmical awareness but suddenly it was not blissful at all but it was *frightening*. Some like real serpent-fear entering the sky. The sky was not a blue hand anymore but like a hand of death coming down on me—some really scary presence, it was almost as if I saw God again except God was the devil. The consciousness itself was *so* vast, much more vast than any idea of it I'd had or any experience I'd had, that it was not even human anymore—and was in a sense a threat, because I was going to die into that inhuman ultimately. I don't know *what* the score was there—I was too cowardly to pursue it. To attend and experience completely the Gates of Wrath—there's a poem of Blake's that deals with that, "To find a Western Path / Right through the Gates of Wrath." But I didn't urge my way there, I shut it all off. And got scared, and thought, I've gone too far.

PAUL PORTUGÉS

The Poetics of Vision

. . . Ginsberg . . . [vowed] never to forget the truths of his Blake visions:

> But I also said at the time, now that I have seen this heaven on earth, I will never forget it, and I will never stop referring all things to it, I will never stop considering it the center of my human existence and the center of my life which is now changed—over the boundary and into the new world, and I'll never be able to go back and that's great, and from now on I'm chosen, blessed, sacred, poet, and this is my sunflower, or this is my new world, and I'll be faithful for the rest of my life, and I'll never forget it and I'll never deny it, and I'll never renounce it.[1]

Being faithful to the "sunflower," in terms of his poetry, meant that he was determined to work out a poetics of vision, a theory and practice of poetry that would allow him to communicate his visions and his heightened awareness of reality to an audience bent on denying the mundane as well as the sublime.

At first, Ginsberg thought the answer lay in successfully re-creating the cosmic consciousness of his vision in his poems. All he had to do was write about the vision itself, and the reader would grasp the nuances and essence of the experience. But how could he accomplish that task? He turned to Blake for practical guidance. He understood very well Blake's own difficulties with his contemporaries, who also thought he was crazy and who

---

From *The Visionary Poetics of Allen Ginsberg* (Santa Barbara: Ross-Erikson, 1978). Reprinted by permission of author and publisher.

were suspicious of his insistence that he wrote his poetry while under the power of a visionary trance. Ginsberg was encouraged when he read that Blake ignored his critics and devoted his energies to the problem of transposing visions into great poetry. Blake knew it would demand a complicated and highly sophisticated method, things "unattempted yet in Prose or rhyme," as Milton, Blake's own model of the poet as visionary, once stated in *his* experiments with the poetry of vision. For years, Blake pondered the problem of writing poetry based on vision. When he wrote his friend Thomas Butts on April 25, 1803, that he had written a long visionary poem, *Milton,* "from immediate Dictation . . . without Premeditation & even against my Will,"[2] he anticipated a tradition of automatic writing, later picked up by Yeats, the Surrealists, and the Beats. Whether he had in fact worked out the problem of creating a poetics based on vision is another question, but it seemed to Ginsberg that he had. Ginsberg was particularly impressed by Blake's final statement on his experiments in poetry "conducted by the Spirits," which he had read in the preface to *Jerusalem.* By this time, in his development as a poet, Blake was completely confident that he had discovered a poetics of vision, and his manifesto on prosody is a strong affirmation of his quest to write a poetry "unfettered" by habitual tradition and contemporary critical standards:

> We who dwell on Earth can do nothing to ourselves; everything is conducted by Spirits, no less than Digestion or Sleep. *I fear the best . . . in Jesus whom we . . .* When this Verse was first dictated to me, I consider'd a Monotonous Cadence, like that used by Milton & Shakespeare & all writers of English Blank Verse, derived from the modern bondage of Rhyming to be a necessary and indispensible part of Verse. But I soon found that in the mouth of the true Orator such monotony was not only awkward, but as much a bondage as rhyme itself. I therefore have produced a variety of syllables. Every word and every letter is studied and put into its fit place; the terrific numbers are reserved for the terrific parts, and the prosaic for inferior parts; all are necessary to each other. Poetry Fedder'd Fetters the Human Race.[3]

. . . The first poem that Ginsberg wrote after his weeks of illumination exemplified the pattern of the poetry that he would design for at least the entire next year—well into 1949. It was one of a dozen poems that were a direct reference to his visionary experience. "The Eye Altering Alters All" is a dense, highly symbolic attempt to assert that everyone could have visions if they would conquer their prejudice against the miraculous and cease to deny the visionary seed in all of us:

> Many seek and never see,
> Anyone can tell them why.
> O they weep and O they cry
> and never take until they try
> unless they try it in their sleep[4]

The "it" in the last line that "many seek" but never try is the visionary consciousness. Ginsberg was convinced that people would be open to visions if he introduced the idea into the general stream of thought and encouraged others to try it:

I thought that perhaps there was some element, you could catalyze it if you were willful or if you really threw yourself into the search for vision, you could bring it about. "Unless they try it in their sleep . . ." How many people had visionary experiences in dream? Has anybody *not* had a visionary experience in a dream?[5]

Though his own vision was definitely not a dream, Ginsberg thought people would accept the possibility of vision if they realized that a similar quality of experience existed in dreams.

Ginsberg's first attempt to recreate his visionary feeling came in a sonnet, "I dwelled in Hell on earth to write this rhyme." Like many of the poems of this period, most of which were not published until 1972 in *The Gates of Wrath,* the style is Elizabethan and metaphysical, reflecting the influence of his early models, Wyatt, Marvell, and Surrey. The poem is decorative, overwritten, full of conceits and poetic diction, with frequent reference to angels, infernos, and even a "blazing stair"—all in the style of the sixteenth and seventeenth century mystics and sonneteers:

> The fame I dwell in is not mine,
> I would not have it. Angels in the air
> Serenade my senses in delight.
> Intelligence of poets, saints and fair
> Characters converse with me all night.[6]

It is as though he were trying to capture the "visionary gleam" by copying the forms and styles of his mystic predecessors, such as the Vaughans, St. John of the Cross, and others. Ginsberg would later characterize this phase of his writing as "overwritten coy stanzas, a little after Marvell, a little after Wyatt."[7] He was consciously trying to perfect a rhymed, punning, "silvery" versification. This was an important effort in prosody that paralleled his misdirection in the search for supernatural realities; he would realize later that he would have to abandon both preoccupations in order to get back to the true spirit of Blake and his spiritual revelations.

For the next three years, however, Ginsberg wouldn't heed Blake's warning that a poet should abandon rhyme and syncopated meter when it meant bondage to the form rather than allegiance to truth. Therefore, his poems, like the above lines quoted from the sonnet, would be obscure, extremely allusive, and often archaic. A reader would have a hard time understanding what was meant by the "intelligence of poets," or "angels in the air," and particularly the vision of mystical light alluded to in the final line, "They vanish as I look into the light." Even with the hindsight of his Harlem experiences, it is difficult to know that "I witness Heaven" alludes to his vision of "Ah! Sunflower" and the heightened perception of the cornices and the late afternoon sunlight that seemed eternal, heavenly.

But Ginsberg was as committed as Blake to becoming a spiritual revolutionary, whose task it is "to explore and record the mysteries of the Human psyche."[8] So, he continued, as best he knew how, retelling his vision, as in the poem "Vision 1948," convinced that, since his annointment by the light, he was "a poet with something to talk about":[9]

I shudder with intelligence and I
    Wake in the deep light
And hear a vast machinery
    Descending without sound,
Intolerable to me, too bright,
    And shaken in the sight
The eye goes blind before the world goes round.
              —East Harlem, summer 1948[10]

In this poem, Ginsberg is trying to communicate to the reader a sense of his Blake vision, as well as attempting to portray a feeling for the cosmic that he assumes, or hopes, might be understood by others. He later characterized this poem as a hermetic communication which he hoped could be appreciated at a deeper, perhaps unconscious, level of thought. In fact, he thought all his poetry should move toward the miraculous, the truly universal experiences of a higher state of being:

> I immediately saw poetry as a hermetic or secret way of talking about experiences that were universal, cosmic, that everybody knew about, but nobody knew how to refer to, nobody knew how to bring it up to front brain consciousness or to present it to social consciousness . . .[11]

Though he assumed "everybody knew about" the cosmic, he wasn't aware that the opaque allusions to his own experience of the mystical light—"Wake in the deep light"—or his sense of cosmic intelligence—"shudder with intelligence"—were clouded by his transmission of the eternal truths in a style difficult for the average reader to comprehend.

Ginsberg would continue to write poems in this fashion for the next year and a half. At least nine poems about his Blake vision were written in 1948 and 1949. The list includes, other than those already discussed, "A Very Dove," "Do We Understand Each Other?," "The Voice of Rock," "A Western Ballad," "On Reading William Blake's 'The Sick Rose',"—and a few others in his journals and letters.[12] However, after all these attempts, Ginsberg began to have second thoughts about writing almost all his poems solely on the subject of his vision. He was gradually becoming aware of the sad fact that no one was taking him seriously, that many were even beginning to express doubts about his sanity. The strangeness of his experience, no less than the turgidity of his style, prevented him in these poems from opening people up to that sense of a cosmic consciousness that was his urgent aim. Consequently, he decided to approach the subject of his visions from another angle, emphasizing those aspects that people might be able to apply to themselves. He found that the general quality of vision itself was completely misunderstood. Even what he had thought was a well-known and well-documented experience—the sensation of light felt by all mystics—was met with bewilderment and doubt by his few readers (either his friends or his teachers). He decided to write a poem about this lack of ability to communicate. It is called "Refrain":

> The air is dark, the night is sad,
> I lie sleepless and I groan.
> Nobody cares when a man goes mad:
> He is sorry, God is glad.
> Shadow changes into bone.[13]

Ginsberg is confessing that nobody cares that he is a visionary and has been given access to unusual insights and eternal truths. His quest had only produced sleepless nights and groaning. The last line, "Shadow changes into bone," is impossible to understand without Ginsberg's own gloss:

> "Shadow changes into bone" was my symbolic language for meaning Thought, high intellectual thought, ambition, idealized desire, and that it can actually come true and you do get to see a vision of eternity which kills you. So shadow, mind, insight changes into three dimensional bone.[14]

In other words, his "high intellectual thought"—the "vision of eternity"—changes from the ecstatic, epiphanous experience into a state of madness, eventually driving the mad visionary to the grave because of his inability to communicate his secret truths. By this time, the great intelligence, the amazing light, had been reduced to a shadow, the burden of which was killing him—"Shadow changes into bone."

Ginsberg's change of direction, therefore, resulted in an abandonment of visionary wonders for a desire to be in the presence of the Creator or Divinity, a state he thought most serious, spiritually minded people would recognize:

> So by this time, a year later, the actual experience had become solidified into the symbol of a god, or the notion of a divinity that I was trying to get to.[15]

The poem that reflects this new focus is "Psalm." Ginsberg did not stop referring to his vision. (He would allude to it throughout the 1950s and 1960s in such poems as "Howl" and "Kaddish.") There are several passages that refer to his desire to infuse the "speechless stanzas of the rose / Into my poem." He is still making a vow to "copy / Every petal on a page" (alluding to his vision of "The Sick Rose") and claiming "Holy are the Visions of the Soul." But the interest of "Psalm" is the question—put rather straightforwardly toward the end of the penultimate stanza—"Am I to spend / My life in praise of the idea of God?" The conclusion is a resounding "yes," with Ginsberg making a new claim to praise the sense of divinity he had felt in his vision by making "the myth incarnate in my flesh," which in the last line of the poem is "Now made incarnate in Thy Psalm, O Lord."[16]

"Psalm" is an interesting poem in two respects. First, Ginsberg modeled it on the classical Christian visionary who, in order to reexperience the presence of the Creator, renounced "this life" in an attempt to achieve more rapidly a promised union with the light/God. Ginsberg had read of this desire and praise of divinity in James's *The Varieties of Religious Experience,* in St. John of the Cross, in St. Teresa, and even in some of the English mystic poets, such as Crashaw and Henry Vaughan. He was now experiencing the mystical death wish himself. It was part of his desire to draw closer to that sense of cosmic awe one felt in the presence of one's Creator. It was partly also a response to the situation of complete alienation he was experiencing. Into the summer of 1951 Ginsberg would write about his "masochistic" wish, as he did in the following poem written in late 1949, "Complaint of the Skeleton To Time":

> Take the art which I bemoan
> In a poem's crazy tone;
> Grind me down, though I may groan,
> To the starkest stick and stone;
> Take them, said the skeleton,
> But leave my bones alone.[17]

He was calling upon death in order to complete the inevitable cycle of his spiritual annointment by renouncing his loves, his thoughts, his earthly possessions in each successive stanza until the last (quoted above), where he even casts aside his poetry: "Take the art which I bemoan / In a poem's crazy tone."

Ginsberg has described this predicament in which he was trapped by his desire to enter the cosmic and eternal, regardless of the consequences:

So then, after a while, the big masochistic psalms of divinity saying I want to die and be part of You. Which is a classic poetic position, which a lot of people get into, trapped into and finally die, too. Thinking, well, I'm going to pursue the beauty to the tomb. So: "Complaint of the Skeleton to Time."[18]

He would bemoan this aspect of his vision in poems such as "Sometime Jailhouse Blues" and "An Imaginary Rose in a Book," with such images as "tears of death," "body to a tomb," and "myth of dust," which illustrate the difficult and obscure style of the earlier poems.

It wasn't until the summer of 1951 that Ginsberg began to realize that he must put an end to this aspect of the visionary cycle. He decided that his quest for death, as well as the subject of divinity and his attempt to recreate the vision of his poems, represented "a whole cycle of inspiration and dead end."[19] He was beginning to consider his work of the past three years as a "broken record."[20] In the poem that registers his disillusionment with his former spiritual path, "Ode: My 24th Year,"

Ginsberg claims that he is giving up his attempts to record the experience of eternity; instead, he will try to accept living in the world of ordinary men. (It is interesting to note that although the poem is an ode to his twenty-fourth birthday, it wasn't put aside until after he was twenty-five, sometime in 1951, when he finally decided to leave it unfinished and dated "1950–1951.")

> No return, when thought's completed;
> let that ghost's last gaze go cheated:
> I may waste my days no more
> pining in spirituall warre.[21]

Though he is still using an Elizabethan voice, "spirituall warre," he is abandoning the classic mystical path of embracing death in order to be taken into the bosom of eternal light. He is claiming that "the visionary gleam" is leading him nowhere, that "here is no Eden,"[22] and that he doesn't want to "waste my days" any longer.

The end of this phase in Ginsberg's poetics came when he received several of his poems back from William Carlos Williams with a note saying: "In this mode perfection is basic."[23] He held Williams in such awe that the gentle but firm reply to his poems by the elder poet was something of a disappointment. Though he himself knew that his poems to this point were imitative and somewhat awkward in their form and style, Williams's advice was the final push he needed to begin a new direction. He started thinking about his visions from a different point of view. After all, hadn't his looking at the cornices of the apartment building and noticing the unusual quality of the sky been the high points of the vision that accompanied his reading of "Ah! Sun-flower"? Hadn't he experienced the sense of eternity he was constantly seeking by looking at a natural object, by observing the detail of craftsmanship in the bricks and cornices?

NOTES

1. Allen Ginsberg, unpublished interview, July 1976.
2. William Blake, *The Poetry and Prose of William Blake,* ed. David Erdman (New York: Doubleday, 1965), p. 696.

3. Blake, p. 144.

4. Allen Ginsberg, *The Gates of Wrath: Rhymed Poems, 1948–1952* (Bolinas: Grey Fox Press, 1972), p. 4.

5. Ginsberg, unpublished interview, July 1976.

6. Ginsberg, *Gates of Wrath,* p. 3.

7. Allen Ginsberg, *Allen Verbatim,* ed. Gordon Ball (New York: McGraw-Hill, 1974), p. 139.

8. S. Foster Damon, *A Blake Dictionary: The Ideas and Symbols of William Blake* (New York: E. P. Dutton, 1971), p. 331.

9. Ginsberg, unpublished interview, July 1976.

10. Ginsberg, *Gates of Wrath,* p. 7.

11. Ginsberg, unpublished interview, July 1976.

12. Ginsberg, letter to Mark Van Doren.

13. Ginsberg, *Gates of Wrath,* p. 7.

14. Ginsberg, unpublished interview, July 1976.

15. Ibid.

16. Ginsberg, *Gates of Wrath,* p. 18.

17. Ibid., p. 19.

18. Ginsberg, unpublished interview, July 1976.

19. Ibid.

20. Ibid.

21. Ginsberg, *Gates of Wrath,* p. 40.

22. Ibid., p. 41.

23. Ibid., p. 55.

PAUL PORTUGÉS

Allen Ginsberg's Paul Cézanne and the Pater Omnipotens Aeterna Deus

I

> I got hung up on Cézanne around 1949 in my last year at Columbia, studying with Meyer Shapiro . . . I think it was about the same time I was having these Blake visions.[1]

In 1948 Allen Ginsberg was completing his last year as a student of literature at Columbia University. The previous summer he had experienced several visionary illuminations under the spiritual guidance of what he perceived as the poet William Blake's raised-from-the-dead, spectral voice. Ginsberg had heard a God-like, cosmic voice; his body had become suffused with supernatural light; and he had, willingly or not, undergone extraordinary, irreversible changes in his personality and his powers of understanding.

One of the many vows he had taken that fateful summer (the mystical experiences were interspersed over several vision-haunted weeks) was the dedication of himself to the investigation of unusual modalities of consciousness. In particular, he wanted to explore states of mind that helped alter one's mundane perception and habits of thought. He began then, at twenty-two, a pursuit of mind-altering experiences that would come to have profound impact—not only on his own psychology, but also on his poetry and poetics.[2]

From *Contemporary Literature* (Summer 1980). Reprinted by permission of author and publisher.

This was Ginsberg's state of mind when he enrolled in Professor Meyer Shapiro's course on modern art in the fall of 1948. Attracted to the dynamic intelligence of his teacher, Ginsberg became entranced by Shapiro's lectures about the considerable impact the postimpressionist Paul Cézanne had made on modern art. Ginsberg, a young sonneteer of modest acclaim (he had won literary awards for his Elizabethan-style sonnets earlier that year), was particularly interested in Shapiro's comments about Cézanne's experiments in perception—specifically his use of perspective, form, and color modulation to alter his own and his viewer's appreciation of the phenomenal world.

Though Shapiro was alarmed by Ginsberg's insistence that he had actually heard Blake's voice and that his own intelligence had increased severalfold as a result of this mystical encounter, the good professor encouraged the young poet (and magna cum laude student) to pursue the visionary side of Cézanne—if indeed there really was such an element in the introverted painter's theories and works. He instructed Ginsberg to go to the Museum of Modern Art and study firsthand some of Cézanne's paintings.

The next few days Ginsberg spent several hours each morning and afternoon pondering the strange canvases of the difficult French painter. While gazing at one of Cézanne's landscapes, Ginsberg began to feel a strange sensation—not unlike the feelings he had had during his Blake visions the previous summer in his sublet Harlem apartment: "there's a strange sensation that one gets, looking at his [Cézanne's] canvases, which I began to associate with the extraordinary sensation—cosmic sensation, in fact—that I had experienced catalyzed by Blake's 'Sunflower' and 'Sick Rose' and a few other poems" (p. 25). This "cosmic sensation" he felt while peering into Cézanne's landscapes was a "strange shuddering impression" and a "sudden shift, a flashing" in his mind that created a momentary "gap" in consciousness caused by the "space gap" in Cézanne's paintings: "Partly it's when the canvas opens up into three dimensions and looks like wooden objects, . . . in three dimensions rather than flat. Partly it's the enormous spaces which open up in Cézanne's landscapes" (pp. 27–29, 25).

Because he associated the strange feelings he got from Cézanne with his Blake visions, Ginsberg felt doubly obligated to find out exactly how Cézanne created these "strange shudderings" in his mind—how he could induce a momentary gap in consciousness simply by playing with color, perspective, and form.

Thus began Ginsberg's dedicated study of Cézanne's techniques, his "intentions and method" (p. 26). Ginsberg examined all the reproductions he could find. Shapiro suggested he study Erle Loran's *Cézanne's Composition,* a fascinating account of Cézanne's inventive composition techniques by a young painter who had himself lived and worked in Cézanne's atelier in Aix-en-Provence. Loran discusses in detail, often using photographs of Cézanne's subjects, the great master's use of color modulation, distorted perspective, and geometric patterning.

In his book Loran includes a photograph of Cézanne's workspace. The usual artist's paraphernalia is evident—in Cézanne's case one's eye is attracted to the familiar bottles, draperies, and tables that appear in his many still lifes. But Ginsberg, in his spiritual state of mind, immediately focused on a human skull, a big black hat, and the artist's cloak. For the young poet, these items were proof positive that Cézanne must have been engaged in some sort of alchemical study, that Cézanne was not a plodding dullard as Ginsberg had been led to believe. Instead, he was convinced that Cézanne was a "hermetic type" like himself, someone devoted to the systematic study of the mystical in the natural world.

Ginsberg's interest in the mystical actually predates his visions in the summer of 1948. In 1945, as a lower division student, he became a dedicated follower of Zen and gnosticism under the guidance of Columbia professor Raymond Weaver. Weaver and Ginsberg, along with Jack Kerouac and William Burroughs, would often meet outside the classroom and discuss Plotinus, Egyptian astrology, and other esoteric subjects. Ginsberg balanced his gnostic interest with a vigorous study of Oswald Spengler. The combination of Spengler's cyclical view of history and the gnostic search for a "Supreme Reality"[3] were the foundation upon which Ginsberg built his respect for, adoration of, and theories about Paul Cézanne.

It is not surprising, therefore, that when Ginsberg studied

Cézanne's *The Black Clock,* he imposed a Plotinian framework on the rather dull still life of a simple black clock surrounded by such items as a vase, coffee cup, and large shell. Here Cézanne fulfilled Ginsberg's mystical needs; for in the painting he found all sorts of hidden meaning: "I began to see that Cézanne had literary symbolism in him, on and off. I was preoccupied with Plotinian terminology, of time and eternity, and I saw it in Cézanne's paintings, an early painting of a clock on a shelf, which I associated with time and eternity, and I began to think he was a big secret mystic" (p. 26). The painting is a study in the play of light and dark in which Cézanne paid particular attention to variations in cool and warm colors. However, for some reason (perhaps the actual clock was broken), Cézanne portrayed the black clock without any hands—a timeless time piece. Ginsberg immediately deduced that the painting was a statement on reality as transcendental, with Cézanne suggesting a perfect Plotinian other world of timelessness and eternal transcendence.

Another painting that interested Ginsberg because of its "Plotinian terminology" was Cézanne's *The Landscape at La Rouche Fuyon.* The painting is an experiment in the manipulation of two and three dimensional planes that interact to give the viewer a distinct three-dimensional feeling—a marvelous technique that Cézanne pioneered. The painting impressed Ginsberg for two reasons. While studying it at length, he would feel a "strange shuddering," the gap in consciousness mentioned earlier. In addition, he was fascinated by the winding road that turns off and out of the painting's borders. To the young student of gnostic thought, this road was a "mystical path" suggesting a journey into the netherworld of secret knowledge, a world beyond time and eternity. Ginsberg's preoccupation with Cézanne's mystical themes (whether real or imagined) led him to write a minor, short poem entitled "Cézanne's Ports":

> In the foreground we see time and life
> swept in a race
> toward the left hand side of the picture
> where shore meets shore.

But that meeting place
isn't represented;
it doesn't occur on the canvas.

For the other side of the bay
is Heaven and Eternity,
with a bleak white haze over its mountains.

And the immense water of L'Estaque is a go-between
for minute rowboats.[4]

Here Ginsberg is obviously mystified by Cézanne's overall composition technique so superbly plotted in his 1886 landscape *The Bay from L'Estaque*. As Shapiro himself has commented, this painting is "without paths or human figures, the world is spread out before his eyes, a theme for pure looking."[5] The interesting point about Ginsberg's poem is his preoccupation with what "doesn't occur on the canvas." He proposes that Cézanne is enticing the reader into a "Heaven and Eternity" that isn't represented on canvas but skillfully suggested by the artist's hermetic method.

Whether or not Ginsberg is "correct" in his interpretation is of little consequence. What is important is that his feelings, intuitions, and musings on Cézanne's methods and intentions inspired him to investigate such possibilities for his own poetry. Ginsberg sought to develop a poetry that would help the reader find "Heaven and Eternity" not beyond the borders of the canvas but between the lines and images of a poem.

During the course of his studies, Ginsberg went to the Museum of Modern Art one day while under the suggestive influence of a "lot of marijuana." While studying *The Rocks at Garonne*, he began "turning on to space in Cézanne." He began to feel disoriented as he stared at the painting, receiving a "very mysterious impression" from the rocks: "you look at them for a while, and after a while they seem like they're rocks, just the rock parts, you don't know where they are, whether they're on the ground or in the air or on top of a cliff, but then they seem to be floating in space like clouds, and then they seem to be also a bit like they're amorphous, like kneecaps or cockheads or faces without eyes" (p. 27). Ginsberg was likewise impressed by *The Card Players*. As in the other paintings, he found "all sorts of sinister symbols," including a portrayal of death, a "fat-faced Kafkian-agent . . . a cosmic card sharp dealing out Fate" (pp. 26–27).

Since Cézanne's paintings had such an overwhelming effect on Ginsberg, he decided to search for material that would shed some light on the painter's ability to produce such a profound impression. Ginsberg began by studying Cézanne's letters, hoping to discover a preoccupation with "Time and Eternity" similar to his own. Not surprisingly he found what he was looking for in a letter quoted in Loran's *Cézanne's Composition:* "I'm an old man and my passions are not, my senses are not coarsened by passions like some *other* old men I know, and I have worked for years trying to . . . *reconstitute* the *petites sensations* that I get from nature" (p. 27). Ginsberg concluded from this statement that Cézanne was no longer concerned with re-creating nature but that he had refined his perceptions to the degree that he was concerned with actually painting his perception of nature—that he was literally intent on painting his emotions (*sensations*), rather than attempting a photographic rendering. To the young Ginsberg, Cézanne had the phenomenological capacity to refine his perception to such a degree that the painter had mastered "optical phenomena in an almost yogic way . . . actually looking at his own eyeballs in a sense" (pp. 27–28).

Another of Cézanne's letters attracted Ginsberg's imagination. Writing to his friend Emile Bernard, Cézanne explained how he had used geometric composition to create a unique portrayal of perspective:

[B]y means of squares, cubes, triangles, I try to reconstitute the impression that I have from nature: the means that I use to reconstitute the impression of solidity that I think-feel-see when I am looking at a motif like Victoire, is to reduce it to some kind of pictorial language, so I use these squares, cubes, triangles, but I try to interknit so that *no light gets through*.[6]

Ginsberg was quite mystified by this famous statement the painter made in his later years. He deduced Cézanne "produced a solid two-dimensional surface" that made it possible to look into it and see a three-dimensional opening:

[Cézanne contained] in his skull these supernatural phenomena, and observations . . . you know, and it's very humble actually, because he didn't know if he was crazy or not—that is a flash of the physical, miracle dimensions of existence, trying to reduce that to canvas in two dimensions, and then trying to do it in such a way as it would look if the observer looked at it long enough it would look like as much three dimensions as the actual *world* of optical phenomena when one looks through one's eyes. Actually he's *re*-constituted the whole fucking universe in his canvases. . . . (P. 28)

As we shall see in a later section, it would take Ginsberg years to transmute what he considered Cézanne's "supernatural" method into his own poetry. Ginsberg not only had to discover for himself the verbal equivalent of Cézanne's perceptual qualities and the technical ability to re-create such phenomena in his poetry; he also had to attempt one more fantastic quality of Cézanne's method, the "Pater Omnipotens Aeterna Deus."

On April 15, 1904, Cézanne explained his theory of nature portrayal in a letter to Bernard:

May I repeat what I told you here: treat nature by the cylinder, the sphere, the cone, everything in proper perspective so that each side of an object or a plane is directed towards a central point. Lines parallel to the horizon give breadth, that is a section of nature or, if you prefer, of the spectacle that the Pater Omnipotens Aeterna Deus spreads out before our eyes. Lines perpendicular to this horizon give depth. But nature for us men is more depth than surface whence the need of introducing into our light vibrations represented by reds and yellows, a sufficient amount of blue to give the impression of air.[7]

When Ginsberg read that Cézanne was attempting to find the "All-powerful Father, Eternal God" in his art, he immediately surmised that Cézanne had discovered a method of depicting the eternal in the everyday world. He believed that Cézanne's experiment with "proper perspective" was actually a true discovery in perception that allowed the artist (and the viewer through the artist's work) to go far beneath the surface of reality and bring forth the eternal, the all-powerful from nature:

> [T]hat [the *pater omnipotens aeterna deus*] was I felt the key to Cézanne's hermetic method . . . you realize that he's really a saint! Working on his form of yoga, all that time, in obvious saintly circumstances of retirement in a small village . . . containing in his skull these supernatural phenomena, and observations. . . . (P. 28)

Ginsberg wanted to be that kind of saint; he wanted to show his readers supernatural phenomena, "the physical miracle of dimensions of existence." Blake had accomplished such miracles in his poetry; Cézanne had created a similar effect in his paintings. How could Ginsberg create that "flash" in his work? What "form of yoga" could create a sense of the eternal in the quotidian world?

In 1954–55 Ginsberg discovered the answers to these questions while writing "Howl." He had learned through various techniques to translate insights gained in his Blake and Cézanne studies into his own art form, for " 'Howl' was really an homage to art but also in specific terms an homage to Cézanne's method, in a sense I adapted what I could to writing" (p. 28).

II

Cézanne: I have my motifs (he joins his hands). A motif, you see, is this . . .

Gasquet: How's that?

Cézanne: Eh? Yes (he repeats his gesture, draws his hands apart, fingers spread out, and brings them together again, slowly, slowly. Then he joins them, presses them together, and contracts them, making them interlace). There you have it; that's what one must attain. If I pass too high or too low, all is ruined. There mustn't be a single link too loose, not a crevice through which may escape the emotion, the light, the truth . . . Our art ought to make us taste nature eternally.[8]

In 1872 a great change came over Paul Cézanne. He had spent his summer painting with his master-teacher, Camille Pissaro. In the fields near Auvers-sur-Oise, Pissaro taught his eager pupil to look at nature with a curious and contemplative gaze. He stressed the necessary mastery of an awareness of self; he insisted his student watch and record, be aware of the processes of thought, and observe the subtleties of personality adding its peculiar tinge to the interpretation of nature.

During this hot and instructive summer, the younger Cézanne learned to comprehend a reality beyond surfaces. He vowed to dedicate his art to a recreation of truth and a celebration of nature and the Eternal by allowing his emotions to be included in his portrayal of reality. He called his approach the *petite sensation*. It was a phenomenological understanding and expression, a means of getting close to the eternal in the everyday, the sensation of the Pater Omnipotens Aeterna Deus.

Cézanne spent the rest of his career refining this preoccupation. He discovered and invented techniques of color modulation and model arrangement that, combined with his experiments in line and perspective, allowed him to portray a phenomenological self observing the secrets of the Eternal, the godliness of nature. In a conversation with Joachim Gasquet he described his method as a rendering of "emotion, the light, the truth."[9]

Seventy-six years later Allen Ginsberg, already predisposed by his studies and visions, discovered Cézanne's experiments with his *petite sensations,* his attempts to generate a feeling of the eternal truths in everyday reality. And for Ginsberg the experiments were successful, for the promising poet felt as though Cézanne had allowed him to glimpse the sensation of Pater Omnipotens Aeterna Deus—that "sudden shift, a flashing." Ginsberg began his own investigation of technique and power under the guidance of Cézanne's achievement.

He discovered in Cézanne's letters a formula for achieving this heightened perceptual ability. Cézanne was lecturing Emile Bernard about the awareness of light sensations on the eyeball:

> An optical sensation is produced in our visual organ which causes us to classify the planes represented by color modulations into light, half-tone, or quarter-tone. . . . Inevitably, while you proceed from black to white, the first of these abstractions being like something to lean on, for the eye as much as the brain, we flounder, we do not succeed in mastering ourselves, in ruling over ourselves.[10]

When Ginsberg read this passage, he deduced that Cézanne was capable of producing the sensation of the Eternal because he had trained himself accurately to reproduce the sensations of light traveling through his optic nerve after it entered the "organ of sight."[11] The key to Cézanne's hermetic method was an almost "yogic perception." The artist (or poet) learns an awareness of the actual physical operations of perception—the phenomenological ability of observing the self observing nature.

Ginsberg's ambition became to learn how to write during such heightened moments of attention. He felt, as did Cézanne, that it was possible to transcend and realize the essence of nature. The art involved in writing (or painting) was to learn how to commit the mind to absolute, "yogalike" attention—a transcendental meditation technique: "The writing itself, the sacred act of writing, when you do anything of this nature, is like prayer. The act of writing being done sacramentally, if pursued over a few minutes, becomes like a meditation exercise which brings on a recall of detailed consciousness that is an approximation of high consciousness. High epiphanous mind. So, in other words, writing is a yoga that invokes Lord mind."[12] Writing is an exercise in perception that, if performed successfully, allows the practitioner to achieve "high consciousness," "Lord mind." First suggested in Cézanne's letter to Bernard, the exercise involves awareness of the actual processes of the mind at work: "You observe your own mind during the time of composition and write down whatever goes through the ticker tape of mentality, or whatever you hear in the echo of your inner ear, or what flashes in picture on the eyeball while you're writing" (*Craft*, p. 58). By paying attention to the forms of consciousness, the artist hopes to achieve a breakthrough in ordinary perception. The only stumbling block is self-consciousness, what Cézanne referred to as "distraction": "If I feel the least distraction, the least weakness (or break in observation), above all if I interpret too much one day, if today I am carried away by a theory which is contrary to that of the day before, if I think while painting, if I intervene, why then everything is gone."[13]

This is precisely Ginsberg's theory of composition, in which the "art consists in paying attention to the actual movie of the mind" (*Craft*, p. 58). Like Cézanne, Ginsberg insists that he not be distracted, that his attention always be focused. Self-consciousness is the great nemesis of this approach—indeed, rational thinking itself is a block because it gets in the way of a pure perception. The poet is the secretary of the consciousness and not its interpreter; he is dedicated to the transcription of the naked, honest, uncontrolled musings of thought and perception.

This method of writing has been dubbed "the spontaneous method of composition" by Ginsberg and by his tutor in prosody, Jack Kerouac. The approach is a commitment to unadulterated attention; the subject matter of the poem becomes the literal workings of the mind: "Such craft or art as there is, is in illuminating mental formations, and trying to observe the naked activity of my mind. Then transcribing the activity down on paper. So the craft is being shrewd at flashlighting mental activity. Trapping the archangel of the soul, by accident, so to speak. The subject matter is the action of my mind" (*Craft*, p. 57).

It took Ginsberg several years to comprehend and utilize the spontaneous method of composition. In 1954–55 as he composed "Howl," he was still learning the process. At that time he was also engaged in a study of Buddhism in the course of which he discovered *Śūnyatā*, a similar approach to transcendental knowledge. *Śūnyatā* is the Buddhist formula for absence of rational, controlled mind. It is pure mind, the same kind of understanding that Cézanne demanded for his art—painting without distraction, an absolute absorption in the workings of perception. *Śūnyatā* is intuitive knowledge; the practitioner is a medium for enlightened sensations. The meditator, like the artist or poet of Ginsberg's conception, trains his mind to watch and record various processes of thought—without conscious manipulation. When he is successful, flashes of eternal consciousness result.

Ginsberg's studies in Buddhism brought him back to his earlier discoveries in Cézanne. His initial Blake visions convinced him that it was possible to achieve transcendental states. When these studies in consciousness finally cohered sometime in late 1954 or early 1955, the result was his great poem "Howl." Written spontaneously (after several false starts), the poem makes use of the trancelike state of mind he had learned from his Cézanne studies and reconfirmed in his subsequent fascination with Buddhism. For Ginsberg, writing had become a successful form of "meditation or introspective yoga" that sought to discover the sensation of Pater Omnipotens Aeterna Deus.

III

> Who dreamt and made incarnate gaps in Time & Space through
>   images juxtaposed, and trapped the archangel of the soul
>   between 2 visual images and joined the elemental verbs and
>   set the noun and dash of consciousness together jumping
>   with sensation of Pater Omnipotens Aeterna Deus
>   —from "Howl"

Ginsberg has said that the last part of "Howl" is a homage to Cézanne. He is referring to the stanza quoted above, with the allusions to his use of Cézanne's "petite sensation" and the Pater Omnipotens Aeterna Deus. Actually the entire poem is a tribute to Cézanne because it is one of the first successful poems Ginsberg wrote using the spontaneous method of composition. But "Howl" is a homage to the great painter in another way. After Ginsberg had adapted the spontaneous method from his studies in Cézanne, he continued to ponder the possibilities of creating in his own poetry the "mysterious impression" that

Cézanne had produced in him. Returning to Cézanne's theories about perspective and color, Ginsberg concluded that it was Cézanne's use of juxtaposition that was the key to his success: "[P]utting it very simply, that just as Cézanne doesn't use perspective lines to create space, but it's a juxtaposition of one color against another color . . . so, I had the idea . . . that by the unexplainable, unexplained non–perspective line, that is, juxtaposition of one *word* against another, a *gap* between the two words— like the space gap in the canvas—there'd be a gap between the two words which the mind would fill in with the sensation of existence" (p. 28). Such a method would allow the poet and reader to experience the Buddhist *Śūnyatā:* "I meant again if you place two images, two visual images side by side and let the mind connect them, the gap between the two images the lightning in the mind illuminates. It is the *Śūnyatā* . . ." (*Craft,* p. 57). The poet traps the "archangel of the soul between 2 visual images" to create a gap in consciousness that results in *Śūnyatā;* the Buddhist equivalent of Cézanne's Pater Omnipotens Aeterna Deus.

The idea of using juxtaposition as a major technique for his poetry was actually first suggested to Ginsberg by Erle Loran. In his analysis of Cézanne, Loran used the word *juxtaposition* to describe Cézanne's method of composition; he proposed, in terms that are almost identical to Ginsberg's descriptions, that Cézanne produced his "shimmering surface quality" and "luminous effect" by the "juxtaposition of multi-colored spots that create atmosphere and light."[14] Loran concluded that this invention was a revolution in art of incomparable magnitude, indeed, one "of the most original achievements in the history of painting."[15] Duly impressed, Ginsberg experimented for the next several years (1948–55) with juxtaposition in imagery, diction, rhythm, and overall structure.

He and Jack Kerouac talked at length about the idea and concluded that the "gap" effect of juxtaposition was successfully achieved in poetry by the classical Japanese haiku writers. In haiku, "you have two distinct images, set side by side without drawing a logical connection between them: the *mind* fills in this . . . space" (p. 29). Ginsberg bought the four-volume set of Blyth's translations of haiku. He spent over a year trying to master the form by writing imitations of the best haiku by Basho, Buson, and Issa. The following haiku by Issa particularly startled him:

> O ant
> crawl up Mount Fujiyama,
> but slowly, slowly.

He felt that this enigmatic poem was a perfect example of the possibilities of juxtaposition, causing the gap in the mind that he so desired for his own poetry. His interpretation of the poem is a good insight into his belief that haiku has the potential of creating *Śūnyatā* through the juxtaposition of images: "Now you have the small ant and you have Mount Fujiyama and you have the 'slowly, slowly' and what happens is that you feel almost like . . . a cock in your mouth! You feel this enormous space-universe, it's almost a tactile thing. Well, anyway it's a phenomenon-sensation" (p. 29).

Convinced that the secret of the desired "phenomenon-sensation" could be mastered in haiku, Ginsberg wrote over two dozen of them while he was writing "Howl." Consider the following two examples:

> The master
> emerges from the movies;
> the silent street

> I don't know the names
> of the flowers—now
> my garden is gone[16]

In the first haiku he juxtaposes the reality of the street with the person emerging from the fantasy world, the movie house. The clash between celluloid reality and the cold reality of deserted streets is supposed to cause a momentary "gap" or "space" in one's sensibility. The reader should emerge with a glimpse of life at its barest. The second example is a similar attempt, juxtaposing the neglected garden with the poet's realization that his garden is barren. Between the two images comes the realization that life passes us by before we realize its essence.

In "Howl" Ginsberg was hoping to accomplish the effect of haiku in combination with his spontaneous method of composition and its use of unaltered mind:

> I was trying to do similar things with juxtapositions like "hydrogen jukebox." Or "winter midnight smalltown streetlight rain." Instead of cubes and squares and triangles . . . I have to reconstitute by means of words, rhythms, of course, and all that . . . The problem is then to reach the different parts of the mind, which are existing simultaneously, the different associations which are going on simultaneously, choosing elements from both, like: jazz, jukebox and all that, and we have the jukebox from that; politics, hydrogen bomb, and we have the hydrogen of that, you see "hydrogen jukebox." (P. 29)

The idea is to "reach different parts of the mind" that exist simultaneously and force them together to create a temporary suspension of habitual thought. The result is the gap that stops mind-flow, arrests normal consciousness, and creates a temporary void. The void is a sensation of *Śūnyatā*. Almost as if he were employing primitive magic, the poet tries to shock, scare, cajole, conjure, or seduce the reader. It is difficult to rationally explain "hydrogen jukebox"—even Ginsberg in the above quotation has a hard time of it. But, as in haiku, one isn't supposed to explain it, not rationally. One is supposed to experience it. It is a visceral approach to poetry in which the mind rejects its own rational sensibility and undergoes a kind of organic alteration.

Ginsberg not only used juxtaposition with his imagery, but made it the basis of his structure. Stanza after stanza of "Howl" follows the others in no logical, predictable pattern. The structure is a series of irrational juxtapositions made with the purpose of altering consciousness itself—something Ginsberg has called an "electro-chemical reaction." Like Artaud, he wanted a poetry that would stimulate in the reader an actual change in perception—at the physiological, chemical level if possible! That's what he thought had happened to him with Blake (and to a lesser degree with Cézanne), and it is that effect he was after, ultimately, with the employment of juxtaposition, the use of spontaneous composition, and the approach to writing as a "sacred act": "the idea that I had was that gaps in space and time through images juxtaposed, just as in the haiku which the mind connects in a flash, and so that *flash* is the *petite sensation*. . . . The interesting thing would be to know if certain combinations of words and rhythms actually had an electro-chemical reaction on the body, which could catalyze specific states of consciousness. I think that's what probably happened to me with Blake" (p. 30).

It is an interesting speculation. In fact, after he had mastered juxtaposition, spontaneous composition, and yogalike states of attention while writing, Ginsberg continued his studies in the exploration of altered states of consciousness. In the late 1950s he experimented with several kinds of hallucinatory drugs, hoping to find new insights into the experience of the Pater Omnipotens Aeterna Deus. In 1962 he journeyed to the Far East to study mantra chanting, hoping to borrow certain Hindu techniques in order to achieve "ecstatic consciousness" in his poetry. In the mid-1970s he returned to Buddhism, searching for meditation techniques that would achieve the void, the *Śūnyatā* he so sincerely desired. These approaches to poetry are all part of the "pragmatic study of consciousness" that began with his Blake visions and his studies of Cézanne. His is a tradition of poetry intent on "the artful investigation . . . of extraordinary states of consciousness," for Ginsberg believes, not unlike Blake, that the true function of poetry is "as a catalyst to visionary states of being" (*Craft,* pp. 69–70).

NOTES

1. Allen Ginsberg, "The Art of Poetry," *Paris Review* 10 (Spring 1966):24; hereafter cited parenthetically in the text.

2. A full account of Ginsberg's Blake visions is given in my *The Visionary Poetics of Allen Ginsberg* (Santa Barbara: Ross-Erikson, 1978).

3. Dennis McNally, *Desolate Angel* (New York: Random House, 1979), p. 79.

4. Collected in *Empty Mirror* (New York: Totem Press in association with Corinth Books, 1961), p. 12.

5. Meyer Shapiro, *Paul Cézanne* (New York: Harry N. Abrams, 1952), p. 62.

6. "The Art of Poetry," p. 26. Ginsberg is paraphrasing Cézanne.

7. Paul Cézanne, *Letters,* ed. John Rewald (London: Bruno Cassirer, 1941), p. 234.

8. Erle Loran, *Cézanne's Composition* (Berkeley and Los Angeles: University of California Press, 1944), p. 15.

9. Ibid., p. 15.

10. Ibid., p. 10.

11. Ibid., p. 10.

12. "Craft Interview with Allen Ginsberg," in *The Craft of Poetry,* ed. William Packard (New York: Doubleday), p. 73. Parenthetical page references, preceded by *Craft,* are to this work.

13. Loran, p. 15.

14. Ibid., p. 14.

15. Ibid., p. 24.

16. The haiku are from a notebook Ginsberg showed me in the summer of 1976.

BRUCE HUNSBERGER

Kit Smart's Howl

When Allen Ginsberg burst upon the literary scene in 1956 with the publication of *Howl,* he carried with him an underground of writers and their work. They were labeled the Beat Generation and their writing was hailed as "the New American Poetry."[1] Oddly enough this "real, unkidding, far-out, truly present scene typewriter-jazz that *matches* the gone world we live in and spin in"[2] carried into notoriety with it the old world poets William Blake and, to a lesser degree, Christopher Smart.

References to Blake that appear in much Beat writing and all of Ginsberg's work indicate that Blake had some influence on Beat writers. Christopher Smart is seldom mentioned, but the fact that he is mentioned at all is an indication that his work was known to them.[3] The blurb on the New Directions paperbook edition of Kenneth Patchen's *Because It Is* reads in part: "Klee and Goya, Edward Lear and Christian Morganstern, Kit Smart and Blake are others [besides Patchen] who have had this genius for inventing a special universe of fantastic revelation." The juxtaposition of Kit Smart and Blake in this context would indicate a similarity in their work and in their influence on other writers. The Beats championed Blake, however, not for any literary debt but for his mystic personality with which they could identify. This would seem to be the case with Kit Smart, also.

Smart was born in 1722 in Kent and died in 1771 in King's Bench Prison, where he was confined as a debtor. He was a scholar, a Fellow of Pembroke and Praelector in Philosophy and Rhetoric at Cambridge until 1749 when he deserted the University to pursue a career on Grub Street. He was a poet, winning

From *Wisconsin Studies in Contemporary Literature* (Winter–Spring 1965). Reprinted with permission.

for Cambridge the Seatonian Prize Poem five times between 1750 and 1755, every time he entered for it. In London he met John Newbery and formed a partnership—Newbery provided the money and Smart the talent—to publish a monthly magazine *The Midwife,* a collection of humor and satire. Smart married Newbery's step-daughter in 1753 and, disregarding his real poetic talent, continued hack writing until 1756 when he became obsessed with religious mania and had to be confined until sometime in 1763, first in a private house (possibly Newbery's) and then in a private asylum, Saint Luke's. In 1759 he was freed for a few months but then was confined again, this time probably at Chelsea. Yet Johnson said of Smart's madness:

> Madness frequently discovers itself merely by unnecessary deviation from the usual modes of the world. My poor friend Smart showed the disturbance of his mind, by falling upon his knees, and saying his prayers in the street, or in any other unusual place. . . . I did not think he ought to be shut up. His infirmities were not noxious to society. He insisted on people praying with him; and I'd as lief pray with Kit Smart as any one else. Another charge was, that he did not love clean linen; and I have no passion for it.[4]

There are several similarities here between Smart's life and the themes of the Beat mystique. There is the religious fervor. Ginsberg was one of the first to insist that the Beat Generation is a religious phenomenon and that Beat really means beatitude. Beat depends on constant revelations, constant mystic visions—"who drove crosscountry seventytwo hours to find out if I had a vision or you had a vision or he had a vision to find out Eternity,"[5] and "who loned it through the streets of Idaho seeking visionary indian angels who were visionary indian angels" ("Howl," I 25). There is also the modified Zen Buddhism practised by the Beats. It is Zen without the Zen discipline. Zen divested of everything but *satori,* the flash of insight which is total awareness—"to find out Eternity."

There is the madhouse theme. Beat writing exhibits a deep interest in psychiatry and mental disorders—although all conventional forms of treatment are considered "square." Ginsberg wrote "Howl" for Carl Solomon who was, at the time of its writing, an inmate at Rockland Hospital. Ginsberg himself spent eight months in a mental hospital in 1949.[6] Throughout Ginsberg's work are references to madmen, madhouses, and madness in general. There is always the feeling that the madman is closer to the center of religious experience. "The madman is holy as you my soul are holy!" cries Ginsberg in "Footnote to Howl" (l. 4).

There is, too, the idea of nonconformity for which the beats are notorious. If we accept Johnson's statement that madness is simply deviation from the usual modes of the world, then the mark of the true nonconformist is commitment papers. (And Johnson's comment on clean linen touches still another, although minor, theme of the Beat Generation.)

There is also the monkish ideal in Beat as a way of life—the turning away from material things and the accepting of voluntary poverty in the tradition of Saint Francis of Assisi. Ferlinghetti, Lamantia, Brother Antoninus, and Kerouac frequently mention Saint Francis in their poetry. Middleton Murry feels that there is only one adjective to describe Christopher Smart's short religious lyrics and, indeed, his whole attitude—"Franciscan."[7] Christopher Devlin says of this, "The adjective Franciscan is sometimes used in a way that has no relation to the actual life history of Saint Francis of Assisi. But in this case there is at least a *prima facie* resemblance—poverty, humiliation and suffering accepted without rancour and even with a kind of joy" (17).

The parallels between the lives of the Beat writers and Kit Smart are obvious and, as in the case of Blake, might be reason enough for Beat writers to bandy his name about. As for Smart's poetry, its outstanding characteristic according to Norman Callan is its egocentricity. Callan says, "Smart's ego seems too often entangled in a pettifogging exhibitionism. His tone is so personal that unless the reader is prepared to make the effort to understand his personality he is continually subject to a feeling of irritation at the self-absorption everywhere apparent."[8] Similar criticism has often been leveled against the Beats.

Smart's premadhouse poetry is glib, facile, and witty, but not very much better or different from the poetry of his contemporaries. His postmadhouse poetry is obsessed with religion. It includes his *Song to David* which is considered by most critics to be his masterwork. Neither category, however, has much to offer the modern poet in technique or inspiration.

But there was found in 1939 a thirty-two page manuscript in Smart's own handwriting—a long poem written in the madhouse. It was called *Jubilate Agno* (Rejoice in the Lamb) which Christopher Devlin describes as, "Written in a sort of free verse, most of the verses beginning with the word 'Let' and the remainder with the word 'For.' The general purpose of the 'Let' verses was to summon different personages, Biblical at first and then non-Biblical to bless God—each in conjunction with some individual of the animal or plant world, so that the total effect would be a chorus of praise from all creation. But after several hundred lines the purpose appears to degenerate into a meaningless list of oddities, while the 'For' verses do not seem to make even the beginning of a coherent plan" (17).

Scholars find the chief value of the *Jubilate Agno* to be its abundant biographical data for Smart's life. A midcentury American reader, however, is struck by the similarities of Christopher Smart's two-hundred-year-old *Jubilate Agno* and Allen Ginsberg's ultramodern "Howl."

Perhaps the most superficial similarity between the two poems is their appearance; they look alike. To illustrate this and to give some of their flavor, here are the first six lines of each poem:

JUBILATE AGNO

Rejoice in God, O ye Tongues; give the glory to the Lord, and the
    Lamb.
Nations, and languages, and every Creature, in which is the breath
    of Life.
Let man and beast appear before him, and magnify his name
    together.
Let Noah and his company approach the throne of Grace, and do
    homage to the Ark of their Salvation.
Let Abraham present a Ram, and worship the God of his
    Redemption.

Let Isaac, the Bridegroom, kneel with his Camels, and bless the hope
of his pilgrimage.[9]

HOWL

I saw the best minds of my generation destroyed by madness,
starving hysterical naked,
dragging themselves through the negro streets at dawn looking for
an angry fix,
angelheaded hipsters burning for the ancient heavenly connection to
the starry dynamo in the machinery of night,
who poverty and tatters and hollowed-eyed and high sat up smoking
in the supernatural darkness of cold-water flats floating across
the tops of cities contemplating jazz,
who bared their brains to Heaven under the El and saw
Mohammedan angels staggering on tenement roofs illuminated,
who passed through universities with radiant cool eyes hallucinating
Arkansas and Blake-light tragedy among the scholars of
war, . . .

Smart uses "Let" as the opening word until the seventh
manuscript page; there he switches to "For" until the thirteenth
page. After that he alternates—some pages having "Let" as the
opening word, most pages having "For." Ginsberg uses the
same repetitive technique in "Howl." In part I he opens each line
with "who." In part II he opens each line with "Moloch." In
part III he opens each line with the phrase "I'm with you in
Rockland."

We can only guess why Smart, who until his confinement had
written in the more conventional poetic forms, forsook them for
the seeming disorganization of the *Jubilate Agno*. Some critics
feel that it is simply a manifestation of his madness (Devlin, 17).
But in Ginsberg's case we have his "Notes Written on Finally
Recording Howl"[10] in which he discusses his poetic intent and
the actual form of his poem. Of his repetitive technique, Gins-
berg writes, "I depended on the word 'who' to keep the beat, a
base to keep measure, return to, and take off from again onto
another streak of invention" ("Notes," 132). This "base to keep
measure" is applicable to Smart's use of "Let" and "For" as

opening words. Smart, it has been said, had at an early stage of composition abandoned any hope of having the *Jubilate Agno* published. He continued it, writing at the rate of one verse per day, as a means of marking off the dates until he would be set free (Devlin, 21). What better method to keep the beat, to achieve cohesiveness, than by using the same opening word "to return to and take off from again onto another streak of invention"?

While idle in the madhouse Smart had time to review his life, and much of it crept into the *Jubilate.* The poem is a storehouse of biographical material. "Howl," too, is an autobiographical poem. As Ginsberg puts it, "I thought I wouldn't write a *poem,* but just write what I wanted to without fear, let my imagination go, open secrecy, and scribble magic lines from my real mind— sum up my life—something I wouldn't be able to show anybody, writ for my own soul's ear and a few other golden ears . . . " ("Notes," 132).

As stated previously, Smart had little hope of ever seeing *Jubilate Agno* published. Perhaps Ginsberg's statement that "Howl" was "writ for my own soul's ear and a few other golden ears" is an indication that he, too, felt that his poem would never be published.

Both poems have a liturgical form. In Smart's case, according to W. H. Bond, Curator of Manuscripts at Harvard (where the original *Jubilate Agno* is housed), the thirty-two manuscript pages of the poem have never been published in the right order. The "For" verses should have been printed alongside the "Let" verses, like the antiphons of Hebraic poetry which Smart was obviously imitating (Devlin, 20). We can have no doubt that Smart's religious zeal had an influence on the form of the *Jubilate Agno*.

Ginsberg writes, "I suddenly turned aside in San Francisco, unemployment compensation leisure, to follow my romantic inspiration—Hebraic-Melvillean bardic breath" ("Notes," 132). Bardic breath is defined as, "Ideally each line of 'Howl' is a single breath unit. My breath is long—that's the Measure, one physical-mental inspiration of thought contained in the elastic of a breath" ("Notes," 133). "Hebraic-Melvillean" is not defined by Ginsberg, but the use of the words "Hebraic" and "bardic" would indicate that his poetic inspiration came from Hebraic poetry, as did Smart's.

In line with the Hebraic influences, we have the titles of the two poems. The English equivalent of Smart's *Jubilate Agno* is "Rejoice in the Lamb." The topic headings which Ginsberg has assigned to the three parts of "Howl" are these:

> Part I, a lament for the Lamb in America with instances of remarkable lamblike youths; Part II names the monster of mental consciousness that preys on the Lamb; Part III a litany of affirmation of the Lamb in its glory. . . . ("Notes," 133).

There is also a similarity in Ginsberg's heading for part III of "Howl" and the first line of the *Jubilate Agno:*

> Ginsberg: Part III a litany of affirmation of the Lamb in its glory . . .
> Smart: Rejoice in God, O ye Tongues; give the glory to the Lord, and the Lamb.

The Lamb is the familiar symbol of Christ, the Lamb of God, and of innocence and love. Smart accepts the Lamb and rejoices in it; his poem is one of faith and glorification. Ginsberg has said his poem is a lament for the Lamb in America with instances of remarkable lamblike youths. The youths he portrays seem anything but lamblike. But this is not their fault, he says, for America has corrupted their innocence. Ginsberg's poem is one of anger and vilification. It is significant that Smart rejoices *in* the Lamb and that Ginsberg laments *for* it. Smart's Lamb has carried him to heaven; Ginsberg's Lamb has dragged him through hell.

Since both poems are autobiographical, they recount actual experiences of the poets. Both poets incur the wrath of the police for their public demonstrations. Ginsberg:

> who distributed Supercommunist pamphlets in Union Square
> weeping and undressing while the sirens of Los Alamos wailed
> them down, and wailed down Wall, and the Staten Island ferry
> also wailed, . . .

who bit detectives in the neck and shrieked with delight in policecars
    for committing no crime but their own wild cooking pederasty
    and intoxication, . . .

(I 32, 34)

Smart's demonstrations are less bizarre, but the result is the same:

For I blessed God in St. James's Park till I routed all the company.
For the officers of the peace are at variance with me and the
    watchman smites me with his staff.

(VIII 19–20)

Smart cautions against putting anything between one's head and the blessing of God:

For it is not good to wear any thing upon the head.
For a man should put no obstacle between his head and the blessing
    of Almighty God.
For a hat was an abomination of the heathen. Lord have mercy upon
    the Quakers.
For the ceiling of the house is an obstacle and therefore we pray on
    the house-top.

(XXIV 53–56)

Compare this to Ginsberg in "Howl":

who bared their brains to Heaven under the El and saw Mohammedan
    angels staggering on tenement roofs illuminated, . . .

(I 57)

Compare Ginsberg's interjection "this actually happened" with Smart's "this is a true case" in the following:

Ginsberg:

who jumped off the Brooklyn Bridge this actually happened and
    walked away unknown and forgotten into the ghostly daze of
    Chinatown soup alleyways & firetrucks . . .

(I 57)

Smart:

For—this is a true case—Cat takes female mouse from the company
    of male—male mouse will not depart, but stands threatening &
    daring.

(XVIII 59)

In his "Notes" Ginsberg describes the actual writing of
"Howl": "So the poem got awesome, I went on to what my
imagination believed true to Eternity (for I'd had a beatific il-
lumination years before during which I'd heard Blake's ancient
voice and saw the universe unfold in my brain), & what my
memory could reconstitute of the data of celestial experiences"
(132). He reconstitutes his experience in "Howl":

incomparable blind streets of shuddering cloud and lightning in the
    mind leaping toward poles of Canada & Paterson, illuminating
    all the motionless world of Time between. . . .

(I 12)

In view of Ginsberg's "beatific illumination" years before, it
is reasonable to assume that the "lightning" he speaks of is
spiritual. Compare it to Smart's lightning:

For The Lightning before death is God's illumination in the spirit for
    preparation and for warning.

(XVI 15)

Later Ginsberg writes of further illumination:

who fell on their knees in hopeless cathedrals praying for each other's
    salvation and light and breasts, until the soul illuminated its hair
    for a second, . . .

(I 62)

And similarly, Smart writes:

For ignorance is a sin because illumination is to be obtained by
    prayer.

(XV 11)

Perhaps it is because of his "celestial experiences" that Ginsberg has described his poetry as "Angelic Ravings" ("Notes," 135), and "Howl" abounds in angels. There are Mohammedan angels, visionary indian angels, a blonde and naked angel, a madman bum and angel, hideous human angels, an archangel of the soul and, of course, angelheaded hipsters. There is, too, an airplane which drops angelic bombs and Moloch in whom Ginsberg dreams angels. Smart is not without his angels. In *Jubilate* we find innumerable angels, blessed angels, cherubic angels, a cherub cat of the Angel Tiger, and the angel gratitude, who is Smart's wife. The sun is described as an improving angel and an angel in human form. The moon is an angel in the shape of a woman.

Both Ginsberg and Smart have very special angels to help them in times of difficulty. These angels are called "my Angel" and are capitalized to designate their unique status in the hierarchy of angels. Ginsberg, for example, tells us in his "Notes" that when he was pondering the possibilities of using the long line in short lyrical poems, "Cottage in Berkeley" and "Supermarket in California" simply "fell in place" the same day. "Not purposely," he says, "I simply followed my Angel in the course of composition" (133).

Although we are not certain if Smart's Angel helped in the actual composition of his poetry, we do know that his Angel saw him through difficult situations:

For my Angel is always ready at a pinch to help me out and to keep me up.

(VII 57)

In opposition to their Angels, who are working on their behalf, Ginsberg and Smart feel that there are forces working against them, depriving them of the realization of their dreams. Ginsberg calls them the three old shrews of fate:

who lost their loveboys to the three old shrews of fate the one eyed shrew of the heterosexual dollar the one eyed shrew that winks out of the womb and the one eyed shrew that does nothing but

sit on her ass and snip the intellectual golden threads of the
craftsman's loom, . . .

(I 40)

Smart calls them "the coffin, the cradle, and the purse":

For the coffin and the cradle and the purse are all against a man.
For the coffin is for the dead and death came by disobedience.
For the cradle is for weakness and the child of man was originally
    strong from the womb.
For the purse is for money and money is dead matter with the stamp
    of human vanity.
For the adversary frequently sends these particular images out of the
    fire to those whom they concern.
For the coffin is for me because I have nothing to do with it.
For the cradle is for me because the old Dragon attacked me in it &
    [I] overcame in Christ.
For the purse is for me because I have neither money nor human
    friends.

(X 55–62)

Christopher Devlin points out in *Poor Kit Smart* that to trample
on the coffin (as Christ does in old pictures of the Resurrection) is
to conquer death by accepting obedience (12). This statement
might also apply to Ginsberg's closing lines of "Notes" when he
states that "Fate tells big lies, and the gay Creator dances on his
own body in Eternity" (135). Smart's rejection of the purse is his
acceptance of voluntary poverty. Ginsberg's "one eyed shrew of
the heterosexual dollar" is one of several statements in "Howl"
which illustrates his feelings about money. He also writes of
"burning their money in wastebaskets and listening to the Terror
through the wall" (I 8).

Smart's statement on his lack of human friends strikes upon
the theme of loneliness which is strong in both poems. For all its
"Eyeball kicks" and loud protests, "Howl" is a poem about
loneliness:

who wandered around and around at midnight in the railroad yard
    wondering where to go, and went, leaving no broken
    hearts, . . .

                      (I 22)

And in Smart's poem as well:

For I am come home again, but there is nobody to kill the calf or to
    pay the musick.

                      (VII 15)

    The poetic line from Kit Smart to Blake has been recognized as has the line from Blake to the Beats. Perhaps there is an unbroken line from the Beats to Kit Smart. From its inception Beat poetry was hailed as "something NEW" and "like all good spontaneous jazz, newness is acceptable and expected—by hip people who listen."[11] But the newness of jazz has in it the echoes of J. S. Bach, and perhaps the newness of that "typewriter-jazz" called Beat poetry has in it the echoes of old Kit Smart.

NOTES

    1. *The New American Poetry 1945–1960,* ed. Donald M. Allen (New York: Grove Press, 1960).

    2. Seymour Krim, in *The Beats,* ed. Seymour Krim (Greenwich, Conn.: Fawcett, 1960), p. 12.

    3. Jack Kerouac, *The Subterraneans* (New York: Grove Press, 1958), p. 89.

    4. *The Portable Johnson & Boswell,* ed. Louis Kronenberger (New York: Viking, 1962), pp. 94–95.

    5. Allen Ginsberg, *Howl and Other Poems* (San Francisco: City Lights Books, 1956), "Howl," Part I, l. 60. Subsequent references to this edition of "Howl" appear in parentheses in the text.

    6. Paul O'Neil, "The Only Rebellion Around," *Life,* Nov. 30, 1959, p. 120.

    7. Christopher Devlin, *Poor Kit Smart* (Carbondale, Ill.: Southern Illinois University Press, 1961), p. 17. Subsequent references to this edition appear in parentheses in the text.

8. *The Collected Poems of Christopher Smart,* ed. Norman Callan (Cambridge: Harvard University Press, 1950), vol. 1, p. xxviii.

9. In *Collected Poems,* p. 249. Subsequent references to this edition of *Jubilate Agno* appear in parentheses in the text. Roman numerals in these references refer to the page numbers of the original manuscript.

10. *Evergreen Review* 3, no. 10 (November–December, 1959):132–35. Subsequent references to this edition appear in parentheses in the text.

11. Gregory Corso, *Gasoline* (San Francisco: City Lights Books, 1959), p. 10.

JOHN TYTELL

The Legacy of Surrealism

. . . Blake, Whitman, and Williams are the figures who have most inspired Ginsberg, but an equally significant, if less finitely measurable, source has been Surrealist poetry and painting. Blake permitted entry into the prophetic tradition; Whitman offered the infusion of democratic optimism; Williams inspired a new diction; but Surrealism suggested the state of mind that proved liberating enough for Ginsberg to see the political realities of his day with passionate clarity.

In a poem called "At Apollinaire's Grave," Ginsberg was to voice his appreciation for the insights learned from the French Surrealist poets:

> I've eaten the blue carrots you sent out of the grave and
> Van Gogh's ear and maniac peyote of Artaud
> and will walk down the streets of New York in the black
> cloak of French poetry
> Improvising our conversation in Paris at Père Lachaise
> and the future poem that takes its inspiration from the
> light bleeding into your grave

Surrealism was very much a part of the *Zeitgeist* surrounding Ginsberg in his youth. During the war, a number of the key Surrealist painters had settled in America, and by 1942 Ernst, Masson, and Tanguy were living in New York City, as well as André Breton, one of the theoreticians of the movement. Breton's belief that subconscious irrationality could provide the basis for a positive social program separated the Surrealists from

From "Allen Ginsberg and the Messianic Tradition," in *Naked Angels* (New York: McGraw-Hill, 1976). Reprinted with permission.

171

the Dadaists, their more nihilistic forebears. Breton's manifestoes contain arguments that anticipate the inner flow of experience Ginsberg was to express so powerfully in his poetry. Breton sought a "monologue spoken as rapidly as possible without any interruption on the part of the cerebral faculties, a monologue consequently unencumbered by the slightest inhibition and which was as closely as possible akin to spoken thought." This "psychic automatism" proposed to express the mind's actual functioning in the absence of controls like reason, or any superimposed moral or aesthetic concern. If Ginsberg was to remain in touch with Blake's tradition of magic prophecy, he would have to find ways to release that vision without unnecessarily tampering, interfering, or distorting, and the Surrealist bias against revision that Kerouac maintained prevented the danger of any fatal loss of impetus.

The Surrealists in France had distinguished between literature as a craft or talent exercised within certain traditional and prescriptive formal limitations and poetry as a mode of visionary discovery. To induce revelation, they pursued their dreams, finding in them a route to the unconscious, and a way of capturing the uncensored maturity of Rimbaud's child-man. Like Blake's idealization of the child, the Surrealists sought a model for wonder, spontaneity, and destructiveness—which, by the way, they interpreted as the end of adult self-control and obedience to conditioning. So Breton began attending with fascination to phrases running through his mind as he fell asleep, just as Williams in *Kora in Hell* was to improvise disconnected passages composed just prior to sleep. Related to such experiments was the Surrealists' interest in Charcot's *Studies in Hysteria* and Robert Desnos's self-induced trances. As Alfred Jarry urged, true hallucination is the sustained waking dream, and this becomes the premise of much of Ginsberg's poetry as he applies the phantasmagoria of dream to everyday reality. As Breton formulated it in his *Second Manifesto:*

> Surrealism aims quite simply at the total recovery of our psychic force by a means which is nothing other than the dizzying descent into ourselves, the systematic illumination

of hidden places and the progressive darkening of other places, the perpetual excursion into the midst of forbidden territory. . . .

It is quite clear that this consciousness was present in Ginsberg's earliest poems. In "Psalm I," the second poem in *Empty Mirror,* Ginsberg refers to his poems as the product of a "vision haunted mind," and writes of "majestic flaws of mind which have left my brain open to hallucination." In the initial poem of the volume, the marvelously understated "I feel as if I am at a dead end," Ginsberg describes a state of psychic and moral impotence whose metaphor is the head severed from the body. This impotence expresses itself as a terrible inability to act in the face of a paralyzing absurdity which stalks through the poems; hallucination, visionary messages from the unconscious, serve to fuse head and body, to reconnect intellect and feeling. A number of the best poems in the collection are called dreams, like the Kafkian "A Meaningless Institution" where Ginsberg invents an enormous ward filled with "hundreds of weeping / decaying men and women." Everyone in the poem is impassive; everything in it is static; there is no interrelationship anywhere—and in the end the observer wanders futilely "down empty corridors / in search of a toilet." The view of the world implied by such a poem is dismal, a miasma of quiescent disappointment and stagnant despair, a pervasive mood in the book appearing with special poignance in "Sunset," "A Ghost May Come," "A Desolation," "The Blue Angel," and "Walking Home at Night." These poems reflect terrible entrapment in mechanical situations revealing men devoid of humanity, like those "cowering in unshaven rooms in underwear" in "Howl." Occasionally, the depression is alleviated by childish rage, as in one of the best poems in *Empty Mirror,* "In Society":

> I walked into the cocktail party
> room and found three or four queers
> talking together in queertalk.
> I tried to be friendly but heard
> myself talking to one in hiptalk.

"I'm glad to see you," he said, and
looked away. "Hmn," I mused. The room
was small and had a double-decker
bed in it, and cooking apparatus:
icebox, cabinet, toasters, stove;
the hosts seemed to live with room
enough only for cooking and sleeping.
My remark on this score was under-
stood but not appreciated. I was
offered refreshments, which I accepted.
I ate a sandwich of pure meat; an
enormous sandwich of human flesh,
I noticed, while I was chewing on it,
it also included a dirty asshole.

More company came, including a
fluffy female who looked like
a princess. She glared at me and
said immediately: "I don't like you,"
turned her head away, and refused
to be introduced. I said, "What!"
in outrage. "Why you shit-faced fool!"
This got everybody's attention.
"Why you narcissistic bitch! How
can you decide when you don't even
know me," I continued in a violent
and messianic voice, inspired at
last, dominating the whole room.

The periodic ending of the poem is a Kafkian delusion, like
Joseph K criticizing court practices in *The Trial* only to learn
later that he had been haranguing his judges instead of visitors to
the court. The aggressively explosive tirade of "Why you shit-
faced fool!" is the culmination of a series of four utterly absurdist
enclosures like the room without room to live, all beautifully
emphasized by the short, abruptly declarative lines. Behind the
subject of the poem is Ginsberg's discomfort with his own ho-
mosexuality, and its most compelling image is the sandwich of

human flesh containing the dirty asshole. Like the talking ass-hole in Burroughs's *Naked Lunch,* Ginsberg's image provides an apt illustration of what Lautreamont thought of as systematic bewildering—the beauty of the "fortuitous meeting of a sewing machine and an umbrella on an operating table." The image of the dirty asshole returns the reader to the uneasiness with the homosexual condition that the poem dramatizes, starting with the shift from queertalk to hiptalk. Calling the fluffy female "shit-faced" creates a continuity of image, just as the emphasis on the hosts' kitchen and cooking apparatus prepares the reader for the dirty asshole. While the continuity from eating food to defecating on those about you does unify the poem, it is by no means an apparent motif, and the categories of kitchen, asshole, and "shit-faced fool" exist like realities on different planes. The asshole image can be taken as an example of what Breton called incandescent flashes linking those different elements of reality together with a vital metaphor, even though those elements seem so far removed that reason alone could never connect them. The impact of the poem, the depth of the anxiety betrayed by its central image, defies a realistic mode. The poem, culminating as it does with a view of messianic anger "dominating the whole room," shares the qualities of self-revelation and honest exposure associated with Robert Lowell's *Life Studies.* As Ginsberg has written in a poem "On Burroughs' Work":

> A naked lunch is natural to us,
> > we eat reality sandwiches.
> But allegories are so much lettuce.
> > Don't hide the madness.

A similar strength occurs in a number of the poems in *Empty Mirror*—little wonder that Ginsberg's critics like the volume—especially in "A Crazy Spiritual," another one of the dream poems that anticipates the bizarrely driving absurdity and fulminating ironies of the songs on Bob Dylan's *Bringing It All Back Home* album ("Maggie's Farm" and "Bob Dylan's 115th Dream" in particular).

The poems in *Empty Mirror* employ short lines predominantly, stripping "yakking down to modern bones" Ginsberg wrote to Cassady, and at one point Ginsberg expresses metaphorical dissatisfaction with Yeatsian terseness:

> I attempted to concentrate
> the total sun's rays in
> each poem as through a glass,
> but such magnification
> did not set the page afire.

He begins to move in the direction of his long-line experiments in "Hymn," a series of five verse paragraphs (animated by such antiprose and surreal formulations as "clock of meat"), or "Paterson," a poem no one seems to have noticed even though it anticipates the rhythmic power of the later poetry as well as the thematic rejection of American materialism. Rather than live in rooms "papered with visions of money," rather than cut his hair, dress properly, bathe, and work steadily for the "dead prick of commonplace obsession," the hero of "Paterson," a Beat code figure, would choose madness:

> . . . gone down the dark road to
>   Mexico, heroin dripping in my veins,
> eyes and ears full of marijuana,
> eating the god Peyote on the floor of a mudhut on the border
> or laying in a hotel room over the body of some suffering man or
>   woman;

The hero prefers to "jar" his "body down the road" of dissipation rather than conform to the conventions of the everyday, and he lists a series of ecstatic excesses, culminating in a screaming dance of praise to an eternity that annihilates reality as in a Dionysian frenzy he impales himself in nature, "leaving my flesh and bones hanging on the trees." "Paterson" is a psychological fulcrum for Ginsberg's early poetry, charging the sense of heavy doldrum and ennui, the sentimentality of his earliest Columbia College verse, with a quality of scatological hysteria he may have learned from Céline. Actually, in a review of Céline's *Death on the Installment Plan* that Ginsberg wrote in his last year at Columbia, he recognized the persona he was later to assume in "Paterson":

The mad author has taken the weird mask of an aggressive character, self-sufficient, skeptical, sentimental, self-disgusted, self-protecting, all because he is convinced of the dangerousness of modern life, and has passed it [the mask] off as a natural, "just" development of mind.

"Paterson" is a poem of excess, an early sign of Ginsberg's surrealism. Breton noted that surrealism acts on the mind very much like drugs, creating a need for the mysterious effects and special pleasures of an artificial paradise, but at the same time pushing men to frightful revolts as that paradise seems unattainable. Like opium-induced images, surrealistic images seem to occur spontaneously, or despotically as Baudelaire once claimed, ringing with unpremeditated juxtaposition. Apollinaire, in *Le poète assassiné,* glorified physical disequilibrium as divine, and Rimbaud, earlier, had called for a violent derangement of the senses.

Ginsberg has heeded this imperative, risking his sensibility to widen the area of his consciousness with drugs. As Coleridge claimed to have composed "Kubla Khan" during an opium reverie, Ginsberg has admitted to writing a number of poems while using marijuana or the stronger hallucinogens like peyote, LSD-25, mescaline, and ayahuasca (yage, the drug for which Burroughs traveled to South America to find the "final fix"). The experiences described in these poems, often titled by the name of the drug employed, are very similar to the effects in Burroughs's fiction: déjà vu, death hysteria, extreme paranoia, disembodied awareness of a decomposing body, demonic mind-monsters, loss of identity as in "The Reply" where the "universe turns inside out to devour me," and only occasionally a sense of ecstatic, spiraling energy. The greatest concentration of drug poems is in *Kaddish,* but they are clearly the weakest part of the volume. Oddly enough, Ginsberg is unable to suggest a convincing state of transport in these poems, and they seem grounded compared to a natural high like the one Emerson described in his first essay, "Nature":

Standing on the bare ground—my head bathed by the blithe air and uplifted into infinite space—all mean egotism vanishes. I become a transparent eyeball; I am nothing; I see all; the currents of the Universal Being circulate through me; I am part or parcel of God.

Ironically, in the *Kaddish* drug poems, just where a reader might expect a sacrifice of intellect and a total involvement with the senses, the intrusion of the poet's questioning mind misdirects the tensions. Ginsberg seems almost aware of this, as when in "Aether" he mentions "the threat to magic by writing while high." "Aether," the last poem in *Reality Sandwiches,* comes closest to fulfilling Ginsberg's ideal of the poem as notation of undifferentiated consciousness (drugs theoretically assisting in such an effort by deemphasizing mind), a quality felt in the poem's movement toward new line arrangements and visual impact.

Over the years, Ginsberg has defended the legalization of marijuana and spoken of his experiences with hallucinogens without proselytizing for them. He regards these drugs as the American and South American Indians have traditionally used them, as potent medicines with ritual significance. When he advocates their use, it is less for pleasure than for the sake of increased consciousness—the necessity of transcending normative behavior, "getting out of one's head" so as to view ordinary realities from an entirely different perspective. On June 14, 1966, Ginsberg testified before a special Senate subcommittee on his own drug experiences. He stated that drugs had helped him overcome stereotypes of habit by releasing inner and latent resources of feeling for other human beings, especially women, and for nature, that had been stymied and almost conditioned out of existence by the mechanization of modern culture with its emphasis on muting the senses, reducing language and thought to uniform patterns, slogans without character, monopolizing attention with packaged news and stale imagery that failed to satisfy his own need for communication. . . .

Although for some, hallucinogens telescope madness, they can prove—for those able to handle the situation, Ginsberg warns—therapeutically restoring. Ginsberg himself has not always been able to contain his drug experiences, and on his trip to India in 1962 he reached an apex with morphine injections and opium that produced a recurrence of the death-terror he felt in 1948 when he tried to deliberately induce the spirit of Blake. Generally, Ginsberg has used drugs as an aid to releasing blocked aspects of his consciousness which are expressed in his poetry, like the Moloch vision in "Howl" which was induced by peyote, or "Kaddish," written while using amphetamines. . . .

PART TWO *The 1960s: Black Magic*
           & Magic Speech

With Ezra Pound and Fernanda Pivano. Portofino, Italy, summer 1967.

SELECTED REVIEWS

A. R. AMMONS

Ginsberg's New Poems

The unit of form (meaning), rhythm, and power in Ginsberg's poetry is the line.

> White electricity
> > in the gaslamp fixtures of the alley.
> > > Bullet holes and nails in the stone wall.
> The worried headwaiter
> > standing amid the potted palms in cans
> > > in the fifteen foot wooden door looking at me.
> Mariachi harmonica artists inside
> > getting around to Banjo on My Knee yet.
> > > They dress in wornout sharpie clothes.

This quotation is from "Havana 1953." I quote it because the three-line organization seems to refute my first sentence. Other early poems have visual organization of lines—the latest in this book is dated 1954. I like the organization, even though it is merely visual; i.e., no principle of duration or repetition seems to be at work in a system of necessity. The later poems are free of visual pattern: each line reaches with ultimate risk into the unknown, the anticipated spaces lining up to be made manifest with word.

> I'll go into the bedroom silently and lie down between
> > the bridegroom and the bride,
> those bodies fallen from heaven stretched out waiting
> > naked and restless,

Review of *Reality Sandwiches,* from *Poetry* (June 1964). Reprinted with permission.

arms resting over their eyes in the darkness,
bury my face in their shoulders and breasts,
    breathing their skin. . . .
        ("Love Poem on a Theme by Whitman")

The first two lines compose almost equal amounts of space. The third line, shorter, seems necessary, inevitable, and complete—etc. Ginsberg's music is felt, instinctive rather than consciously metrical, but it's true, I think, by inexplicable gift.

The lines don't shape, predict, and limit whole-poem forms. Most of the poems might have been shorter or longer. The reason is that external reality (time, place, event) dictates Ginsberg's means, so the means are outside the poem and, though unrecoverable, are more complete there. Certain things happened in a certain city at a certain time: a journal, or cata-travelog of accidentals. Opposite (for clarification) is the internal vision, selecting, transfiguring, making new and whole; the poet servant to the poem that exists apart in terms of its own reality. The unity in Ginsberg's work is Ginsberg in search of unity, so that the poems are fragments of the search. The greater poem is possible when the poem is the sought unity, the poet providing the fragments to the whole from his fragmentary experience.

The poems in this volume date from 1953 to 1960, poems both before and after *Howl*. They mostly lack the desperately earnest cry for truth and the sung-tension accuracy of Ginsberg at his best.

JAMES SCULLY

A Passion in Search of Two Boards

Wallace Stevens once wrote that authors are actors. Well, every actor needs a stage: if the world will not provide it ready-made, one must be improvised. In the theater of his poetry, Ginsberg is a grand and tawdry passion in search of two boards, any two, upon which it may play itself out.

And Ginsberg works at it. Wherever his ambition falters, as in "Aether," there's either a lapse of mental integrity or a breakdown of language. The former is exposed in the pompous conclusion, ascending the sennet of capital letters, that God is meaningless. In attempting to discover ultimate bedrock beneath the "Universe," he tends to fall headlong into God, Angels, Cosmos, Time, Eternity, and other graveyards of the sentimental intellect. He then resembles the shade of the second-rate sociologist who stuffed all his categorical jargon into a rucksack and marched off, one day, toward bloody-gold horizons of evangelical light. An admirable move, surely, if only because any passion is preferable to none at all. In the end, however, it will not suffice. So flimsy a passion is liable to dissolve, more or less insensibly, from speech to babbling and from histrionics into hysterics.

Yet Ginsberg's metaphysical probings frequently do touch home, particularly when he ceases daydreaming of naked Eternity and concentrates instead on its "hieroglyphs." These are the only realities we can sink our teeth into. So the finest poem in this collection, "Siesta in Xbalba," embodies neither Hell nor Heaven but a strangely palpable, pulsating world in which both those extremes are implicit; it recalls not Blake, but the quieter

Review of *Reality Sandwiches* from the *Nation*, 16 November 1963. Reprinted with permission.

vision of Henry Vaughan. At indefinite moments the real be-
comes unreal, even while the persistent sensation of reality
swells and envelops one's mind:

> palms with lethargic feelers
> rattling in presage of rain,
> > shifting their fronds
> in the direction of the balmy wind,
> > monstrous animals
> sprayed up out of the ground
> > settling and unsettling
> as in water . . .

"And later in the night," it continues, "a moment of premoni-
tion / when the plenilunar cloudfilled sky / is still and small."
How often do we find such an image, one undergoing such
dramatic metamorphoses, which yet remains precise and invio-
lable throughout? It makes our ordinary distinction between
illusion and reality seem piddling or even perverse. Nor is this
an isolated moment in the poem: it spreads out and sustains
itself, before and after.

Ginsberg, too, sustains himself. One wonders how, for he is
the unacceptable human being whom the Brahmins thought
they had transformed into a bearable, if not entirely acceptable,
screwball. What was it that unnerved them? The brain, the ego,
the extravagant wit, the obscenity, the broadly humorous self-
perspectives, the oftentimes cauliflowered inner ear? Perhaps
they were disturbed by the humanity which informs so much of
the poetry, especially the *Kaddish* volume. In *Reality Sandwiches,*
he manages to imbue even a scatological insight with that sense
of humanity. For "even the ugliest will seek beauty," and of a
crippled girl, "her hips askew":

let her roll her eyes in abandon & camp angelic through the campus
    bouncing her body about in joy—
someone will dig that pelvic energy for sure.

Such a joyously obscene suggestion hardly undercuts the crip-
ple; in fact, it catches her radiance. In a crazy way, what might

have been merely pitiable has become desirable: an agony has evolved into a celebration. This is what a sense of humanity does. And in a society of cliques Allen Ginsberg is one who has made an attempt, more apparent in his poetry than in his publicity, to uncover a community. It is in this, not in the religious or sexual abstractions, that the passion realizes itself. Then the Allen emerges from behind the Ginsberg; the man breaks through the paper wall.

ALAN BROWNJOHN

Fblup!

Allen Ginsberg has always somehow slipped out of the grasp of criticism. That public image has been too eccentrically powerful: either you absorb the message wholly, or you just don't think it's worth complaining. On the page, the hectoring, large-scale verses race you on past any attempt to sort out something rational and paraphrasable, defying objections with scatological exuberance and a crazy, ranting benignity. In "Uptown" in the new book, a "hatted thin citizen hurrying to the barroom door" shouts at the poet, " 'If I had my way I'd cut off your hair and send you to Vietnam . . . And if I couldn't do that I'd cut your throat.' " Replies Ginsberg, in admirable, imaginable fashion, " 'Bless you then . . . Bless you sir.' " One feels that the poems answer in a similar vein to the mildest sort of critical reproach.

In *Planet News,* nothing has changed very much. There are two major poems of considerable length: one called "Television Was a Baby Crawling Toward That Deathchamber"—

I am the Intolerant One Gasbag from the Morgue & Void,
    Garbler of all Conceptions that myope my eye & is Uncle Sam
    asleep in the Funeral Home?—

and the other "Wichita Vortex Sutra," which anchors more successfully in time and space and has some of the most coherent and sustained political invective Ginsberg has ever achieved. The other poems are, by this poet's standards, short—many of them pieces of personal meditation in places visited on his travels. Bombay, Warsaw, Prague, London and Wales receive the same

Review of *Planet News* and *Ankor Wat,* from the *New Statesman,* 10 January 1969.
Reprinted with permission.

hectic treatment as Hollywood and New York, Ginsberg working, as before, to pile up vast accumulations of topical images and references, switching and mixing them with heady rapidity, yoking together the repellent and the mystical in a manner he's made his own.

Ankor Wat is an extended, but less striving, exercise in the same vein: a poem written under morphine-atrophine in one night in 1963 and published separately in a handsome edition illustrated with Alexandra Lawrence's photographs of the famous ruins. Ginsberg has a clear eye for things when he stands still and works it all out; and the illustrations here point up vividly the patches of visual description which occur in the midst of a long, jerky monologue on Cambodian scenes, Buddhist disciplines and murky political events. It all hangs together, just; but there are passages of embarrassing badness.

Ginsberg stands at the end of a long line of American poets who have striven to embrace and comprehend everything in sight, but his poetry lacks the compensations of his predecessors'. He doesn't have Whitman's sweeping lyrical cadences, he has abandoned Hart Crane's quest for "a formal integration of experience," he doesn't manage the clever and pointful anecdotes and maxims that relieve Carl Sandburg's resounding periods. It is difficult not to see Ginsberg's work as the final collapse of this style, a last self-indulgent plunge into chaos and nonsense. And to what effect? In the black mood of "Morning," he sees the limitations of the liberty society has granted him, to be a licensed rebel, while it gets on with its own brutalities—the "total Freedom! To / Do what?" The poem breaks down into a terribly sad, inarticulate self-hatred—it is the freedom "To be a big bore! . . . Paper words! Fblup! Fizzle! Droop! . . . Go fuck / yourself, / everybody Ginsberg! / And when you've exhausted / that, go forward? / Where? kiss my ass!" One answer *might* be to go *back*, forget the mysticism and the egocentric sexuality, and use that fine camera eye which even here focuses with haunting clarity in one or two memorable patches (as in "Wichita Vortex Sutra"):

> Red sun setting flat plains west streaked
>   with gauzy veils, chimney mist spread

around christmas-tree bulbed refineries—aluminum white
    tanks squat beneath
winking signal towers' bright plane-lights,
        orange gas-flares
beneath pillows of smoke, flames in machinery—transparent
    towers at dusk

("Bless you, reviewer.")

DAVID LEHMAN

Review of *Ankor Wat*

Allen Ginsberg's *Ankor Wat* is retrospective—a long poem from
his journals—written in Siemreip, Cambodia in 1963. It's a very
moving poem, in some ways a prophecy, in some ways a shout
with a nervous laugh trailing it. Ginsberg manages, by the sheer
passion of his writing, to convince us of his personal agony and
turmoil—

> Nothing but a false Buddha afraid of
>   my own annihilation, Leroi Moi—
> afraid to fail you yet terror

—amid the impending disasters in Southeast Asia. And Gins-
berg's "I" is always engaging:

> They need conscience-striken analysts, I'm
>   a conscious-stricken panelist on this
>   university show.
>   Forward March, guessing
>   which bullet which airplane which nausea
>   be the dreadful doomy last
>   begun while I'm still
> conscious—I'll go down and get a cold coffee at
>   Midnight

To read Allen Ginsberg is to enter his "conscious-stricken"
mind, to feel the poem being written, to be "there." And so we
shift with the poet from the dangers of eating "So much pork
they'll make a butcher shop /restaurant of the whole white folks

From *Poetry* (September 1969).

universe" to "Everywhere it's the fear I got in my own intestines"; from "chinese smooth limbed workmen" outdoors to sordid interiors of "journalists itching with neon."

Ginsberg keeps his poem moving at an incredibly speedy pace. Like an Eisenstein film, he gets a montage effect out of a series of basic oppositions; on the one side, the politicos ("I'm just doing my / Professional duty"), the military ("the beefy marine," "speaking hot dog guts") and the journalists ("Discussing the manly truth Gee Fellers"); on the other, "the praying young / head shaved peasant," the poet, and the central motif of the poem, the temples of Ankor Wat, in which, as in hashish, he must take refuge:

> Buddha, save me, what am
>> I doing here
> again,   dreamed of this
>> This awful stone moment

Even in the snatches of dialog, we are never really hearing anyone other than the poet, his interpretation, characterization, and embodiment of all that he describes. Solemnity alternates with wit and verbal virtuosity in this always present "I." Notice, for example, the spacing and syntax here, and the continued use of the metaphor of digestion:

> in the wetness my shirt
> covered with green plastic
>> apron shivering
>>> and throat choking
>>>> with upsurge
>>>> of stroke fear
>>>>> cancer Bubonic
>>>>> heart failure
>>>>> bitter stomach juices
> a wart growing on my rib
> Objection! This cant be
>>>> Me!

Or the characteristic juxtapositions:

Moils of New Frisco San York Orleans
Castro Bomb Shade Protest Shelter.

The photographs, by Alexandra Lawrence, enhance the
book, illustrating well the poet's perception of Banyan trees
growing like hair, like snakes, "out of [the] ruined walls and
temple roofs" of Ankor Wat:

> at the knees of greater trees, one

> needed a haircut, root-hair sprouting
> on branches.

I think it's a marvelous book. I'm afraid that my quotations
may not do it full justice, though; the poem should be read
straight through: the nonstop movement from scene to scene,
voice to voice, so vitally builds and sustains an undercurrent of
urgency and dread.

PAUL ZWEIG

A Music of Angels

Communicating vases: so the French Surrealists described them. Between the inner and the outer vase, a boil of suffering; memories churning over the psychic obstacles, on their way to be captured in the nets of grammar and consecutive statement. If there is one man who has helped us to believe in and to practice the mystery of these communicating vases, it is Allen Ginsberg, whose new book, *Planet News,* contains some of his finest poems. Between the planet earth and the planet Ginsberg, a banter of loves and disasters has been carried on; between this aging space of ecstasies, who insists aloud:

> I am that I am I am the
> > man & the Adam of hair in
> > my loins   This is my spirit and
> > physical shape I inhabit
> > this Universe

and that other jet-diminished globe, riddled with places: Warsaw, New York, Calcutta, Wales . . . titles of so many personal, gritty moments from which poems arise.

What Ginsberg forced us to understand in "Howl," twelve years ago, was that nothing is safe from poetry. His argument was not for new poetic subjects, for speech rhythms, for more emotions, or for mysticism. Argument in fact, is not the word for the unsettling spell Ginsberg-as-shaman chanted, suffered and danced in "Howl." In life, as in poetry, the shaman does not argue. He climbs the psychic hill, beyond the last familiar stone,

Review of *Planet News,* from the *Nation,* 10 March 1969. Reprinted with permission.

and then disappears. Later the wind will blow disquieting noises back to us. Morality has pursued him like a clean razor and dismembered his body; his spirit has been assaulted by righteous chancres; rumors abound that he has been nailed to a tree, where the animals will play upon his bones forever, like a harp. But then the poet-shaman reappears, carrying the sick soul he had gone to save: anyone and everyone's soul, his own too, for the shaman must have suffered from all the ills he can cure. He comes back, but he is changed, for he has seen, played before him, all the fantasies of the hidden psyche, and all the possibilities of the will. He has learned the demanding truth that Montaigne discovered in his tower: "I am a man, and nothing human is foreign to me." Here, I think, lies the generous fantasy of *Planet News*. Ginsberg has brought back the sick soul—his own, mine, yours. In payment, he has received the gift of love. Now nothing human is foreign to him.

We know how much what we are is bound up in what, and how, we remember. Our character, and therefore what we do, depends upon—and is—the style of our remembering. I insist upon the word "style," for quantity, the sheer bulk of what we have been, has nothing to do with it. It is like stringing beads out of a huge box of beads. I work in reds, you in shades of green, and you in sharp edges. The "I" is selective, distrustful. And when, beguiled by travel, drugs or women, I recklessly string a rainbow stone, or a piece of turd, that too is part of the pattern. I have learned to be selectively reckless. On principle I open a certain third eye, let if flicker on the marvel of endless possibility, and then hurry it shut, afraid I will be convicted of "too much."

Ginsberg has made "too much" the affair of his life. Like Whitman, Blake, Traherne, Rabelais, he has enacted what it means to say: "I am the greatest lover in the universe." It is the mystery of seeing, and not judging, of understanding, and not discriminating. If such a life can have a program, then Whitman formulated it:

> This is the meal equally set, this the meat for natural hunger,
> It is for the wicked just the same as for the righteous, I make
>   appointments with all,

I will not have a single person slighted or left away,
The kept-woman, sponger, thief, are hereby invited,
The heavy-lipp'd slave is invited, the venerealee is invited;
There shall be no difference between them and the rest.

In *Planet News,* the quintessential poem of "too much," is "Television Was a Baby Crawling Toward That Death-chamber." It is a poem which, like electricity, is sustained by its own movement. And the movement arises from Ginsberg's magical ability to know all the beads, and yet select none, for he selects all. Here as elsewhere, Ginsberg opens a hot line to every recess of his roomy, endless body. Like the infinite interconnection of all phenomena in the physical world (when I spit into the ocean, it rises; when I blow, the wind changes direction), the tangled relationships of everything with everything speak in Ginsberg's poem. He has faith that this is so; that all fishing in the dark water is successful. When Ginsberg is at his best, his mad leaps of association are perfect; they imitate the ideal knowledge of a Monad linked, lovingly, to the whole planet: even to cat vomit, Peruvian skulls, disappointed old body, or LSD pastoral worships:

That's what I came here to compose, what I knocked off my life to
    Inscribe on my grey metal typewriter,
borrowed from somebody's lover's mother got it from Welfare, all
    interconnected and gracious a bunch of Murderers
as possible in this Kalpa of Hungry blood-drunkard Ghosts—

The shape of "Television . . ." is the shape of "too much," which is to say that it works against the very idea of poetic form. And yet, by creating the experience (or enchantment) of "too much," it claims for itself all the privileges of form, i.e., the privilege of being this irreplaceable, absolutely achieved word-vision. Ginsberg, like Whitman, does not forget the place he occupies in the spectrum of cultural forms. He has the pleasure of knowing, from some shy Victorian refuge in his own psyche, that he is being a bit ridiculous. And so he acts out for us our temptation to judge his "too-muchness," and to contain it.

197

What I mean is that Ginsberg, like his spiritual godfather, Walt
Whitman, has a sense of comedy. He is an American humorist:

> Dusty moonlight, Starbeam riding its own flute, soul
>> revealed in the scribble, an ounce of looks, an Invisible
>> Seeing, Hope, The Vanisher betokening Eternity
> one finger raised warning above his gold eyeglasses—
>> and Mozart playing giddy-note an hour on the Marxist
>> gramophone—
>
> . . . .
>
> The Bardo Thodol extends in the millions of black jello
>> for every dying Mechanic—We will make Colossal
>> movies—
> We will be a great Tantric Mogul & starify a new
>> Hollywood with our unimaginable Flow—
>> Great Paranoia!

The humor is part of the generosity of *Planet News*. Ginsberg, in
his expansive way, is trying to convince us to wade out from the
moralizing beaches where we have learned too well to string our
beads. The water is fine, he says. If only we could stop judging
and disdaining, we would realize how simple it is to paddle
around in the world (and in ourselves).

Often *Planet News* modulates from the glutted, sexual fantasy
of "too-muchness," to a quieter, more intimate vision. When
the Kalpas of extended space collapse momentarily, Ginsberg
remembers himself: the citizen of an aging body, uprooted, hu-
manly unhappy, and yet far from lament, for—and this is the
peculiar strength of these moments—he has learned to love even
his own aging despair:

> Allen Ginsberg says this: I am a mass of sores and worms
>> & baldness & belly & smell I am false Name the prey
>> of Yamantaka Devourer of Strange Dreams . . .
>
> . . . .
>
> and I lay back on my pallet contemplating $50 phone bill,
> broke, drowsy, anxious, my heart fearful of the
> fingers dialing, the deaths, the singing of telephone
> bells

Ginsberg in *Planet News,* has given us a music of angels. Not Christian holy angels, but the angels of which Rilke spoke: "those almost deadly birds of the soul." They are almost deadly, because they ask what is most difficult to do: to love even what is not lovable, to serve up the meal for everyone, to love fate while seeing with intelligent, discriminating eyes what fate is.

I have insisted on evoking the ancestry of Ginsberg's vision because there is in this poetry of "too-muchness" a tradition and a genre which deserve to be noticed. In "Journal Night Thoughts," for example, Ginsberg echoes a conventional form and uses it, with humor, to express his continuous fantasy. It is a poem of night images, traveling a path of the mind's peregrinations in New York. One thinks, inevitably, of Young's "Night Thoughts," of Whitman's lovely poem, "The Sleepers." Ginsberg has confidence that form, once rhetorical shapes have been discarded, can arise from life itself, referring backward and forward, in the fashion of a psychic genre, to a larger shape of human experience. Here Ginsberg writes the "night-ode" or whatever name we give it: a form more ample for our total needs than sonnet, epic, or other hanger for old clothes.

REED WHITTEMORE

From "Howl" to OM

. . . Because of "Howl," poets writing in the sixties became ill-at-ease manufacturing their tried-and-true delicate nuances. Fashion decreed that they howl instead. Ginsberg's poem had the effect of a sort of natural disaster. The country deserved it—and poetry deserved it—but it was a disaster nonetheless, one that left us in a state of poetic emergency. Rightly or wrongly, "Howl" knocked hell out of earlier images of what best minds say and do. Not only was it descriptive of a vast social-spiritual death, but it provided a villainous cause, the god Moloch who in the poem is simply the System. Not since the thirties had the System had such an inclusive raking over—in fact, "Howl" singlehandedly did much to restore the thirties vogue of super-colossal system-damnation we are still suffering from, and it did so without providing a Marxist antidote. It was what D. H. Lawrence would perhaps have called a death-energy poem.

Having dropped his bomb, Ginsberg looked around for a next step—and that of course was to rehabilitate us. Any powers effectively restorative of the blasted American landscape would obviously have to come from outside the country; and so, with the remarkable timing that has marked his career Ginsberg went thoroughly Eastern. His *Indian Journals* (March 1962–May 1963) describe in prose and verse his heavily hallucinatory (morphine) daily experiences in India where, with Peter Orlovsky, he scouted out nirvana and suchlike for us: "heaven: a place beyond shit and desire."

My impression is that he didn't find it (heaven), nor did he escape "clinging to my human known me, Allen Ginsberg." He

Review of *Indian Journals,* from the *New Republic,* 25 July 1970. Reprinted with permission.

also failed—if the Journals are evidence—to get very close to India. He describes encounters with a variety of holy men—and provides us with a few snapshots of them—but the encounters are touristlike in their brevity and incompleteness. The significant life of the book is (1) the inner life of the poet reflecting on poetry, America, death, love, personality; (2) the private life of the poet in a room with Orlovsky; and (3) the life of the astonished alien observer seeing for the first time India's squalor and grandeur. The squalor he is good on; it offends him far less than American tawdriness; he displays no middle-class goose pimples about dirt and starvation, and he has an understandable obsession for the constant proximity of death in India—the skeletons living and the corpses burning:

> boy chased three cows out of the rectangle garden of fire—they were eating up a corpse litter prematurely—or horsing around in the way—the nearby corpse masked in white shroud lay back in the flames & turned black, knees hanging down, the veil burning away and one ear sticking too far out . . .

On the grandeur, particularly at the Taj Mahal, he is weaker; he is driven to tears and exclamation points like Richard Halliburton himself: "O Spoken with Stone! O Socialist Architecture!" Indeed? But whether meditating, making love or touring the streets and temples, he emerges forever as A. G. from Paterson, N.J.—*not* made over by drugs or by the cultural distancing.

I must confess to what must by now be obvious, a passionate disapproval of all the sudden easy Easternness that descended on the American sensibility in the sixties. To me it was, and still is, a screaming defeat for the whole revisionary machine of youth; and so I naturally look on Ginsberg as a wicked Pied Piper. My "error" here, however, has not been, I believe, in failing to respect Eastern thought as she is thought in a loin cloth under the Howrah Bridge in Calcutta, but in failing to respect it in young middle-class Americans, to whom a guru is like a new exotic flavor at Howard Johnson's.

For the devotee the fascination of the *Indian Journals* will presumably be in seeing where and how the saint who brought OM to Chicago had his basic—i.e., oriental—training. For me, the nonbeliever, the fascination is mostly less pleasant; it is the fascination of seeing close-up the kind of cheaply acquired religious experience—hop the plane, get the drugs—that has come to take hold of so many so fast in the last few years. For me this second stage in the Ginsberg saga has been even more calamitous than the "Howl" stage. The first had the genuineness of anger and despair about it—it was home-grown and home-felt—but the second has been clouded by great expectations, expectations that Ginsberg himself sometimes manages to temper with solid observations and with his striking death-obsession, but that his devotees infallibly leave raw: nirvana in the pad, nightly, forever. There is terror for me in their misconceptions of what inner fantasy-life can make of the stony world; and Ginsberg is one of the breeders of that terror. Saintly he may indeed be as a private sinner—I do not question his private credentials—but he has also been a most influential loudmouth, an eccentric evangelist for an apocalyptic faith (and aesthetic) that has in my opinion competed pretty well with Moloch in mind-destroying. In various parts of *Indian Journals* he runs down the apocalyptic most effectively:

> Skin is sufficient to be skin, that's all
> it ever could be, tho screams of pain in the kidney
> make it sick of itself . . .

Yet the fantasy-Ginsberg is what the destroyed ones pick up. . . .

HELEN VENDLER

Review of *The Fall of America*

The fall of America is not Ginsberg's real subject in this book, in spite of his title. He has two subjects: the state of America and the state of his life, the first now almost eclipsing, on the pages, the second. Balked by the roadblock of middle age, Ginsberg marks time around it, baffled, like other poets, by the moment when poetry thins out, everything is already known, and everything has stopped happening.

Too many times the cycle of life has turned all the way through to death; Neal Cassady is dead, Jack Kerouac is dead, it is only a matter of time for everyone else. Friends are now what they will be for good; no one will change. Everything has been encountered: sex, love, friendship, drugs, even fame, even the boundary-dimensions of self. War has come and gone; peace has come and gone; a moon-landing has come and gone. After Europe and India, after the Orient, what is left to do but to come back to America, an America already endlessly crisscrossed in the past, in cars, in buses, on trains, on planes—the interchanges, the highways, the cities, the airports, the bars, the lecture halls, the apartments.

Motion, in the face of this fixity, becomes more imperative: more and more places, more trips, more excursions, more visits; and noise, to fill the silence, rises more and more intrusive, in radios, headlines, TV, singers, rock, gospelers. An addictive sociability coexists now in Ginsberg with a pall of solitude; willed prophecy inhabits a religious void; and of empty necessity topographical description supersedes familial drama.

Ginsberg's version of the crisis of middle life is everywhere in the *Indian Journals* (1962–63):

From the *New York Times Book Review*, 15 April 1973. Reprinted with permission.

I wanted to be a saint. But suffer for what? Illusions? . . .
Next the rest of India & Japan, and I suppose later a trip:
England, Denmark, Sweden & Norway, Germany, Poland,
Russia, China & then back home again. And that'll be the end
of that world, I'll be about 50, the relatives'll all be dead by
then, old ties with the boys of yore be loosed or burnt, un-
faithful, in so many decades it's best to let it all go—is Jack
drunk? Is Neal still aware of me? Gregory yakking? Bill mad
at me? Am I even here to myself? I daren't write it all down,
it's too shameful & boring now & I haven't the energy to
make a great passional autobiography of it all. . . . I guess I
have nothing to contribute to general edification by this
vague haphazard slow motion death.

Like Oblomov, he says, he lies "in morphined ease" in
Benares, wondering "what possible poem to imagine any
more":

Now seem the thrills of scanning the scaly dragon dream universe
equal in endlessness boredom to passing my moons playing Cards
in third class trains circling the equator. . . .

"Washed up desolate on the Ganges bank, vegetarian & silent
hardly writing," Ginsberg ends the *Indian Journals* saying:

Now all personal relations cold exhausted.
I'll be on impersonal curiosity hence flying round the world. . . .

The poems written in India, some of them published in *Planet
News* (1968), fix on the life of beggars and lepers:

Today on a balcony in shorts leaning on iron rail I watched the
        leper who sat hidden behind a bicycle
emerge dragging his buttocks on the grey rainy ground by the
        glove-bandaged stumps of hands,
one foot chopped off below knee, round stump-knob wrapped
        with black rubber
pushing a tin can shiny size of his head with left hand (from
        which only a thumb emerged from leprous swathings)

beside him, lifting it with both ragbound palms down the curb
    into the puddled road,
balancing his body down next to the can & crawling forward on
    his behind
trailing a heavy rag for seat, and leaving a path thru the street
    wavering
like the Snail's slime trace—imprint of his crawl on the muddy
    asphalt market entrance—stopping
to drag his can along stubbornly konking on the paved surface
    near the water pump.

Concentration and exactness of focus are, when he is able to summon them, among Ginsberg's undeniable powers. "Kaddish," his elegy for his mother, is full of visualized moments comparable to the presented isolation of the leper; and Ginsberg's shorter poems, like the wonderful "American Change," depend equally on making us see, to paraphrase Yeats, "as though a sterner eye looked through our eye." Ginsberg had cried to the crowds at Sather Gate in Berkeley: "I have a message for you all—I will denote one particularity of each!" and for years he believed, with Blake and Yeats, that it was necessary that "eye and ear . . . silence the mind / With the minute particulars of mankind."

The trouble with the present book is that the minute particulars of mankind seem to be vanishing from Ginsberg's latest verse in favor of the minute particulars of geography. In the *Indian Journals* Ginsberg declared that since we now know that visions are "no longer considerable as objective & external facts, but as plastic projections of the maker & his language," we must stop being concerned with these "effects," eliminate subject matter, and concentrate on language itself. With a penitence we can only regret, he admits, "I seem to be delaying a step forward in this field (elimination of subject matter) and hanging on to habitual humanistic series of autobiographical photographs—although my own Consciousness has gone beyond the conceptual to non-conceptual episodes of experience, inexpressible by old means of humanistic storytelling . . . as my mind development at the year moment seems blocked so also does my 'creative' activity, blocked, revolve around old abstract & tenuous sloppy political-sex diatribes & a few cool imagistic photo descriptions (which contain some human sentiment by implication)."

In *The Fall of America,* then, we see the disappearance or exhaustion of long-term human relations, an unwillingness to continue the "old means of humanistic storytelling," a persistent wish (evident since *Howl*) for some "non-conceptual episodes of experience," and a theory of poetry intending to "include more simultaneous perceptions and relate previously unrelated (what were thought irrelevant) occurrences."

Under these pressures, Ginsberg has become a geographer, and his one inexhaustible subject is the earth and what it looks like. There are precedents for this sort of subject in the past, though then, it is true, the earth looked rather more natural. Drayton's "Polyolbion," for instance, meanders unhurriedly through England, describing rivers and mountains, woods and dales, shepherds, nymphs, and worthies of past history. Ginsberg's effort is not far distant in its kind from Drayton's: Ginsberg has it in mind to write a long "poem of these states" (incorporating earlier poems like "Wichita Vortex Sutra"), which will finally sum up the physical and spiritual map of America—its natural rivers, mountains and coastlines, its man-made cities, superhighways, and dams, its media (radio, TV, magazines, newspapers, movies), its social life (bars, universities, dance-halls), its political activity (especially its isolationism, suspicion, and hatred of foreigners), its poets and musicians (including rock and pop) its mythology (comics and S.F.), its graffiti, its religion (a poisonous fundamentalism), its banks, its wars, its violence, its secret police, its history, its seasons—in short, the whole of our common life. This text of the common life is crossed, less often than one could wish, with the text of the life of Ginsberg.

Mostly, the conclusions of the Ginsberg census are apocalyptic ones. America is going to fall because of its sins, chiefly the sins of crushing its dissidents and conducting war:

Jerry Rubin arrested! Beaten, jailed, coccyx broken—
Leary out of action—"a public menace . . . persons of tender

years . . . immature judgment . . . psychiatric examination . . ."
i.e. Shut up or Else   Loonybin or Slam

Leroi on bum gun rap, $7,000 lawyer fees, years' negotiations—
SPOCK GUILTY headlined temporary, Joan Baez' paramour
    husband Dave Harris to Gaol
Dylan silent on politics, & safe—having a baby, a man—
Cleaver shot at, jail'd, maddened, parole revoked,
Vietnam War flesh-heap grows higher.

The indictment is made repeatedly through the book, because
The Fall of America is really a daily newspaper—a "chronicle
tape-recorded scribed by hand or sung condensed, the flux of
car bus airplane dream." What spontaneity gains, reiteration
loses. But as soon as that easy criticism rises to the lips, a
countertruth stills it: it may be boring to read the map aloud—
West Coast to East, East to West, "L.A. to Wichita," "Kansas
City to St. Louis," "Bayonne Turnpike to Tuscarora," and so
on, but it is true that Ginsberg lights up territory when it is land
familiar to me, and so maybe the ideal reader of this poem is
someone who knows Kansas City and Wichita and Salt Lake and
Bixby Canyon and Sonora Desert as I do not. "Know me, know
my map," says Ginsberg: it's not an unfair demand for a poet to
make.

    Ginsberg's avalanche of detail is like the rain of dust and lava
that preserved Pompeii—here lies America, in literally thou-
sands of its emanations, recorded in such minute particularity
that quotation from this time-capsule (because it would have to
go on so long) is impossible. I still tend to prefer the shorter
poems, because they allow some drawing of breath for relief
from Ginsberg's ardent atlas. And I like best the poems where
Ginsberg is still visited by evanescent flashes of his old humor,
too often now in abeyance.

    There are faults in the book: the Eastern mantras get in the
way, for instance. It is one thing to end an English poem with
"Shantih, shantih, shantih," but to end "Om Om Om Sa Ra Wa
Bu Da Da Ki Ni Yea," and so on for three more lines is disaster.
Then, too, Ginsberg strikes certain prophetic attitudes whose
irony is their own undoing:

Oh awful man! What have we made the world! Oh man capitalist
exploiter of Mother Planet!

The book allows sentimental confessions ("When he kissed my
nipple / I felt elbow bone thrill") and masochistic self-abasement
(in "Please Master") unaccompanied by (so far as I can see) any
redeeming poetic value, except a programmatic confessional
one.

But Ginsberg belongs, if we accept Blake's two categories of
the Prolific and the Devouring, to the Prolific: there will always
be more of him, and more of his excesses, than we can quite
want. On the other hand, he is never negligible, and he is often
(the only true test) unforgettable. This book, for instance, in the
midst of a lot of ephemeral poetry, contains the supreme sum-
ming-up of this decade, a perfectly finished fourteen-page poem
wittily called "Ecologue." Ginsberg has bought himself a farm
and lives there in a tragicomic mixture of live animals, killed
animals, cows who eat his Blakean sunflowers, batteries that
fail, detergent-fouled creeks, the Pleiades, the day's radio news,
memories of the dead, books, rain, returnable Ginger Ale bot-
tles, quarrels, abashed recollections of Marie Antoinette playing
milkmaid, bugs on the potatoes, thoughts of Ezekiel and the
FBI, Indian Summer, and the *New York Times*.

The poem has all the earnestness and absurdity of the com-
mune movement in it, the despair of a "return to nature" com-
bined with a horror of "civilization": it walks a tightrope be-
tween the intimate and the international, it embeds in every
phrase (except, perhaps, in its rather strained prophetic begin-
ning) the incompetent New Yorkers trying out country life. But
it pits against that initial comic incongruity the tale-within-a-tale
of the poet frightened by death and ennui back into the company
of the hillsides and the stars.

It belongs, in its fine casual descriptiveness and open personal
truth, with Ginsberg's slowly cumulative Indian Summer poem
"Autumn Gold: New England Fall," a poem that passes from
depression to almost Emersonian sight, from the wrenched ad-
mission that "even sex happiness [is] a long drawn out scheme /
To keep the mind moving" to the beautiful visions near the end.

Entering Whatley,
> Senses amazed on the hills,
> bright vegetable populations
>> hueing rocks nameless yellow,
veils of bright Maya over New England,
> Veil of Autumn leaves laid over the Land,
> Transparent blue veil over senses,
>> Language in the sky.

Sadness, and not his intermittent hysteria, underlies Ginsberg's most eloquent poems. Though he is recognizably the native heir of Emerson, Whitman, and Williams, he was not born with their regenerative sporadic optimism; nor does he participate, like Whitman, in heroic human action, nor descend, for that matter, as far as Whitman into despair. "Elegy," said Coleridge in his "Table-Talk," "is the form of poetry natural to the reflective mind. . . . Elegy presents everything as lost and gone or absent and future." Ginsberg, a naturally elegiac poet, is at present repressing his own elegiac spirit, attempting a poetry where, to quote Coleridge again, "all is purely external and objective, and the poet is a mere voice." The elegiac side of Ginsberg still seems to me the winning one, but it may be that in the sparseness of middle age Ginsberg needs the plurality of notations and enumerations accumulating to fill these pages. It is nothing new for a poet to need filler: what else was play-writing to Tennyson or thinking up *A Vision* for Yeats?

It may be that later, in the subsidence and condensation of this tireless relief-map of America, we will have from Ginsberg the sort of quintessential late poetry of old age that we have already received from Yeats and Stevens. For the present, we cannot begrudge Ginsberg his painstaking record of his microcosm, "empty-lov'd America."

CHARLEY SHIVELY

Allen Ginsberg

A Prophet on the Electric Networks

. . . Among the ways to enlightenment, the Tantric path may be most misunderstood in Ginsberg's poetry. This path leads to an exploration and celebration of sensual pleasure—not a simple wallowing in lust (as Christians might say in their pornographic, one-way way) although that is not excluded. "Even Tantric path (exploration of sensory limits) leads to liberation (relaxation) from sensory grasping (i.e., desire). Because senses are mechanical and repetitious" (Ginsberg's preface to *The Bhagavad Gita As It Is*). In repeating the sexual acts like mantra the person is released from an overweaning desire for more. Repression never stops the desire for more, the obsession; repression closes off more than it opens.

Iron Horse is partly a tantric meditation following masturbation in a train. The words are printed over railroad pictures—illuminations in half-tone lying under the tracks of the song, bringing it all back home. The poet sees and hears soldiers, their white bellies arousing, their crotches turning on a man who knows these are the killers of the Vietnamese whom he should enlighten not worship. "Ninety nine air force boys / lined up with their pants down forever." But the "prophet on the electric Networks" cannot speak to them in person so well as he can masturbate to their singing flesh, so different from their nauseating words—and the monied network of death in which these

From a review of *The Fall of America, Iron Horse, Bixby Canyon,* and *The Gates of Wrath,* in *Gay Sunshine* (June–July 1973). Reprinted with permission.

studs are encased. Seeing, feeling this disparity between the freshness and beauty of their bodies and the hideousness of their network sponsors, in detumescence, Ginsberg sings, seeing

> same electric lightening South
>> follows this train
>>> Apocalypse prophesied—
>> the Fall of America
>>> signalled from heaven.

Through the electric networks, networds through the train, there is only one hope: "I wept, How soft flesh is—"; "only boys' flesh singing / can show the warless way— / or miracle"; "open yr ass to my mouth— / a poem to thee!" . . .

Much of Ginsberg's poetry has been a struggle through flesh and song to find a liberation from the haunting master-images of Neal Cassady and Jack Kerouac. In *The Gates of Wrath, Rhymed Poems: 1948–1952* there is a whole section of love poems from 1947 for Neal Cassady. These are mostly interesting for historical purposes; they show the immense imprint of Blake's visionary verses on Ginsberg. There are some interesting lines predicting more to come: "Behold thy myth incarnate in my flesh / Now made incarnate in Thy Psalm, O Lord"—a good summary of Ginsberg's whole body of poetry. And there are interesting experiments (called bop lyrics) like "Fie My Fum": funny, happy, playing with language: "Pull my daisy, / Tip my cup, / Cut my thoughts / For coconuts" which really sounds great when sung.

But what about Neal Cassady? I suspect he was just another free-wheelin' stud—who brought out love in both Kerouac and Ginsberg because he was himself incapable of love. Nothing is so blind to judgment as fantasy-love: for instance, was the buddha enlightened as Ginsberg claims in his *Howl* dedication, by reading Cassady's *Autobiography?* What are we to say about our mad, divine impassioned loves for these superstud he-men such as Neal or Jack? Elegies for Neal Cassady are haunting and beautiful, and Ginsberg's elegy for Kerouac, "Memory Gardens," is a high part of *The Fall of America:*

      I threw a kissed handful of damp earth
            down on the stone lid
                  & sighed
         looking in Creeley's one eye,
      Peter sweet holding a flower
      . . . .
      Well, while I'm here I'll
            do the work—
      and what's the Work?
            To ease the pain of living.
      Everything else, drunken
            dumbshow.

At this moment Ginsberg throws in the line "& *Time* has a ten-page spread on / Homosexual Fairies!" They obviously don't inspire his respect nor engender quite the poetry Cassady or Kerouac do. Nor do Herbert Huncke and William Burroughs, bold and clear homosexuals who were also early companions of Ginsberg and from whom he probably picked up more poetry and insight than from the straight studs. Huncke & Burroughs get ample praise from Ginsberg, but they have never inspired the intimate love, devotion, ecstasy and poetry of Cassady or Kerouac's images (even in decay and ashes). Nor has Peter Orlovsky (who is evidently now settled down with a woman but with whom Allen still shares his life) ever brought out such beautiful poems as the blondish demigods—Kerouac & Cassady.

Why is it that the stud image can bring us faggots sooner to poetry and tears than few other things? Had Ginsberg refused to love Neal or remember or worship that beautiful body would he have fought in all the battles he has? Would he have written half the poems he has? Would they have been half so powerful and moving ("and all the times I came to myself alone in the dark dreaming of Neal or Billy Budd"? I feel myself that some of my best poems have come from the trials of unrequited loves. Being guilty is no way out at all: shouting *mea culpa, mea culpa* and enjoying the sinning all the more. I don't know the answer, but I do respect Allen Ginsberg's struggle with the memories of Cassady and Kerouac; in the quiet peace of "Ecologue" he comes near to transcending while living in their images.

Allen Gisnberg is weak in his understanding of "sexism." Many in the women's and gay movement would argue that the money nexus is less at the root of "the fall of America" than male supremacy. We would say that the madness for Cassady-Kerouac keeps the dollar floating as much as eating scab lettuce or smoking cigarettes. Much of the butch disrespect for women in Cassady and Kerouac has rubbed off onto Ginsberg. (We'll pass over the unkind things he says about "closet queens" and "teacup faggots.") In Ginsberg's poetry and conversation, women are always called "girls" and their names are seldom used. In the vast array of Beatdom, almost no reference is ever made to such poets as Diane di Prima or Lenore Kandel; and, although Allen's entourage through the years has included many women, they (unlike the men) are seldom if ever named in the poems. The move to Vedic and Buddhist wisdom has often been a way of forestalling not facing the issues of sexual politics (e.g., Gary Snyder or Rennie Davis).

I can cite one recent example of Allen Ginsberg's sexism which is probably not atypical. At a reading in Salem, Massachusetts, (a Jack Kerouac symposium-memorial-festival), one woman in the audience said (during a question period) that among the performers (Peter Orlovsky, Gregory Corso & Allen Ginsberg) only Peter in his spiel against smoking and drinking had shown any real concern for the people there. Allen shut her up saying that she was just on an ego trip. While that may be true, little had been said to the klunk studs with their canteens of wine whose long-winded & irrelevant questions had been entertained patiently.

This question of faggots and women as against the blue-eyed blond stud such as Neal Cassady raises a hard question about the communal comradely love prophesized by Whitman and others. *The Fall of America* is dedicated to Walt Whitman and begins with a quotation from *Democratic Vistas:* "It is to the development, identification, and general prevalence of that fervid comradeship, (the adhesive love, at least rivaling the amative love hitherto possessing imaginative literature, if not going beyond it,) that I look for the counterbalance and offset of our materialistic and vulgar American democracy, and for the spiritualization thereof." Fine, but can everyone be included in this circle, or will it just be the beautiful, young blonds? Will brunettes be in? Fat people? Bald people? Jews? Sioux? Faggots? The old? Children? In celebrating so much adhesive love for the on-the-road companions, Ginsberg leaves someone like me outside (a faggot—and I drive just like a woman, as Kerouac pointed out about someone in derision in *On the Road*). Whitman's love theory is hardly adequate for an androgynous society—he views it all from a male man's viewpoint: amative love (love of men for women) should be balanced by adhesive love (male bonding, love of man for man). No provision is really made for women as *active* lovers—choosing their own love "objects."

Another objection to the adhesive love is its link to "America." We must break ourselves of the habit of nations and nationhood. Those map lines were not drawn by the landscape; they were drawn across America by straight white men, agents of Western civilization. I see national lines (for instance, those between Canada, Mexico, the United States and Cuba) to be "real"—but real in the way prisons are real. Celebrating "America" in "these states" is no good, not liberating—it perpetuates the nation-myth which is totally antipeople, anti-adhesive love, anti-amative love. For example, it is a national vanity (a very real imperialism) to assume that these United States are responsible for every evil befalling the earth—as does "September on Jessore Road." The poem is a work of perfection in probing starvation and horror, but the failures on Jessore Road and the Indian subcontinent are at least partly the work of Pakistani & Indian "leaders." It is arrogant to presume "our" country controls everything. Thinking in "national" categories perpetuates "these states" and prevents any real community from forming.

Ginsberg is imperfect, he's human, he's a man—that's not news. Faggots shouldn't let his "mistakes" go by without objection, but we must never forget, he is a *poet*. He is not just a cultural phenomenon, not just a prophet, not just a Beatnik, not just a liberator, not just a grand old man for us to play our fantasies on—he is a *poet*. And it's no easier being a poet in these states than it is being a woman, or being a Cherokee, or being a faggot, or being black, or being anything that doesn't fit the straight network. Poets have no more license to commit crime than anyone else, but they should have a special claim to our love, understanding, help and (in Allen Ginsberg's sense of the word) "prayers."

JOHN SEELYE

The Sum of '48

Allen Ginsberg's voice is here transcribed from tapes, ad lib lectures and conversations on issues that are fast receding with the sixties. These issues raised the poet from the relative obscurity of a minor literary movement into national and even international prominence, made him a leader in another kind of movement, political in cast but largely an expression of mass consciousness. If rock was a kind of religion, then Ginsberg was its pope, a quizzical Peter peering out from behind glasses and beard under the absurd canonical miter of a star-spangled, red-white-and-blue-striped top hat, part saint, part seer and part (like the hat) put-on.

The speed with which that moment is receding is shown in Ginsberg's ritualistic praise of Timothy Leary in this book. The poet has more recently gone on record denouncing Leary for a liar, the former martyr—"persecuted for his philosophy and his professional practice"—having declared himself willing to inform on his former associates in return for early parole. But cruel ironies like the souring of Leary are not needed to demonstrate Ginsberg's dilemma. In an epilogue to this collection of his attempts during a lecture tour in 1971 to raise the consciousness of America to the dangers of monolithic capitalism, despoilation of nature, institutionally enforced conformity, the Vietnam war, the complicity of police in the drug trade at home and the CIA in poppy fields abroad, the poet assails his own addiction to bodily comforts, bemoans his apparent inability to inspire action concerning the drug problem, and broods over the death of Jack Kerouac. He comes at last to a terminal sigh: "And I keep think-

Review of *Allen Verbatim*, from the *New Republic*, 12 October 1974. Reprinted with permission.

ing I'm too comfortable in this chamber of horrors, so my own future I think will probably be more meditative and ascetic." The issues remain relevant, but "everybody's so inured to rape and catastrophe it's like a fatigue: nobody can take it in any more, nobody cares." The despairing prophet retires to Patmos, perhaps to reform the world through the force of his own silent witness, at least to save himself, to crawl above the "great wave of horror."

At that time early in 1973, Watergate (no mention of which is found here), the final expression of the Age of Aquarius, the bursting of a gigantic waterbed of false optimism and ease, had not happened. Nor had Allen Ginsberg as yet received the National Book Award. His receiving it was proof that an age had ended, buried with Kerouac, not merely the ballyhoo of Aquarius but a larger epoch, a quarter-century of creative explosion that began with the Beats and declined with the death of two of its great poetic resonators, Charles Olson and Ezra Pound. Two of the most interesting conversations included here, to my way of thinking, are between Ginsberg and Robert Duncan, representing the New York and California brackets of the Beat movement, in which the poets rehearse the circumstances that brought a number of individuals of different backgrounds together as a group.

Their conversations move as inexorably toward accumulative accord as did the diatoms of people and events that became the Beat movement. Having paid tribute to Pound, W. C. Williams and Olson, Blake and Whitman, having kicked T. S. Eliot in his pin-striped pants ("deficient on a formal level; that's why he talks about form"), having heaped praise on their contemporaries, Corso, Creeley, et al., Ginsberg and Duncan come at last to that moment when the Beat "community . . . came to total clear consciousness with accompanying explosions of mystical visions and epiphanies around 1948, I'd say" (this is Ginsberg speaking), "I'd put 1948 as the date of this emergence into a flash, because '48 was when I had my Blake epiphany experiences."

RD: '48, my "Venice Poem."
AG: '48 Robert's "Venice Poem." '48 also the Berkeley Ren-

aissance community, which would be Jack Spicer, and oddly enough, you know, Timothy Leary was there.

RD: '48 was the time for Charles Olson's Call Me Ishmael.

AG: Yeah. In 1948 Gary Snyder in Portland finished his Amerindian anthropology unified field theory honors thesis to graduate, and that morning when he wrote the last words saying sumpin' about consciousness, about primitive consciousness, and then went down to the Willamette River and sat down in dawn silence, kind of exhausted, musing over the silence of nature, just as the sun rose, he heard a rushing of many wings, and thousands of birds rose up from the trees, and he looked around and his head turned inside out, and he suddenly realized "everything is alive"—the entire universe is alive. Every sentient being is alive, like myself. So that was '48, also. Do you know about that?

RD: No, I didn't know that.

Duncan was also a year off on *Call Me Ishmael,* but 1948 remains a great time for the wilder aspects of American modern letters, and the date sounds like a refrain throughout Ginsberg's discussions of his own personal and poetic development. So these conversations, which end in 1973, provide a punctuation mark of sorts to a quarter-century that began with the Beats, who conceived Hip, which begat Hippies who spawned a legion of foster children in faded blue jeans and light brown hair floating on the breeze. This book is therefore a sum, not necessarily a final figure but a tallying of the score to date, and it must be said that the figures are discouraging, that poetry like the economy is faced with hard times. Ginsberg in the epilogue regards himself as a star-crossed Whitman, and in mourning for Jack Kerouac he grieves for himself: "In a nation which is itself so messed up, what is he going to be—a happy singer? Happy healthy singer of a dying, decadent destructive world? Happy joker?" Exit Ginsberg as he entered the public view, on an apocalyptic note, schlepping toward Armageddon, not now with a *Howl* but a groan.

This collection of lectures and conversations is a pocket epitome of the Beat genesis, for it too begins in hope, in 1971, and ends two years later in sadness and a sense of defeat. It begins by sortieing out into Young America, Ginsberg launching a private campaign against institutional corruption, and ends by a threatened withdrawal into a sanctuary of silence. Toward the end of the book Gordon Ball includes an interview not given until 1972, an impromptu and touching tribute to Ezra Pound, inspired by the announcement of the poet's death. "He was like Prospero," said Ginsberg, "wise, and a great teacher—and a great guru, and a great silent man at the end." By his own admission Ginsberg is one of the "younger poets" who "learned from him . . . derived from him," and though he himself is certainly, as maker or mentor, no Pound, no Prospero, Allen has attained a certain mythic stature: a Yorick, perhaps, a loving-wise jester jingling his finger-cymbals or wagging his head in smiling accompaniment to his harmonium as he plays his music set to the poems of Blake. And Yorick too has his wisdom of silence, expressed through Hamlet, a muteness of mortality toward which Ginsberg points in his own last soliloquy. A Pied Piper, he has led the kids on a merry dance through the sixties and as he opens the door into his mountain, I wonder how many will follow him inside. Somehow the silence that follows the dying fall of *Hair* seems to me like the proper sound for the seventies. It is not, as many have observed, the same thing as the silence of the fifties, when it all began, not the silence of dull acquiescence but of resignation, of presidents and poets alike.

Ginsberg, by his own account, began as a poet of love, working out in derivative verse his unrequited passion for Neal Cassady, who was for the Beats what Maude Gonne was for the Irish Renaissance. But Ginsberg was at the same time—in that *annus mirabilis,* 1948—in love with Jack Kerouac, an "engagement" that began "with a long conversation in which I described leaving a room that I'd lived in for half a year (where I'd originally fallen in love with him and some other friends, simultaneously), and when I left the room to move to a hotel, turning around as I left the seventh floor and went down the steps, and looking back at my door and looking back at the hall and saying, 'Good-bye door, good-bye hall, good-bye step number one, good-bye step number two, good-bye step number three,' down seven flights. And so I told him that story, and he said

'Oh, that's what I do!' So I suddenly realized that my own soul and his were akin. . . ." This recollection provides the incantatory refrain for the last piece in Ball's collection, "What Would You Do If You Lost It?," a poem that Ginsberg wrote last year while confined by a broken leg, meditating on how he was "still getting and spending in a world too much with me." In it he bids hypothetical farewell to all his "own treasures" to

old souls worshipped flower-eye or imaginary auditory panoramic
   skull—
good-bye old socks washed over & over, blue boxer shorts, subzero
   longies
. . . .
good-bye to my room full of books, all wisdoms I never studied, all
   the Campion, Creeley, Anacreon, Blake I never read through.
. . . .
Attic full of toys, desk full of old checks, files on N.Y. police & CIA
   peddling Heroin,
Files on Leary, files on Police State, files on ecosystems all faded &
   brown,
notebooks untranscribed, hundreds of little poems & prose my own
   hand,
. . . .
good-bye poetry books, I don't have to take you along any
   more. . . .

The cadence is Walt's, but the catalogue is undeniably Allen's, luggage he has acquired in his minstrelsy following that magical year when he heard Blake's voice and went tripping down the stairs empty-handed and lighthearted, bidding farewell to that momentary room, skipping into the soul of Jack Kerouac and from there taking flight across America. "Bom Bom!" he ends the poem, "Harekrishna faretheewell forever more! / None left standing! No tears left for eyes, no eyes for weeping, no mouth for singing, no song for the hearer, no more words for any mind." Alas, poor Yorick! We'll miss thy panoramic skull, subzero longies, boxer shorts and all.

DOCUMENTS & REFLECTIONS

FRED MORAMARCO

Moloch's Poet

. . . The long, meditative "Siesta in Xbalba and Return to the States" is the centerpiece of [*Reality Sandwiches*], which is based on some of Ginsberg's experiences in Mexico during the first seven months of 1954.[1] The poem is built around the contrast indicated by the title. Lying in a hammock in a small Mexican village, Ginsberg toys with the idea of staying forever, of never returning to his complex, intense, citified life in the States:[2]

> —One could pass valuable months
> and years perhaps a lifetime
> doing nothing but lying in a hammock
> reading prose with the white doves
>   copulating underneath
> and monkeys barking in the interior
>   of the mountain
> and I have succumbed to this temptation—

The feeling here is much like that generated by James Wright's brief but wonderfully evocative lyric, "While Lying in a Hammock on William Duffy's Farm in Pine Island, Minnesota." In both poems the withdrawal from "civilization" and "society" that occurs as the poet lies in the hammock observing the scenery around him is treated ambiguously. Are the months "valuable" *because* he is lying in the hammock, or is he losing "valuable" time by "doing nothing"? Ginsberg's reminiscence of urban life intrudes:

From the *American Poetry Review* (September–October 1982). Reprinted with permission.

Dreaming back I saw
an eternal kodachrome
souvenir of a gathering
of souls at a party,
crowded in an oval flash:
cigarettes, suggestions,
laughter in drunkenness,
broken sweet conversation,
acquaintance in the halls,
faces posed together. . . .

The narrator's attention shifts back and forth from the hammock to the party in New York, and the experience of straddling the two worlds in his imagination allows him to objectify both of them by stepping outside of himself and observing his participation in both. This is a wonderful moment in the poem—a metamorphosis reminiscent of Ovid via Ezra Pound:

As I leaned against a tree
            inside the forest
expiring of self-begotten love,
I looked up at the stars absently,
            as if looking for
something else in the blue night
            through the boughs,
and for a moment saw myself
            leaning against a tree . . .

. . . back there the noise of a great party
            in the apartments of New York,
half-created paintings on the walls, fame,
            cocksucking and tears,
money and arguments of great affairs,
            the culture of my generation . . .
. . . .
—uncanny feeling the white cat
            sleeping on the table
will open its eyes in a moment
            and be looking at me—.

The Poundian echoes are from both Pound's early poetry ("I stood still and was a tree amid the wood / Knowing the truth of things unseen before") and the *Pisan Cantos,*[3] where Pound observes a prowling cat outside his cell in the DTC while reminiscing about the culture of *his* generation.

The illumination leads the narrator to speculate on objectifying not only his immediate surroundings and imaginings, but his very relationship to the earth itself. The poem moves outward from the poet's mind to the contours of the landscape around him to the curvature of the earth itself. It is, Ginsberg indicates, a drug-induced vision (prefiguring the LSD-inspired ecological vision of his later poem, "Wales Visitation") but it is also one of the most beautiful descriptions of a natural landscape that occurs in his poetry:

> One might sit in this Chiapas
> recording the apparitions in the field
>   visible from a hammock
> looking out across the shadow of the pasture
> in all the semblance of Eternity
>
>   . . . a dwarfed thatch roof
> down in the grass in a hollow slope
> under the tall crowd of vegetation
>   waiting at the wild edge:
> the long shade of the mountain beyond
>   in the near distance,
> its individual hairline of trees
> traced fine and dark along the ridge
>
>   against the transparent sky light,
> rifts and holes in the blue air
>   and amber brightenings of clouds
> disappearing down the other side
>   into the South. . . .

The meditation on the landscape around him becomes a meditation on time, death, and eternity as day turns to night in the poem. An image of the rising moon supplants the image of the "late sun" which began the poem, and Ginsberg's attention is captured by an ancient sculptured figure on the wall:

> I can see the moon
> moving over the edge of the night forest
> and follow its destination
> through the clear dimensions of the sky
> from end to end of the dark
> circular horizon.
>
> High dim stone portals,
> entablatures of illegible scripture,
> bas-reliefs of unknown perceptions:
> and now the flicker of my lamp
> and smell of kerosene on dust-
> strewn floor where ant wends
> its nightly ritual way toward great faces
> worn down by rain.
> In front of me a deathshead
> half a thousand years old

The narrator continues his "skully meditation" studying the "alien hieroglyphs of Eternity." He becomes highly sensitive to the sounds all around him: birds, crickets,

> The creak of an opening
> door in the forest,
> some sort of weird birdsong
> or reptile croak.

The poem moves deeper and deeper into the night and early morning hours, and its language, by incorporating Mexican place names, becomes more exotic, dreamlike, apparitional. In a note, Ginsberg tells us that "Xbalba, translatable as morning Star in Region Obscure, or Hope, and pronounced Chivalvá, is the area in Chiapas between the Tobasco border and the Usumascintla River at the edge of the Peten Rain Forest; the boundary of lower Mexico and Guatemala today is thereabouts. The locale was considered a Purgatory or Limbo, the legend is vague, in the (Old) Mayan Empire." The note clarifies certain references in the poem as the reader moves further from the stability of the physical world into the strange, dark limbo of the unknowable:

> Pale Uxmal,
> > unhistoric, like a dream,
> Tuluum shimmering on the coast in ruins;
> Chichen Itza naked
> > constructed on a plain;
> Palenque, broken chapels in the green
> > basement of a mount;
> lone Kabah by the highway;
> > Piedras Negras buried again
> by dark archaeologists;
> > Yaxchilan
> resurrected in the wild,
> and all the limbo of Xbalba still unknown—

After evoking the names of the pre-Columbian civilizations which flourished in this place, Ginsberg surveys the surviving ruins and notices how they have become intertwined with the natural landscape. Nature's work, and man's, has become one with the passage of time:

> > floors under roofcomb of branch,
> foundation to ornament
> > tumbled to the flowers,
> pyramids and stairways
> > raced with vine,
> limestone corbels
> > down in the river of trees,
> pillars and corridors
> > sunken under the flood of years:
>
> Time's slow wall overtopping
> > all that firmament of mind,
> as if a shining waterfall of leaves and rain

226

> were built down solid from the endless sky
> > through which no thought can pass.

Here, then, is another example of Ginsberg's "aggression upon the unseen to make it seen": the passage of time made visible through a description of ruins conjoined with nature; it is a technique he surely learned from Pound, the "ply over ply" method used extensively throughout the first thirty Cantos.[4]

A burst of daylight intrudes upon the meditation at this point, and we are made to see time's passage from another perspective. The poem's night has turned into day, and the traditional symbol of morning—of the affirmation and continuity of life—disrupts the narrator's reverie:

> A great red fat rooster
> mounted on a tree stump
> in the green afternoon,
> the ego of the very fields
> screams in the holy sunlight!
> —I can't think with that
> supersonic cock intensity
> crucifying my skull
> in its imaginary sleep.

The disruption is momentary. The narrator closes his eyes (to shut out the present) and returns to ruminating on the ruins of the past. The meditation appears to awaken in him a sense of a personal connection with past civilizations and previous human achievements. He wants to see more of the "ancient continent" before the physical remains of the past are totally obliterated by "the ultimate night / of war."

But his realization of a connection with the past also makes him aware of a specific tradition to which he—as a contemporary American poet—is related, as well as a future to which he has an obligation. In a remarkable passage which embodies imagery from America's greatest literature—Whitman, Melville, Crane (both Stephen and Hart), Pound, and others—Ginsberg appears to *become* the American literary imagination searching for a direction:

> So I dream nightly of an embarcation,
>   captains, captains,
> iron passageways, cabin lights,
>   Brooklyn across the waters,
> the great dull boat, visitors, farewells,
>   the blurred vast sea—
> one trip a lifetime's loss or gain:
>
> as Europe is my own imagination
>   —many shall see her,
>   many shall not—
> though it's only the old familiar world
> and not some abstract mystical dream.

"Toward what city/will I travel?" Ginsberg asks, "What wild houses / do I go to occupy?" The poem's first section ends with the recollection of a mystical experience Ginsberg had in his New York apartment in 1948. At that time, Ginsberg believes, he heard Blake's voice and saw "the motionless buildings / of New York rotting / under the tides of Heaven." That recollection evokes a symbolic rendering of Ginsberg's divided muse: is he to be the poet of Moloch or the poet of the inner self? Does his imagination owe its allegiance to America or to the human spirit? This part of the poem ends with the question unanswered:

> There is a god
> dying in America
> already created
> in the imagination of men
> made palpable
> for adoration:
> there is an inner
> anterior imagine
> of divinity
> beckoning me out
> to pilgrimage.
>
> O future, unimaginable God.

The second section of the poem is more easily summarized than the first. There is a "Jump in time" to the future when Ginsberg begins his return to the States, carrying with him some lingering images of his Mexican experience: a busload of blue-hooded nuns, some mummies he saw at Guanajuato, and the memory of a voyeuristic moment as he watched two couples dancing from "the patio at San Miguel / at the keyhole: 2 A.M." Looking at death (the mummies) on the one hand and life (the two dancing couples) on the other, Ginsberg identifies what he regards to be the fundamental tragedy of human experience:

> The problem is isolation
>   —there in the grave
> or here in oblivion of light.

He feels his solitude deeply, but as he nears the American border he braces himself for the task he sees as his destiny. He is to be Moloch's poet, the heir of Whitman and Pound, the contemporary embodiment of America's poetic soul:

> —Returning
>   armed with New Testament,
> critic of horse and mule,
>   tanned and bearded
> satisfying Whitman, concerned
>   with a few Traditions,
> metrical, mystical, manly
> . . . and certain characteristic flaws
>
>   —enough!
> The nation over the border
> grinds its arms and dreams
>   of war: I see
> the fiery blue clash
>   of metal wheels
> clanking in the industries
>   of night, and
> detonation of infernal bombs

                    . . . and the silent downtown
         of the States
                    in watery dusk submersion.

These concluding lines signal Ginsberg's intention to confront
the chaos of contemporary America directly in his poetry—to
awaken from the "siesta in Xbalba" and return to the States both
in person and in the subject matter of his poetry. The life of the
imagination is to be put to work transcribing the world that
worships Moloch. . . .

NOTES

1. A prose account of these months, including a description of
Ginsberg's reading during this time is included in Gordon Ball, ed.,
Allen Ginsberg's Journals (New York: Random House, 1977), pp. 29–87.

2. The quotations from "Siesta in Xbalba and Return to the States"
are from *Reality Sandwiches* (San Francisco: City Lights Books, 1963),
pp. 21–39.

3. Included on Ginsberg's reading list while in Mexico are *The Pisan
Cantos, XXX Cantos,* and a work indicated as "An Examination of Ezra
Pound."

4. See especially "Canto XVII."

TIMOTHY LEARY

In the Beginning,
Leary Turned on Ginsberg and Saw
That It Was Good . . .

. . . November 26, 1960, the sunny Sunday afternoon that we gave Allen Ginsberg the mushrooms, started slowly. First in the cycle of breakfasts at noon were my son Jack Leary and his friend Bobbie, who had spent the night. Bobbie went off to Mass. When I came down I found Donald, an uninvited raccoon hipster-painter from New York, solemnly squatting at the table gnawing at toast and bacon. Frank Barron, who was visiting, and the poets, Allen Ginsberg and Peter and Lafcadio Orlovsky, remained upstairs and we moved around the kitchen with that Sunday-morning hush, not wanting to wake the sleepers. Lafcadio, Peter's brother, was on leave from a hospital.

About twelve-thirty the quiet exploded into family noise. Bobbie was back from church where he had excitedly told his father about the party we had given the night before for the Harvard football team and how I had given the boys, Bobbie and Jack, a dollar each for being bartenders.

I toted up the political profit and loss from this development. The Harvard football team rang up a sale. But the boys bartending? Bobbie's father is Irish so that's all right. All okay.

Then wham, the door opened and in flooded Susan Leary, my daughter, with three teenage girls, through the kitchen, upstairs to get clothes, down to make a picnic lunch, up again for records, out, and then back for the ginger ale.

By now the noise had filtered upstairs and we could hear the

From *Esquire* (July 1968). Reprinted with permission.

late sleepers moving around and the bathroom waters running, and down came Frank Barron, half-awake, to fry codfish cakes for his breakfast. And then, Allen Ginsberg and Peter. Allen hopped around the room with nearsighted crow motions cooking eggs, and Peter sat silent, watching.

Afterward the poets fell to reading the *Times* and Frank moved upstairs to Susan's room to watch a pro football game on TV. I told Allen to make himself at home and got beers and went up to join Frank. Donald the painter had been padding softly around the house watching with his big, soft creature eyes and sniffing in corners and at the bookcase and the record cabinets. He had asked to take mushrooms in the evening and was looking for records of Indian peyote drum music.

At dusk, Allen Ginsberg, hunched over a teacup, peering out through his black-rimmed glasses, the left lens bisected by a break, started telling of his experiences with ayahuasca, the fabled visionary vine of the Peruvian jungles. He had followed the quest of Bill Burroughs, sailing south for new realms of consciousness, looking for the elixir of wisdom. Sitting, sweating with heat, lonely in a cheap hotel in Lima, holding a wad of ether-soaked cotton to his nose with his left hand and getting high and making poetry with his right hand, and then traveling by second-class bus with Indians up through the Cordillera de los Andes and then more buses and hitchhiking into the Montaña jungles and shining rivers, wandering through steaming equatorial forests. Then the village Pucallpa, and the negotiations to find the *curandero* [guide], paying him with *aguardiente,* and the ritual itself, swallowing the bitter stuff, and the nausea and the colors and the drums beating and sinking down into thingless void, into the great eye that brings it all together, and the terror of the great snake coming. The old *curandero,* wrinkled face bending over him and Allen telling him, *culebra,* and the *curandero* nodding clinically and blowing a puff of smoke to make the great snake disappear and it did.

The fate of fire depends on wood; as long as there is wood below, the fire burns above. It is the same in human life; there is in man likewise a fate that lends power to his life.

—I Ching

I kept asking Allen questions about the *curandero*. I wanted to learn the rituals, to find out how other cultures (older and wiser than ours) had handled the visionary business. I was fascinated by the ritual thing. Ritual is to the science of consciousness what experiment is to external science. I was convinced that none of our American rituals fit the mushroom experience. Not the cocktail party. Not the psychiatrist. Not the teacher-minister role. I was impressed by what Allen said about his own fear and sickness whenever he took drugs and about the solace and comforting strength of the *curandero,* about how good it was to have someone there who knew, who had been to those far regions of the mind and could tell you by a look, by a touch, by a puff of smoke that it was all right, go ahead, explore the strange world, it's all right, you'll come back, it's all right, I'm here back on familiar old human earth when you need me, to bring you back.

Allen was going to take the mushrooms later that night and he was shaping me up to help him. Allen was weaving a word spell, dark eyes gleaming through the glasses, chain-smoking, moving his hands, intense, chanting trance poetry. Frank Barron was in the study now, and with him Lafcadio Orlovsky.

A car came up the driveway and in a minute the door opened, and Donald, furry and moist, ambled in. He had brought his friend, an anthropology student from Harvard, to be with him when he tripped. Donald asked if his friend could be there during the mushroom session. I liked the idea of having a friend present for the mushrooms, someone to whom you could turn at those moments when you needed support, so I said, Sure, but he couldn't take the pills because he was a university student. Everyone was warning us to keep our research away from Harvard to avoid complications with the university health bureau and to avoid the rumors. He wasn't hungry so I mixed him a drink and then I got the little round bottle and pulled out the cotton topping and gave Donald 30 mg. and Allen Ginsberg 36.

Allen started bustling around getting his cave ready. I brought Susan's record player up to his room and he took some Beethoven and Wagner from the study and he turned out the lights so that there was just a glow in the room. I told him we'd be checking back every fifteen minutes and he should tell me if he wanted anything.

233

By the time I got downstairs Donald was already high, strolling around the house on dainty raccoon feet with his hands clasped behind his back, thinking and digging deep things. I stayed in the study writing letters, reading the *Times*. I had forgotten about the anthropology student. He was waiting in the kitchen.

After about thirty minutes I found Donald in the hallway. He called me over earnestly and began talking about the artificiality of civilization. He was thinking hard about basic issues and it was obvious what was going on with him—clearing his mind of abstractions, trying to get back behind the words and concepts.

And if he succeeds in assigning the right place to life and to fate, thus bringing the two into harmony, he puts his fate on a firm footing. These words contain hints about the fostering of life as handed on by oral tradition in the secret teachings of Chinese yoga.

—I Ching

The anthropology student was standing by, watching curiously, and Donald asked if he minded leaving so that he could talk to me privately. Anthro went back to the kitchen and Donald continued talking about the falseness of houses and machines and deploring the way man cut himself off from the vital stuff with his engines and structures. I was trying to be polite and be a good *curandero* and support him and tell him, great boy, stay with it and work it out.

Susan came back from her friends' about this time and went upstairs to her homework, and I followed her up to check on Allen. He was lying on top of the blanket. His glasses were off and his black eyes, pupils completely dilated, looked up at me. Looking down into them they seemed like two deep black, wet wells and you could look down them way through the man Ginsberg to something human beyond. The eye is such a defenseless, naïve, trusting thing. PROFESSOR LEARY CAME INTO MY ROOM, LOOKED IN MY EYES, AND SAID I WAS A GREAT MAN. THAT DETERMINED ME TO MAKE AN EFFORT TO LIVE HERE AND NOW. —Allen Ginsberg.

Allen was scared and unhappy and sick. And still he was lying there voluntarily, patiently searching, pushing himself into panics and fears, into nausea, trying to learn something, trying to find meaning. Shamelessly weak and shamelessly human and greatly classic. Peter was lying next to him, eyes closed, sleeping or listening to the record. I GOT NAUSEOUS SOON AFTER—SAT UP IN BED NAKED AND SWALLOWED DOWN THE VOMIT THAT BESIEGED FROM MY STOMACH AS IF AN INDEPENDENT BEING DOWN THERE WAS REBELLING AT BEING DRAGGED INTO EXISTENCE.

On the way downstairs I checked Susan's room. She was curled up on the carpet, with her books scattered around her and reading in the shadows. I scolded her about ruining her eyes and flicked on the two wall bulbs. Downstairs Frank was still at the study desk. Anthro was wandering in the living room and told me that Donald had gone outside. The rule we had set up was that no one would leave the house and the idea of Donald padding down Beacon Street in a mystic state chilled me. Out on the front porch I turned on the two rows of spotlights that flooded the long winding stone stairs and started down, shielding my eyes and shouting Donald. Halfway down I heard him answering back and saw him standing under an oak tree on the lower lawn. I asked him how he was, but he didn't talk, just stood there looking wise and deep. He was barefoot and higher than Piccard's balloon. I want to talk to you, but first you must take off your shoes. Okay, why not? I sat down to unlace my shoes and he squatted alongside and told about how the machines complicate our lives and how cold and hot were abstractions and how we didn't really need houses and shoes and clothes because it was just our concepts that made us think we needed these things. I agreed with him and followed what his mind was doing, suspending for a moment the clutch of the abstract but at the same time shivering from the November wind and wanting to get back behind the warm glow of the windows.

The young anthropology student was standing in the hallway. I told him that Donald was doing fine, great mystical stuff, philosophizing without concepts. He looked puzzled. He didn't want a drink or food. I walked upstairs and found the door to Allen's room closed. I waited for a while, not knowing what to do and then knocked softly and said softly, Allen I'm here now and will be back in a few minutes. *Paradise Lost,* A BOOK I'D NEVER UNDERSTOOD BEFORE—WHY MILTON SIDED WITH LUCIFER THE REBEL IN HEAVEN.

I GOT UP OUT OF BED AND WALKED DOWNSTAIRS NAKED, ORLOVSKY FOLLOWING ME, CURIOUS WHAT I WOULD DO AND WILLING TO GO ALONG IN CASE I DID ANYTHING INTERESTINGLY EXTRAVAGANT. URGING ME ON IN FACT, THANK GOD.

Susan was sitting cross-legged on her bed brushing her hair when there came a patter of bare feet on the hallway carpet. I got to the door just in time to see naked buttocks disappearing down the stairway. It was Peter. I was grinning when I went back to see Susan. Peter is running around without any clothes on. Susan picked up her paraphernalia—curlers, brush, pins, and trotted up to the third floor. I headed downstairs.

When I got to the study Frank was leaning back in his chair behind the desk, grinning quizzically. In front of the desk looking like medieval hermits were Allen and Peter, both stark naked. I WENT IN AMONG THE PSYCHOLOGISTS IN STUDY AND SAW THEY TOO WERE WAITING FOR SOMETHING VAST TO HAPPEN, ONLY IT REQUIRED SOMEONE AND THE MOMENT TO MAKE IT HAPPEN—ACTION, REVOLUTION. No, Allen had on his glasses and as I came in he peered out at me and raised his finger in the air. Hey, Allen, what goes on? Allen had a holy gleam in his eye and he waved his finger. I'm the Messiah. I've come down to preach love to the world. We're going to walk through the streets and teach people to stop hating. I DECIDED I MIGHT AS WELL BE THE ONE TO DO SO—PRONOUNCED MY NAKEDNESS AS THE FIRST ACT OF REVOLUTION AGAINST THE DESTROYERS OF THE HUMAN IMAGE.

Well, Allen, that sounds like a pretty good idea. Listen, said Allen, do you believe that I'm the Messiah. THE NAKED BODY BEING THE HIDDEN SIGN. Look, I can prove it. I'm going to cure your hearing. Take off your hearing machine. Your ears are cured. Come on, take it off, you don't need it. AND GRABBED THE TELEPHONE TO COMMUNICATE MY DECISION—WANTED TO HOOK UP KHRUSHCHEV, KEROUAC, BURROUGHS, IKE, KENNEDY, MAO TSE-TUNG, MAILER, ETC.

Frank was still smiling. Peter was standing by, watching seriously. The hearing aid was dumped on the desk. That's right.

And now your glasses, I'll heal your vision too. The glasses were laid on the desk too. ALL IN ONE TELEPHONE LINE AND GET THEM ALL TO COME IMMEDIATELY TO HARVARD TO HAVE SPECTRAL CONFERENCE OVER THE FUTURE OF THE UNIVERSE.

Allen was peering around with approval at his healing. But Allen, one thing. What? Your glasses. You're still wearing them. Why don't you cure your own vision. Allen looked surprised. Yes, you're right. I will. He took off his glasses and laid them on the desk.

Now Allen was a blind Messiah squinting around to find his followers. Come on. We're going down to the city streets to tell the people about peace and love. And then we'll get lots of great people onto a big telephone network to settle all this warfare bit.

Fine, said Frank, but why not do the telephone bit first, right here in the house. Frank was heading off the pilgrimage down the avenue naked.

Who we gonna call, said Peter. Well, we'll call Kerouac on Long Island, and Kennedy and Khrushchev and Bill Burroughs in Paris and Norman Mailer in the psycho ward in Bellevue. We'll get them all hooked up in a big cosmic electronic love talk. War is just a hang-up. We'll get the love-thing flowing on the electric Bell Telephone network. Who we gonna call first, said Peter. Let's start with Khrushchev, said Allen.

Look, why don't we start with Kerouac on Long Island. In the meantime, let's pull the curtains, said Frank. There's enough going on in here so I don't care about looking outside. Allen picked up the white telephone and dialed Operator. The two thin figures leaned forward wrapped up in a holy fervor trying to spread peace. The dear noble innocent helplessness of the naked body. They looked as though they had stepped out of a quattrocento canvas, apostles, martyrs, dear fanatic holy men. Allen said, Hello, operator, this is God, I want to talk to Kerouac. To whom do I want to talk? Kerouac. What's my name? This is God. G-O-D. Okay. We'll try Capitol 7-0563. Where? Northport, Long Island. There was a pause. We were all listening hard. Oh. Yes. That's right. That's the number of the house where I was born. Look, operator, I'll have to go upstairs to get the number. Then I'll call back.

Allen hung up the receiver. What was all that about, Allen?

Well, the operator asked me my name and I said I was God and I wanted to speak to Kerouac and she said, I'll try to do my best, sir, but you'll have to give me his number and then I gave her the number of my mother's house. I've got Kerouac's number upstairs in my book. Just a minute and I'll get it.

Back at the phone, Allen was shouting to Jack. He wanted Jack to come up to Cambridge and then he wanted Jack's mother to come too. Jack had a lot to say because Allen held the phone, listening for long spaces. Frank was still sitting behind the desk smiling. Donald and the anthro student were standing in the hallway looking in curiously. I walked over to explain. Allen says he is the Messiah and he's calling Kerouac to start a peace and love movement. Donald wasn't interested. He went on telling me about the foolishness of believing in hot and cold. It occurred to me that Allen and Peter were proving his point. The phone call continued and finally I walked back in and said, Hey, Allen, for the cost of this phone call we could pay his way up here by plane. Allen shot an apologetic look and then I heard him telling Jack, Okay, Jack, I have to go now, but you've got to take the mushrooms and let's settle this quarrel between Kennedy and Khrushchev. BUT NEEDED MY GLASSES—THOUGH HAD YELLED AT LEARY THAT HE DIDN'T NEED HIS EARPIECE TO HEAR THE REAL VIBRATIONS OF THE COSMOS. HE WENT ALONG WITH ME AGREEABLY.

Allen and Peter were sitting on the big couch in the living room and Allen was telling us about his visions, cosmic electronic networks, and how much it meant to him that I told him he was a great man and how this mushroom episode had opened the door to women and heterosexuality and how he could see new womanly body visions and family life ahead. BUT THEN I BEGAN BREATHING AND WANTING TO LIE DOWN AND REST. Peter's hand was moving back and forth on Allen's shoulder. It was the first time that Allen had stood up to Jack and he was sorry about the phone bill but wasn't it too bad that Khrushchev and Kennedy couldn't have been on the line and, hey, what about Norman Mailer in that psychiatric ward in Bellevue, shouldn't we call him.

I don't think they'd let a call go through to him, Allen. Well, it all depends on how we come on. I don't think coming on as

Allen Ginsberg would help in that league. I don't think coming on as the Messiah would either. Well, you could come on as big psychologists and make big demanding noises about the patient. It was finally decided that it was too much trouble.

Still *curandero,* I asked if they wanted anything to eat or drink. Well, how about some hot milk. IF I ATE OR SHIT AGAIN I WOULD TURN BACK TO MERE NON-MESSIAH HUMAN. Allen and Peter went upstairs to put on robes and I put some cold milk in a pan and turned on the stove. Donald was still moving around softly with his hands behind his back. Thinking. Watching. He was too deep and Buddha for us to swing with and I later realized that I hadn't been a very attentive *curandero* for him and that there was a gulf between Allen and him never closed and that the geographic arrangement was too scattered to make a close loving session. Of course, both of them were old drug hands and ready to go off on their own private journeys and both wanted to make something deep and their own.

Anthro's role in all of this was never clear. He stood in the hallway watching curiously but for the most part we ignored him, treated him as an object just there but not involved and that, of course, was a mistake. Any time you treat someone as an object rest assured he'll do the same and that was the way that score was going to be tallied.

We ended up with a great scene in the kitchen. I bustled around pouring the hot milk into cups, and the poets sat around the table looking like Giotto martyrs in checkered robes. Lafcadio came down and we got him some food and he nodded yes when I asked him about ice cream and Allen started to talk about his visions and about the drug scene in New York and, becoming eloquent, wound up preaching with passion about the junkies, helpless, hooked, lost, thin, confused creatures, sick and the police and the informers. I SAW THE BEST MINDS OF MY GENERATION DESTROYED BY MADNESS, STARVING HYS-TERICAL NAKED, DRAGGING THEMSELVES THROUGH THE NEGRO STREETS AT DAWN LOOKING FOR AN ANGRY FIX. And then we started planning the psychedelic revolution. . . .

E. KLINGENBERG

Ginsberg's Czech Expulsion

Prague's best known jazz club, the Viola, where avant-garde poets recite their verse, has lost its birghtest star, and the largest concert hall in Prague, the strictly *art nouveau* Smetana, its warmest admirer.

"On May 7th, 1965, Irwin Allen Ginsberg, American poet, born on June 3, 1926, in New Jersey in the U.S.A., was summoned before the passport and visa section of the local administrative branch of the Ministry of the Interior in Prague where he was told that his presence was no longer considered desirable and that he was required to leave Czechoslovakia immediately. Allen Ginsberg accepted this pronouncement without protest, and on May 7th at 17.30 hours flew from Ruzyne Airport to London."

That is the brief official statement which says nothing about the reasons for his expulsion.

When Allen Ginsberg arrived in Czechoslovakia in mid-February honors were showered on the high priest of the anti-bourgeois Beat generation. *Literární noviny,* the organ of the Czechoslovakian Writers' Association, printed his photograph on the front page of its no. 10, and called him "the most unusual representative of nonacademic American poetry whose poems are already known to our readers and will soon be published in book form."

In no. 12 of the journal Igor Hájek wrote a longer article (notable for its well-intentioned objectivity) in which he introduced Ginsberg to the public and also allowed him to speak for himself: "When we set out to write a novel or a poem or to paint a picture," Ginsberg said, "we have no idea of the outcome of

From *Censorship* (London), Summer 1965.

the process. The concept of a creative plan is alien to us. It would therefore be difficult for me to be an artist in an environment where art has a specific program and where an ideology prevails. I try to grasp the world without labels, categories or ideology— only with an open mind." Hájek added (without criticizing Ginsberg's theses): "Polemics against Marxism? Although brought up among Communists, Ginsberg is certainly no Communist."

It is quite clear that despite his atheism and his polemics against everything bourgeois, despite his stay in Cuba and in the Soviet Union, Ginsberg is no Communist. He is basically an anarchist and is not prepared to give any state the loyalty demanded of him nor will he conform to the prevalent social outlook anywhere.

Nevertheless, all the literary journals in Prague, from *Kulturni tvorba* to *Světová literatura,* were available as his forum. Hájek wrote in his article that "Ginsberg is a large blackbird standing on one leg and listening until the music of life reveals itself to him . . . and whose visit reminds us that the complexity of the world does not allow us to close our eyes to any human problem."

Ginsberg and his unkempt anarchist's beard, his shabby light coat and white tennis shoes, in which he used to trudge through the deepest snow and slush in Prague, soon became a well-known sight in the city. He could be seen strolling on the Hradschin, in the squares where Kafka worked, on the Charles Bridge, whose muscular statues fascinated him, and in the small pubs of Prague with their grey-haired, rosy-cheeked waiters who were the embodiment of his conception of Central Europe. His name and reputation as an unconventional and revolutionary poet opened all doors to him. He reached the zenith of his popularity on May 1 when he was elected King of the May by the youth of Prague at the big student festival, the *Majales.* Arrested by the police for disturbing the peace on the nights of May 3 and 5, he was taken to his hotel after his friends spoke up for him.

But the storm was gathering around him. On May 6 a Prague citizen handed over to the Vinohrady police station a notebook he had found on the evening of May 3 in front of the *Spejbel and Hurvinek* theater. Ginsberg's name appeared on the front page.

The notebook contained notes written in English, various addresses and a few drawings, among them a self-portrait which Ginsberg had sketched in the Globus Jazz Club on February 23. After Ginsberg had affirmed that the diary was his, it was confiscated under Paragraph 79 III of the Czech criminal law, on suspicion that its contents were unlawful.

The authorities' assumption was confirmed. In his diary the poet had written detailed accounts of his numerous escapades with handsome youths, actors and writers in Prague and Bratislava. On May 16th *Mladá fronta,* the organ of the Czechoslovak youth organization, published an indignant, full-page article about Ginsberg's conduct entitled "Ginsberg and Morality" and sneered at Hájek's and Kusák's appreciative and sympathetic articles in *Literárni noviny* and *Kulturni tvorba.*

Full of philistine indignation and writing in the spirit of the maxim "Even if I don't know anything about Homer, at least I know that he had v.d.," *Mladá fronta* quoted intimate passages from Ginsberg's diary in an attempt to win its readers' approval for the poet's expulsion. Deviation, however, is not an offense in Czechoslovakia, and the reason for Ginsberg's expulsion can therefore only be indirectly attributed to these proclivities.

The real stumbling block was rather Ginsberg's criticism of leading officials, of the Czech people, and of the country itself. Notes like "The whole history of the Iron Curtain is true," and "All capitalist views of communism are correct" might well have been written by Ginsberg, although they must have seemed unfair and malicious in view of the hospitality he had received. But he could not easily be forgiven general calumnies such as "It seems that everyone in Czechoslovakia is always drunk," and his thumping abuse of the authorities.

A person like Ginsberg—an anarchist hostile to any regime or regimentation, a revolutionary par excellence who says exactly what he thinks and feels—can be a nuisance in any state. Ginsberg is awkward because he attacks everyone—Communists, capitalists, aesthetes and believers alike. He is a satyr whose mischievous aggressiveness stamps on majority values while defending with diabolical zeal everything the majority repudiates. Thus one evening among close friends in Prague he sang a panegyric to the monarchy and pleaded for its reestablishment. His mastery of paradox, well-aimed aphorisms and sophistries, impulsiveness and unconventional life won him a large audience of young companions in Prague who followed his free-ranging intuition as if bewitched by the pipes of Marsyas. Open and obvious as his violation of the explicit and tacit canons of a foreign guest's behavior may have been, it is a great pity that the Czechoslovak state could not muster the self-confidence to put up with a somewhat badly behaved, sharp-tongued angry young man.

"In Our Files"

(from a Memorandum, Federal Bureau of Narcotics, New York Office)

[U.S. Customs officials subjected Ginsberg to an intensive drug search when he returned from his 1965 trip to Europe. This and other events led him to write a letter to his congressman, Charles Joelson, Jr., asking if he would call upon the responsible agencies to account for their behavior. Ginsberg's letter was sent from Joelson's office to the New York office of the Bureau of Narcotics, which replied with a four-page attack on the poet, a section of which is reprinted here.

Part of what is interesting here is that within three months of its publication in Prague, some United States agency had translated the Czechoslovakian party-line denunciation of Ginsberg's work and character and made a copy available to the Bureau of Narcotics, which dutifully incorporated it into their assessment of the poet. The irony, says Ginsberg, "is the parallel mind-set of the two police bureaucracies supposedly engaged (otherwise) in cold war against each other."

This document was obtained by Ginsberg under the Freedom of Information Act.—ED.]

. . . GINSBERG, in his letter to Congressman [censored], stated that he had come back to New York after six months in Prague, Moscow, London, etc. Nowhere in this letter was it mentioned by GINSBERG that he was in fact expelled from Czechoslovakia. In an [censored] contained in our files, the [censored] quotes the May 16, 1965 issue of the Czechoslovakia publication *Mladá Fronta* in which an editorial appeared regarding GINSBERG, parts of which are quoted below.

> Ginsberg's visit, instead of contributing to the recognition of cultural values created by leading American poets, has a negative effect because Ginsberg, in his extreme independence and

irresponsibility, submits from his life those things which must be condemned: bisexuality, homosexuality, narcomania, alcoholism, posing, and a social extremism verging on orgies.

The [censored] report continues to quote another article in the May 17, 1965 issue of the publication *Rude Pravo* regarding GINSBERG, parts of which are quoted below:

If he had delighted in the shadowy lanes and in the beauty of the Charles Bridge, if he had read his poems at literary evening, nobody would have hindered him in any way. Our country is known for its hospitality and it is polite to each foreigner it invites. It cannot and does not tolerate, however, anyone bringing manners to our country which a normal man—sorry to say—spits upon.

Three Documents from
Allen Ginsberg's FBI File

(Obtained under the Freedom of Information Act)

UNITED STATES DEPARTMENT OF JUSTICE

FEDERAL BUREAU OF INVESTIGATION

WASHINGTON, D.C. 20535

April 26, 1965

In Reply, Please Refer to
File No. Bureau file 105-137059
New York file 105-71471

Chief
United States Secret Service
Department of the Treasury
Washington, D. C. 20220

Re: Irwin Allen Ginsberg
Internal Security - Cuba

Dear Sir:

The information furnished herewith concerns an individual who is believed to be covered by the agreement between the FBI and Secret Service concerning Presidential protection, and to fall within the category or categories checked.

1. ☐ Has attempted or threatened bodily harm to any government official or employee, including foreign government officials residing in or planning an imminent visit to the U. S., because of his official status.

2. ☐ Has attempted or threatened to redress a grievance against any public official by other than legal means.

3. ☒ Because of background is potentially dangerous; or has been identified as member or participant in communist movement; or has been under active investigation as member of other group or organization inimical to U. S.

4. ☐ U. S. citizens or residents who defect from the U. S. to countries in the Soviet or Chinese Communist blocs and return.

(a) [X] Evidence of emotional instability (including unstable residence and employment record) or irrational or suicidal behavior;

(b) [X] Expressions of strong or violent anti-U. S. sentiment;

(c) [X] Prior acts (including arrests or convictions) or conduct or statements indicating a propensity for violence and antipathy toward good order and government.

6. [ ] Individuals involved in illegal bombing or illegal bomb-making.

Photograph [ ] has been furnished [X] enclosed [ ] is not available [X] may be available through *U. S. Secret Service, New York, New York*.

Very truly yours,

John Edgar Hoover
Director

SECRET

1 - Special Agent in Charge (Enclosure(s) (2)
U. S. Secret Service , New York, New York
ENCLOSURE

Enclosure(s) (1)   *(Upon removal of classified enclosures, if any, this transmittal form becomes UNCLASSIFIED.)*

Registered Mail

105-137057-6

DISTRICT NO ::

GEN. FILE T DATE: Allen GINSBERG —

REPORT NO.

REPORT NO.

RELATED FILES

OTHER OFFICERS

AT: New York, N.Y.

DATE: September 28, 1967

BY: Narcotic Agent

RECOMMENDATION

PENDING: XX

CLOSE:

FURTHER INVESTIGATION:

SUBJECT OF THIS MEMORANDUM

Photograph of Allen GINSBERG.

DETAILS (if report is over two pages in length summarize in first paragraph)

1. On this date, I received a photograph of Allen GINSBERG where he is pictured in an indecent pose. For possible future use, the photograph has been placed in a locked sealed envelope marked "Photograph of Allen GINSBERG - Gen. File: Allen GINSBERG". The locked sealed envelope has been placed in the vault of this office for safekeeping.

UNITED STATES DEPARTMENT OF JUSTICE
FEDERAL BUREAU OF INVESTIGATION

Copy to:

Report of:
Date: 10/10/68

Field Office File #:

Title: IRWIN ALLEN GINSBERG

Character: ANTIRIOT LAWS

Synopsis:
██████████ advised he observed
GINSBERG at Grant Park in front of the Conrad
Hilton Hotel in conversation with associates.
GINSBERG chanted unintelligible poems* in Grant
Park on 8/28/68. AUSA declined prosecution of
GINSBERG.

Office: Chicago, Illinois

Bureau File

2 - USA, Chicago

---

*The "unintelligible poems" mentioned here was Blake's "The Grey Monk." — ED.

ALLEN GINSBERG

A Letter to Richard Helms, Director of the Central Intelligence Agency

[In March, 1971, Ginsberg met Richard Helms at a reception before a poetry reading at the Corcoran Gallery in Washington, D.C. Long interested in the question of police involvement in the drug trade, Ginsberg told Helms that he believed the CIA had a hand in the opium traffic in Southeast Asia. Helms denied the charge, whereupon Ginsberg offered a wager: if he was wrong he would give Helms his *vajra* ("a Buddhist-Hindu ritual implement of brass symbolizing the lightning-bolt doctrine of sudden illumination"), but if he was right, Helms would meditate an hour a day for the rest of his life.

The issue was never resolved, though articles written at the time supported Ginsberg's side of the wager (see "The New Opium War," *Ramparts,* May 1971, or the two columns that Flora Lewis wrote for *Newsday,* 1 May and 6 May 1971).

A conflict between two kinds of intelligence—"central intelligence" and "empty mind intelligence," let us say—bears on Ginsberg's politics, of course, but also on his prosody, which is one of the reasons why this letter is here reprinted.—ED.]

Cherry Valley, N.Y.
June 1972

Dear Mr. Helms:

Om Ah Hum! (Body Speech Mind.)

I will be in Miami for the [Democratic National] Convention (c/o Yippies) rejoicing meditating and keeping the peace. Mantra for this occasion will be *AH* (not Om as last time)—*Ah,* open blue space, something to breath into without anxiety.

I notice that Cuban refugees have been so far the sole causers of much loud mouth stink bomb strong arm anxiety preparatory to the convention. I suggest that if lower echelon C.I.A. folk are involved in this silliness it be stopped if possible. I have no idea.

Are you yet interested in some silent open space empty mind intelligence? I am more adept at it now than I was when we made the bet about Long Cheng being opium trafficking center for Xieng Quang Province.

I think by now you must admit that I was rightly informed and that you were not, to put it as kindly as possible.

It will do you no harm to meditate daily, and if the hour daily you agreed to is too heavy a burden, fifteen minutes or even five minutes daily is a good beginning. I wish I could introduce you to my meditation teacher, and can and will if you have time, and that could be done discreetly and sensibly.

If this is too much, try sitting crosslegged, back straight, on soft rug, pillow under your butt to ease straight spine—breathing slowly relaxed with whole abdomen & breast—use no mantra eyes open Zen style & follow breath—or use any mantra suitable—like *Ah!* or *Om Ah Hum*—Ah is most natural and American.

My abuse of your confidence in betting with me may be excused if you sit empty minded peaceful—at least forgiven.

Yours as ever—Strange Friend

Allen Ginsberg

FLOYCE ALEXANDER

Metapolitics

. . . Ginsberg is engaged in what Norman O. Brown calls "the real fight," which is "not the political fight," but the fight "to put an end to politics." The metapsychologist Brown advocates the turn from politics to metapolitics, or poetry:

> Legislation is not politics, nor philosophy, but poetry. . . .
> Poetry, art, imagination, the creator spirit is life itself; the real
> revolutionary power to change the world; and to change the
> human body.[1]

Political revolution is only "a temporary break-down followed by the reinstitution of repression, a cycle of explosion and repression, activity and passivity, in eternal recurrence." Metapolitics is engaged in a dialectical revolution of "intellect seeking union with energy," creating "a logic of passion" in which "nothing is stable, movement is all." Whereas politics is a "systematic reified permanent form" which "creates an elite who possess the secret," poetry is a form of "mass-mysticism" in which the masses share "an open secret," namely that " 'the truth is in the whole,' " and "the whole is in any part."

Poetry is "the solvent which dissolves the rigorous stereotypes of political ideology, the numb automatism of political reflexes, the somnambulist gravity of literal believers," and in place of these forms of ossification offers "the language which unifies, the language of healing, or making whole," which expresses "the transforming spirit of . . . metaphorical play."[2]

Ginsberg's poetry embodies his effort to break through the

From "Allen Ginsberg's Metapolitics: From Moloch to the Millennium," in *Research Studies of Washington State University* (June 1970). Reprinted with permission.

crust of a civilization which exalts the static, rational virtues of the mind and denies the body its dynamic power to generate an imaginative alternative to the contemporary political and spiritual decay. He is fully aware that the spiritual utopia in his poems is solely of his own making, and that any actual utopia to be realized will not be created through his, or anyone's, poetry. He is merely insisting upon the right to create through his own language a vision to oppose to the reality of the world that political systems have created. He has learned the lesson of William Blake's creed,

> I must Create a System, or be enslav'd by another Mans
> I will not Reason & Compare: my business is to Create. . . .[3]

NOTES

1. Norman O. Brown, "A Reply to Herbert Marcuse," in Marcuse, *Negations: Essays in Critical Theory* (Boston: Beacon Press, 1969), p. 246.

2. Brown, "From Politics to Metapolitics," in *Caterpillar* 1, ed. Clayton Eshleman (October 1967):75–93.

3. Blake, "Jerusalem," in *The Poetry and Prose of William Blake,* ed. David V. Erdman (New York: Doubleday, 1965), p. 151.

JAMES A. W. HEFFERNAN

Politics and Freedom
Refractions of Blake

. . . "Howl" is aggressively polemical, and as such, it tends to summon up the Blake who was a prophet against empire, the champion of an essentially *political* freedom. "The best minds of my generation," says the poet (and here the very word "generation" has a Blakean ring), "passed through universities with radiant cool eyes hallucinating Arkansas and Blake-light tragedies among the scholars of war."[1] I do not know how to connect Arkansas with "Blake-light tragedies," or even what those tragedies are, but it is clear at least that students of Blake are being contraposed to "scholars of war," that the maker of illuminated books is being called upon to light the way of protest against the makers of war. Thomas Vance calls this line "uncannily prophetic" because it seems to anticipate the confrontations between war protestors and university administrations which convulsed the sixties.[2] But if we now "nostalgically" remember the fifties as a decade of peace and complacency, we should not forget that they began with two years of war in Korea and were dominated by the jingoistic voice of Joseph McCarthy, who helped to create the mood that sent the United States into Vietnam. In any case, one of the most vivid passages in "Howl" represents young draftees appearing for their physical examinations, "who broke down crying in white gymnasiums naked and trembling before the machinery of other skeletons." With its faint reminiscense of the creature in Blake's "Infant Sorrow" ("Helpless, naked, piping loud"), the line depicts the crushingly humiliating process of induction: stripped of their bodies as well

From "Politics and Freedom: Refractions of Blake in Joyce Cary and Allen Ginsberg," in *Romantic and Modern,* ed. George Bornstein (Pittsburgh: University of Pittsburgh Press, 1977). Reprinted with permission.

as of their clothes, men are turned into machinelike skeletons, into functioning parts of the all-consuming war machine. And as a Jewish poet writing just ten years after the end of World War II, Ginsberg may well be alluding also to those naked and trembling figures led to the "gymnasiums" and crematoria of Dachau and Auschwitz, bodies consumed by the juggernaut of Nazism.

Ginsberg's conception of the war machine as juggernaut becomes explicit in part two of "Howl," and here the warmongering that Ginsberg finds in America is specifically linked with the Blakean figure of Moloch. According to Frye, Blake regarded Moloch (or "Molech" in Blake's spelling) as the presiding spirit of the brazen age, the second of the seven great periods of the Fall. In this period the Titans worshiped Urizen, "thundergod of moral law and tyrannical power . . . in a cult of death consisting largely of human sacrifices. Since then, the belief that somehow it is right to kill men has been the underlying cause of all wars." And Frye goes on to say: "This is the period of Druidism, when giants erected huge sacrifical temples like Stonehenge and indulged in hideously murderous orgies."[3] In Blake's *Milton,* Moloch is plainly the juggernaut of crematoria, pestilence, and war:

> loud his furnaces rage among the Wheels of Og, &
> pealing loud the cries of the Victims of Fire:
> And pale his Priestesses infolded in Veils of Pestilence,
>   border'd
> With War . . .[4]

It is this figure that Ginsberg specifically and repeatedly invokes in part two of "Howl." For Ginsberg, Moloch becomes the specter of the military-industrial establishment, the embodiment of everything in modern American civilization that feeds on the sacrifice of human blood or human imagination:

Moloch the incomprehensible prison! Moloch the crossbone soulless
    jailhouse and Congress of sorrows! Moloch whose buildings are
    judgement! Moloch the vast stone of war! Moloch the stunned
    governments!

Moloch whose mind is pure machinery! Moloch whose blood is run-
ning money! Moloch whose fingers are ten armies! Moloch whose
breast is a cannibal dynamo! Moloch whose ear is a smoking tomb!

Moloch whose eyes are a thousand blind windows! Moloch whose
skyscrapers stand in long streets like endless Jehovahs! Moloch
whose factories dream and croak in the fog! Moloch whose smoke-
stacks and antennae crown the cities!

Moloch whose love is endless oil and stone! Moloch whose soul is
electricity and banks! Moloch whose poverty is the specter of ge-
nius! Moloch whose fate is a cloud of sexless hydrogen! Moloch
whose name is the Mind!

Ginsberg's language is at once contemporary and Blakean.
Amid smokestacks and television antennae, skyscrapers appear
as the new Jehovan thundergods of tyrannical power, the new
Druidical megaliths. Near the Congress of sorrows, he implies,
stands the Pentagon, the new Stonehenge of war. The war ma-
chine whose fingers are ten armies (fingers here become cyber-
netically mechanized) recklessly consumes both blood and mon-
ey, and Ginsberg's concentrated account of the way it wastes
them both ("whose blood is running money") recalls the equally
concentrated imagery of war in Blake's "London": "And the
hapless Soldier's sigh / Runs in blood down Palace walls."
Dreaming is left to factories—cruelest of ironies—because, as
the first line of part two tells us, the brains and imagination of
men have been eaten up by that "sphinx of cement and alumi-
num" named Moloch. Finally, then, Moloch is a Urizenic fig-
ure, the embodiment of a tyrannical pure reason that is pitiless
alike to body, imagination, and soul: "Moloch whose mind is
pure machinery! . . . Moloch whose name is the Mind!"
Ginsberg himself has said that while part one of "Howl" is "a
lament for the Lamb in America," part two "names the monster
of mental consciousness that preys on the Lamb."[5]

To this extent, Ginsberg is implicitly using Blake as a prophet
of psychological freedom—not merely of political freedom.
Ginsberg's relation to Blake is in fact anything but categorically
neat. In the first place, Blake is only one of the many influences
on Ginsberg, who owes at least as much (if not more) to Whit-
man, to his Paterson mentor Williams, and to his contempo-

raries Kerouac, William Burroughs, and Neal Cassady. Secondly, Ginsberg has said that "the only poetic tradition is the voice out of the burning bush."[6] Yet it is precisely his conception of the poet as prophet that prompts Ginsberg to admire the resoundingly prophetic Blake, just as Blake's own obsession with the Bible led him to admire the author of *Paradise Lost*. Moloch, after all, was both a Biblical and a Miltonic figure before he became a Blakean one, and his appearance in "Howl" perfectly demonstrates the continuity of what Ginsberg calls "the only poetic tradition." For Ginsberg, then, Blake is a good deal more than a prophet against political empire, and although he uses Blake in the cause of political freedom, he also knows that Blake is a prophet of ultimate freedom: the kind of freedom that comes from the individual imagination. Reflecting this side of Blake, Ginsberg's poetry seeks to liberate man not only from the machinery of war, government, and industry, but also from the machinery of a purely conceptualizing, abstracting, Urizenic mind. . . .

NOTES

1. I quote from *Howl and Other Poems* (San Francisco: City Lights Books, 1967), p. 9. *Howl* was first published in 1956.

2. "American Poetry of Protest, from World War II to the Present," in *Amerikanische Literatur im 20. Jahrhundert,* ed. Alfred Weber and Dietmar Haack (Göttingen Vandernhoek & Ruprecht, 1971), p. 257.

3. Northrop Frye, *Fearful Symmetry* (Princeton: Princeton University Press, 1947), p. 129.

4. I quote from *The Poetry and Prose of William Blake,* ed. David Erdman with commentary by Harold Bloom (New York: Doubleday, 1965), 37.21–24.

5. "Notes for *Howl* and Other Poems" (1959), in *The New American Poetry,* ed. Donald M. Allen (New York: Grove Press, 1960).

6. Quoted in Richard Howard, *Alone with America: Essays on the Art of Poetry in the United States since 1950* (New York: Atheneum, 1971), p. 146.

ERIC MOTTRAM

Anarchic Power

. . . Brought up as a communist Jew, Ginsberg is in the major American tradition of anarchism—Thoreau's "majority of one." . . . But the anarchist position is notoriously difficult to maintain without it degenerating into a crude iconoclasm, the mirror image of the crude authoritarianism of the world it opposes, equally simplistic and equally intolerant. Ginsberg has generally been able to avoid this because he has the intelligence of his body's convictions for freedom. There was time when he could be a manically disintegrative power on those open to his energy—Carl Solomon records his submission and opposition in those passages of *Mishaps, Perhaps* which concern their relationship, in and out of the New York Psychiatric Institute, in 1949. The two young men sustained a state of mutual hallucination in order to become real:

> Shortly after my mummification and defiance of Amenhotip, I encountered what appeared to be a new patient, to whom I mumbled amiably, "I'M KIRILOV". He mumbled in reply "I'M MYSHKIN". The cadence of the superreal was never challenged; not one of us would dare assume responsibility for a breach of the unity which each hallucination required.

And later:

> Dear Allen:
>   YOMOLKA and all I have escaped from the lunatic rathole which your perverted old auntie antics drove me into.[1]

From *Allen Ginsberg in the Sixties* (Brighton/Seattle: Unicorn Bookshop [1972]), a twenty-six-page pamphlet. Reprinted with permission.

Only recently has Ginsberg been able to shake off hallucinatory relationships with his followers and audiences; his prophetic power is now clear of the early Beat image—necessary in its anarchic program of projective verse and exhibitionist nakedness, but insufficiently explicit in its political and psychological aims. The Beat had a violent freshness which barely concealed a suicidal retreat into self-exploration and cosmic consciousness. Ginsberg created himself as a laboratory of experiment for the expanded consciousness out of an experience of poetry, religion and drugs. Within that search lay the hunt for an adequate decision on what the term "God" could mean for him; that is, his energy has been directed towards a definition of power in the self, by the self and beyond the self. Although this has meant a fusion of a great deal of information, there is little sign that Ginsberg has a manic desire for epic grandeurs; John Clellon Holmes is exaggerating when he says that Ginsberg's mind operates "as if the nerves of a Rimbaud were harnessed to the immense, synthesizing vision of a Spengler."[2] The poet's vision certainly does not extend to that kind of vitalism, associated with fascism, within which Eric Bently has included Spengler. He is far too conscious of his own messianic obsessions and the positions of easy oracular and charismatic leadership towards which his aims and the conditions of the world push him. A man without laws is peculiarly vulnerable to his own gifts of power.

"In Society"[3] ends with ironic, comic self-mockery within its protest against the predations of inevitable social rounds: he shouts at some insulting woman "in a violent / and messianic voice, inspired at / last, dominating the whole room." Ginsberg wants to dominate the room but only for a purpose: the expansion and regeneration of mutual consciousness. It is the aim of his poetry, and is remote from art for its own sake or the artist's sake. His safeguard is a painful one: to be fundamentally alone and write out of that loneliness:

> Alone
> in that same self where I always was
> with Kennedy throat brain bloodied in Texas
> the television continuous blinking two radar days . . .

The rest of this poem, "November 23, 1963" (Now Now, 1965), describes the circle of friendship, which he values particularly and at which he is adept, but which is a set of contacts within which he must remain alone. He is fond of those passages in *The Tempest* where Prospero, the white magus, relinquishes the instruments of his magic power (he refers to them at the end of "The Change," for example, and in the conversation with Ernie Barry in *City Lights Journal* 2, 1964) and requests release by pardon from his audience. He once said of Elise Cowen, who typed the primary copy of "Kaddish," "she has that quality of alert solitude": it is the silent area of Allen Ginsberg himself.[4] He is acutely conscious of any movement in himself or other people towards tyranny; "A Dream" (*Gnaoua 1,* Spring 1964) gives the form of a recurring routine in his works and journals—he is an "international European city" in 1962, experiences the streets, apartments, young writers, girls with flowers, "walls pockmarked with bullet-holes," sounds of machine-gun fire. In bed with Elise Cowen he dreams of Buchenwald figures, Stalin, Roosevelt, Hitler, choruses of Russian communists, and a stroboscopically blinking death's head. But the dream ends with choruses of yellow, black and Jewish people all singing: "We will have our victory!" In one of the selections from his journals in *Boss,* Summer 1966, he writes

> If I was in Power / I would also be closed in by certain / necessities of Power? No I would take / off my clothes and go naked on Television / with Kruschev—

Nakedness and tenderness are his constant instruments of anarchic power because in this condition he is vulnerable to little of the black magic of the Faustian magus which lies inside his consciousness. In "Genocide" (*War Poems,* edited Diane di Prima, 1968) he dreams of LeRoi Jones, incarnated as an Afro-American, and laying with him, "our legs wrapped and twined round each others bodies, soft cheeks together":

> He wanted to protect me in the War
> storm, but was unable
> for the great force that was

                    upon us, of strangeness and
                    alien white mind in America . . .

   His solution to the American Dilemma, as he told Paul Car-
roll, is in the same belief: "my understanding is that present race
hostilities is obviously frustrated relationship, frustrated love.
The *ground* is desire. All hate energy is a conversion of that desire
when blocked." "Kaddish," "To Aunt Rose" and "History of
the Jewish Socialist Party of America" at least partly state
Ginsberg's necessary evolution out of that commitment to polit-
ical party action which is a version of a more general madness
threatening human lives: the organized system of manipulation.
"New York to San Fran" (1965), in *Airplane Dreams: Composi-
tions from Journals* (1968) is a meditational structure about power.
The poet in a plane is in the later twentieth-century area of
space-time, combining movement and rest in a semihallucinato-
ry journey over the Earth. Against Adlai Stevenson's Grosvenor
Square death he chants the syllable of assent, "om," the sound of
the universe. The sense of potential life and potential death gives
way to the ironies of musical associations with the sublime and
divine, heard from loudspeakers while reading newspaper head-
lines of the Vietnamese war. He retreats from this electronic
idiocy by "breaking the 'Law'": "Hashish in the Bathroom."
But the euphoria is shortlived. He watches a movie called "Spi-
derweb of Evil," a coincidence which might appear to be too
oppressively pat but represents the kind of grim coincidence
possible in modern conditions. He resists by asserting godhead
in himself; war on Satan, prophecy against political killers, Sta-
lin, capitalism—in fact, the poem becomes what too often hap-
pens in Ginsberg's recent works, an hysterical and dull denun-
ciation of the obvious: evil men of power. The music over
headphones fuses the guilty land over which he passes, with its
CIA, police, state prisons and scientific laboratories, with the
movie which is "about the most secret chemical / warefare sta-
tion on this hemisphere," and therefore "projecting / the same
angst as my hashish / bathroom— / So I share in this vast
fantasy / which rises like poison gas / from the man-warmed
farmlands / approaching Missouri River."
   Ginsberg's theme of power and paranoia, both in himself and

in his environment, is in the sixties the center of his concern, his vulnerability, the experience of this century. But once again the black humor of self-criticism prevents egotism—"Shit the movie's attacking / us Messiahs"—and he considers the possible treasons to be committed by the Beatles, Yevtuchenko and himself, risking imprisonment. He resists paranoia in his customary way: "I must come back to my body." . . .

In 1960, Ginsberg's international tenderness was not overtly political:

> people are beginning to see that the Kingdom of Heaven is within them, instead of thinking it's outside, up in the sky and that it can't be here on earth! It's time to seize power in the Universe, that's what I say—that's my "political statement." Time to seize power over the entire Universe. Not merely over Russia or America—seize power the moon—take the sun over.[5]

In 1963 he picketed in the San Francisco anti-Madame Nhu demonstration—"the first time I've taken a political stand"—but his sign read in part: "Till his humanity awakes says Blake / I am here saying seek mutual surrender tears / That there be no more hell in Vietnam / That I not be in hell here in the street / War is black magic . . ."[6] Mutual surrender was the only answer to mutual bankruptcy. In 1965 he attempted, with some success, to deflect the Hell's Angels from disrupting Californian peace demonstrations against the war, and provided instructions on "How to make a March/Spectacle," as well as an address to the Angels themselves (reprinted in *Liberation,* January 1966):

> The parade can be made into an exemplary spectacle on how to handle situations of anxiety and fear/threat (such as Specter of Hells Angels or Specter of Communism). To manifest by concrete example, namely the parade itself, how to change war-psychology and surpass, go over, the habit-image-reaction of fear/violence.

The appeal to the Angels to realize their own "Anxiety Para-noia" did not, of course, work beyond the immediate situation ("All separate identities are bankrupt—Square, beat, Jews, negros, Hell's Angels, Communist and American"). But from this point on, in America and Europe, and in India through the new younger poets, Ginsberg has been unavoidably political in the most revolutionary way: "the revolt of the personal. War-saw San Francisco Calcutta, the discovery of feeling."[7]

. . . In Ginsberg's world, his own nation expends "its deepest energies in wars . . . against the yellow and other races," and expands the poverty of the world: "prosperity . . . really a great psychic hoax, a mirage of electric mass-hypnosis, the real hor-ror, the real evil latent in America from the days of Poe to the Days of Burroughs." So that beyond the political lies personal survival in order to speak out in poetry:

> Finally it becomes too much to fight. But the stakes are too
> great to lose—the possession of one's feelings intact.

The basic outrage is "to live in a country which supposedly dominates the entire planet and to be responsible for the out-rages of one's own country!" His tenderness is endangered in battle against the exhausting forces of "the military machine non-person rage that dominates the thinking feeling massmedia family life publishing life universities business and budgetary government of my nation." Poetry opposes the Unreal and its manipulatory centers of power: but in the fight "how can the soul endure?"— "what happens to real bodily human feelings confronted with inhuman response? The feelings and the re-sponse become seeming unreal. Total disorganization." Poetry must be "the renaissance of individual sensibility carried thru the vehicle of individualized metrics," and that is exactly why the police attack the avant-garde. In "Kansas City to St. Louis," one of the long sections of the poem on "These States," Ginsberg puts the problem in its most urgent form: the condition of power in America.

He shows the culture of the people of the Middle West as a treachery called "We the People" seething inside a vitalistic pro-gram of terror: Fulton—

where Churchill rang down the Curtain
                on Consciousness
and set a chill which overspread the world
                one icy day in Missouri
                        not far from the Ozarks—
Provincial ears heard the Spenglerian Iron
                Terror Pronouncement
                        Magnificent Language, they said,
                for county ears—

The lyrical impassioned movement—Ginsberg at his finest—
moves towards his own position:

The hero surviving his own murder,
                his own suicide, his own
                        addiction, surviving his own
poetry, surviving his own
                        disappearance from the scene—
returned in new faces, shining
                through the tears of new eyes.
                . . . .
                . . . the wanderer returns
                from the west with his Powers,
the Shaman with his beard
                in full strength,
the longhaired Crank with subtle humorous voice
                        enters city after city
to kiss the eyes of your high school sailors
and make laughing Blessing
                for a new Age in America . . .

Planet News is a record of his right to be that laughing proph-
et. Today his poetry is a continuous record of space-time travel
in the Cold War. He is a media man, fearful of global electronic
communications networks but trying to employ them for his
own ends of humane communication—the condition of every
peaceful revolutionary. Ginsberg's voice and image are available
internationally in the flesh, on film, on records, in books, on
posters and on television. With the other major American poets

266

of our time—Williams, Pound, Zukofsky, Olson, Duncan—he is making the continuous open-ended epic which will end with his life: the information program for these men is endlessly exploratory, continually forming, disintegrating and re-forming. Ginsberg's scroll is not encyclopedic, as it is in Duncan and Olson—he does not have their manic desire for the inclusive myth of all myths, the geography of all history. His self-centerdness does make for a certain monotony of urgency, despair, reiteration of disasters and tyrants, and disgust with his alternately melancholic and exuberant self. *Planet News* is the book of a busy social man agonized in private, a traveler recorder who has vowed to maintain his impressions in notebooks and on tape. The poems, "journal notations" and journal compositions have a vitality of manic need to define, to master complexity and universality, and to keep off self-distrust, despair and impotence. . . .

NOTES

1. Carl Solomon, *Mishaps, Perhaps* (San Francisco: City Lights Books, 1966), pp. 36ff and 57.

2. John Clellon Holmes, *Nothing More to Declare* (New York: Dutton, 1967), pp. 53ff.

3. *Empty Mirror* (Corinth, N.Y.: Totem, 1961), p. 18.

4. Allen Ginsberg and Lucien Carr, "Some Thoughts about Elise Cowen," *City Lights Journal* 2 (1964).

5. Quoted in David Ossman, *Sullen Art: Interviews with Modern American Poets* (N.Y.: Corinth, 1963).

6. Ernie Barry, "A Conversation with Allen Ginsberg," *City Lights Journal* 2 (1964).

7. Allen Ginsberg, "A Few Bengali Poets," *City Lights Journal* 2 (1964).

CZESLAW MILOSZ

The Image of the Beast

. . . Meaning does exist, beyond the reach of all reason in the meeting of eyes, hands, in the play of pronouns—I-he, I-she, in identity and nonidentity, in perpetual regeneration, in the places ready and prepared, places forever taken anew by children, the young, old women, in happiness and unhappiness, in love and hate, a fluency of becoming, a river. It is impossible not to mention the name of Walt Whitman here, but not because Walt Whitman is America. The truth contained in the ecstatic stammering "to be alive among the living" exists separate and apart from him, and even before I read Whitman, his sense of things compelled me to search for words and was the source of all my curiosities and passions. The electric current of Whitman's *en masse* was certainly stronger in America than anywhere else, and that bard, more complicated and more cunningly circuitous than is generally thought, closed the conduits in himself that were too private and refractory and opened those favoring that great current. When the poets of Europe were cursing the *cité infernale,* populated like Hades with restless specters, Whitman extolled, glorified, and blessed the human element and its irrepressible onward rush. His work has suffered a defeat because, though our experience of collective life is still strong, it has now been seasoned with a bitterness which he forbade himself. The young American poets turn to him, the progenitor, the father of their line, crying: "Walt Whitman, come see what's become of your prophecy, your hymn." . . .

What sphinx of cement and aluminum bashed open their skulls
　　　　　and ate up their brains and imagination?
Moloch! Solitude! Filth! Ugliness! Ashcans and unobtainable
　　　　　dollars! Children screaming under the stairways! Boys
　　　　　sobbing in armies! Old men weeping in the parks!
Moloch! Moloch! Nightmare of Moloch! Moloch the loveless!
　　　　　Mental Moloch! Moloch the heavy judger of men!
Moloch the incomprehensible prison! Moloch the crossbone
　　　　　soulless jailhouse and Congress of sorrows! Moloch whose
　　　　　buildings are judgement! Moloch the vast stone of war!
　　　　　Moloch the stunned governments!
Moloch whose mind is pure machinery! Moloch whose blood is
　　　　　running money! Moloch whose fingers are ten armies!
　　　　　Moloch whose breast is a cannibal dynamo! Moloch whose
　　　　　ear is a smoking tomb!
Moloch whose eyes are a thousand blind windows! Moloch whose
　　　　　skyscrapers stand in the long streets like endless Jehovahs!
　　　　　Moloch whose factories dream and croak in the fog!
　　　　　Moloch whose smokestacks and antennae crown the cities!
Moloch whose love is endless oil and stone! Moloch whose soul is
　　　　　electricity and banks! Moloch whose poverty is the
　　　　　specter of genius! Moloch whose fate is a cloud of sexless
　　　　　hydrogen! Moloch whose name is Mind!

　　　　　　　　　　　　　　　　　　　　　　　　("Howl")

Chanting his song, Whitman's turned inside out, Allen Ginsberg
was Everyman. The very body of a person, whether he be edu-
cated or not, recoils from a cold, brilliant, perfectly consistent
slab of metal, glass, concrete, or synthetic materials which can-
not be embraced by sight or touch, and it recoils from the power
residing behind that armor, as well. Thus, a caterpillar adapted
to the roughness and porosity of plants is at a loss on the waxed
hood of an automobile; the grotesque efforts of a bee knocking
against a pane of glass indicate how ill prepared it is to meet with
a transparent obstacle resembling solidified air. A slab, wall, or
steamroller begins to move all by itself, its movement unique,
mathematically necessary, it looms larger and larger—then you
wake up in a cold sweat after a dream of being crushed. Of
course, seen from an airplane, this continent is desolate, the skin

of an antediluvian beast, flaxen, bluish, yellow, sometimes furry with forests; sometimes an hour passes without proof that the land below is inhabited, and only here and there does the mildew of cities thicken, at night emanating a many-colored light, the gigantic neon honeycomb of the three megalopolises of the East, the West, and the Midwest. Of course, America has a dusting of brushwood, green trees and lawns, wooden sheds, fences, weeds swaying over rusted cars. But still the sign of Moloch is everywhere and all the cities are one city, all the highways are one highway, all the stores one store, and to travel a thousand miles becomes meaningless, for wherever you turn, you come up against that same moving wall.

Why does a person tremble, recoil, withdraw into his own fragile, threatened flesh? After all, what surrounds him is his creation, his doing, he brought it into existence out of himself, to serve as his own contradiction. But that isn't true—he, the individual, touching himself, the color of his eyes and hair appearing in the mirror, does not admit to a causal role, and he is right. It is not he who is responsible but that other in him who acts as a statistic; clutched by others and clutching to them, in the most human way, submitting to his needs and desires, he creates something which is inhuman, beyond the human, which turns against his needs and desires, eluding his control. There it stands before him, and though it would seem to be his, it is not, it is *on the outside*. It is no accident that I have spoken a great deal about nature. The greatest trick of this continent's demons, their leisurely vengeance, consists in surrendering nature, recognizing that it could not be defended; but in place of nature there arose that civilization which to its members appears to be Nature itself, endowed with nearly all the features of that other nature. It is just as alien and hostile to me, a single, tangible man, impenetrable in its opposition to meaning; it rules by its own laws, which are not the same as mine. The difference is that the old nature would offer itself temptingly, ready to submit. We were able to bore tunnels through mountains, irrigate dry plains, plant orchards and vineyards where buffalo and stags had grazed. The new nature, containing such great energy and achievements that forces greater than the individual have been compressed into it, casts me, you, everyone into impotence, evasion, a solitude with phonograph music and a fire in the fireplace.

To what degree one plus one plus one can influence that new, second nature and give it direction does not pertain here, because any semblance of a political treatise was ruled out in advance. Impotence resides not only in consciousness but, it can be said without exaggeration, deeper than consciousness. The higher the consciousness, the better it will comprehend the mutual meshings of the gears, the self-perpetuating mechanisms, and the clearer becomes the incommensurability between the channel once assigned to the turbulent stream and the stream which has spilled out of its former channel. Intellectual fashions, slogans, programs rallying people under one banner or another are weakened from within by their tacitly accepted transience. There has been a great deal of all that, but it was digested, broken down, and assimilated by the Behemoth with all the impassivity of a second nature, and the more it changed, the more it stayed the same. A lower consciousness trusts textbooks on civics, but they stop at arithmetic, at one plus one plus one, and pay no attention to the complex determinants concealed behind the arithmetic. However, just beneath the threshold of consciousness, there is a doubt, perhaps peasant in origin, of the possibility of any change—the constant conspiracy of the mighty somewhere behind the scenes seems to predetermine a social order as regular as the seasons. But this is naïve; the higher consciousness knows there is no such conspiracy, that function begets function for the sake of function, and what terrifies the higher consciousness is precisely this impersonal monolith, its glacierlike advance.

Weak, warm-blooded, what can a man do against it, not man as a concept, but the given individual? Never has the division between man as a unique creature and man as a cipher, the cocreator of the unintended, been so clear-cut, and perhaps it was the calling of America, Europe's illegitimate child, to compose a parable of universal significance.

LASZLO GÉFIN

Ellipsis
The Ideograms of Ginsberg

. . . The central method and the main form of modernism I call the *juxtapositional* or, to use the name given to it by its "inventor" Ezra Pound, the *ideogrammic* method. To juxtapose, of course, means to situate side by side two or more things. The method may also be called *paratactic,* based on the Greek verb παρατάσσω, to place beside one another. Parataxis is the opposite of hypotaxis, from ὑποτάσσω, to arrange under, which signifies a dependent construction or relation of parts with connectives. On the simplest rhetorical level such a mode is an asyndetic composition (from the Greek ἀσύνδετος, unconnected), where connectives have been omitted. The Chinese ideogrammic method, in Ernest Fenollosa's view (from which Pound built a poetic theory), relies in its juxtapositions on a close observation of natural processes. In his view the basis of the method is metaphorical: the juxtaposed "material" images imply "immaterial" relationships. From a deliberate juxtaposition of pictures of things, without any connectives, the Chinese written language can draw not only more pictures of things (that, too), but more important, it can point to concepts and universals. For example, the juxtaposition of the pictograms of "man" and "fire" produces a new meaning, the color "red." For Pound, the setting side by side, without copulas, of verbal pictures will perforce establish relationships between the units juxtaposed. Such juxtapositions he called *images.* The image is the basic form of ideogrammic composition; it is not simply a

From *Ideogram: History of a Poetic Method* copyright © 1982 by the University of Texas Press. Reprinted by permission of the publisher.

visual impression but a union of particulars transposed onto the conceptual plane. . . .

The method of the ideogram asserts that a true representation of reality (one that is in accord with nature's own movements) is possible in poetry (and in art in general) by an asyndetic juxtaposition of linguistic (or pictorial, spatial, tonal) particulars which the mind of the reader (onlooker, listener) will organize into a coherent whole just as he or she does with particulars in the real world. Not only are connectives relics of an outmoded transitional practice, but they are redundant, in fact, because they are not present in nature. To use Wittgenstein's example, in the descriptive sentence "The book is on the table" we can point to objective referents in the world of "book" and "table," but we cannot point to the copula "is on." The ideogrammic method obviates such artificial "meddling" with and intrusion upon nature. Herein lies perhaps the source for Pound's (and the ideogrammic poets') mistrust of metaphor; hence their move "TOWARD ideogram" as an accurate mode of depicting reality. . . .

Some readers and critics may object to the use of the term "ideogrammic" in describing the Poundian method of composition. But whether we substitute "paratactic" or "juxtapositional," or talk about a vorticist combination of "pattern units," or employ phrases like "qualitative progression," "nontransitional sequence," "fugal construction," "montage," or "collage," or, specifically, "Poundian juxtaposition," we are really speaking about the same thing: the literary or poetic version of the *forma mentis*. Similarly, the poets in the ideogrammic tradition have given new names to the method to fit their own individual poetics. For Olson, for instance, it is "composition by field"; for Zukofsky it is the fugue; for Duncan it is "collage," while Snyder describes his method as "riprapping" and Ginsberg calls attention to his "elliptical" mode of composition. But in spite of the shades of meaning, the same organizing principle is behind their diverse methods. . . .

Ginsberg started writing when he was still a high-school student in Paterson, New Jersey, and continued it as an undergraduate at Columbia. In college, he recalls, John Crowe Ransom and Allen Tate were the "supreme literary touchstones," but Ginsberg was not impressed. So he turned to imitating six-teenth- and seventeenth-century poets like Wyatt and Marvell. After his expulsion from Columbia he continued to write in this vein, and in 1948 sent a half-dozen of his poems to William Carlos Williams, who sent them back with the stern verdict, "In this mode, perfection is basic, and these are not perfect."[1] Then Ginsberg began to read Williams's poetry, and he tried to rearrange his lines as he saw them in Williams, according to emotional and breath patterns. He began to concentrate on "more detail, more minute particulars, less ideas, more things,—'icebox, cabinet, toasters, stove'—*presenting* material, rather than recombining symbols that I had appropriated from Yeats or Blake or Marvell."[2] The result pleased Williams, but the real turn in Ginsberg's poetry came when he *heard* Williams read for the first time at the Museum of Modern Art:

> I suddenly realized he [Williams] was hearing with raw ears. The sound, pure sound and rhythm—as it was spoken around him, and he was trying to adapt his poetry rhythms out of the actual talk rhythms he heard in the place that he was, rather than metronome or sing-song archaic literary rhythms he would hear in a place inside his head from having read other writings.[3]

He grasped that Williams's form was identical to his content, it *was* the content as it is uttered in daily life. The poem ("The Clouds") ended in midsentence, not as formally constructed poems do, but as a piece of conversation might end in reality. This was completely new and exhilarating to Ginsberg:

> . . . to arrive at a poetry that really means what it says, a poetry with a meaning which is identical with its form, with a rhythm identical with the arrangement of the words on the page, and the words on the page arranged identically with what you want to say and how you want to say it, was like a revelation of absolute common sense in my entire universe of complete bullshit.[4]

Ginsberg literally learned to speak as a poet from Williams, and his poems in *Empty Mirror,* published with Williams's foreword, attest to his amalgamation of Williams's lessons. But there is also another aspect to be noted there: Ginsberg is not proposing to merely reproduce faithfully what he observes; he aims at an imaginative transfusion of things, as can be seen in "A Poem on America." In this poem a seemingly photographic reproduction of industrial desolation is juxtaposed to an image from Dostoevski's *The Possessed*.* The effect is not quite ideo-grammic, for the poem begins with a "conclusion of fact," as Reznikoff would say, which in fact it would be the reader's task to arrive at after having meditated on the sequence of particulars. But the absence of logical connection between the lines "and dreamed of classical pictures" and "The alleys, the dye works" is an indication that Ginsberg was already on the lookout for nonlogical modes of poetic expression.

In the early 1950s the influences multiplied. Most important among them, pertaining to form, were Whitman, Kerouac, and the Japanese haiku. After having experimented with Williams's terse line patterns, Ginsberg turned his attention to the problem of how to sustain a long line in poetry without lapsing into prose. The example was Whitman's long line, ignored for more than a century as an uncontrolled and uncontrollable prosaic outpouring, and Ginsberg saw its potential as a vehicle that could carry his own "Hebraic-Melvillian bardic breath"—the kind of total expression he wanted to put in poetic form. Ginsberg's fastening on Whitman's line as a valid precedent was precipitated by the realization that his speech, his "breath," was different from Williams's; it was longer, more ecstatic and excit-ed. Interestingly, breath length as organizer of the line came to him not from Olson but from Kerouac, who in turn was influ-enced by jazz musicians, particularly saxophone players like Lester Young and Charlie Parker. As Kerouac noted, the sax-ophone player, especially when improvising, is "drawing in a breath and blowing a phrase on his saxophone, till he runs out of breath, and when he does, his sentence, his statement's been made."[5] Similarly, Ginsberg's long lines in "Howl" and his other poems written in the middle and late fifties were organized according to his long breath, which became the unit for the

---

*Ginsberg says that the image is actually from Dostoevski's "A Raw Youth."— ED.

line—"one physical and mental inspiration of thought contained in the elastic of breath."[6]

But the organization of the long line and breath, the "how" of sustaining it, came from a different source. Shortly before writing "Howl" Ginsberg read R. H. Blyth's collection of haikus and promptly began to compose in that form. He wrote some twenty-odd pieces in a brief period of time, only a few of which are successful. The majority are not strictly haiku but spontaneous juxtapositions, records of Ginsberg's actual flow of mind. The long line, then, is supported by seemingly incongruous, antithetical images:

> It is natural inspiration of the moment that keeps it moving, disparate thinks put down together, shorthand notations of visual imagery, juxtapositions of hydrogen jukebox—abstract *haikus* sustain the mystery and put iron poetry back into the line. . . .[7]

"Hydrogen jukebox" is a memorable image from "Howl," one of several elliptical juxtapositions which Ginsberg crammed into his lines in Part I—such as "stale beer afternoon," "unshaven rooms," "angry fix," and "heterosexual dollar." Just as Whitman's long line was an example of his own long breath, the haiku excited Ginsberg because in it he saw a precedent of his own naturally elliptical habits or patterns of speech. After his experiments with haiku and his own individual use of them in "Howl," he discovered that "all my talk is haiku"; that is, any conversation like "I need a spoon to eat soup" is "bridging Ellipse," filling up the gaps between essential facts with connectives, which he would normally omit from his hurried talk of telescoped, heaped-together perceptions. The study of the "primary forms of ellipse," Ginsberg concluded, is "useful for advancement of practice of western metaphor," toward a kind of "naked haiku" like his "hydrogen jukebox." Ginsberg's conception of "advancement" on metaphor can be seen from his description of his understanding of haiku:

> Haiku = objective images written down outside mind the result is inevitable mind sensation of relations. Never try to

write of relations themselves, just the images which are all that can be written down on the subject.[8]

Ginsberg's phrase is clearly an echo of Fenollosa's "Relations are more important than the things they relate," which may also indicate the direction of his search: from metaphor toward ideogram, or, in his word, the "ellipse."

In feeling his way toward a theory of the ellipse, Ginsberg received corroboration of his experience with haiku from another source: the paintings of Paul Cézanne. As had Williams before him, Ginsberg noticed that in Cézanne's works visual structuring is not based on perspective—"it's just juxtaposition of one color against another color." So the idea came to him that "by the unexplainable, unexplained non-perspective line, that is, juxtaposition of one *word* against another, a *gap* between two words" would be created "which the mind would fill in with the sensation of experience."[9] While many of the ellipses in Part I of "Howl" are ironic in their incongruity (Plotinus, Poe, and St. John of the Cross are mentioned in the same breath with Kansas, Idaho with "visionary indian angels," Baltimore is seen gleaming in "supernatural ecstasy"), the elliptical juxtapositions of Part III are more arcane and the gaps between the images are wider. The rhetorical connectives "I'm with you in Rockland" are a form of parallelism, but they do not logically link up the lines. The images remain as they are, unrelated to one another, and they have relevance because the poet and Solomon are *related*. Ginsberg's imaginative juxtapositions are as condensed as those of Creeley, but of a different order. They are not scrupulous compressions of factual data taken from nature but, as Ginsberg says, "verbal constructions which express the true gaiety & excess of Freedom . . . by means of spontaneous irrational juxtaposition of sublimely related fact."[10] The juxtapositions in the above lines, and in several other places in "Howl," seem to be influenced less by Cézanne than by the method of the surrealists, and not so much the painters as the poets. During his "Howl" period Ginsberg was immersed in surrealist poetry and poetics, and saw Kerouac's advocacy of spontaneity reinforced by the basic tenets of this important European literary movement. Spontaneity corresponded to the surrealists' automatic writing, and Ginsberg's juxtapositions of "hydrogen jukebox," "nitroglycerin shrieks," and "catatonic piano" are reminiscent of Eluard's *"nuit hermaphrodite"* and Breton's *"coqs de roche"* and *"revolver à cheveux blancs."* In "At Apollinaire's Grave" Ginsberg paid homage to the forefather of surrealism and acknowledged its influence:

> I've eaten the blue carrots you sent out of the grave and
>   Van Gogh's ear and maniac peyote of Artaud
> and will walk down the streets of New York in the black
>   cloak of French poetry.

Automatism meant a total disregard for logical and rational ordering of experience, because the experience the surrealists were interested in recording had to do with the inner, not the external, world. This setting a higher value on dreams, reveries, and hallucinations struck a sympathetic chord in Ginsberg because he was also interested in finding a way to re-create the unimpeded flow of his mind, and he experimented with various means of expanding consciousness by drugs, meditation, or mantra chanting. By releasing the forces of the unconscious he was attempting to reach a state of higher consciousness, or cosmic consciousness, an attainment of mystical illumination. Poetry, then, had to deal with the transmission of such spiritual/physical enlightenment, with what Kerouac termed "the unspeakable visions of the individual." The self is the center from which true knowledge is to emanate, and it is not difficult to see that Ginsberg took over from Whitman much more than the long line. Whitman had put his faith in the supremacy of the self, and poetry for him could not be anything else but "the outcropping of my own emotional and other personal nature, an attempt, from first to last, to put a *Person,* a human being (myself, in the latter half of the Nineteenth Century, in America) freely, fully, and truly on record."[11] Accordingly, Ginsberg saw the poet as prophet and visionary, and however he disordered his consciousness, and by whatever means, the sublime fact remained that it was *his* consciousness, and it was his duty to register its fluctuations.

Such a view of the function of poetry and poet obviously goes against the grain of Poundian modernism and the ideogrammic method proper. It is on these themes, the subjects of self and spontaneity, that the later ideogrammic poets show the greatest divergence from Pound's ideas, or, more precisely, his attitudes vis-à-vis Whitman and surrealism. Pound's ambivalence to Whitman is well known, and so is his coolness toward the surrealists, in spite of some initial enthusiasm. It is also a fact that this champion of all types of avant-garde artists had, in the 1930s and 1940s, begun to view with suspicion the work of even the greatest experimenters, such as James Joyce and Gertrude Stein. Because of his economic, political, and historical preoccupations during that period, Pound simply lost touch with contemporary currents in the arts—hence his oft-repeated lament to Olson during his confinement at St. Elizabeth's: "Thirty years behind the time."[12]

Yet the conceptual basis of surrealism is not markedly different from that of the ideogrammic stream in American poetry, and this accounts in part for the positive attitude of Williams, Duncan, and Ginsberg to the aims of the movement. One of these crucial notions is that the human being is not the apex of being in this, or any other, universe. As Breton put it in *Arcane 17:*

> En tête des erreurs initiales qui nous demeurent les plus préjudiciables figure l'idée que l'univers n'a de sens appréciable que pour l'homme, alors qu'il en manque, par exemple, pour les animaux. L'homme se targue d'être le grand élu de la création.[13]

> [At the top of the old delusions still with us and the most detrimental stands the notion that the universe has appreciable meaning only for man, while lacking any, for example, for animals. Man boasts of being the great elect of creation.]

Small wonder, then, that this essentially antihumanist attitude, coupled with the creative and imaginative freedom afforded by actual poetic practice, made surrealism attractive to Ginsberg.

But it is important to note that Ginsberg did not become a committed or dogmatic surrealist. In his search for a nonlogical, "elliptical" mode of expression, he utilized all possible manifestations of the form, whether found in haiku, Williams,

Cézanne, or surrealism. Like Provence or Fenollosa for Pound, surrealism for Ginsberg had been just one area among many to be "dug up" and the findings integrated into the large process of discovering form, *his* form. And while his affinity to Whitman was genuine and pervasive, his beliefs in the self and the importance of the poetic personality were never held exclusive of other ideas. They were in fact continually complemented and balanced by his own brand of "sincerity and objectification," his concern for perceptual detail *outside* the subjective consciousness—the space of America and the material world. Ginsberg's poetics can actually be seen as an attempt at synthesis, at unifying the divergent traditions of American poetry, what Roy Harvey Pearce termed "Adamic" and "mythic." It is through the ellipse, his personal variant of the ideogrammic method, that Ginsberg sought to integrate self and space in a unified theory.

Absorbing and benefiting from the variety of nontransitional methods, Ginsberg in the 1960s arrived at his own poetics. He put them to use in an open sequence, begun in the volume *Planet News* and continued in *The Fall of America*. Ginsberg came to the realization that the mind is not all-powerful; it did not invent the world, but in fact it owes its being *to* the world. But by this same token the flow of consciousness cannot be essentially different from nature's flow, and if consciousness is permitted to stream forth unobstructed, it will realize both itself and the cosmos. Poetry, therefore, fulfills its function if it re-creates the mind's movement, which is no longer a law unto itself but a counterpart of the larger mind of nature. Poetry, Ginsberg affirmed, is "a Composition of Elements," the elements being discrete words, and words are "solid objects"; in the same way, "life itself is a composition of elements outside words." The mind does not think in rigid patterns, so artificial forms in poetry cannot be justified. "We think in blocks of sensation & images," said Ginsberg. Ginsberg's oft-quoted axiom follows from this: "IF THE POET'S MIND IS SHAPELY, HIS ART WILL BE SHAPELY." He goes on to explain that "the page will have an original but rhythmic shape—inevitable thought to inevitable thought, lines dropping inevitably on the page, making subtle infinitely varied rhythmic SHAPE."[14] Ginsberg does not elucidate further what he means by a "shapely" mind. One could perhaps say that in a dream or in a drug-induced state the mind still has a "shape," though quite different from the one it has when its attention is fastened on the particulars of the world. Shut off from the world, the mind feeds on itself, on its accumulated bits of reality which it rearranges just as subjectively as the purely rational mind does: both reorder the world in their own image. Ginsberg in his syncretic theory attempts to avoid the pitfalls of either. He does not relegate poetry to a kind of substitute therapy, and whatever evidence of such use there may have been in "Howl" and "Kaddish," they are definitely not present in his long poem, *The Fall of America*. The mind acquires its particular shapeliness in that sequence from the variegated shapes and turns and breaks of American reality, both spatial and temporal, and from its own relation to that space-time entity, a relation which is not just physical but moral as well. The form arises from this relationship; it is an open, ideogrammic, or projective form, the basis of which Ginsberg clarified for himself well before he started writing the poem, during his trip to India. This basic statement on form he put down in *Indian Journals:*

Interest in the awkwardness
               accidents
               rhythm
jump of perception from one thing to another breaking
               syntactical order
               punctuation order
               logical orders
               old narrative order
               meaning order.
Notations of process of mind
               & relative natural process
               Uncensored by
                    grammar
                    syntax
                    order
because these Conventions
               we find not a
               rational ordering of
                    experience

```
                    but an attempt to
                            censor experience
        & keep out certain
                    facts which embarrass
        & throw doubt on
                    whole of previously
                    accepted
                    Human
                    Humanistic
                    rational
        Reality.15
```

The poem is thus a union of "mind flow" and the *relative* natural process, "with space jumps to indicate gaps & relationships." *The Fall of America,* subtitled "Poems of These States," is not the record of a mental trip, but of actual crisscrossings of the entire continent. In these poems Ginsberg goes beyond the "hydrogen jukebox" type of elliptical juxtaposition. As in *The Cantos* and *Paterson,* larger blocks of material, ostensibly unrelated, are placed side by side to enact the complex reality of America.

Ginsberg had read some of Pound's poetry before embarking on his long journey, and, as he later said, for his own elliptical method he was "drawing from Pound's discovery and interpretation of Chinese," both through Williams and Pound himself. During a side trip to Europe in 1967 he visited Pound and spent several days with the aged poet, who was already sunk in a deep depression and a silence he rarely broke. Ginsberg was undaunted, however, and told Pound that his perceptions had been "strengthened by the series of practical exact language models scattered through *The Cantos* like stepping stones."16 His own long poem, which he continued with renewed vigor after his meeting with Pound, is an epic in the vein of *The Cantos,* "a poem containing history," of which Ginsberg was already conscious in 1967. He had said in an earlier interview that in the fabric of his poem he wanted to include

all contemporary history, newspaper headlines and all the pop art of Stalinism and Hitler and Johnson and Kennedy and

Vietnam and Congo and Lumumba and South Africa and Sacco and Vanzetti—whatever floated into one's personal field of consciousness and contact. And then compose like a basket—like weave a basket, basket-weaving out of all those materials.[17]

In order to be even more faithful to "mind-flow," Ginsberg in some of the poems composed directly and spontaneously not on the typewriter but on the tape recorder, signaling the end of a breath-perception unit with a click on the microphone for transcription of the poem onto the page. The "basket-weaving" is the abrupt juxtaposition of (1) perceptions—newspaper and radio reports put down either verbatim or compacted by Ginsberg; (2) related mental associations—memories and spontaneous responses answering or advancing the external material; (3) observational detail of immediate happenings during the journey, to fix the floating of the mind to the actuality and specificity of space. The various elliptical passages make up incidental, not consciously preplanned ideograms or groups of related units around a central theme and place which touch and overlap in the manner of Williams's juxtapositions in *Paterson*. Yet Ginsberg did not abandon his compressed elliptical juxtapositions of seemingly incompatible material, particularly adjective-noun pairs or series of adjectives. But instead of simply baffling the reader's mind, these juxtapositions are now made to function like sudden electrical discharges, jolting the mind to grasp relations where there seemed to be none before, or which were obscure until Ginsberg's projective act illuminated them.

In "Wichita Vortex Sutra," perhaps the most important among the "Poems of These States," the second part is a huge ideogram of language, its use and abuse in America during the Vietnam war. It begins with Ginsberg's sitting in the car, as it moves through the bleak winter scenery of the Kansas prairie, and taking down images of the passing landscape. These images are interspersed with his running commentary on the language of government dispatches, television news reports, magazine articles, and the declarations of the president, senators, and generals. Certain elements are repeated, at times rhythmically, at other times unexpectedly, in a new and different context. One such recurring element is Defense Secretary McNamara's "bad guess" as to who the *real* enemy is in Vietnam.

The other fact which reappears in various places in the poem is the number of Viet Cong losses per month as announced by the U.S. government. Ginsberg first presents it in the context of the manipulated media:

> Put it this way on the radio
> Put it this way in television language
> > > Use the words
> > > > language language:
> > > > > "A bad guess"
>
> . . . .
> Put it *this* way
> > > Declared McNamara   speaking language
> > > Asserted Maxwell Taylor
> > General, Consultant to the White House
> Vietcong losses leveling up three five zero zero
> > > > per month
>
> . . . .
> > > the latest quotation in the human meat market—
> > > > Father I cannot tell a lie!

Set among the other headlines, General Taylor's assertion is just another piece of news, but this added unit is not merely cumulative or contrastive—it is both. Washington's apocryphal statement at the end of the section is at once ironic and antithetical to the previous linguistic abuse, and it is also Ginsberg's own declaration of poetic truth-telling. By inference it is he who carries on and embodies the ideals of the founding fathers. The "father" he calls on, though, is not Washington, but Whitman, the author of *Democratic Vistas,* the "national expresser" of "adhesiveness," of "fervid comradeship." (The epigraph to *The Fall of America* is an extended quotation from *Democratic Vistas.*)

Washington's words are later echoed by the seemingly unequivocal statement of another president: "We will negotiate anywhere anytime," to which Ginsberg juxtaposes a newspaper report based on an Associated Press dispatch to the effect that the

Americans do not encourage the South Vietnamese to negotiate with the Viet Cong. "The last week's paper is Amnesia," comments Ginsberg, and in contrast to the mendacities and travesties of language he builds another section containing a different regard for language:

> Headline language poetry, nine decades after Democratic Vistas
> and the prophecy of the Good Grey Poet
> . . . .
> Ezra Pound the Chinese Written Character for truth
> defined as man standing by his word. . . .

Whitman, Pound, Fenollosa, and the Chinese word for truth are Ginsberg's "ideogram of the good," which is "different from a bad guess," the "black magic" of the manipulators and distorters of language. The intrusion of the line, "Ham Steak please waitress," has a double-edged quality. It serves to pinpoint the actual circumstance, the "space" where the poet "lives" his imaginative particulars. But it is also a reminder of Ginsberg's position in the larger framework of American reality: he, the Buddhist, the advocate of vegetarianism, is caught up in the world-wide slaughter and eats not merely meat but, as he knows, the flesh of once-alive fellow creatures. In spite of his heightened moral sense he is not above the flow of the present, of the space and time of history. He is in it and of it, exerting his poetic force in the force field of language.

Ginsberg's synthesizing act in language enacts the parallel progress of individual consciousness and universal consciousness through the method of the ellipse. He knows that elliptical or paratactic composition is not an enemy of continuity but in fact a *real* way in which the ongoing process can be re-created and revealed. The contingent aspect of elliptical poetry, as in the Homeric and all other archaic poems, is its oral dimension, and one of Ginsberg's preoccupations has always been to bring to fruition Pound's ideas about the unity of words and music. Most of the ideogrammic poetry is written for the human voice and not for the eye, for silent reading. But Ginsberg's lines, as they come fully formed by his own voice during oral composition, are made to be chanted and even sung. In his work subsequent to *The Fall of America,* he has even experimented with writing songs, mainly influenced by the blues and Bob Dylan's compositions. With Ginsberg's poetics and oral-elliptical method the ancient art of poetry comes full circle. His works are at once the synthesis of ideogrammic modernism and Whitman's heritage, and a revival of the archaic oral tradition within the context of authentic, modern poetic expression. . . .

NOTES

1. Allen Ginsberg, *Allen Verbatim: Lectures on Poetry, Politics, Consciousness,* ed. Gordon Ball (New York: McGraw-Hill, 1974), p. 139.

2. Ibid., p. 141.

3. Ginsberg, "A Talk with Allen Ginsberg," with Alison Colbert, *Partisan Review* 38 (1971):295–96.

4. Ginsberg, *Allen Verbatim,* pp. 144–45.

5. Jack Kerouac, "Interview," with Ted Berrigan, *Paris Review,* no. 43 (Summer 1968):83.

6. Ginsberg, "Notes for *Howl and Other Poems,*" album cover, Fantasy Records 7013.

7. Ibid.

8. Ginsberg, *Journals, Early Fifties Early Sixties,* edited by Gordon Ball (New York: Grove Press, 1977), p. 95.

9. Ginsberg, "Interview," *Paris Review,* no. 37 (Spring 1966):28–29.

10. Quoted by Stephen Stepanchev, *American Poetry Since 1945* (New York: Harper & Row, 1965), p. 133. Ginsberg distinguishes sharply between closed form and spontaneous composition: "The difference is between someone sitting down to write a poem *in* a definite preconceived metrical pattern and filling in that pattern, and someone working with his physiological movements and *arriving* at a pattern, . . . arriving at it organically rather than synthetically" ("Interview," *Paris Review,* no. 37 [Spring 1966], pp. 15–16).

11. Walt Whitman, "Backward Glance O'er Travel'd Roads," *Leaves of Grass* (N.Y.: New York University Press, 1965), pp. 573–74.

12. See Olson, *Charles Olson and Ezra Pound* (N.Y.: Grossman, 1975), p. 97.

13. André Breton, *Arcane 17* (1947; reprinted Paris: Collection 10/18, 1975), p. 37.

14. Ginsberg, *Indian Journals* (San Francisco: City Lights Books, 1970), p. 41.

15. Ibid., pp. 93–94.

16. Quoted in Michael Reck, "A Conversation between Ezra Pound and Allen Ginsberg," *Evergreen Review,* no. 55 (June 1968):29.

17. Ginsberg, "Interview," *Paris Review,* no. 37 (Spring 1966):30.

CHARLES MOLESWORTH

Public Events, Private Musings

Robert Lowell and Allen Ginsberg, arguably the best poets of their generation, have perhaps succeeded most notably in surviving their own publicity. They have been able to write good poetry for thirty years in part because the publicity that surrounded them was generated by others who were quick to attend not so much to talent as to popularity. Lowell and Ginsberg became well known in different ways, of course, but both ways grew out of their talents for an endless, often *driven* form of speaking that at one and the same time clarified itself and grew more inclusive of the historical complexity it recorded. This speaking—one often thinks of both poets as "commentators"— has a confessional cast to it, and both men have made the private order into public occasion more than once. But their fullest voices were achieved through their ability to make the public events they often deplored into something like private musings. . . .

Ginsberg's poetry has developed out of an aesthetic of immediacy and produced a snytax that mediates between a flat, uniform perception and a swirling, flashing registry of states of consciousness in which perceptions are constantly disarranged, even deranged, by fissures or leaps in awareness. Ginsberg's poetry often reads like a conscious mix of newspaper headlines (the ephemeral cast into the forms of "mass production," made at once striking and easily assimilable) and tape recordings (the simultaneous made into circuitry, the moment wrapped into a continuous spool, the mind spun into a paranoid Möbius strip). Such a poetry relies more on paratactical orderings than on any-

Reprinted from "Republican Objects and Utopian Moments: The Poetry of Robert Lowell and Allen Ginsberg," in *The Fierce Embrace,* by permission of the University of Missouri Press. Copyright 1979 by the Curators of the University of Missouri.

thing like a recognizably ordered syntax. This parataxis, this parallel placing of "notations," resembles a litany, of course; and Ginsberg's public reading voice is an extremely pleasurable instrument that at its best seems to partake of the structural complexity of an Eastern raga and the improvisational push of jazz. This language, at its fullest in a poem like "Wichita Vortex Sutra," needs a voice analogous to the field of vision in a hallucinatory state: constantly changing, yet made continuous by a dampening of tone or affect, loosely attentive yet not so alert as to become self-seeking, trusing in the absence of structure in the short run to vindicate a larger, more inclusive ordering. Ginsberg's language always includes, but is seldom conclusive. The end of things, in a temporal or chronological sense, gets indefinitely postponed lest it disrupt or betray the end, the goal, or telos, in the messianic sense. The notion of a sentence as a "complete idea" makes the sentence a foreign substance in Ginsberg's poetry; almost all sentences are made or spoken by the enemy, namely, the government in all its various duplicitous forms. Hallucination and the posthallucinatory moment both share a privileged status, since either can yield a perception just beyond the borders of established or official reality. Ginsberg's lyric shaping often begins with a chanting, meditative flattening out of the daily order, an unwinding of the logical mind's coils of expended pressure. His poems then often end with an anagogic leap, a sudden breakthrough of new awareness; less often, but perhaps more movingly, they end with a breakdown in the sustaining vision of things, a rupture in the cohesive will to love and observe without violence or force. The apocalyptic is clearly as much a source of dread for Ginsberg as it is a point of triumphant release or vindication. The nonordering, nonsubjugating syntax results finally from a deep, underlying sense that the outcome is still in doubt. The victories of order are either false or momentary, and this makes Ginsberg's language kaleidoscopic, fitful, even perfervid, whether it is busily celebrating or warily cautioning. The period is for Ginsberg only a breathing space. . . .

From the beginning of his career, Ginsberg has constructed a poetry made up of a special blend of two voices: one, a putatively universal voice that would claim implicitly of its lonesomeness that "it's Ours"; the other, a frankly personal voice that insistently chronicled the growth and movement of a discrete, historically singular people. As the mores and life-styles of his affinity group came closer to the "mainstream" of American manners, or perhaps vice versa, since the early beatnik-hipster was eventually taken up by a later generation as an unspectacular, matter-of-fact alternative, Ginsberg's prophecy was fulfilled in all but the more meaningful ways. When drugs and drifting became almost commonplace, Ginsberg's daring use of these subjects in his defiant appropriation of a prophetic voice lost its force. This threw Ginsberg's poetry back onto its personalist voice, and concurrently his earlier technical breakthroughs and his insistence on a body-centered mysticism were being diversely adopted by other poets. We cannot say of Ginsberg what Auden said of Freud, that he became a climate of opinion, but what began as daring and distinctive had by the early 1970s become so widely assimilated as to be barely distinguishable. All the while, the "materialistic and vulgar" aspects of American life continued to exercise the fascination of the abominable.

In *The Fall of America*, we're told at one point that "grey twilight falls on rolling robotland," and it's as if Ginsberg's dedication to a poetry "composed directly on tape by voice, and then transcribed to page," has shaped his subjects and his attitude into this bleakly nontranscendent mood. At its weakest, Ginsberg's music has become the victim of its instruments.

The climactic moment in "Wichita Vortex Sutra" comes when the poet says,

I lift my voice aloud,
	make Mantra of American language now,
		pronounce the words beginning my own millennium,
			I here declare the end of the War!
				Ancient days' Illusion!

It stands as a moment of poetic daring, an attempt to use the words of the language for their proper ends of communication and community, rather than for deceit and destruction. But in the roll call of deities that precedes this climactic moment, the names Ginsberg invokes are drawn predominantly from Eastern religion. It is hard to transplant Krishna and Shiva to Wichita, Kansas, as Ginsberg must surely know; the only way to "rectify" the geography is to correct the temporal order. But the putative start of a new millennium is cast in personal terms; as long as Ginsberg is forced, either by poetic "logic" or by a greater awareness to say "my" millennium, the poem must remain lyric rather than prophetical. . . .

PAUL CARROLL

"I Lift My Voice Aloud, / Make Mantra of American Language Now . . . / I Here Declare the End of the War!"

Is "Wichita Vortex Sutra" a major American poem? The great act of imagination at the core of this long work seems to demand that the reader consider the poem either as a notable and even monumental achievement or as a roaring and pretentious failure. Either this poem is incandescent in that Allen Ginsberg succeeds in assuming the role of poet as priestly legislator and as Baptist of a mantra whose dispensation brings peace and love or it is opaque in that he fails to become little more than mock creator of a harangue whose dispensation brings bad rhetoric and banality.

This is of course relentlessly univocal. Yet the poem demands such univocal judgment due to the sheer heroism and daring of its declared intention. With admirable sincerity and making no bones about it, Ginsberg attempts to assume the role called for by Shelley in the celebrated if somewhat petulant assertion that poets are "the unacknowledged legislators of the world." Ginsberg assumes this role when he attempts to legislate by declaring the end of hostilities in Vietnam in these astonishing lines which occur about two-thirds of the way through the poem:

From *The Poem in Its Skin* (Chicago: Big Table, 1969). Reprinted with permission.

I lift my voice aloud,
      make Mantra of American language now,
            pronounce the words beginning my own millennium,
                        I here declare the end of the War!
                              Ancient days' Illusion!
Let the States tremble,
      let the Nation weep,
            let Congress legislate its own delight
                        let the President execute his own desire—
this Act done by my own voice,
                        nameless Mystery—

What makes this assertion so original is the means by which
Ginsberg strives to give validity and authority to his act of legis-
lation: he declares the end of the war by making a mantra. More
specifically, it is a mantra of the American language. The central
implication seems clear. If the mantra of the American language
"works," then it should be able in some vigorous, magical or
religious way to end the slaughter in Vietnam. But first, what
exactly is a mantra?

The dictionary explains that mantra comes from the Sanskrit
term for sacred formula or counsel and defines it as "a mystical
formula or invocation or incantation in Hinduism or Mahayana
Buddhism"; but since I am ignorant about Eastern religions, I
asked Ginsberg if he would explain his understanding of mantra,
as well as to indentify some of the important but obscure allu-
sions to Hindu or Buddhist mysticism—for example, the litany
of gurus, swamis, yogis, saints and demigods whom he invokes
in the section beginning: "I call all Powers of imagination / to
my side in this auto to make Prophecy. . . ." In August 1966,
the poet generously replied in the form of a letter and notes
written in the margins of a xerox copy of the poem. Here is
Ginsberg's definition of mantra: "a short magic formula usually
invoking an aspect of the Divine, usually given as meditation
exercise by guru to student, sometimes sung in community or
'kirtan'—the formula is considered to be identical with the god
named, and have inevitable power attached to its pronunciation.
Oft used in chanting or invocation."

The mantra made in "Wichita Vortex Sutra," then, seems to consist of three parts. First, there is the litany beginning "I call all Powers of imagination," invoking the holy men, demigods and gods from whom the poet asks assistance in the making of his mantra. Then there is the creation of the mantra itself: "I lift my voice aloud, / make mantra of American language now. . . ." Finally, the mantra is put to work as the poet announces his act of declaring the end of the war and then pronounces benediction on the United States, Congress and President Johnson; and then as part of the mantra he ritualistically enumerates the five "leaps" or "skandas"—the areas of apportionment of consciousness mentioned in the Buddhist Sutras: the liberation of his own form, sensations, thought, imagination, and "all realms within my consciousness."

The intention of the mantra is heroic and ambitious. If it works, it functions as a magic formula whose power can end the war and also as the formula which invokes that which is eternal and divine and free in the poet himself, as well as that which is holy and free in the members of Congress and in the president. Clearly here is one of the supreme moments of imagination in American poetry. There has been nothing to equal its grandeur, it seems to me, since Whitman's "Passage to India."

What is impressive about this mantra is that it isn't merely a Hindu or Buddhist prayer for peace and for the liberation of the holy in the poet and in his fellow Americans. Instead, Ginsberg attempts to make a mantra out of the American language itself. What exactly could this mean? The poet explains in his reply to my original letter in which I mentioned that I'd been thinking of his poem as fulfilling Shelley's assertion that poets are the unacknowledged legislators of the world: "Not *only* a question of legislator as Shelley's formula. Merely that the war has been created by language . . . & Poet can dismantle the language consciousness conditioned to war reflexes by setting up (mantra) absolute contrary field of will as expressed in language. By expressing, manifesting, his DESIRE (BHAKTI in yoga terminology—'adoration')."

Here, then, is the dramatic and crucial tension created by the making of the mantra: the poet expresses his desire for peace and the liberation of the divine and free in himself and his countrymen by creating a mantra made with American words; but the mantra will succeed in bringing peace and liberating the holy and free in Americans only if its language can oppose and finally dismantle the corrupt and evil language which has conditioned the American people to "war reflexes"—the corrupt and evil language which (according to the poet) created and sustains the current Vietnam war. In brief, the mantra is one of true or beatific language; its job is to dissipate and annihilate the slaughter and moral barbarism created by false or evil language. In this sense, "Wichita Vortex Sutra" is primarily a poem embodying an experience of contemporary American language and what that language can or cannot accomplish.

When read in the light of this tension between false and true language, the poem divides into three parts. The first section is the longest, containing five stanzas of some 365 lines, all of which document in one way or another aspects of the false and evil language which created and sustains the Vietnam war. The second section, beginning with the stanza "I call all Powers of imagination / to my side in this auto to make Prophecy . . ." depicts in some 50 lines the creation of the mantra. The final section opens in "the chill earthly mist" sixty miles from Wichita and contains some 130 lines in two stanzas in which the mantra of true language is put to work in opposing the false words of the first section.

Let us look at some of the outstanding examples of the false and evil use of the American language in the first section and attempt to see how such perverted uses drive the poet to declare: "The war is language, / language abused / for Advertisement, / language used / like magic for power on the planet: / Black Magic language, / formulas for reality . . ."

At the very beginning of the poem, the poet encounters an example of black magic language as he hears the voice of Senator Aiken [Republican, Vermont] on the interview program "Face the Nation" coming over the radio in his Volkswagen driving on a Sunday morning in February 1966 past Hickman, Nebraska, along Route 77, bound south for Wichita. The Senator claims that Secretary of Defense McNamara made "no more than a Bad Guess" when he predicted in 1962 that only "8000 American Troops [could] handle the / Situation." Here are at

least two examples of misused or twisted "formulas for reality."
By calling McNamara's miscalculation only a bad guess, the
Senator distorts what that miscalculation in all events actually
was: namely, a calculated sop thrown to pacify the American
people and soften or quiet whatever moral opposition they may
have felt against our involvement in Vietnam, as well as a sop to
mollify whatever objection they might feel in the near future to
the increasing escalation of aggression by American pilots
against Viet Cong troops and civilian villages. What makes the
Senator's description false is that the Secretary of Defense might
possibly have known in 1962 that America would increase its
"commitment" and aggression on the large scale that it actually
did.

A minor but equally false perversion of language occurs when
Senator Aiken describes the war as "the Situation." To call
napalm bombing, machine-gunning and destruction of helpless
villages by United States pilots—not to speak of the massacre of
our own soldiers by the Viet Cong—a "situation" is precisely
that kind of official gobbledygook which refuses to call an event
by its correct name (however ugly that name is) and by so
refusing only helps to blunt moral perceptions of what that real-
ity might be. Bombing with intent to destory and kill, intricate
tactical strategies, abortive attempts to negotiate peace, and
swelling rosters of dead or wounded on both sides: this is not a
"situation": this is war.

Other examples of perverted use of words bombard the poet
as he reads newspaper headlines. "Rusk Says Toughness Essen-
tial for Peace" declares the *Omaha World Herald*. Toughness?
What's accomplished by the use of this virile noun? Such a word
only flatters a nation's image of itself and helps to dissipate what-
ever reservations Americans may have about the morality of our
slaughtering in Vietnam by conjuring the image of the American
as Wild West hero who refuses to let anybody push him around
or make a sissy out of him. What the use of the word tends to
ignore or varnish over is the moral reality: What right do Ameri-
cans have to act "tough" with Oriental peasants who are fight-
ing for what is, after all, their own country? Thirty years ago, a
German newspaper could have said: "Hitler Says Toughness
Essential for Final Solution"—meaning the extermination of

countless Jews who were in no rational or legal sense enemies of the Third Reich. Then there's the headline: "Vietnam War Brings Prosperity." Here the perversion exists in the word "prosperity." By claiming that the war brings prosperity, the headline implies that the aggression is not only reasonable and valuable but condoned by the god of capitalism. No sensible man denies that prosperity is a good thing; but the use of the word here blunts the vital issue: Prosperity at what moral cost? Antebellum slavery brought prosperity to Southern planters and to the entire economy of the South. Barbaric working conditions and immoral wages brought prosperity to owners of Chicago meat packing houses and New England textile mills in the late nineteenth century. And so on.

Examples of perverted black magic language heard over the radio or read in the newspapers continue to assault the poet throughout the long first section of the poem as he comes to know how persuasive and corrupting the perversion has become. One example is the old misuse of the word "Communism" to encourage a growing "war reflex" both in American statesmen and military men and in the citizens as a body. While eating ham steak in the warm cafe, the poet broods how "Communism is a 9 letter word / used by inferior magicians" and funky warlocks which resulted in the "Communion of bum magicians / congress of failures from Kansas & Missouri / working with the wrong equations / Sorcerer's Apprentices who lost control / of the simplest broomstick in the world: / Language . . ." whose perversion may erupt in the "deluge of radiation" flooding the living rooms of America.

Nor is the black magic language limited only to the present. In one of the most memorable passages in the poem, Ginsberg recalls an episode of the perversion of the Word which occurred in 1956 when President Eisenhower "knelt to take / the magic wafer in his mouth / from Dulles' hand / inside the church in Washington . . ." Here the "magic" communion wafer given by Dulles (acting as lay presbyter) seems to symbolize all of the abuses and perversions of the American language: it is the Word abused. Presumably the wafer represents the false advice given by the then Secretary of State that America should continue its involvement in the Vietnam civil war, although on strictly moral grounds this country had no justification whatsoever for its increasingly active participation in that Asian conflict.

Misuses of language also occur in the examples from mass communication (symbolized by the almost comic monster NBCBSUPAPINSLIFE) and from the advertising industry. Not only does "Time Mutual" present the "World's Largest Camp Comedy" by turning the Vietnam reality inside out but the poet also notices the pathetic but droll misuse of words by advertising companies. One billboard informs him that his generation is not the Lost Generation or the Generation of 1776 or the one of Manifest Destiny: it is "the Pepsi Generation"; another billboard tells him how Marines are "in love" with a local bread made by a Pop Art icon called Aunt Betty.

On a more profound level, one also notices how the poet himself suffers from the abuses done to the American language by fork-tongued politicians, hysterical columnists, mass media and by those Barnums of exaggerated and phony language—the gentlemen of advertising. What could be more trite, flat and prosaic, for example, than his own description of the Nebraska landscape: "icy winter / grey sky   bare trees lining the road / South to Wichita"? Here is an ultimate indignity created by false language: it leaves a contemporary American poet with only shabby equipment with which to try to do his job. Even his grasping at those masters of the spoken American idiom—Walt Whitman and Ezra Pound—as possible antibiotics to counteract the infections in our language turns into a buffoon episode in which the only words Ginsberg has are: "Ham Steak please waitress."

What do all of these examples of perverted black magic language add up to? The poet tells us clearly in the desperate passage quoted a moment ago, beginning: "The war is language . . ." All of the perversions of black magic language in the opening section, the passage implies, not only helped to encourage and condone the original involvement of America in the internal affairs of Vietnam but the false, evil idiom helps to perpetuate that involvement by distorting the bald reality that United States troops are engaged in a murderous aggression waged against Oriental peasants who have never threatened or harmed America in any way whatsoever.

Then what must the mantra accomplish? It must oppose and dismantle the "war reflexes" conditioned by the false, evil misuses of the American tongue. How? Through language. Fire must fight fire.

For one thing, the true and beatific language must call events and moral realities by their correct names. And it must accomplish this tough task by embodying a vocabulary which is not only accurate but powerful and *magical* in the profound and mysterious sense of that word. Indeed, this true language must be something like the idiom used by the mystical alchemists of the Middle Ages—those extraordinary men who (as Jung documents in his important study *Psychology and Alchemy* [1953]) were hardly concerned with such trivial, childish goals as discovering how to transform cheap iron or matter into gold; rather, they were striving to create out of gross matter nothing else than the God Incarnate.

The true and beatific language, in short, must be brilliant and memorable enough to create and sustain the "absolute contrary field of will" which alone can cure the moral disease resulting from the false and evil idiom and, by so doing, end the war in Vietnam. The language of the last 180 lines must be the language of great poetry.

Is it?

The language of the creation of the mantra certainly is if not great, then memorable poetry. In strong, vivid and lucid words Ginsberg not only creates the possibility of an original supernatural reality for the American consciousness but he calls for the liberation of the holy and free in himself and in his fellow countrymen. [1]

But what about the language in the stanzas following the making of the mantra? Does it have the ring of great or memorable poetry?

No.

On the contrary, the shocking thing seems to be that the language of the final section of "Wichita Vortex Sutra" sounds much the same if not even worse than the black magic vocabulary of the first section. One hears the same flat, boring descriptions of the landscape, the same type of newspaper headlines, the same Rand-McNally catalogue of Kansas towns and cities, ending with a doggedly accurate map of Wichita streets and the names of office buildings, gas stations, the McConnell Air Force Base and the Lutheran Church of the Redeemer past which the poet's Volkswagen drives, heading for the Hotel Eaton on Douglas Street.

Not only is the language undistinguished and prosy but in several crucial instances the diction disintegrates into bad or flashy rhetoric. Take the section in which Bob Dylan is invoked as an Angel of Glad Tidings. As the Volkswagen speeds past the "endless brown meadows" and the small Kansas town of Burns, the folk-rock singer's voice floats over the radio, singing "Won't you come see me, Queen Jane?" Here is the entire Dylan section:

Oh at last again the radio opens
    blue Invitations!
           Angelic Dylan singing across the nation
                "When all your children start to resent you
                Won't you come see me, Queen Jane?"
    His youthful voice making glad
           the brown endless meadows
    His tenderness penetrating aether,
        soft prayer on the airwaves,
             Language language, and sweet music too
             even unto thee,
                hairy flatness!
             even unto thee
                despairing Burns!

In what sense is Dylan "angelic"? And why does his voice gladden the brown, endless meadows? Why should the town of Burns be in despair? And even if its citizens are suffering from despair, why should Dylan's "soft prayer" and "sweet music" alleviate their unhappy condition? Answers to such questions remain in my mind a total blank: the poem does nothing to clarify them. Instead, it seems to fall back on an adolescent rhetoric in which the mere mention of Dylan and the epithet "angelic" are supposed to persuade the reader that here is an angel of language who embodies the true and beatific American idiom which puts to rout the effects of the earlier language of black magic. Even worse: Burns is in despair presumably because its small-town natives are writhing in unhappiness (the reader is encouraged to imply) because they don't hear Dylan often enough. Unfortunately, the melancholy effect of such rhetoric is to make the reader suspect that such writing is no better in kind than the rhetoric of Senator Aiken and the copy writer who describes the "love" of Marines for Aunt Betty's loaves of bread.

An even more glaring example of bad rhetoric occurs in the (by now) celebrated final lines:

> The war is over now—
>> Except for the souls
>>> held prisoner in Niggertown
> still pining for love of your tender white bodies O children of
>> Wichita!

Even if one understands children here in the metaphysical sense which translates into "white citizens," one doubts if it is their bodies for which the ghetto Negro pines: it is more likely their necks. In a less melodramatic sense, it's neither white bodies (the hoary Caucasian fantasy that black men possess magical sexuality which if not castrated will lure white females away forever) nor white necks for which most Negroes "pine": rather, it's the more mundane opportunity to obtain and earn the jobs, prestige and buying power taken for granted by the majority of whites. Here I'm not interested in the compassion of Allen Ginsberg (he clearly is the speaker in the poem) for the American Negro; I am concerned with why the concluding lines disintegrate into piously liberal but sentimental rhetoric. Nothing in the body of the poem justifies the switch from Vietnam to the Negro Revolution. Even less organic is the creation of the figure of the Loving Negro.

Notice that until these lines the poem hasn't once mentioned civil rights or the Negro Revolution. Then why does the speaker switch horses, as it were, in midstream? To argue that, after all, both the Vietnam conflict and the Black Revolution are both "wars" and that the victims of both are victims of White American aggression and that the poet here attempts to end all types of war and aggression: this is pious liberal sentiment which has nothing to do with this poem as a poem. What the sudden and unprepared introduction of the loving Negroes of Wichita accomplishes, on the other hand, is to create the nagging suspicion that the speaker himself feels his mantra has failed, despite his assertion that "the war is over now," and that he tries to gloss over or even to ignore the suspicion of failure by turning to that last resort of the rhetorician: the instant cliché or self-righteous sentimentality. The conjuring of the loving Negroes is part of the same kind of rhetoric one hears from a rhetorician of the John Birch Society who invokes the cartoon of the Pilgrim Father with the White Face or the Henry Ford of Free Enterprise in an argument attempting to annihilate all that is not white or capitalistic or Protestant Christian.

Still a third example of bad rhetoric occurs in the Carry Nation section. The reader is asked to believe that the crusader for temperance—who in the 1890s marched into saloons throughout Kansas to hurl vituperations at the drinkers and smash furniture and fixtures with her hatchet ("hatchetation" of "joints," as she put it)—is responsible for beginning the "vortex of hatred" evident in Wichita today. Moreover, this vortex now defoliates the Mekong Delta and also murdered the poet's mother by driving her insane "one decade long ago." One accepts the existence of the vortex discovered by the poet in the same sense that one accepts the wasteland discovered by Eliot. No reasons exists within "Wichita Vortex Sutra," however, to clarify how Miss Nation created the vortex or why the vortex is responsible either for the war in the Mekong Delta or for the insanity of Mrs. Naomi Ginsberg. (I trust this doesn't sound flippant: I don't intend it to be.) Obviously his mother's insanity is a moving memory for Ginsberg—as the reader may recall from that great elegy "Kaddish"—but he still fails to perform the ancient task of the poet: to render why or how any connection whatsoever exists between her insanity and Carry Nation or between the two women and the current aggression of the United States against the Viet Cong. To feel that the connection should be obvious merely because of the poet's wounded feelings is not enough, in my opinion. Such a reading, in fact, only responds to the sentimental rhetoric of the lines and not to the lack of genuine poetry in them.

And this brings us to a final and perhaps profound issue: Why does the language fail to be great poetry? One approach to a possible answer would be to explore still another question: Does the mantra "work"?

As far as additional news of war is concerned, the mantra seems to be working: we hear only of conflicts which happened a few days or even few hours ago as the poet reads an edition of the *Wichita Eagle-Beacon* of the 100 Viet Cong deaths near Bong Son and how soldiers "charged so desperately they were struck with six or seven bullets / before they fell." And he tells us clearly that he feels the mantra is working because:

> The War is gone,
> > Language emerging on the motel news stand,
> > > the right magic
> > Formula, the language known
> > in the back of the mind before, now in black print
> > > daily consciousness

Even though we hear no more of present conflict, however, there seem to be several more subtle ways in which the poem itself suggests doubts that the mantra is "working" not only in the sense of the cessation of war but also in the sense of releasing the holy and free in both the speaker and in his countrymen. The most obvious of these doubts occurs when we hear what does come over the radio now that there's no more news of war. What the poet hears are the voices of angels.

We've seen how the voice of the first angel—Bob Dylan as the Angel of Glad Tidings—fails in an important way to embody the incandescent language promised by the making of the mantra: his "blue invitation" disintegrates into sentimental rhetoric. Then the poet hears the voices of the Angels of Apocalypse—"Now radio voices cry population hunger world / & unhappy people"—who also prophesy the nativity of the new American Adam who presumably will overcome the Whore of Babylon of Famine and who also seems to fulfill the prophecy made in the first section of the poem: "I claim my birthright! / reborn forever as long as Man / in Kansas or other universe— Joy / reborn after the vast sadness of War Gods!" But the new Adam is parodied and rendered merely comic by the voice of the mock Angel of Advertising which suddenly floats over the air waves with a fragment from a soap commercial: "*you certainly smell good* / the radio says . . ." False or evil language, in short, infects what at first appear to be the healthy voices of the new dispensation made possible by the creation of the mantra.

On still another level, the poem corrodes one's hope that the mantra is working in the sense that it has released the divine and free in the speaker and, by extension, in his countrymen. And that is: it ends in a loneliness or lack of love more exacerbating than the loneliness and hatred which pervades the opening section and which the poet discovers in himself and in his fellows and which he cries out against in the moving stanza beginning: "I'm an old man now, and a lonesome man in Kansas / but not afraid / to speak my lonesomeness in a car, / because not only my lonesomenesss / it's Ours, all over America, / O tender fellows . . ."

Loneliness pervades all of the stanzas leading up to the creation of the mantra. One notices how desolate the loneliness feels in that the Nebraska landscape through which the speaker drives is without people. All one hears are faceless voices. In fact, the only faces seen are in the grotesque photo in *Life* depicting adolescent Marines "blowing the air thru their cheeks with fear." And it is this loneliness which compels the speaker to feel:

All we do is for this frightened thing
        we call Love, want and lack—
    fear that we aren't the one whose body could be
        beloved of all the brides of Kansas City,
        kissed all over by every boy of Wichita—
    O but how many in their solitude weep aloud like me . . .

But is this acute American loneliness and lack of love alleviated by either the making of the mantra or the realities experienced once the mantra begins its dispensation?

At first, it appears that both loneliness and lack of love are dispelled—particularly in the intimacy between poet and the Indian holy men summoned in the litany at the beginning of the creation of the mantra. Notice the vividness of detail in the summoning of the ten saints: "Shambu Bharti Baba naked covered with ash / Khaki Baba fat bellied mad with the dogs / Dehorahava Baba who moans Oh how wounded, How wounded"—and so on. This is the kind of specific, intimate knowledge of another person that only a close friend or lover has. But the reader may also begin to notice a paradox: once the speaker begins to summon the supernatural beings whom the saints worship, the sense of intimacy evaporates. The poet calls on them in increasingly formal and depersonalized epithets: "Allah the Compassionate One / Jaweh Righteous One"—and so on. Here the irony is that the speaker seems to end lonelier than he began.

And the loneliness only becomes more exacerbated as he continues driving toward Wichita. Even voices disappear as he enters Wichita itself and sees only a gas station, factory, supermarket, "crowds of autos moving with their light shine," an insurance company and the De Voors Gurad's funeral home. At the end his only companions are ghosts and faceless abstractions—the ghosts of Carry Nation and his mad mother, and the anonymous souls of Negroes and the bodies of the "children" of Wichita. The poem ends, in truth, in a nightmare vortex of loneliness.

Still a third way in which the poem suggests that the mantra hasn't worked its "right magic / Formula" is in the spiritual vacuum which pervades the final section. As we've seen, the mantra promises a release of the divine in both speaker and fellow countrymen. Instead of continued communion with the gods or an awareness of divinity in Americans, however, the poet sees statues commemorating the only god this country knows: the god of the pragmatic, concrete, materialistic present. It is as if Wichita itself becomes a cathedral filled with "statues" of signs advertising hamburgers and Skelley gas, the Kansas Electric Substation, Texaco, the Lutheran Church, the (felicitously named) Titsworth Insurance Company, the funeral parlor—and so on. And instead of the release of divine energy in Americans, the poet experiences only the re-release of hatred (in the figure of Carry Nation), paranoia (his mother), and racial violence (the Negroes of the ghetto). In short, the concluding stanzas depict a spiritually empty whirlpool, irresistible and cat-astrophic in power, in which the poet suffers the desolation of existence in a nation without gods or spiritual realities.

All of these doubts of the mantra's efficiency raised by the poem contribute to suggest that "Wichita Vortex Sutra" fails to achieve the intention stated by the poet: namely, to dismantle "the language consciousness conditioned to war reflexes by set-ting up (mantra) of absolute contrary field of will as expressed by language."

But does the poem itself fail? The answer might seem ob-vious. If the mantra fails and the language continues to be dis-eased by false or evil idioms, then Ginsberg's act of legislation fails too and obviously the poem itself is a failure.

But such a verdict depends of course on discursive analysis. Such analysis can help to reach an intelligent grasp of some aspects of a poem but it is almost useless if not a hindrance once the reader moves (as he should move) beyond what the poem *appears* to be saying and begins an adventure into the deeper and more obscure areas of the complex of experience which the poem may *in reality* embody.

In short, it should prove valuable to explore: *Why* does the mantra fail?

How could it have succeeded? When we examine the irony created by the meeting of the two equal but separate powers in the final section—the poet as holy man and America as secular nation—it should become clear how and why the mantra must fail.

On the one hand, there's the religious act of the poet as holy man. As priestly legislator, he invokes saints and deities to help in the creation of the mantra; and then as Baptist, he announces the dispensation of the mantra by calling on "Proud Wichita! vain Wichita" to repent of its sin in having sustained the vortex of hatred, and he announces in the composite figure of the Lov-ing Negro and the white "children" of Wichita the advent of the Lamb of peace, love and brotherhood. The Lamb is of course the new American Adam proclaimed earlier by the Angel of Apocalypse. The Baptist arrives in Wichita, in short, to make the prophecy announced in several passages throughout the poem.

But to whom? The America to whom the Baptist speaks is, on the other hand, clearly alien if not hostile ground for such a dispensation and Messiah.

How is America depicted in the poem? As we've seen, it seems a wilderness containing expanses of fields and meadows vacant of people but infested by the voices of "angels" of evil or false language, and containing small towns and the secular cathedral called Wichita—both of which are also empty of people (with the exception of the faceless crowd in Beatrice, Nebraska). In addition, Wichita contains statues commemorating the gods of commerce and technology, as well as a vortex of hatred filled with war reflexes, paranoia and ghettoes.

To think of this America as merely the wilderness surrounding the Jordan, however, would be an understandable but serious error. Notice how the poet himself responds to the alien reality, strength and beauty contained not only in the farmlands of Nebraska and Kansas but also in some of the small towns and in Wichita itself. Rural elegance is acknowledged in lines such as: "A black horse bends its head to the stubble / beside the silver stream winding thru the woods / by an antique red barn on the outskirts of Beatrice— / Quietness, quietness / over this countryside"; and in the view glimpsed through the chill earthly mist of "houseless brown farmland plains rolling heavenward / in every direction." And the excitement of a happening is contained in the haiku of the burning garage in Beatrice: "Water hoses frozen on the street, / Crowd gathered to see a strange happening garage— / Red flames on Sunday morning / in a quiet town!" Wichita too contains elegance and a kind of muscular or existential beauty: the poet responds to its "mysterious families of winking towers" grouped around the quonset hut on the hill, the aluminum robot of the Kansas Electric Substation signalling through thin antennae towers to the solitary derrick that "pumps oil from the unconscious / working day and night," the "green jewelled" traffic lights, the Texaco sign "starred / over streetlamp vertebrae"— and so on.

In short, the America here is the everyday middle class America which in its natural resources, standard of living, and commercial and technological genius is the most prosperous nation men have ever known. The "alien gods" of this country are of course the gods of the practical, existential present. And the implication seems clear, in my opinion, that such gods condone this nation's continued commitment to the South Vietnamese in their civil war with the North for the most obvious reason: it might be most practical to protect this American middle class life by helping to defeat Communism in Vietnam and truncate its potential growth.

The irony, in brief, is this: the Baptist announces the coming of the Lamb in a country which neither desires nor recognizes the authority of such a Messiah.

And the irony cuts of course both ways. As we've seen, the Baptist is himself a distinguished victim of the black magic language which created the vortex of war and hatred he would oppose with the Lamb of peace and brotherhood: the Baptist speaks in the idiom of the New Testament Pharisee and not in the tongue of the Old Testament prophet. And the irony at the expense of middle-class America cuts as deep. The greatest nation in the sense of material prosperity and power the world has known is capable of producing a language which is perhaps among the most barbaric the world has ever heard. Contemporary American language not only conditions "war reflexes" which result in a harvest of slaughter among Oriental peasants but in its banality, its glut of clichés and adolescent vocabulary with which to express complex adult feelings and ideas, this language affords no decent words with which a powerful American poet might express desire for peace and love and brotherhood.

The mantra fails, then, because it couldn't possibly have succeeded. If the mantra had "worked," the poem would have been false. How could the religious act of the poet, which is doomed to expression in language which embodies worship of alien gods, affect that language and what it has created and sustained?

One problem still remains: Does the failure of the mantra contain all of the complex of experience within this poem? What prompts me to raise the question is the heroic quality in the final image of the poet as Baptist.

308

Although the concluding lines with the image of the Loving Negro and the white children contain an ironic example of that false rhetoric which the mantra attempts to oppose, the lines when read from another view also contain genuine poetry. What makes the final lines moving, it seems to me, is the fact that they are spoken at all. Everything opposes this last and almost desperate attempt to make the mantra effective: the poet stands as Baptist crying in a false language in a secular wilderness; yet he refuses to stop his attempt to dismantle the vortex of hatred and death which seems about to envelop him.

In this sense, "Wichita Vortex Sutra" can be read as a poem of noble desire. The desire it embodies is the ancient one: that the Lamb of God come among this people, bringing peace, love and salvation. This desire not only seems to inspire the creation of the mantra in the first place but also encourages the poet to continue trying to build a Jerusalem of peace and brotherhood in the teeth of such a hostile or indifferent environment. In a striking sense, this is the same desire which we have heard in Blake's famous lines from "Milton":

> And did those feet in ancient time
> Walk upon England's mountains green?
> And was the holy Lamb of God
> On England's pleasant pastures seen?
>
> And did the Countenance Divine
> Shine forth upon our clouded hills?
> And was Jerusalem builded here
> Among these dark Satanic Mills?
>
> Bring me my bow of burning gold!
> Bring me my arrows of desire!
> Bring me my spear! O clouds, unfold!
> Bring me my chariot of fire!
>
> I will not cease from mental fight,
> Nor shall my sword sleep in my hand,
> Till we have built Jerusalem
> In England's green and pleasant land.

Finally, the nobility of the desire of the poet who refuses to cease from mental fight accounts, it seems to me, for some of the memorable passages throughout the poem which in their intensity and magnanimity seem unequalled by any American poet since Whitman.

Reread that passage on United States Foreign Policy, for instance, which occurs a little over half way through the second section as the Volkswagen nears Marysville, Kansas, beginning: "Is this the land that started war on China?" and ending with the indictment of the Dulles law firm for the alleged greed which prompted its support of the overthrow in 1954 of the Guzmán regime in Guatemala which had favored agrarian reform and encouraged Communists to hold key posts in government. Then there's the section depicting the Human Mystical Body which begins as the station wagon passes through Waterville, Kansas and which ends: "When a woman's heart bursts in Waterville / a woman screams equal in Hanoi." Or take the Loneliness of Americans section (which some might censure for its sentimentality but which I find genuine poetry because of the incandescence of the desire) which opens with the confession: "I'm an old man now, and a lonesome man in Kansas" and continues with the meditation on God the Creator and concludes with the poet searching for the language "that is also yours."

In the light of such passages embodying Ginsberg's desire for peace and brotherhood, we should reread the Indictment of Wichita section, beginning with the entrance of the Volkswagen into the "Centertown ganglion" and ending with the final exhortation to the children of Wichita. When seen in the broader context of the poem as statement of desire, this section no longer seems, in my opinion, as rhetorical or sentimental as it once did. Now it blazes with compassion.

When the entire poem is seen as being a statement of desire, it seems irrelevant to circumscribe our critical appreciation by such questions as: Does the mantra fail? or Is this an anti-Vietnam poem? What matters is that the poem embodies and sustains throughout the statement of Ginsberg's complex desire to assume the function of poet as priestly legislator and as Baptist announcing the dispensation of peace, compassion and brotherhood for all Americans. In this sense, then, "Wichita Vortex Sutra" is a major work.

[From an appendix to the essay. References to the poem appear first, in italics, followed by Ginsberg's own comments.]

Aiken Republican on the radio: In my own mind Sen. Aiken's "bad guess" was just straight forward facts—that the whole $50 billion a year war machine was operating (comically enuf) on sheer subjective guesswork (like Laurel & Hardy trying to find oil). That's all I meant. "Bad Guess" as distinct from Orwellian pseudoscientific think-touch-Time-Life con that all higher decisions are options taken by Men of Distinction on basis of inevitable non-subjective Necessity.

that never worked for Ike who knelt to take / the magic wafer in his mouth / from Dulles' hand: Two grown men with destinies of planet in hand were dealing w/each other in a magic-subjective intimate way. Poem makes claim that much magic's going on unnoticed in US & I cited the above fact to nail it down in awareness, since taking sacrament's so common no one notices the anthropological fact of weird magic practices going on there. Also it's an evidence of white Christian Black magic conspiracy against nonchristian World.

Ham Steak please waitress: Ham steak not intended as buffoon episode—merely a nailing down of common lunchtime fact in midst of overheated imagination runs re Pound + language. Rueful, but not buffoonish, in my opinion.

Sacred Heart my Christ acceptable . . . Jaweh Righteous One: Re the gods: & selected *aspects* of each God, i.e., sacred heart, compassionate, & righteous—in which I had personal faith, wherein I made personal identification, or found the ancient forms equivalent to the saints I met or my own heart's desire. This selection of aspects is done in this context at variance or oddness with most commonly held images of—say, Christ. Who as Christian gets really hung on the red-meat *Sacred Heart?*

the end of the war: "I here declare the end of the war" is a fact, whether the war ends for everyone or not. I end the war in me and anyone who's affected by my gesture . . . I didn't pronounce the mantra to work on all literal levels automatically. I pronounce it w/faith—& cast bread on waters.

Oh at last again the radio opens / blue Invitations! / Angelic Dylan singing across the nation: I think Dylan's "Queen Jane" is a great lyric poem, done as it is in blues style, an invitation to return to relationship—of course interpretation of this does depend on knowledge of lyrics & music by Dylan and in this particular song the passage means exactly what it says . . . Angelic because he looks like an angel & has spiritual or transcendental instinct & manifests them in music and poetry. If you feel there's no place for this type in Xtian [Christian] Angelology I'm sure we could find some variant Angelology in the new book by Davidson that wd. fit. After all, there is not "literally" an angel. Or better, Dylan is as literally angelic type as anything in history or literature.

despairing Burns: N.Y. Times today says whole Midwest is restive and unhappy and I was simply noting a Judgment: and given the Shelley and Warbroadcast data in the poem a judgment surrounded by facts.

the souls / held prisoner in Niggertown / still pining for love of your tender white bodies O children of Wichita!: As far as poesy & accurate language, my own favorite line in the poem is the last about pining for tender white bodies . . . I really dig the ending line as the perfect inspired element, switch, & focussing of the problem of awareness of Sacred Heart right on Wichita Streets. Quite flatly: my understanding is that present race hostilities is obviously frustrated relationship, frustrated love. The *ground* is desire. All hate energy is a conversion of that desire when blocked. That's obvious intellectually. I simply put it in the lover-like language it basically deserves: "still pining . . ."

NOTE

1. I will never forget the feeling that swept over me as I heard the poet recite the lines of the creation of the mantra at the University of Chicago one evening in February 1967. Here was an American poet calling—for the first time in our literature perhaps and certainly for the first time since Whitman—for the possibility of the existence of the

ancient verities in the life of these States. Ginsberg was calling for communion with the gods and for release of love and peace in the souls of Americans. He was calling, in truth, for the realization by himself and by all of us that the Kingdom of God is within everybody. And as I remember the figure of the poet chanting his prayer on the stage of Mandel Hall, I hope that never again will I have to hear or read the widespread but boring criticism of Ginsberg which scolds or condemns him because he is supposed to be the Rasputin of American Poetry: the degenerate who is out to subvert or tarnish the Stars and Stripes, Mom, Home, and the Boys of the 4-H Club, as well as *The Oxford Book of American Verse*. The man on stage that evening was a holy man.

SHEPHERD BLISS

Men, Poetry, and the Military

A Memoir

It's not exactly that I went to hear Allen Ginsberg read/chant his poetry during the sixties and then resigned my commission as an officer in the U.S. Army. But almost.

There I was in Lawrence, Kansas, not a bad place. Only a few miles from my family at the Strategic Air Command headquarters in Omaha, Nebraska. I had just completed basic training at Ft. Riley, Kansas, with the Big Red One, First Division, "backbone of our fighting forces in Nam." I was about as straight as could be—red, white, and blue—planning a career in the military, like my father. And his father, and his father, back to Gen. Tasker Bliss.

I recall visiting Ft. Bliss, Texas, as a child, named after one of the generals in the family. I was then living in Panama with the U.S. military occupying forces. We kids used to run out on the runway, military police chasing us, B-52s screaming above. Most of the first twenty years of my life were spent on military bases, in the military, and otherwise enveloped in that total institution.

Before hearing Ginsberg, I had requested assignment in Nam, hoping to move more swiftly up the ranks to general. I wanted to put that chess strategy I had been practicing since childhood into action. So far the only action had been beating up "pinko-commie-faggot" members of the Student Peace Union. They called us "paid killers" and "death merchants." Their strategy to organize us out of the military did not work, it only hardened our hearts to such long-haired rebels.

Then one day a wandering, bearded poet arrived in Law-

Previously unpublished.

rence. I recall a large room, probably a gym, lots of excitement. And he read: harmonium and all, waving of arms, chanting. I had never experienced anything like this during twenty years in the military mind and the military body. Something shook loose, inside. That shaking continued, through the efforts of Martin Luther King, Jr., and others. Poetry and preaching. Gay and Black, other ways of being, radically other. Finally, after all that shaking, something broke.

There are many ways of moving through the world: one with rigid, directed body moving constantly forward, sharp changes, militarily trained. Ginsberg's movements were quite different: fluid, spontaneous, bobbing up and down and around, moving in more than one direction at the same time, poetically inspired. Poetry doesn't just touch the mind, it embraces our entire being, enters the body and modifies its motions.

The ears absorb sound. So, too, do the pores, through the skin. Sound affects motion: stifling it or encouraging it. Sounds of basic training: "Kill! Kill! Kill!" "What does it take to be a man? A rifle, sir?" Aggressive sounds, internalized, externalized through fight. Such sounds activate certain movements toward certain goals. Male sounds, loud and powerful.

Other sounds make their way in, softer, opening up new passages. More musical, less assaultive. Such sound surrounds, rather than penetrates, creating comfort rather than anxiety. And it has the power to cause the armor to drop away.

Peaceniks. Gradually the boundary between them and me, once so clear, became diffuse. My commanding officer, more aware of this than I, was one of the first to notice. "Well, who are you going to march with today—we men or them sissies?" I didn't even know, consciously, what he was talking about. But I guess my behavior was already reflecting doubts about the military and its program for men; I was inclining toward another vision of what it means to be a man, a vision which seeks to incorporate aspects more often associated with women.

Allen and his lover Peter Orlovsky were said to have taken a trip to Topeka, Kansas, to visit the Menninger Clinic. Apparently a black-tie event, some kind of evening party. It's said that Peter took off all his clothes. And came down the stairs—hard-on and all. I'm told the psychiatrists and their ladies hardly batted an eye. Control. I'm not sure it's fact, but I remember it as truth. Somehow it's all in there together for me—that relationship between freedom in sexuality and the loosening ties to the military.

A few years later I drove Allen and Peter from O'Hare Airport to the National Democratic Convention in Chicago. Windows up, harmonium sounds filled the car's echo chamber. Chants and incantations. Filled with these sounds, I was arrested the following day for "infiltrating military lines," the National Guard. Thrown in the clink for a few days. Found guilty.

I joined the resistance, Chicago Area Draft Resistors, but stayed in the army reserves to organize. I began writing some poetry, as well as organizing a street theater group, Rapid Transit Guerrilla Communications. Then I went to Puerto Rico to work with the independence movement, trying to regain control for the people of a tiny island, Culebra, which the navy used for practice bombing, much to the inhabitants' dismay. I resigned my commission as a U.S. Army officer in protest of this bombing; this was the late sixties, end of a decade.

I'm glad I missed combat. I'm glad I did not kill anyone in Vietnam. Yet I also remember something playful and magical about that all male community in basic training. I'm glad I lived with those men under those harsh physical conditions. I wish there were more channels for the intimate connection among men which the military affords. Sometimes I feel it when dancing with men. Such a contradiction, the military. I still like to march to a marching band—music, movement, people together.

Dear General Tasker Bliss, long deceased ancestor, I carry you in my body. And in my voice. If only you could see me now. My family thinks of me as some kind of commie-faggot. I guess I am, though I sleep with women and can no longer honestly call myself the Marxist-Leninist I was when I worked in Allende's Chile, Torrijos' Panama, Manley's Jamaica, and visited Cuba. That got shaken loose, too, another prison.

That was the seventies. We all change, or at least we all have that potential. And for me, for two decades, Allen Ginsberg's poetry has been one of the powers of change.

PART THREE *Sit and Follow the Breath: Recent Work*

Meditating with friends on the railroad tracks leading to the factory where the Rockwell Corporation uses plutonium to manufacture nuclear bomb triggers. Rocky Flats, Colorado, June 1978.

ALLEN GINSBERG

Remark

. . . At the time [of *Howl*] I believed in some sort of God and thus Angels, and religiousness—at present [1976] as Buddhist I see an awakened emptiness (*Śūnyatā*) as the crucial term. No God, no Self, not even great Whitman's universal Self, it's still Self, as God would be. The defect in these [early] poems . . . is the insistence on a divine self rather than a relatively heavenly emptiness. But it was implicit that mindfulness insight and perfection of Self would lead to no-Self. . . .

From *To Eberhart from Ginsberg* (Lincoln, Mass.: Penmaen Press, 1976). Reprinted with permission.

ALLEN GINSBERG

From an Interview

Interviewer: How, if at all, has your work with Trungpa—your extensive meditation practice—changed your outlook on North American or world politics?

Ginsberg: It has changed it somewhat from a negative fix on the "fall of America" as a dead-end issue—the creation of my resentment—into an appreciation of the fatal karmic flaws in myself and the nation. Also with an attempt to make use of those flaws or work with them—be aware of them—without animosity or guilt; and find some basis for reconstruction of a humanly useful society, based mainly on a less attached, less apocalyptic view. In other words, I have to retract or swallow my apocalypse! (Laughs.)

Trungpa's been pushing me to improvise, to divest myself of ego eventually, kidding me about "Ginsberg resentment" as a national hippie characteristic, and warning me to prepare for death, as I registered in a poem called "What Would You Do If You Lost It?"

From an interview with Peter Chowka, printed in *New Age Journal,* April 1976. Told of this excerpt, Ginsberg wrote: "I'm a little worried that that brief paragraph be taken as reneging on Apocalypse rather than development of same, i.e., some humor of Negative Capability is involved here, not just 'either/or' renouncing of youthful folly. . . . When Prospero burnt his books it didn't mean he was denouncing his youthful follies."—ED.

HAYDEN CARRUTH

Chants, Oracles, Body-Rhythms

Allen Ginsberg's poems of the 1970s are a marvel, his new book, *Mind Breaths,* presenting a half-dozen poems, probably more, that are first-rate Ginsberg. The fact that they are as good as anything he has ever written delights me (and, I hope, many others), because I feel that his poems of the 1960s in *The Fall of America* were generally not so good, too full of random, unassimilated political rage; neither were his experiments with consciously composed blues a few years ago, as I remarked at the time.

You know how Ginsberg writes. Long circular movements, syntax irregular and interfused, catalogues of parallel thoughts and images extending sometimes for pages: chants, oracles, body-rhythms. Hopeless to try quoting them in a review. To excerpt a few lines would serve no purpose, and it would be a positive disservice to the poem.

But let me describe one poem from the new book, called "Ego Confession." A wonderful poem; I've read it five times. It is a mockery throughout: a mockery first of the convention of confessional poetry in recent decades, and then a mockery of the poet himself; it lays bare all his fantastic desires, to be the great poet, the great saint, to stop war, to eradicate viciousness, to gather in from the universal spirit that singing tenderness that will unite us all, etc., etc.; and it is, finally, a mockery of us, the readers and bystanders, silly, fantasizing, unavoidably messianic creatures that we are.

Yet the mockery transcends itself, not at the end of the poem, but all the way through, each statement moving in a process of

Review of *Mind Breaths,* from the *New York Times Book Review,* 19 March 1978. Reprinted with permission.

self-transcension toward the higher compassionate understanding that makes our silliness sane, our pathos holy, our "ego confessions" authentic significations of human spiritual desire. The poem is infused with passionate tenderness.

I once referred to Ginsberg's books, as they are published by City Lights Books in their little, square formats, as "mousetraps of love," which is exactly what they are.

Ginsberg is no simple poet, though some people would like him to be—in fact, the technical means by which he achieves his effects are difficult, even obscure. Consider structure. Categorically speaking, there are three kinds in poetry: first, conventional structure imposed from without; second, archetypal structure risen from within; and third, random structure derived, again, from without. In reality these categories are far from explicit, and they shift and meld together; yet I do believe that all great poems, no matter how rigid or free in their styles and appearances, fall within the second category, and this includes the best of Ginsberg's earliest work (though whether or not those poems are truly "great" is something we won't know in our lifetimes).

In his poems of the 1960s Ginsberg strayed into the third category. Structure was derived from random external events, newspaper stories or things seen from the window of an airplane. The result too often was declaration, not poetry. The structure, if it was structure at all, was disintegrative, literally incoherent.

But now he has returned to poems of the imagination, poems arising from within, complexes of feeling that come to consciousness with their own structure already in them. This doesn't mean that they are of necessity profoundly mythological, in the Jungian sense. No, the political feeling of the sixties— and of the present—can be as much a part of these inherent complexes as anything else. But the structures are integrated, assimilated; they are products of Ginsberg's unified, multiplex personality. As a result, he can now utter explicit political curses against the whole nark segment of modern life in such a way that they not only become genuine political statements but also function esthetically and commensurately as elements of his entire poetic vision. They are part of the prophesying. And this has been at least one of the chief poetic objectives through all ages, from Homer and Isaiah down to our own time.

Enough theorizing. The poems are there—on the page, in the book. They are called "mind breaths." No need to speak of kinds, qualities, degrees, the intellect's inevitable meanderings. The poems *exist*. Think of all the millions of things that might have gone otherwise, so that they might not exist. Our times are bleak enough, heaven knows, but at least we have this.

RICHARD ELMAN

Beyond Self-Absorption

One of Allen Ginsberg's finest poems of recent years is pastoral,
a sort of quirky nature ode on the subject of Bixby Canyon near
Big Sur, California, a landscape that is part natural and part the
detritus of Mammon; and what brings the delight on this deli-
cately worked piece is the interest in very small things, bits of
the palpable, a flower, or insect seen up close, the experiential
world felt as seen, and a relationship of eye to sound which is
accurate, wonderful, alive:

> Ash branch's tender
> pine cone cluster
> proffered by leathery
> sawtooth rib leafs. . . .

This poem startles by interjecting pieces of manufactured
wreckage and flotsam with vivid Wordsworthian landscape no-
tations, as if to imply the pollution of a perfectly alive ecosystem
detail by detail; and yet even these excrescences of a manufac-
tured and intruding world are wonderfully observed now as
intertwined, through observations as specific and accurate as the
journals of any committed imagist:

> Car's rusty
> under carriage
> kelp pipes
> and brown chassis,

Review of *Journals: Early Fifties, Early Sixties,* from the *Nation,* 12 November
1977. Reprinted with permission.

                    one rubber wheel
                    black poked from
                    Sand mattresses
                    rock wash. . . .

There is much of this sort of objectivist wonder, too, in Ginsberg's published journals of the 1950s and 1960s in New York, Berkeley, Mexico, Paterson, and in his trips abroad to the Mediterranean, and East Africa. Living across from the Port Authority Building, downtown, in New York, dawn comes "rust red" for Ginsberg, time is perceived as "a shower," and an ordinary rock becomes a "huge stone tear."

This is the time of visits back home to Paterson and Dr. W. C. Williams and father Louis (with whom the father figure Williams is sometimes confused in Allen's dreams), when the poet is so desperate to break through into life that the clanking of New York City garbage cans carries a "hollow sullen roar like that of a dog," and, under peyote for the first time, Ginsberg imagines himself sketching "like Cézanne." He knew Burroughs by then, and Carl Solomon and Corso, and Lucienne Carr, and Neal Cassady, and Kerouac, and these are very much the years of apprenticing himself to Art through poetry, years of monthly list-making of books read, and a lot of melancholy solitude, captured in bits of unfinished prose, and poetry:

                    Up from my books.
                    The moon in the window,
                    Summer night and solid sky.

                    Black hollow of buildings,
                    A hundred different chimneys.
                    I see lit windows but no humans. . . .

But then in the trip to Mexico Ginsberg's writing truly comes alive in moments, such as this prose-poem observation on a Durango park:

Suddenly there were a million children playing in the park, stubborn, on skates and scooters or bicycle astridden, fighting and running to grab arms, stumbling and staring about hand in mouth, circling the bandstand on single skates, jiggling one-foot or in carriage, conversing solemnly astride a bicycle, running down aisles and stopping short, carried aloft by mothers and brothers, chasing in threes, swirling around of girls on one foot, ringing bells, racing broadside, skipping ropes in circles, bumping each other absently, lifting each other up squealing, falling down hitting arms, waiting, imitating airplanes and horses, getting dizzy, lying crucifix on the grass, dropping money, walking single file in zigzag, playing tag, shaking empty paper bags, making sucking noises; faces besmirched by chocolate, plumped down on the pave, scooping shitty water out of the pool, pushing sailboats, sinking woodscraps, smirking & screaming for bubblegum, tearing up flowers by the roots, presenting them to elders with chubby hands; hairless and ribboned, in rags and diapers, levis and pants too short, in shirts with circles, in neckerchiefs, sitting on the grass, swinging balloons and pocketbooks, hair cut off braided or in ribbons, yellow, red, brown, and black of hair, bald, or leaning on great knees and having their dresses adjusted and hair put in place, staring in white dresses—and when the band began all began screaming.

This aliveness to a tropical landscape among exotic faces involved an extraordinary absorption with place and its intricacies. Ginsberg's joyous ability to perceive unblocked was what he seemed to be seeking in going to Mexico. He wanted to hear his own thoughts, trust his own eye, and these journal entries, like those of the later East African trip, are dotted with direct, moving observations. In this portion of his apprenticeship to writing Ginsberg has finally been able to sustain an interest in the world beyond his own self-absorption, and his writing has become more specific, informational, caring, less vague:

The plaza by night—Kiosk Bon Ampak—bottles of tamarind&peach and lime syrup, as well as grape&orange& chocolate, pan dulces, dulces, blue bottles of Alkaseltzer, straws&glasses&paper cartons of cigarettes.

Man with serape & overalls, and the dark Tumbala boy I

have seen for last few days from over the mount in town for a visit—2 days walk home with carga on his head, past the last chance cantina . . . etc. . . .

The Berkeley journals, composed at the time he was writing and publishing *Howl* and making a large commotion on the poetry scene, are scantily represented here to my disappointment, but the New York entries of 1959 through 1961, after *Kaddish* and much else, when he had become an international figure, are full of interesting first drafts, speculations, notes to himself, dreams and odd encounters.

There are some amusing political diatribes, an advisory to Corso on the CIA, politics, and drugs, and a bemused erotic recollection of Kerouac, presumably, for October 12, 1960:

Jack in for 3 days, finally ending in bed w/ me & Peter like Silenus nekkid—his big thighs & belly.

It is during this period, I believe, that he has come to form the chief romantic attachment of his life with Peter Orlovsky, after the unhappy crush on Neal Cassady, and this, along with a renewed proliferation of the dreams and reading lists and the *shmecking* of various intoxicants and hallucinogens, gives the journal a busy, staccato notational style with which Ginsberg may have felt so uncomfortable, at times, that he springs from it to expatiating to himself:

Read at Gaslight, rainy night, 3 a.m. Mist walking along Avenue D to E, 2 St. and up E. 2 St., in the blue haze of rain, overbright street lamps screaming down their mechano radiance onto the street, a violent-red damp sky above, walking into the Dream, remembering Shelley's insight, I repeated in my mind
                    The One remains
and glimpsed the One behind the transient clouds in the haze. . . .

The dreams and the journals proliferate with names from the scene: Leroi Jones, Gilbert Sorrentino, Harry Smith and a number of jazz musicians. But it is William Blake, more than his contemporaries, who persists as the dominant influence on Ginsberg's practice as poet and seer in the journals. It is Blake, the autodidact, who displaces Ginsberg's costly education with his visionary legions. Nevertheless, even during Ginsberg's most strenuous efforts at disorganization and dissociation, a strong, organic hold on language as notation persists: "At the mouth of Aqaba has been a circle of green shallows in the azure water and the stream out of that (caused by a wrecked iron ship) a feather current of iridescent malachite, shining & unreal as a hummingbird's wing. . . ."

Ginsberg's friend and admirer, Gordon Ball, has provided an excellent introduction and copious, unobtrusive footnotes to these journals; they are readable, bawdy, and, in places, frightening. I got the sense they were carefully edited, though not necessarily cleaned up, so that I was able to see the young man struggling to become an artist, and the developing artist as a man on almost every page. It is a book that should be read by Ginsberg's detractors (if there still are any), for they might learn something about his accuracy, and sense of wonder, his craft, diligence, and studiousness. All of us may learn to appreciate the innovativeness behind the bold public stance and wide open manner which we find being worked out, *or through,* here. Not all of these notations later appeared as poems; some remained just notebook sketches. Gordon Ball has indicated relationships between journal notes, rants and published poems.

For those who have loved Ginsberg's works all along, the persona as well as the writings, it may come as a surprise to read that, along with wearing a suit and tie for some occasions in those days, he had earlier contemplated a straight job, a straight life, and that he could be very much on the make. But while these journals record, among other things, Allen Ginsberg's ambition and adjustment to fame, they are chiefly gobbets of experience and work experiments, not another effort to promote a *persona.* Ginsberg comes very much alive here, showing throughout the courage of a lover of poetry whose large genius for publicity has sometimes obscured his very real poetic talents.

By the time Ginsberg had composed "Kaddish," (and, again, much later, I believe, at the time of the very moving on-the-spot

328

Bangladesh dirge), some of his difficulties with expressing what he thought he should say and what he could actually write down had been worked out. But in Mexico he still *saw* "palmtrees . . . shifting their fronds in the wind with a dry soft rattle sound, so much like animal hairy windmills . . ." and when some of that was later incorporated in "Siesta in Xbalba" as poem it became "palms with lethargic feelers / rattling in presage of rain, / shifting their fronds in the directions of the balmy wind, / monstrous animals / sprayed up out of the ground / settling and unsettling / as in water," which loses something, by being a little more wordy and Latinate and less specific, but it also gains something with the extended visual image: "Sprayed up out of the ground / settling and unsettling / as in water. . . ." It is being able to do just this sort of comparing of the published works to the journals that yields one of the very special pleasures I got in reading this book; and, as there are very few living poets of his stature who have made themselves as vulnerable to those who know their finished work, it's an inspiration and a joy to see how Ginsberg's art is so strongly shaped from the materials of his senses.

Reading these journals is also an aid in demystifying the Ginsberg of visions, dope and religiosity (though there is a lot of that stuff mentioned here) while, at the same time, perceiving that his art is very solidly based on his pleasure, his self and its wonders, on curiosity, and the esteem he has always had for life. For his contemporaries, this is among his many innovations: a devout acceptance of himself dispensing with false modesty and self-deprecation, until, after much effort, he was no longer this ordinary Jewish paranoid genius, angry, lugubrious, and closed off but a maker of brilliant and moving poems out of things at hand and with the people he knew, in a language that became as available to him as breathing. His grandiosity was the measure of his talents educated by his reading and his perceptions; his "acting out" became a way of perceiving his adversity and, through genius, overcoming it.

SELDEN RODMAN

"The Expense of Spirit"

. . . Ginsberg's stereotypes . . . are addressed to himself, and without joy or humor. There is not a trace of passion or tenderness in the homosexual encounters he describes with clinically repulsive detail. His hatred of America and his reiterated complaint that the CIA exists to subvert good government abroad, carry no more supportive evidence than the well-known statement at the beginning of "Howl" that his mentally deranged friends are the "best minds" of his generation. The poem relies for its power on a Whitmanesque litany of hatred and despair, just as "Song of Myself" derives its torrential force from Whitman's affirmation of love for himself and America. But in the entries of a prose journal obsessions become absurd and pitiful. Ginsberg seems to recognize this, unconsciously, for toward the end almost all the entries are reports of his dreams. And since these dreams are neither beautiful nor terrifying, and are put down without any attempt at interpretation, the result is boredom. The one really moving entry comes at the beginning, when the (then humble) Ginsberg runs into the already ravaged Dylan Thomas in a Greenwich Village bar and is too shy to introduce himself and tell him "my true feeling, and its importance to you." Maybe Thomas would have told him, as the stricken William Carlos Williams didn't or couldn't, that self-love inflamed by drugs can lead only to "the expense of spirit in a waste of shame."

Review of *Journals: Early Fifties, Early Sixties,* from the *National Review,* 1 September 1978. Reprinted with permission.

MARK SHECHNER

The Survival of Allen Ginsberg

We have three new books from Allen Ginsberg: a selection of recent poems, a second transcription of entries from his vast archive of journals, and an exchange of letters with Neal Cassady, who was once the elusive object of his tumultuous affections. But there is little to catch the eye here; two of the books—the journals and the correspondence—are sentimental journeys to familiar terrain: the mind of Allen Ginsberg. For years, Ginsberg has been the most accessible of our writers, conducting his affairs very much in the open, if remarkably beyond the reach of talk shows, book chat, and general literary blather. Nor do the poems break any new ground, thematically or technically. They put forth the standard brew of homosexuality, metaphysics, pacifism, stirring declamation and muddled prophecy, and home-cooked Buddhism, which is as familiar now as the morning coffee and about as shocking.

Ginsberg has long since graduated from being a subterranean and "know-nothing Bohemian" (Norman Podhoretz's tactful phrase) to being everyone's favorite prophet. He is our anarchist-in-residence, queer and avuncular, whose open passion for young boys and tirades against empire, oppression, and, lately, heroin are disarmed and domesticated by his irony. He reads poems about shit to packed houses in the prep schools. Even Diana Trilling, ever watchful for bad influences on the young, glowingly remembers him, in *We Must March My Darlings,* as a warm and comforting presence in the sixties. As an added ingratiating feature, Ginsberg is that rarest of figures among

Review of *Journals: Early Fifties, Early Sixties; As Ever: The Collected Correspondence of Allen Ginsberg and Neal Cassady;* and *Mind Breaths.* An earlier version of this essay appeared in *Partisan Review* 46, no. 1 (1979). Reprinted with permission.

American poets, a survivor, working vigorously into his fifties, despite the script he was handed early in life which called for a spectacular crack-up or a slow descent into alcohol or madness in the grand American tradition. He was cut out to be a *poète maudit:* a Poe, a Berryman, a Delmore Schwartz, a Plath, a Kerouac, and much of his initial impact in the fifties derived from the impression he gave that he had privileged insight into the tragic fate of the imagination in America: "I saw the best minds of my generation destroyed by madness." But his own was not among them. Unlike Kerouac, he eventually recoiled from the allure of martyrdom, sparing us another tiresome lesson in how America abuses her poets and yet another case-history in poetry as a by-product of terminal euphoria. He was finally too ironic and willful for martyrdom, and, despite his rages against America and her wars, too enamored of the *idea* of America, which he confused with the idea of Walt Whitman, to renege on his initial promise: "America I'm putting my queer shoulder to the wheel."

Credit for Ginsberg's survival belongs to his Buddhism, which has taught him how to marshall and conserve his energies and to suspend his urban, Jewish agitation in passive, Eastern repose. The aroma of wise passiveness that wafts through his public appearances these days is a studied calm, a calculated vigilance over seething emotions which he has learned to hold in check and sublimate into a keening, sonorous delivery. In a recent poem on the subject of being mugged in his own neighborhood ("Mugging" in *Mind Breaths*) Ginsberg tells of surrendering to a troop of young thugs while frantically intoning a mantra to keep his terror and rage under control: "I went down shouting Om Ah Hūm to gangs of lovers on the stoop watching." But whatever such methodologies of self-discipline have contributed to his durability and his public figure—that is, to the pedagogic example—they have brought little to the poetry save heavy breathing and a treasury of lambent phrases to be sprinkled lightly over a poem like curry over a stew, for oriental pungency. Sanskrit scans marvelously in English meters, while spreading little wavelets of mystical illumination. Thus several of the poems in *Mind Breaths* are graced with such sweet cadences as "Bom Bom! Shivaye! Ram Nam Satyahey! Om

Ganipatti, Om Saraswatti Hrih Sowha!" which mean something, we may be assured, in the original, but which, for most of us, might just as well be "Hey nonny nonny no." Yet, despite the airs of Tagore or Lao-Tze that drift like incense through his poetry, Ginsberg has kept faith with his earliest mentors—Williams, Whitman, and Blake—and nothing he has done since the poems in *Kaddish* (1961) shows any advance in vision or technique.

In *Mind Breaths,* except for a strange bit of romantic allegory, "Contest of Bards," which Ginsberg himself has hailed as a gift from the muse, but whose studied Blakeisms ("Icy intellect fir'y beauty wreck") sound false to an ear trained on his more vernacular, American line, most of the poems seem like refrains from earlier books, and far less inspired ones at that. This is Ginsberg's coolest book; its dithyrambic surges, at any rate, aim no higher than the foothills of the Adirondacks. The spontaneous composition that was a boon to earlier poetry, summoning up the long, rabbinic chords of "Howl," "Kaddish," and "Wichita Vortex Sutra," looks more and more like a recipe for instant altitude: a shortcut to the poetic high. The paraphernalia of inspiration that serve Ginsberg so well in performance—what with the harmonium and the receptivity of audiences just dying for enchantment—are no promise of poetry that works in print, especially now that Ginsberg devotes so much of his attention to pure voice and pure breath, biomusic, if you like, that does not translate easily into words.

> Zalmon Schacter Lubovitcher Rebbe what you say
> > Stone Commandments broken on the ground
> > Sufi Sam whaddya say
> > > Shall Prophet's companions dance circled
> > > > round Synagogue while Jews doven bearded
> > > > > > electric?
> Both Gods Terrible! Awful Jaweh Allah!
> > Both hook-nosed gods, circumcised.
> Jaweh Allah which unreal?
> > > Which stronger Illusion?
> > > > Which stronger Army?
> > > > > ("Jaweh and Allah Battle")

One turns almost in relief from antiwar dovenning* such as this to poems like "Sweet Boy, Gimme Yr Ass," and "Under the World There's a Lot of Ass, a Lot of Cunt," where, at least, the old sexual frankness shows signs of life, largely because Ginsberg's sexual imagination is so aggressive, so downright violent. "Under the world there's a lot / of ass, a lot of cunt / a lot of mouths and cocks, / under the world there's a lot of come, and a lot of saliva dripping into brooks" makes its raunchy statement with the same peevish assertion that Ginsberg could always summon up when aggravated, though now that these sentiments are tolerated in the prep schools, even his gnashing of teeth begins to sound like good cheer, which is not entirely his fault.

At this stage of the game, rather than try to push ahead poetically, Ginsberg has taken to doubling back upon himself, and the journals, correspondence, memoirs, and *obiter dicta* (see, for example, Gordon Ball's *Allen Verbatim*) that now tumble onto the market suggest that what we can henceforth look forward to are neither breakthroughs nor refinements in poetry, but Ginsberg's efforts to clarify his image and carve out a place in American cultural history. One suspects that Ginsberg understands these days that he matters less as a poet than as a figure, an exemplary life. Certainly he has grown influential without being consistently great, or even consistently engaging as a writer, and most of us can count on one hand the poems that survive rereading, let alone study. As an exemplary figure, however, Ginsberg is something else again, and it is to the clarification of the example that the journals and letters are devoted.

But in what sense is such a life admirable? Are we compelled to admire the conspicuous alienation and rootlessness that has made of Ginsberg America's foremost wandering Buddhist-Jew? Are we *really* that comfortable with the aggressive homosexuality? Neither of those qualities is unambiguous. If his alien-

---

Doven or *davenen* is a Yiddish word which, according to Samuel Rosenbaum's *Yiddish Word Book,* means "to pray, to recite the prescribed prayers, alone or in the midst of a congregation."—ED.

ation has afforded him a critical distance from American society and institutions and given him a place to stand in opposition to it, has it not also separated him from poetry as well? Has not his writing been flawed over the years by his refusal to study his craft, to brighten his language, to learn from others? As for the public homosexuality, even granting that as a campaigner for sexual pluralism Ginsberg has been instrumental in creating the current social climate in which coming out is encouraged and gay-baiting is on the defensive, except perhaps in the deep south or at *Commentary* magazine, doesn't the studied *épatism* grow tedious after a while? What surely *is* exemplary on Ginsberg's part is the risk he has taken in placing his own sexual nature out in the open; proclaiming it, writing about it, worrying over it, and insisting on its right to gratification, thus keeping himself clear of the enervating compromises of closet homosexuality. Ginsberg's acceptance of his own constitution as the very condition of his life and his poetry is certainly one of the sources of his strength and durability. Blakean that he is, he has not let himself be undermined by his own repressed desires. Admiration for the *idea* of sexual openness, however, does not make it any easier to read a poem like "Sweet Boy, Gimme Yr Ass." Even as an honored senior poet and a quasi-saint, Ginsberg can still make us squirm.

But Ginsberg's long involvement with mind-altering drugs is more problematic. His exalted testimonials on behalf of his pharmacological experiments gave sanction not only to the use of drugs in the sixties, but to their glorification as the elixir of cosmic consciousness. Though Ginsberg has campaigned against heroin, and now writes, "Nobody saves America by sniffing cocaine," his basic line on dope, as on everything else, has been the libertarian's *laissez faire,* and let every man find out for himself. But hallucinogenic drugs once meant more to him than just another degree of American freedom; they occupied a place in his romance with madness, which, as Kerouac shrewdly saw, served his need to justify his mother. Though he eventually outgrew his illusions about redemptive insanity and took up spiritual self-discipline after the Indian trip in 1962–63, he had, by then, already made his contribution to the myth of the mad-man as antinomian saint "who drove crosscountry seventytwo hours to find out if I had a vision or you had a vision or he had a vision to find out eternity." Some of those visions, we now know, were the mental vapors of neurons boiling away in the skull. Yet all this in Ginsberg: the aggressive homosexuality, the rootlessness, the anarchism, the celebrated expeditions in search of a better hallucinogen, cannot be seen apart from what is to be admired in him, for they are, however ambiguous, his efforts at salvation. The accumulating documentation of his life is slowly amounting to the authentication of a saint's life, a chronicle of beatitude whose theme, like that of all saints' lives, is crisis, conversion, and trial. The famous Blake vision, of which we have a half-dozen accounts, is like Paul's vision on the road to Damascus or Martin Luther's fit in the choir, a token of annoint-ment, and the torments that follow are steps in the realization of a mission. The mother's madness had to be suffered and purged; the humiliating love for Neal Cassady had to be indulged and worked through; imprisonment and institutionalization had to be endured and made use of; shame and guilt had to be admitted and overcome. Allen Ginsberg's youth was an apprenticeship in failure, and in light of the dismal lessons he suffered his heroism would appear to lie not in his resistance to money or power or social convention but in his refusal of the original emotional ground rules of his life. He altered the deadly prognosis: by way of Blake and Buddhism he became that mythic American, the self-made man. He is an anarchist Horatio Alger. More bookish, more resolutely literary than any of the other Beats, he trans-formed and rescued himself through the medium of books. What else shall we make of the Blake vision that set into motion his career as a poet but this—that here was a man on his way down who was rescued by poetry? Little wonder that he is honored these days in the academy, to whose basic values— dispassionate toil, restraint, objectivity—he is seemingly so anathema, for he is a living defense of the literary vocation.

These journals and letters, by and large, have little to tell us about Ginsberg's survival, but much to show us about his early desperation. The *Journals* cover two periods, 1952 to 1956, and 1959 to February 1962, the eve of his departure for India. The *Indian Journals,* previously published (1970), take up where these leave off. The correspondence with Neal Cassady extends farther back, to 1947 and the tender years at Columbia, and plots the vicissitudes of that difficult relationship into 1963. The Ginsberg who emerges from these pages is the lost and driven young poet seeking respite from his pains through determined reading, mysticism, and sex.

The letters to Neal, especially the very earliest, are the most readable and touching of these documents because they are the most thoroughly grounded in common humanity. Ginsberg's mysticism would later cast a veil of metaphysics over the emotions, making portions of the journals tough sledding for the reader in search of more ordinary revelations. But the letters are direct and ardent, full of passionate declarations of emotional dependency and pleas for punishment and love. Writing in 1947, a year after first meeting Cassady in New York, Ginsberg declared, "I am lonely, Neal, alone, and always I am frightened. I need someone to love me and kiss me & sleep with me; I am only a child and have the mind of a child. I have been miserable without you because I had depended on you to take care of me for love of me, and now that you have altogether rejected me, what can I do, what can I do?" I scarcely know of more abject appeals anywhere in literature or published correspondence. Yet even at his most desolate, Ginsberg would turn his sexual dependency into intellectual advantage, urging Neal, in a postscript to one letter, to read *Nightwood, Wings of the Dove,* and *The Idiot.* Cassady, who had received his education on Denver's skid row, where he earned advanced degrees in deprivation and drift, was vulnerable to learning, and Ginsberg knew how to gain leverage over him with exhibitions of Columbia erudition. The letters reveal the emotional quid pro quo of homosexuality, the give and take of power that became for Ginsberg the basic rule of psychic accounting. As applied to his relationships it took the form of the strategic dependency, the manipulative weakness. As applied to himself, it was the conversion factor in reconstructing paranoia as enlightenment, persecution as hypostatic union. His later messianism sprang full grown from his early masochism, his transcendence from his lessons in abasement. It is easy to understand the appeal of Cassady for someone like Ginsberg, though Cassady's magic does not come through in the letters. He was not an intellectual or even much of a reader;

he tried to write and, for the most part, failed,[1] and even his letters are garbled. "I hate words," he complained to Ginsberg. "They are too much." What captivated Ginsberg and Kerouac was the rough and ready masculinity, the suggestion of complete male competence. They were Reichians, and he was a vessel of molten libido, blissfully pansexual and yet carelessly masculine. Moreover, he was almost a dead ringer for Kerouac, which surely played into the latter's exalted conception of him. Kerouac mythicized him in his books as Dean Moriarty and Cody Pomeray; Gary Snyder saw him as the last cowboy, a Jedediah Smith hemmed in by the modern world; Ginsberg just loved him. He was their link to frontier manhood, their own urban cowboy, though they understood too that his skid row disorientation was an alienation not unlike their own. He was born to lose. After marrying his second wife, Carolyn, in 1949, he wrote to Ginsberg, "From what I can unerstand of them your doldrums are fine. All I can see is the long, continuous doldrum I'm in." Seeking release from the doldrums in spontaneous flights from one end of the continent to the other in search of the ease that always eluded him, he served Kerouac and Ginsberg as a tour guide to the American heartland and introduced them to an authentic American high, the high of the fast car and the open road. The rolling cadenzas of *On the Road* owe everything to Cassady and his cars, as do the lilt and flux of Ginsberg's highway poems, which are among his best: "The Green Automobile" (*Reality Sandwiches*), a poem about Cassady, "Wichita Vortex Sutra" (*Planet News*), and the cross-country "vortex" poems in *The Fall of America*.

But the open road is only a high while one remains in motion, savoring the illusion that trouble is back down the road somewhere. Cassady's fretful activity was only a scheme for buying a moment away from his panic and his incredible bad luck. Indeed, while William Burroughs and Lucien Carr could get away, literally, with murder, Cassady would eventually get caught for possession and sale of marijuana and wind up doing two years at San Quentin, from 1958 to 1960. Imagine that today. After his release he was reduced to doing his routine in miniature, driving the bus for Ken Kesey and his Merry Pranksters, hitting the road as a parody of himself. He died in Mexico in February, 1968, under mysterious circumstances, though probably of alcohol fatally spiked with barbiturates.

Ginsberg and Cassady had already begun to drift apart after their reunion in 1954. Ginsberg met Peter Orlovsky, while Cassady attended fitfully to his family and his job as a railroad brakeman for the Southern Pacific. In the midfifties, Ginsberg was also discovering his own strength and his calling, spiritualizing his emotions and consigning his torments to his poetry. He was discovering *the heights*. The movement of the journals is away from the lucid, personal, and tortured writing of the early letters toward an elliptical and mystagogic style that is difficult to penetrate. Relationships surrender to casual impressions and dreams; almost half the contents of these journals are Ginsberg's transcriptions of his own dreams, though without the associations that might make them accessible. Indeed, there is a refractory quality to these journals, and the *Indian Journals* are the most resistant of them all. Despite their painstaking documentation of the inner life, they obscure personal qualities in a blizzard of fragmentary notations, alternately banal and dharmic, and shuttle back and forth between runaway empiricism and runaway mysticism.

> *Oct. 22.*
> Read at Gaslight, rainy nite, 3 a.m. Mist walking along Avenue D to E. 2 St. and up E. 2 St. in the blue haze of rain, overbright street lamps screaming down their mechano radiance onto the street, a violent-red damp sky above, walking in the Dream, remembering Shelley's insight, I repeated in my mind
> The One remains
> and glimpsed the One behind the transient clouds in the haze—The Many change and pass, as I was walking down the street, I passing this life toward my ever-menacing present Death—Inevitable—

Here, as practically everywhere else in these journals, the odd empirical/metaphysical blend crowds out all more mundane preoccupations, making the most intimate revelations sound impersonal, oddly dreamlike. The journals, indeed, document the triumph of the religious imagination over the social, and only constant infusions of Ginsberg's irrepressible irony save the whole venture from collapsing into worship and trance.

> Bullshit Artist of Reality,
>   Ginsberg,
> Give up,
>   Forever
> To your Truth,
>   and Lose thy shoe on
> the Great Step.
>   * * *
> Allen—Does the Capitoi
>   Believe that
>   in the Imagination?
> Jack—Yes—they do—but it isn't official yet.

The appeal of Ginsberg in the sixties lay in the appearance he gave of seeing through or beyond the veils and blinders of ordinary social thought. I remember vividly a moment in the mid-sixties when Ginsberg, operating as only he could, through the medium of power poetry, affected a truce between antiwar marchers in the Bay area and the Hell's Angels, who, egged on by local officials and police, were poised to assault the demonstrators. Appealing to the bikers that, more or less, "we're all social outlaws together," not only did Ginsberg pacify them, but apparently mollified the surly Oakland police as well. Moreover, the truce was sealed, as I recall, by the reading of a poem, "To the Angels," at a rally in the East Bay. Who could help at such moments but believe that here was a truly transcendent figure, someone who just, by his presence alone, dissolved the ordinary social categories. Strange it is, then, to find so little social reflection in his journals, as if the social and political self were to be treated as a stepchild and of relative unimportance compared to the prophet. We expect poetry that is sufficiently inspired to leap from one plane of meaning to the next, to zoom upwards from sensory data to the higher realms, but what seems like thrilling prophecy when spoken in biblical accents does not satisfy in the form of a journal entry. Which is another way of saying that the journals and most of the letters to Neal are disappointing except for the light they shed on other things that may matter to us: Ginsberg's poetry, or American social history in the postwar decades. And that light is dim.

There is no reason for Ginsberg *not* to have published such journals and letters or to withhold the additional materials which will soon be forthcoming. Public self-examination of this sort is a rare and valuable gesture, even when, as in this case, what is actually disclosed will interest few. Understandably, a confession, even to oneself, is a bargain struck with the superego to permit some more difficult and compromising knowledge to be withheld, though it is odd to find such a case in which primal fears and sexual anxieties are laid bare and social relations suppressed. But that reversal is in the antinomian manner of Ginsberg's life. He always does things differently than we do.

NOTE

1. Cassady's writings are not without their interest, however, for the life they depict. See Neal Cassady, *The First Third and Other Writings* (San Francisco: City Lights Books, 1971.) The reader might also want to have a look at Carolyn Cassady's memoir—letters strung together by a thin narrative, actually—of Cassady and Kerouac, in *Heartbeat: My Life with Jack and Neal* (Berkeley: Creative Arts, 1976).

PAUL BERMAN

Intimations of Mortality

Just what did happen to Allen Ginsberg in East Harlem in 1948? According to his original account, one day he suddenly heard William Blake reciting "Ah! Sun-flower" and "The Sick Rose" in a "deep, graven" voice from beyond the tomb. Then he looked out the window and saw the sky as the "blue hand" of God and the bricks and cornices of old tenements as manifestations of an eternal creativity. This experience flabbergasted him. He interpreted it as a call to become a messianic prophet with a mission to inform the world of profound truths. He thought he had become a "seraph." Immediately, he climbed out on the fire escape to tell the news to two girls who lived next door. "I've seen God," he said. Subsequently, smaller mystical tremors shook him in his kitchen and across town on the Columbia campus.

One of the peculiarities of this famous Beat epiphany is that Ginsberg, the least shy of all poets, has been reticent to write or at least to publish much about it, though he has been willing to discuss it with interviewers. For some reason the experience has been difficult to communicate. The girls next door slammed the window on him; his professors at Columbia thought him mad; his early attempts to describe it in verse were not successful. The *Journals* from the Fifties and Sixties published by Grove Press begin four years after the vision, in 1952, and show that during that period Ginsberg had very little to say about it, even in the privacy of his own notebooks. References to the vision are scattered and partial.

Nevertheless the mark of the experience is on these journals. Plainly Ginsberg took it as a sign of vocation. He expected to have

Review of *Journals: Early Fifties, Early Sixties,* and *Mind Breaths,* from *Parnassus: Poetry in Review* (Fall–Winter 1979). Reprinted with permission.

more visions, and a visionary life. Ginsberg has always been a diligent and disciplined worker, and the journals show that he went about preparing for his visionary career quite as systematically as he went about learning the art of poetry. He experimented with peyote, mescaline, acid, heroin, psylocybin, different amphetamines, laughing gas, ether, marijuana, hashish, morphine, and an Amazon psychedelic called ayahuasca. He filled his notebooks with descriptions of his dreams. The impression arises that he peeked through every mental and pharmaceutical door in sight, looking for the one that opens on the universe. "What is needed is an *actual* vision," he writes in a notebook for 1954. This was the crux of the matter. "When it comes I will know that I have been preparing for it. . . . The main theme of my thought has been in preparation for understanding or achieving a moment that is to come."

Unfortunately—and this is the most poignant reference to his mystical calling in the *Journals,* perhaps the most poignant confession of his life— "It never came," a 1976 footnote adds. There were no more visions. William Blake never arrived again. In an interview in 1976, Ginsberg goes so far as to say that the fifteen or twenty years he spent pursuing what he calls "visionary consciousness" were a mistake. He counsels: "Avoid that mountain of ego vision!"[1]

What, then, of the original Blake epiphany? Ginsberg has a new retrospective analysis of this, too. Perhaps the mystical vision wasn't what it seemed at the time. In a second footnote in the *Journals,* Gordon Ball, its editor, tells us that "in later years, Ginsberg has come to view the voice that he heard in 1948 as that of his own mature self." He did not hear William Blake at all; or at least he did not *quite* hear William Blake; what he "heard" was a sense of his own potential.

This is quite an admission, and presents a quandary for Ginsberg. His persona as visionary seer with a proven record is not something that can be tossed away lightly. This persona has a place in the national history. A mere handful of American poets have ever had substantial following outside of literature— Whittier; the Yiddish radicals of the 1890s Morris Winchevsky and David Edelstadt; the Italian-American syndicalist Arturo Giovanitti; and the ex-Beat black militant LeRoi Jones (Amiri

Baraka). Anyone who spent time during the appropriate years on Haight Street, San Francisco, or Eighth Street, Greenwich Village, knows that the visionary prophet and militant community exorcist Allen Ginsberg belongs in this company. More to the point, his visionary persona has a central place in all those little black and white volumes that City Lights has published. He did, after all, develop and master a mode of vatic poetry and write a large number of excellent poems that leave the impression of extraordinary mystical strength. What, then, is to happen to the accumulated legend, to his spiritual dash and bravura, to his characteristic assurance of vast otherworldly power? What is to happen to the public persona that he and his friends and his colleagues have labored so many years to create? How should we judge his visionary, prophetic poetry?

What happens in this edition of the *Journals* is that Ginsberg has it both ways. The brace of footnotes about his mystical failure is supported by an occasional mark of sobriety in the editor's Introduction and Notes, testifying to Ginsberg's mature recognition of personal limits. But in other passages the Introduction can't resist a new go-around for the old boast about mystical abilities. Ball observes that Ginsberg's dreams recorded in the notebooks predict uncannily the future of various famous personalities. There was a dream of John Kennedy in 1959 in which the future president had a hole in his back; a dream of Nixon breakfasting in a San Clemente-like pastorale; a dream of Eleanor Roosevelt shortly before Ginsberg chanced to meet her in real life. This is tacky stuff, reminiscent of nothing so much as the silly religious briefs made on Whitman's behalf by that poet's overawed acolytes. But there it is. Americans may not like to celebrate their great poets, but they do love to beatify them.

In any event, the very thinness of Ginsberg's mystical boasts leads one to wonder whether his spiritual exuberance all these years may not have been concealing a deeper anxiety about his visionary potential. The anxiety is certainly visible in the notebooks, and as long ago as the early fifties. He worries that his spiritual development will not keep pace with Kerouac's and William Burroughs's. Above all he frets that politics, in which he was passionately interested but they were not, will do him harm: too much attention to the "tricks of power" will thwart his "seraphic potentialities." There was a plausible basis for this worry. Excessive reading of the *New York Times,* which Ginsberg gives indication of having indulged in for many years now, might chill anyone's otherworldly capacities. Then too the *Journals* show that he had a childhood and youth directed more toward politics than toward religion and mysticism. He was picketing Boss Hague at the age of twelve, at fourteen he was a communist and wanted to be president, at nineteen an anarchist and at twenty-six, he notes, a registered Democrat. And this political interest continued. At age thirty-five he undertook a passage to India for spiritual reasons, only to find himself on shipboard daydreaming about forming a new political party to oppose Adlai Stevenson—a most disheartening sign, one might suppose, for an aspiring seraph.

It would be wrong to conclude from this that Ginsberg's religious qualities are somehow fraudulent. He may brag and exaggerate—he is a maestro at this—but he is obviously not a fraud. "Strange, mad, but genuine," Gershom Scholem once said of him. It would also be wrong to emphasize uncategorically the dampening effect of politics on his spiritual ardor. Whitman was a journalistic hack for the Democratic party in Brooklyn, and he managed to keep his mystical skin intact (though a case can be made that the Democratic party was a lot more transcendental in those days). At any rate discovering something of Ginsberg's political background is certainly valuable because, whether or not it inhibited his mysticism, it does account for much of the actual content of his prophetic poetry. The breadth of his social outrage, his alertness to political and cultural oppression, his appreciation that injustice under capitalism and the imperial state is systematic, his unshakeable suspicion of the military and his facility for spotting devious concealments in United States foreign policy—these features of his political personality, which Louis Simpson calls Ginsberg's "paranoid view of life in the United States,"[2] are implicit in the radical working-class tradition of his background and explicit in the notebooks.

A remarkable thing about Ginsberg's political perspectives is how fixed they are in his subconscious, so fixed that they register regularly in his dreams. Not only are there dreams of famous figures, but also a couch-full of dreams in which policemen chase, harass, and arrest him. In one dream the police book him "on suspicion of orgies" and in another round up the Jews and Puerto Ricans in Tompkins Square. These are dreams of persecution, and someone might take them to indicate that Ginsberg's view of life in the United States is "paranoid" in a narrower and more psychological sense than is suggested by the usual political meaning of that word, which connotes an exaggerated fear of capitalist or governmental conspiracies. I do not think Ginsberg's view is distorted. Even paranoids have enemies, Delmore Schwartz said, and Allen Ginsberg, as can be seen in the *Journals* and elsewhere, has certainly had them. The man is, after all, a drug-taking homosexual Jewish anarcho-pacifist-leaning Buddhist poet from a Communist Party background who matured in the repressive Cold War years—and therefore is the very sort of figure in whom agencies of government have long taken a malign interest. He has been confined eight months in a mental institution for a crime he did not commit, harassed outside his home by the local police, obliged to watch his closest friends be persecuted sometimes for their private drug habits and other times for their public literary creations. Federal agents tried to entrap him in a drug bust. His own first book was subject to police nuisance-making and his publisher was forced to spend an afternoon in jail. "Howl" was made the object of an attempted legal suppression. Then there was Cointelpro, the FBI counterintelligence program which was used to persecute radicals—including many of Ginsberg's cronies and political allies—and to poison the political atmosphere on the Left. Documents published in *City Lights Journal* (number 4) show that the FBI not only had a file on Ginsberg (and on his current publisher Ferlinghetti) but had plans to disgrace him or damage his reputation. A certain kind of political sanctimoniousness popular at the present moment requires that upon mention of such things, gratitude be expressed that Ginsberg has never drawn what the Russians call a "tenner" to chop ice in Alaska. It might have gone harder for him in other countries—this is true. Nevertheless the history of Ginsberg's treatment by the American state shows that a large part of his prophetic force—namely the spectacular rage and emotional charge that light up his political insights with a cosmic incandescence—can be explained without invoking William Blake's shade or William James's theories. Like Diego Rivera in the witty poem by E. B. White, Ginsberg paints what he paints, he paints what he sees.

If there must be a mystery about the sources of Ginsberg's poetry, it is to explain how he has managed to create the voice that could give expression to this cosmic rage. The *Journals* record his meetings with William Carlos Williams, which influenced him considerably, and a beery run-in with Dylan Thomas in a Greenwich Village bar, which influenced him not at all, and they show how highly he regarded the work of his fellow Beats. There are reading lists of Pound, Eliot, Rimbaud, Gertrude Stein—the authors one would expect. I was curious to see whether there would be a mention of Dos Passos, since it has occurred to me that Ginsberg's verse stands in close relation, politically as well as prosodically, to Dos Passos's prose poems, but Dos Passos never comes up. The most striking aspect of the *Journals* is how much closer Ginsberg's early unconsidered prose stands to his mature poetry than does his early poetry. Ball points out that whole phrases written in prose in the notebooks later emerged in verse, for instance this jotting during a visit to Chihcen Itza in 1954:

> Great stone portals, entablatures of languages gone, poetry gone, spirit gone, bas reliefs of unknown perceptions: in front of me a minute ago I saw a death's head half a thousand years old—and have seen cocks a thousand years old grown over with moss and batshit in a dripping vaulted room of stone, stuck in the walls (like C.'s plasticine cock at Columbia dormitory).

This paragraph later became a part of "Siesta in Xbalba" in *Reality Sandwiches,* with a number of words changed or cut:

> High dim stone portals,
> entablatures of illegible scripture,
> bas-reliefs of unknown perceptions

And later:

> In front of me a deathshead
> 　　　　　half a thousand years old
> —and have seen cocks a thousand
> old grown over with moss and batshit

The close visual perception, the words, even the rhythms move straight from the prose jottings into the poetry. It is apparent in the *Journals* that Ginsberg's transition from prose to poetry developed gradually over several years. The entries from the early fifties are almost all in prose. Poetry increases in the middle fifties, and by the late fifties and early sixties has become as spontaneous or more spontaneous than his prose.

For some reason, Ginsberg's notes for "Howl" are missing from this edition of his *Journals,* which is very disappointing. There is an early draft of "America" from the fall of 1955, the same period as "Howl," whose ending

> I Allen Ginsberg Bard out of New Jersey take up the laurel tree
> 　　cudgel from Whitman

is not as good as the published ending, "America I'm putting my queer shoulder to the wheel," but interesting to see. There are only a few notes for "Kaddish": a record of a dream of his mother and some preliminary jottings. But there is, interestingly, a different, earlier kaddish—this one for his uncle, Harry Meltzer—which uses ideas that would later turn up in the "Kaddish" for his mother:

> My God!
> 　　Uncle Harry, what happened
> to you—are you really gone
> already past the deathbed to the grave,
> disappeared into B'nai Israel Cemetery
> with the rest of the ancestors we knew
> and watched go by, and ate our Seder
> Suppers over again every year at your house?

Presumably the notes that are missing here will be published in some future volume.

By the early sixties Ginsberg's full mature voice thunders forth in the notebooks in long rants on a variety of topics, especially on politics. Some of these are lively.

> What good are all our washmachines if our hair's dirty with
>   Algiers blood?
> If the Vice President sits around telling lies about Guatemala what
>   good television except get mad?
> What good being reasonable talking public if movie stars're afraid
>   they're queer?
> What good being Senator you can't confess your inmost thought?
> What good utmost thoughts if murder gets away with the
>   newspapers?
>
> ("Politics on Opium")

Or again:

> One million editorials against Mossadeq and who knows who
>   Mossadeq is any more?
> Me a Democracy? I didn't know my Central Intelligence was
>   arming fascist noodnicks in Iran
>
> ("Subliminal")

Mossadeq was of course the Iranian nationalist whom the CIA overthrew in 1953 in order to establish the Shah on the throne, more or less on behalf of the oil companies.

In these spontaneous poems we can see the familiar long-breathed rolling rhythms, the insistence on fact, the open-throated volume and the building energy, the imprecations that sometimes seem grandly biblical and other times like a homely, funny Yiddish curse. This is the voice that Ginsberg in one passage calls, apparently quoting someone else, the "cosmic-ferocious." In these poems we also see an early expression of one of Ginsberg's great themes: the hypocrisy and criminality of American politics, especially overseas policy, and the terrible impotent frustration that an anti-imperialist such as himself feels at trying to communicate his outrage. Frustrated outrage of this sort was one of the characteristic political emotions of the sixties and early seventies (it has not entirely disappeared today); Ginsberg's achievement is to have given vent to this feeling better than anyone else.

One of the merits of *Mind Breaths,* his most recent collection, is that it includes a number of "cosmic-ferocious" poems of this kind. Consider the opening lines of "Hadda Be Playing on the Jukebox":

> Hadda be flashing like the Daily Double
> Hadda be playing on TeeVee
> Hadda be loudmouthed on the Comedy Hour
> Hadda be announced over Loud Speakers
> CIA & Mafia are in Cahoots
> Hadda be said in old ladies' language
> Hadda be said in American Headlines
> Kennedy stretched & smiled & got doublecrossed by low life
>   goons & Agents
> Rich Bankers with Criminal Connections
> Dope pushers in CIA working with dope pushers from Cuba
> working with Big Time syndicate Tampa Florida
> Hadda be said with big mouth

This is a particularly simple example of Ginsberg's force and rhythmic flexibility. "Hadda be" hits the downbeat: the measure which follows varies in length according to the type and intensity of emotion, from the short statement, "Hadda be playing on TeeVee," to the long six-line statement that begins, "Hadda be said in American Headlines." The effect is that of a chest heaving with indignation.

The phrase "Hadda be" also has an ambiguous meaning, which makes the poem interesting. In the political context of the poem—the avalanche of revelations associated with Watergate and the collapse of the Vietnam war effort—"Hadda be" expresses the poet's disgust that nothing less than sensational headlines could convince a naive public that terrible crimes had been committed by the government, as if he were really saying, "It had to be nothing less than this to convince them." On the other hand "Hadda be" expresses his sense of fatality about these crimes: they "had to be." Still again, "Hadda be" expresses his regret and sorrow, as if he were saying, "Why did it have to be you, America, that these things happened to?" The connotation of the phrase changes as continuously as the rhythm which its sound establishes.

The *Journals* reveal that Ginsberg used to worry about political poems of this type. "I shouldn't waste my time on America like this. It may be patriotic / but it isn't good art." True enough, there are some wastes of time in *Mind Breaths,* most tediously a bit of Marxist sociology set to verse that is so astonishingly leaden it drops off into a scholarly bibliography at the end. Normally, though, politics quickens his blood to just the right pace. His prophetic identity may have been wobbling a bit recently, but these political poems continue to exercise civic responsibilities—to name one of the less transcendental aspects of the prophetic mode—in the same old manner as before. Perhaps the lack of political development is a problem. The political poems in the new collection echo with political poems past, and those early poems can't be beat. But this is not the worst problem that a poet can face.

The signs of Ginsberg's growth are elsewhere in *Mind Breaths:* in new forms, a variety of conventional structural devices, and a retreat from the spontaneity whose development is illustrated in the *Journals.* Song and rhyme, actually, are not new for him—he used them in his previsionary youth—but I do not think he has ever sounded entirely at ease in any form other than the several he has developed himself. At least he is not afraid to sound awkward. The worst failure in the collection is a long, florid poem called "Contest of Bards," which narrates in a pseudo-mythic style an encounter between an old prophet who has lost his youthful prophetic powers and a beautiful poetic lad who has come to remind him of these powers. Doubtless some of Ginsberg's thoughts and hopes about his own lost visionary vocation are buried here, but the dramatic device is so heavy, the language so obscure in places, and the message so vague that the poem can only be read with great effort, and yields no pleasure.

The resounding successes in *Mind Breaths* are in those poems that, without excessive artifice, confront head-on Ginsberg's new estimations of self and world outlook. "I want to be known as the most brilliant man in America," one of these poems begins, just to prove that the old egomania can still fly its colors. He wants to be known as the man "who overthrew the CIA with a silent thought," "who prepared the way for Dharma in America," who triumphed over the "trickery of the world," and more, too—the chorus of "who's" lightly mocking "Howl" of two decades ago. He would like to be known for all these things, even if only some are true. "Ego Confession" is the apt name of the poem.

So Ginsberg's wry humor, which left him during the terrible years of repression and war in the sixties and early seventies, has returned in force. In "Mugging" he tells us how abashed he was when a blast of "Om" failed to disarm his muggers. "The tone of voice too loud," he conjectures while picking himself up off the ground. He means it, which makes the remark touching; but it is also funny, quietly. The quietness is a new quality in his sound, a shift down to the humble-tender, as it were, in which the wit serves dramatically to deflate the bombast. A good example is this quatrain from a seven-part poem about the last months and death of his father, called "Don't Grow Old":

> I read my father Wordsworth's *Intimations of Immortality*
> ". . . *trailing clouds of glory do we come*
> *from God, who is our home . . .*"
> "That's beautiful," he said, "but it's not true."

"Don't Grow Old" is yet another kaddish, which means that like the political poems it too chimes with earlier works. But here the echo is one of contrast, not repetition, for where the "Kaddish" for his mother was huge and cosmic, the poem for his father is modest and down to earth, and where "Kaddish" drew cadences from somber religious chants and especially from the Bible, "Don't Grow Old" uses the light rhythms of song (indicated in the appropriate section by one of the irritatingly amateurish musical transcriptions that Ginsberg has been availing himself of) and children's chants: "What will happen to my bones? / They'll get mixed up with the stones." In my opinion "Don't Grow Old" is one of Ginsberg's most memorable poems. But it is hardly the work of a visionary. It points in an entirely different direction from his early vatic poetry, which becomes apparent in the poem's exquisitely sad conclusion:

What's to be done about Death?
Nothing, nothing
Stop going to school No. 6 in 1937?
Freeze time tonight, with a headache, at quarter to 2 A.M.?
Not go to Father's funeral tomorrow morn?
Not go back to Naropa   teach Buddhist poetics summer?
Not be buried in the cemetery near Newark Airport some day?

Ginsberg's resigned tone avoids the unctuousness and smug preening that characterizes so much of American Buddhist poetry. It is an honest poem. If a grandiose ambition underlies "Don't Grow Old," it is, as he says in "Ego-Confession," "to set surpassing example of sanity. . . ." Mad no more, in short. The old visionary, in his persona, has been inching along into Good Gray Poet-hood for some time now, but here we have the poetic evidence, and no one will be disappointed.

NOTES

1. The interview is an excellent new study of his work, *The Visionary Poetics of Allen Ginsberg,* by Paul Portugés (Santa Barbara: Ross-Erikson, 1978).

2. Louis Simpson in *A Revolution in Taste* (New York: Macmillan, 1978), p. 74.

CHARLEY SHIVELY

25 Rainbows on My Windowsill

Since the San Francisco police tried to suppress publication of *Howl* (1956), Allen Ginsberg and Peter Orlovsky have been publicly known homosexuals. Authorities feared the openly explicit homosexual lines (censored as late as 1970 in the ninth printing of Thomas Parkinson's *Casebook on the Beat*); rulers panicked at people

> who bit detectives in the neck and shrieked with delight in
> policecars for committing no crime but their own
> wild cooking pederasy and intoxication . . .
> who let themselves be fucked in the ass by saintly
> motorcyclists, and screamed with joy,
> who blew and were blown by those human seraphim,
> the sailors, caresses of Atlantic and Caribbean love,
> who balled in the mornings in the evenings in rosegardens
> and the grass of public parks and cemeteries scattering
> their semen freely to whomever come who may . . .

Those lines remain (and I think will always remain) as startlingly fresh as the day they were written. What has changed is the context in which they can be heard. Gay Liberation groups have at least chastened the San Francisco police while gay newspapers, poetry groups, hotlines, health clinics, bookstores and publishers are building a culture of our own, a culture of freedom and new life. Within this culture, Allen Ginsberg and Peter Orlovsky no longer appear as oddities or freaks but as clues, examples. They are not something to avoid, but lives to study, to build upon. We

Review of *Straight Hearts' Delight: Love Poems and Selected Letters 1947–1980* by Allen Ginsberg and Peter Orlovsky, from *Gay Sunshine* (Autumn–Winter 1980). Reprinted with permission.

look to them for echoes, previously silenced, deadened, hidden. In gathering together love poems, photographs, drawings and letters, Winston Leyland exposes two extraordinary bodies—living literature, literary lives; ass suckers, cornholers, jerk-offs, fuckers, cocksuckers, poets—never before seen in such clear, transparent beauty/totality.

Supposedly all happy families (like business suits) are the same. But no two homosexuals are quite the same; and our sexuality consists of much more than what we do in bed. *Straight Hearts' Delight* leaves a lot out (don't we all withhold evidence?); yet it provides wonderful clues and questions about how love, poetry, sex, relationships, the world and revolution are (and can be) linked together. Within a gay context, Peter Orlovsky emerges both as a poet and a person—a creative force much more exciting than the companion/counterpart some would see. And Allen Ginsberg's achievement becomes all the more remarkable when seen through the prism of his loves/lovers.

Ginsberg's latest poem "Love Forgiven" (March 10, 1980) reads pure and delightful as one of Blake's songs:

> Straight and slender
> Youthful tender
> Love shows the way
> And never says nay
>
> Light & gentle—
> Hearted mental
> Tones sing & play
> Guitar in bright day
>
> Chanting always
> Poetries please
> Speak sweetly, say
> Hello, for you may
>
> Voicing always
> Melodies, please
> Sing sad, & say
> Farewell if you may

> Righteous honest
> Heart's forgiveness
> Woos Woes away,
> Gives love to cold clay.

Orlovsky's poems are more earthy and direct—"more athletic and physical"—and will appeal to some like myself for just that reason. Peter needed no spirits or metaphysical cover to just do it; his latest "Dildo Song   Note for Note on Guitar" comes out totally guiltless: "my sweet little dil-do." Peter seems to be searching for a direct fix with experience—no interventions, no gods or goddesses to "clean it up"—only sex in itself. Ginsberg himself testifies to the liberating experience he found in Peter's body: "so frank, so free and so open that I think it was one of the first times that I felt open with a boy." And Peter's very explicit "Sex Experiment" poems will be hard to swallow for the antisexuals:

> He takes his cock out of my ass, gently—a ball of shit falls on the
>   pillow—looks like shape of chicken heart—Allen thought it was
>   come—but no—he puts it on white paper & carries it—get
>   behind me & wipes my ass with underpants & krinckles my shit
>   up to throw away—my ass feels free—& easy relaxed—now I
>   go to bathroom—like I always do when he screws me &
>   wash—he goes for cig—& says that felt very good—

There is a remarkable absence of jealousy on both sides. Peter writes from NYC (20 March 1958) that "the next time I see him [Henry Schlachter] alone I give him a blast about jealousy. . . ." And while the events in Tangiers are somewhat obscure, Peter seems to have left rather than be caught in back-biting jealousies between Burroughs, Leary, and some of the literary leaches hovering around the circle. Ginsberg replies "I think one trouble here was you were isolated, I was confused and since I was clinging to my identity with you I could not see thru your identity to your heart, and I think you wound up over-affirming your identity and pressing down harder on it while it was under attack, instead of just giving it up & coming out free" (3 Aug 61).

The ideal was to find a system that would exclude no one, that would draw everyone into a circle of love. "Got on big discussion with Bill of means of extending Love-Bliss to others & spreading the connection between us (told him we had intended that in Tangiers with him, even if it didn't work) without sacrificing intimacy)." (20 Jan 58) Easier said than done! When I first met Orlovsky and Ginsberg in 1963, that was just the suggestion: why don't we (five in the room) just take our clothes off & do it. Uptightness prevailed, but not because of either Peter or Allen, nor I think because of my friend Edmund or myself (we'd both been in several orgies together before), but because of the cute SNCC boy who was passing as straight (he didn't want the public to know there were queers in SNCC). Probably too, nothing happened because Edmund, Allen and myself all wanted the pretty boy more than we wanted each other. What Peter wanted then was not entirely clear, but from his letters it would seem that Allen's love was the prize he sought.

Peter's not hot after the straight men, or if he is, he doesn't show it in letters or poems. Indeed I suspect he has been cursed with having to pass as bisexual in order to keep up Allen's interest in him. Allen is very clear about who he has loved in "Many Loves":

> My first love Neal Cassady
> He ran away from me
> Second love Kerouac
> He began to drink, alack
>
> Peter the third
>   took Speed quite long . . .
> He's back in the World now . . .

There are also those hopeful young poets; Peter takes them in stride, perhaps a bit sadly: "it seems to me that you will never have no piece for the rest of yr life for all hands want poetry & you know how many hands there are . . ." (24 Mar 60). A number of supposedly straight poets think that all they have to do is sleep with the great poet & their career will be made. This flock are physically beautiful insofar as one worships (and who

357

of us doesn't in some fashion) conformist, advertising standards of beauty; but we need to find a way of seeing more the beauties in each other (that to me is at the heart of gay liberation) than running after those who would kill our love. If only they could learn to love the gay energies within themselves (instead of their careers)—but then perhaps it is just us worshipping their straightness (calling it beauty) that keeps them from being liberated.

"Love" is just another word for dependency and endurance. In these letters, that is certainly clear. What drew Allen to Neal Cassady, Jack Kerouac and Peter Orlovsky was not only their beautiful hair: it was also their sweet dependency. Neal and Jack were great drinkers (did they get drunk before they let Allen love them?) and Peter became a speed quean [sic]. Peter's dependency and Allen's dominance are spelled out honestly in the letters and poems. As early as 1947, "In Society," Allen dreamed of his "messianic voice, inspired at / last, dominating the whole room." And Peter wrote, 23 June 60: "maybe I am yr Child & you dont know it Allen." 15 Sept 63: "I take you as my divine Love Gerhu you kept humming belley-Love in my ear & letters until I got yr meaning—swing open yr Blake gates." 25 Sept 63 signed, "Peter Your Slave Happey." Ginsberg is quite clear in his understanding of their relationship in their first sex: "emboldened, I screwed Peter. He wept afterwards, and I got frightened, not knowing what I'd done to make him cry, but completely moved by the fact that he was so involved as to weep. At the same time the domineering, sadism part of me was flattered and erotically aroused."

The letters and poetry are so completely honest because the authors and editors have undertaken a minimum of deletion and disguises. Consequently warts do show through; the great evil of polite society is to pretend that there are no flaws. Allen's weakness for blond straight men has been noticed. And Peter (at least in the printed letters) hasn't worked through his discomfort with Blackness. Thus he writes "I hope Leroy [Amiri Baraka] is happey & alright. Sorrey I dident make love with him when he wanted me to. John [Wieners] was right when he said I was scared." (25 Sept 63) And both Peter's and Allen's letters are studded with comments about women which are sadly short of seeing them as human beings.

The questions of how to end such social, sexual and racial inequalities is not easy. Both Allen and Peter have been active in all sorts of campaigns to save the earth and its people. But they seem clear that communism is not the answer. Having traveled to both Cuba and Czechoslovakia and having been expelled, Ginsberg underlines the weaknesses of existing communist regimes: "I still feel sympathy for revolution but I don't think they dig how puritan conformist & brainwashing dangerous it is . . . I told someone, a reporter, I'd had sex fantasies about Che Guevara & that almost precipitated an explosion in the Casa de la Americas" (4 Feb 65). And Peter comments on Allen's expulsion from Czechoslovakia after being crowned King of May: "Its too bad about being bosted out of Prague, it shows that sex love talk & suck is a big exploseive—if not more than the Hydrogen bomb" (14 May 65).

Both communists and academic formalists have been moving to dismiss the "sixties." What they really mean to say is that they want to kill the core in *Straight Hearts' Delight*. What is represented there goes much deeper into history (and I hope much further into the future) than the mere ten years from 1960 to 1969. The ancient Gnostics, the heretics, Blake, Rimbaud, Whitman—these have not been fads. At their core in different ways issues have come up about expanded consciousness, drugs and madness. At a Culture Conference in Chile in 1960, Ginsberg "read them Wieners' queer poems, Lamantia's 'Narcotica' & Gregory's Bomb—plus a long lecture on prosody, Jazz, Drugs, Soul, etc" (24 Jan 60). Many gay liberationists would sanitize (get rid of the crazies); while they fight the American Psychiatric Association to remove homosexuality from the sickness list, they are eager to disassociate "us" from, say, "schizophrenics."

Neither Peter nor Allen have fallen back from their early pledge of struggle. Orlovsky: "we'll change the world yet to our desire—even if we got to die—but OH the world's got 25 rainbows on my window sill . . ." (10 Feb 58). And Ginsberg: "there's too much to do, in public, & it's reaching proportions of religious revival, & we got to be absolutely pure to lay down a golden rose & not just goofy ego—& in a way it's important that we help save ourselves & everybody right now so we got to come forth & sing anyway even if afraid, like we laid out our task in eternity & now Voice of Eternity calling us out to dance to our own music & suffer forth our humancy where every eye can see . . ." (1 April 1958). That struggle did not begin in any of our lifetimes; and (something the sixties did not understand well enough) it will not end in our lifetimes. As long as people live who struggle to change the world, these letters, poems, documents will have meaning.

PAUL BERMAN

Untitled Review of
Plutonian Ode

What is a political-minded poet to do in an era of doom and
gloom? You could see the problem when Allen Ginsberg took
his turn at the mike a few weeks ago at the Town Hall protest
meeting for Polish Solidarity. From his seat on the stage,
Ginsberg had spent the evening nodding agreement while vari-
ous speakers gravely denounced communism, capitalism, the
defense budget, and other odiousnesses of the present day. His
own contribution was less grave: he brought out a guitarist,
dedicated his performance to Pete Seeger, and sang the poem
"Capitol Air" from his new book. "Capitol Air" is an extended
ditty, familiar to everyone who has seen Ginsberg perform over
the last year, which begins: "I don't like the government where I
live / I don't like dictatorship of the Rich." It continues in a less
than Panglossian fashion:

> No hope Communism no hope Capitalism Yeah
> Everybody's lying on both sides Nyeah nyeah nyeah
> The bloody iron curtain of American Military Power
> Is a mirror image of Russia's red Babel-Tower

Ginsberg danced to the vigorous strumming of the guitarist,
wagged his head in a fetchingly loose-jointed manner, and pro-
vided a pantomime subtext throughout. When he got to the line,
"I don't like Castro insulting members of my sex," he held up a
limp wrist to show which sex he meant. The effect was charm-
ing and funny, since the direness of his bill of political particulars

---

From the *Village Voice*, 23 March 1982. Reprinted with permission.

contrasted with the hamming, the silly-sounding rhymes, and the deadpan melody. The audience of sober leftists cheered and laughed appreciatively. The performance fit the occasion.

But there is no getting around the fact that the pessimism which lay beneath it presents a problem for Ginsberg's poetry. Not that a giant dose of disillusionment and outrage is anything new for him. As long ago as the middle fifties Ginsberg was hip to the CIA and its evil machinations—and denounced them in long poetic tirades. His political values have always been, by necessity of circumstance, mostly anti—anti stupid wars, anti gross imperialism, anti lunacy in government, anti *Time* magazine, anti nightstick as a tool of morality. But in earlier years his despair about such things stood against a background of other sentiments—sentiments that were often unstated but present nonetheless, such as naive idealism and youthful optimism. You can see this in an early poem like "America," where political indignation conflicted poignantly with naive optimism and even seedlings of patriotism. "America when will you be angelic?" he asked.

He is not asking this question anymore. Political despair has swept the field, and the underground naiveté and optimism are gone. In recent political poems there is no tension between text and subtext, stated emotion and unstated emotion—at least there is no tension when you read the poems on the printed page. In performance he is able to conjure some of his youthful whimsy and innocence, and pose the contrast. But most of this is lost in print.

The flatness of Ginsberg's recent political poetry points to a larger problem. Perhaps society has reached a stage where our language can no longer cope with the mess we find ourselves in. We certainly seem to have reached this stage with regard to the nuclear calamity that nearly everyone believes is impending. The words to discuss this calamity seem not to exist. Language fails us; we don't know how to describe our own danger and predicament convincingly, which is why we twiddle our thumbs and wish someone else would come up with an intelligent solution. Ginsberg, in "Plutonian Ode," has made a major effort to grapple with this situation. He has scrounged up what seems like every possible element for a new nuclear language—Greek myth (Pluto, Hades, and Nemesis), Buddhism and Buddhist numerology, the exorcist formulas of his own anti-Vietnam conjurings, the language of Whitman, even what seems like a hint of Eliot, via "Waste Land" type footnotes. In an interview about this poem he dragged in Milton and Blake as well. It is as if he has thrown everything he can think of at the nuclear industry, and is now hurling the kitchen sink. But, alas, the industry survives.

The bulk of the new collection consists of minor and light poems following lines laid out in his last, much more substantial, book, *Mind Breaths*. There are rueful Blakean love songs of the sort that are greatly improved in performance. There is an experiment in rigid sapphic metrics. There are three minor additions to "Don't Grow Old," the moving kaddish for his father—his tenderest, most distinguished poem of the last decade. And there are a couple of vivid cityscapes, or rather Avenue A-scapes, which he has always been very good at.

The one significant advance from the last book, and the one major success, is an adaptation of Neruda (done with Sidney Goldfarb from an old *Masses & Mainstream* translation). The poem is a Whitman-like invocation of Abraham Lincoln, striking for its combination of the vatic and the humorous, the political and the American mythic:

> Let the Railsplitter Awake!
> Let Lincoln come with his axe
> and with his wooden plate
> to eat with the farmworkers.
> May his craggy head,
> his eyes we see in constellations,
> in the wrinkles of the live oak,
> come back to look at the world
> rising up over the foliage
> higher than Sequoias.
> Let him go shop in pharmacies,
> let him take the bus to Tampa
> let him nibble a yellow apple,

> let him go to the movies, and
> talk to everybody there.
>
> Let the Railsplitter awake!

and so forth. Maybe here lies a way out of the present dilemma of political poetry—a return, via the Spanish, to American historical sources, a language to be scooped up out of the American past. For the poet who wrote, "America I feel sentimental about the Wobblies," and who cites Sacco and Vanzetti at the drop of a hat, reaching back into history would be less of a departure than one might think.

PART FOUR   *Thinking Back*

Working at home on East Twelfth Street. New York City, 1982.

WILLIAM A. HENRY III

In New York
Howl *Becomes a Hoot*

Night, the hour of poets, on a windy street in the part of New York City where academe meets Harlem. Outside a nondescript building, a man calls to an acquaintance. The second replies, "Allen Ginsberg reading 'Howl'? It's tempting, but . . ." He walks on.

Inside McMillin Theater at Columbia University, an audience of about 900 assembles. Most appear to be younger than the poem they are to hear. A few are bearded hippies loyal to the Movement. A few are enervated, gentle, Buddhistic Wasps. A handful are black. All around are flannel shirts, funny hats, sleeping children, the emblems of safe bourgeois funk. Not many in the crowd notice, let alone cheer, the arrival of one honored guest, Radical and Felon Abbie Hoffman.

Most wait quietly, unsure of what to expect. Ginsberg is reading his epic poem of outrage and lament to commemorate the twenty-fifth anniversary of its publication. Media announcements have recalled the public theatrics of the poet, an ostentatious nonconformist, a self-described "Hebraic Melvillean bardic breath." He drew together the strident Beat Generation of the 1950s, led the flower children of the 1960s into Eastern religions, hymned the antinuclear movement of the 1970s. Throughout, he sustained his vernacular yet visionary voice— marked, said one admiring fellow poet, by a "note of hysteria that hit the taste of the young."

There is nothing obviously theatrical about the Allen Ginsberg who scutters among friends and fumbling technicians. One thirtyish woman in the audience, a "fan," fails to recognize him. Says she: "He looks like any college professor." Gone are the flowing beard, the Zapata mustache, the ragbag tatters. He wears a gray-blue business suit, a blue shirt, muted red-and-blue striped tie, dark socks, black shoes. Offstage he talks with the measured deliberation of a statesman-celebrity.

Half an hour late, Poet Anne Waldman rises to introduce the aging *enfant terrible,* now fifty-five. She arouses the crowd to nostalgia for dissent with the code language of the anti-Establishment. She describes Ginsberg as a product of "postwar materialist paranoid doldrums." She proclaims, to the audience's laughter, that "Howl" was "written while Allen was living on unemployment compensation."

At last Ginsberg is ready to stand and perform, as he has at coffeehouses and on campuses since the late 1950s. "Howl" begins with one of the bitterest and best-known lines in American poetry: "I saw the best minds of my generation destroyed by madness, starving hysterical naked."

But something has changed. This puckish little figure, this professorial imp with the loony grin, does not sound angry. He is not wailing about the wickedness of his time. He is mocking the past—mocking the angry radicals, mocking the dreamers, mocking the quest for visions. The audience is laughing with him. They are howling, but in pleasure rather than anger, as he thrusts an arm up for each of the jokes. They hear satire, not nobly expended pain, in these lines: ". . . who vanished into nowhere Zen New Jersey leaving a trail of ambiguous picture postcards of Atlantic City Hall"; "who scribbled all night rocking and rolling over lofty incantations which in the yellow morning were stanzas of gibberish"; "who drove cross-country seventy-two hours to find out if I had a vision or you had a vision or he had a vision to find out Eternity"; "who demanded sanity trials accusing the radio of hypnotism and were left with their insanity and their hands and a hung jury."

Some, perhaps, do not understand the poem. After a long litany using the name Moloch, a biblical god demanding human sacrifice, to invoke nearly every American banality and evil, two girls turn to ask a man behind them, "What is a Moloch?" Others, perhaps, are reflecting on their own older-but-wiser bemusement about antiwar and anti-Establishment excesses of the 1960s, a decade later than the poem. But Ginsberg's humor is intentional. His contemplative, rounded voice has tightened into singsong waggery.

Mockery is his theme through much of the night. He speaks of a poem by William Blake, whose work once plunged Ginsberg into perception of "a totally deeper real universe than I'd been existing in," as "a country-western S-M song." He then sings several of Blake's visionary eruptions, to cheerful nurserylike ditties of his own composition. Near the end of the evening he reads from recent verses describing himself as a failure. In one he confesses: "My tirades destroyed no intellectual unions of the KGB and CIA . . . I have not yet stopped the armies of entire mankind on the way to World War III . . . I never got to heaven, nirvana, x, whatchamacallit. I never learned to die."

After the reading he is surrounded by youths asking the usual hesitant questions of the star-struck. Does he remember a mutual friend? (Yes.) Does he still have a following in Europe? (He seems to remember, and cite, his every public reading scheduled within the past two years.) What younger poets does he like? (He mentions Punk Novelist Jim Carroll, Rock Singer Patti Smith and "a guy named David Pope in Grand Rapids, who doesn't get published.")

In Europe, where 100,000 Prague youths once elected Ginsberg King of the May, the young are once again marching against war. On campuses there are teach-ins about the threat of nuclear holocaust. But this night, at this Columbia campus, sartorially and spiritually the most volatile and un-Ivy of the Ivy League, Allen Ginsberg is chatting, singing, wearing a necktie and making his howl a thigh-slapping hoot. His last words are prophetic, but not in the stirring way of the years gone by. He plays a worn squeeze-box and sings: "Meditate on emptiness, 'cause that's where you're going, and how."

GEORGE BOWERING

How I Hear "Howl"

(Poetry is a vocal art. In the following impression of Allen
Ginsberg's poem, I will refer not so much to the printed versions
as to his spoken version on the Fantasy LP 7005, *Howl and Other
Poems*.)

. . . The central image of "Howl" is the "robot skullface of
Moloch," the mechanical monolith that eats the children of
America. The original Moloch was just as fearful, tho not so
widely powerful. This was the old Canaanite god that appealed
to the wives of the original Solomon, & earlier to the followers
of Moses. He was figured as a giant stone statue with arms held
out & giant flames burning all round him. It was the practice of
religious women to worship Moloch by casting their children
into the arms of the statue & watching them burn alive, held by
that mockery of affection & care. So Ginsberg's image of a
present day monster, as much more terrible as the Empire State
Building is taller than an ancient Hebrew statue.

(Here the reader should hear Part II of "Howl")

(Then listen to the whole poem)

Depending on whether you are for or against Moloch, the sacri-
fice can mean two things. A ravenous murder of children by
their self-interested parents, or a chance for the children to pu-
rify themselves thru flames & torture & death. The latter strikes
close to the Christian way to paradise, or what Ginsberg calls
"the starry dynamo in the machinery of night." All thru the
poem, heaven & eternity are in sight, are being called upon, or
bitterly regretted, so that a cynical second best stands as an ironic
refuge from the world of present Moloch. In a haunting parallel

From *Beaver Kosmos Folio* (Calgary, Canada), no. 1 (1969). Reprinted with
permission.

to the sermon on the mount, Ginsberg substitutes for "theirs shall be the kingdom of heaven"—"their heads shall be crowned with laurel in oblivion."

Christ went on to say: "Blessed are ye, when men shall revile you, and persecute you, and shall say all manner of evil against you falsely, for my sake. Rejoice, and be exceeding glad: for great is your reward in heaven: for so persecuted they the prophets which were before you."

These are the people seen by Ginsberg in the first broad scene of his poem: "I saw the best minds of my generation destroyed . . ." In seeing them, he has his eyes wide open, all three of them, & his mind opens outward, opening with long torrential lines rolled out together on an axle of sound, the words propelling one another, as in the rime & consonant leading of:

> who chained themselves to subways for the endless ride from
>   Battery to holy Bronx on benzedrine until the noise of
>   wheels and children brought them down shuddering
>   mouth-wracked and battered bleak of brain all drained of
>   brilliance in the drear light of Zoo

But woe betide the scholar man who says a man dont have time to see precise truth when he is lipping off this way. Let me say the great poet (& in this poem speaks he) comes to truth world thru the sounds he picks out of it. So I will mention some things I hear in Part I of "Howl," & I say that in his rapid setting down, Ginsberg was in the happy poet experience where the true sounds of the galaxy are there with true sightings, & the man's pen is hard presst to get most he can down, in frantic pursuit.

Here I return to the "vast conspiracy to impose one level of mechanical consciousness on mankind,"* & the means by which

---

*Bowering has earlier referred to a remark of Ginsberg's printed in the *Village Voice*, 25 August 1959: "Recent history is the record of a vast conspiracy to impose one level of mechanical consciousness on mankind and exterminate all manifestations of that unique part of human sentience in all men, which the individual shares with his Creator."—ED.

the Occupation does this. The agents of the Occupation wield their control by controlling money, time, machines, institutional education, & all the means of communication.

Ginsberg goes underground against the tyranny of Time, finding some refuge in the eternity that is sanctuary of artists & religious martyrs, where Shadrach, Meschach & Abed-nego really walkt when Nebuchadnezzar thought he had them in his Moloch furnace. So Ginsberg's martyrs are "burning for the ancient heavenly connection to the starry dynamo in the machinery of night," the antithesis to the machinery operated by the social state.

Ginsberg itemizes the true story staggering of his martyrs who cower, get busted, purgatory their bodies, see lightning in their brains that illuminates "all the motionless world of Time." He is interested in motion, soul motion, emotion, to break thru the motionless world of Time. Time, Standard Time, Time Magazine, Time Payments, There's A Time For Everything. The face of Moloch is a clock. The martyrs (I have to call them that now) sit for hours waiting doom-crack, talk continuously for seventy hours, disgorge in total recall for biblical seven days & nights. Section I of "Howl" shows portraits of people the poet knows, caught in the eye of Time.

Finally, in one great gesture of rebellion, they throw their watches off the roof "to cast their ballot for Eternity outside of Time, & alarm clocks fell on their heads every day for the next decade." The insurgents, now, the insurgents demonstrate, & the Occupation answers by dropping bombs, clocks, the terrible measure of bombs for a decade, the weapon of Time. In retaliation the insurgents smash "phonograph records of nostalgic European 1930s German jazz"—captured Time broken loose in the smashing, the motionless world liberated for a second of Eternity; but in Eternity a second is all Eternity, & a blow can be struck against the duly invested authorities.

The insurgents keep active, barreling "down the highways of the past" & driving crosscountry in 72 hours of time, looking for Eternity, a vision of Eternity, a hope. They make a seige on Denver, defy Death & Time for a moment, only to be defeated again, to go away again, "to find out the time." To try again in a bombed out cathedral where hope, "the soul illuminated its hair for a second," but a second from Eternity where the soul is; a second in Eternity is all Eternity, but shown in Time it is only a second. & Carl Solomon, hero of the poem, is torn from cathedral, thrown into institution madhouse, into the "total animal soup of time," where he still dreams freedom, making "incarnate gaps in Time & Space." He is, as Allen is, "putting down here what might be left to say in time come after death," for a time after Time, for, obviously, Eternity, when the cities will be destroyed, when Moloch will fall on his back. This is hope & prophecy. This from Solomon, from Allen, from each martyr, who is "the madman bum and angel beat in Time."

At the same time the martyrs demonstrate against the other oppressions, money & academy, prisons where not criminals but children are lockt up, bent, warpt, trained to pass thru the sacrifice fires of Moloch. Ginsberg gives a clue to what *Life* magazine (yes, where is *Death* magazine) calls the "Beat mystique" when he first presents the insurgents as "poverty and tatters and hollow-eyed," deviants from the control center instructions like "Clothes make the man—Physical fitness keeps America strong."

Opposed to academy control of developing brains, Ginsberg proffers the direct vision, religious, hallucinatory, a flash of light, what happens in that revealed second of Eternity. So the insurgents "bared their brains to heaven," seeing "Blake-light tragedy among the scholars of war." Here is personal Ginsberg biography, as everyone must know by now, & apt—Blake is anathema to the scholar approach, he doesnt fit, he baffles the overconscious mind, & professors generally dismiss him or try to make him something he is not—politician, patriot, moron. So the young insurgents, the young in one another's arms, preferring their Blake visions, are like him, "expelled from the academies for crazy & publishing obscene odes on the windows of the skull." (Strange tough variation on Petrarchan image.)

"Crazy" still, & making archetypal protest, they leave the university & burn their money (the "heterosexual dollar"), not only a plain facts crime against the American state, but an insult to that control as sure as the other insult to the academy's programs of lassitude: "who studied Plotinus Poe St. John of the Cross telepathy and bop kaballa because the cosmos instinctively vibrated at their feet in Kansas."

A clear sight into "Howl," you see, needs not interpretation, needs only listening ear, maybe rearrangement like mind that remembers qualitatively—that is, I am sure the Gysin Burroughs cut-up suggestion, done many times would also reveal here—the objects, the nouns speak out, group together, they speak out.

The martyrs, insurgents, wanderers now, seek out visionary indian angels, insulting the professor at Columbia Berkeley Reed Iowa State University—the visionary indian angel is not caught in motionless time; if he were he wouldnt be around, alive this century. & they throw Dada potato salad at CCNY lecturers on Dadaism, making moment of gooey vision in sordid program of a prof trying to intellectual footnote chapter heading discourse organize the unorganizable—itself, the lecture, hopeless Dada that can only invite & be pointed out by a handful of potato salad on vest front. Organic communication.

As opposed to mechanistic control of machine & communication.

"Excuse me, I think my phone's tapt by the FBI."

"Then use instant soul semaphore, or like jazz."

I think the first part of "Howl" deals largely with that major concern of modern writers—that thing about communication. The heroes of the poem are broken & punisht & trained for sacrifice thru the control center's hold on the machinery of contact; & when they become insurgents they have instinctively, religiously sought (Ginsberg makes good use of the verb, "seek") communication that transcends the machine.

So they drag themselves down long straight communication streets, the city's way to Harlems, looking for a visionary connection. It is only under the communication El that they can bare their brains, looking for the heaven fix. They get busted at communication Mexican border for transporting grass illumination—the control center machines must keep their human machines in the dark. They wander in a maze of blind streets looking for heaven lightning to transport them impossibly to "Poles of Canada & Patterson." They jolt along in communication subways, tunneling away from brilliance in that above-board underground machine. They return & return to, & finally leap off the big American successful communication Brooklyn Bridge, into dirty rivers that go nowhere but down. In their prisons they wait for the light that crackt the gloom dark cell of Peter & Simon. The jukebox in the background is trapt mechanical singer of this age, & Ginsberg sees it as "hydrogen jukebox" where the crack of doom will be communicated, broadcast.

The railroad in the nineteenth century (Whitman) pusht west to the Pacific, opening the country & closing it too, around all caught in the continent; the railroad was the communication network that made America big & was supposed to make America great. Now Ginsberg's heroes "wandered around and around at midnight in the railroad yard wondering where to go, and went, leaving no broken hearts." They are lost in America's communication center, outsiders, not even able to participate in the grand design as does Pauline of the Perils, who at least knew what was going to happen as she lay there trusst to the Union Pacific tracks—the vibrations along the rails were news.

Thru the streets of New York, Idaho, blitz purgatory, deep in subway tubes, on bridges, they are lost where men should find. They sit cold in "boxcars boxcars boxcars," racketing thru unknown snows of farmland America, prisoners of the long train in the night. Better to be inside something timeless, the Volcanoes of Mexico, for instance, volcanoes that are ancient & revered as supernatural; they reach for the sky, but they have deep holes in them, where gods can enter the earth. In America the volcanoes thin out, & they are definitely not supernatural; to the American they are noted for their size, or their names as national monuments, a thing of the Time. (See Shelley on volcanoes.) "To converse about America and Eternity, a hopeless task," Ginsberg says.

At this point I want to say something about every single Ginsberg phrase in the poem—they all arrest, they exfoliate. But it cant be done, & should not. Let me touch finger to some, reader do it himself.

For instance, though, you know, you *know* where Ginsberg is & where the control center is, & who is doing what with the means of communication, when you see the martyrs "howled on their knees in the subway." The subway, how is it not the cattle train to Dachau? (This writ before we ever saw *The Pawnbroker*.) Who has not dreamed the "horrors of Third Avenue iron dreams?" But even in the shadow of the great control center communication machines, the insurgents arise betimes to construct their own holy machines of worship, to reach beyond the steel sky—"who sat in boxes breathing in the darkness under the bridge, and rose up to build harpsichords in their lofts . . . rocking and rolling over lofty incantations," doomed songs of freedom. Their songs are drowned out by the Orwell "radio of hypnotism" in the end. But outside Time there is no end. There is a place to reach. & so they reach, the martyrs, & they try to communicate in their own underground networks:

> to recreate the syntax and measure of poor human prose and
> stand before you speechless and intelligent and shaking
> with shame, rejected yet confessing out the soul to conform
> to the rhythm of thought in his naked and endless head.

This is the enemy of Moloch, & in Part II of "Howl," Ginsberg howls his defiance as his fathers carry him toward the fire & gleamy eye, the final torture & death at the grim hands of the monster lurking thru Part I, where he is seen in concrete, stone, lead, iron, ugly flames. In Part II Ginsberg starts by asking: "What sphinx of cement and aluminum bashed open their skulls and ate up their brains and imagination?" Formally, the poet is working from the first line of Part I, the image of the best minds of his generation destroyed, here eaten out of basht-open skulls.

At the Chicago reading (on the Fantasy record) the poet begins Part II with a suddenly deliberate pace, after the high flight that ended Part I. By the time the fifteenth & last line of Part II is reacht, there is an exciting tension in the voice, great emotion of pain & defiance. Moloch he confronts, maybe a moment before his own brains are to be slurpt down.

As Part I was one long exhausting sentence, Part II is the natural series of noun clusters & exclamation (!) points that come from the throat of a son about to be sacrificed, the outcry that has little time. When there is little time & no place for decorum, the noun comes out: "Moloch! Solitude! Filth! Ugliness! Ashcans and unobtainable dollars!" Here Ginsberg strips his statement to essentials: "Moloch whose mind is pure machinery! . . . Moloch who entered my soul early!"

Here Ginsberg switches from the survey of the American Occupation in Part I, to first person confession & defiance. He rips thru formal logic in presentation, to the bare communication available in words direct from the soul, as adjective becomes noun, & noun becomes adjective which is noun: "Crazy in Moloch! Cocksucker in Moloch!" The control center ways of communication are removed entirely, & Ginsberg's poem at this point becomes lesson—what difference here from the abstract sludge of business jargon evasion ("due to circumstances beyond our corporate control") or evasive poetry language ("You would think the fury of aerial bombardment / Would rouse God to relent; the infinite spaces / Are still silent.")

"They broke their backs lifting Moloch to Heaven!" says Ginsberg of the martyrs, & he tells in four great powerful long lines, the tragedy of lost sold-out American dream gone down the choked-out American river, or again, "down on the rocks of Time!" the treacherous killer of the drifted mind removed from hope Eternity.

Part III is addresst to Carl Solomon, & now Ginsberg has passt "thru the fire to Moloch" (2 *Kings* 23:10). "I'm with you in Rockland," he says. Rockland is name of loony bin, but this way—Rock Land—the metamorphosis of America, rock being the material of Moloch, the mountain of American machine, the "incomprehensible prison" of Part II.

Carl Solomon is addresst as a crazy Jesus, so apt, Jesus the enemy of Canaanite Moloch, & now we must think of hope, resurrection, peace, direct ascent to heaven, the connection by way of soul to the starry dynamo. This crazy Jesus has murdered his twelve secretaries, cries that "the soul is innocent and immortal," & his soul will never be returned to its body "from its pilgrimage to a cross in the void." Solomon (the wives of Solomon betrayed him to worship Moloch—this happened in the Old Testament), Carl Solomon is rebel Jesus, plotting against the "fascist national Golgotha," or Moloch again.

Ginsberg predicts victory for this sacrificial leader of the insurrection, saying they will "split the heavens of Long Island and resurrect your living human Jesus from the superhuman tomb." In fact resurrection is the prelude to revolution war, uprising of the sacrificial victims, angelic bombardments by the souls' airplanes to counter the Time bombardments of alarm clocks. The stakes are America & freedom.

> Moreover
> thou hast taken
> thy sons & thy daughters
> whom thou hast borne unto me,
> & these hast thou sacrificed
> unto them to be devoured.
> Is this of thy whoredoms
> a small matter,
>
> that thou hast slain my children,
> & delivered them
> to cause them to pass thru
> the fire for them?
>
> (*Ezekiel* 16:20–21)

WARREN TALLMAN

Mad Song

Allen Ginsberg's San Francisco Poems

"Howl" Part I, tells Carl Solomon's story, or is it Neal Cassady's, or is it North American Everymadman's? Whichever, it is also night pangs and ay cries as Allen Ginsberg is born into knowledge of the ruins in which he and his friends have what being they have been able to muster—which isn't much. How little is explained at the climax of the poem just after it has happened to mother

> and the last fantastic book flung out of the
> tenement window, and the last door closed at 4 AM and the last
> telephone slammed at the wall in reply and the last furnished
> room emptied down to the last piece of mental furniture, a
> yellow paper rose twisted on a wire hanger in the closet, and
> even that imaginary, nothing but a hopeful little bit of
> hallucination—

These are not hysterical actions of the destroyed minds. They are an emphatic if rueful catalogue of resourcelessness, not a counting up but a counting down under and out of what is left when the books, the telephones and the doors—knowledge, communication, contact—are all shut and slammed and smashed. Not much is left, only a flower. And not much of a flower, paper in fact, a yellow rose head twisted onto coat hanger shoulders there in the closet of being there in the empty apartment. But still, a flower—paper head dream of coat hanger hope, deep in the heart of Madtown.

I should mention the lickety-split mind speed at which Ginsberg sends his measure vehicle yacketayakking down the

From *Open Letter*, 3d ser. (Winter 1976–77). Reprinted with permission.

incomparable blind streets. It is this speed which sustains and controls the kind of trip he takes in Part I. The underlying pace doesn't falter until he reaches the full pause in near nonbeing. But way out west in the Berkeley cottage the pacing in "Transcription of Organ Music" is exactly opposite. Yacketayak-yak-yak gives way to an almost motionless motion of thought. There are a series of slow starts which lapse into stops which open out as the leaves of actual flowers might into other slow starts. Ginsberg explains the process as "strange writing which passes from prose to poetry and back, like the mind" and as "long units and broken short lines spontaneously noting prosaic realities mixed up with emotional upsurges, solitaries." The words falter in this most naked of the San Francisco poems because being itself falters under awareness that all creation lies open to the gaze of his "mental open eye." The faltering traces to an absence in which no human object or objective other than himself appears to return his open, receptive gaze. Attention shifts, pauses, almost floats under influence of the music: from ordinary objects in the cottage to remembrance of times past to the flowers outside in the dooryard, "red blossoms in the night light," to the flower inside, "in the glass peanut bottle," to the one in the pallet on the floor, "I am so lonesome in my glory," to the sound flower that "descends as does the tall bending stalk of the heavy blossom."

I suppose that "Transcription" is in many ways an unsuccessful poem just because Ginsberg can find no means to carry his yearning for fullness of being beyond yearning—"I want people to bow when they see me and say he is gifted with poetry, he has seen the presence of the creator." Wanting is not having. Yet in the chronology of Ginsberg's flowers the incomplete yearnings of "Transcription" stand as a long stride on the road back from near nonbeing in the Madtown closet. The eye of paper flower head has opened in hope and the world of the western cottage has opened eyes back: the actual flowers "their leaves too have hope and are upturned top flat to the sky to receive"; the closet door, which "kindly stayed open for me its owner"; the light socket, the entrance to the kitchen, the kitchen window—all open to receive. In this way the poem confesses for Ginsberg to a direct if imperfect knowledge of and strange faithful confidence in his capacity for being, even under these adverse conditions in which peanut bottles, disconnected phones, and closet doors are among his nearest of kin and kind. Nor is the poem to be understood without recognizing his peculiarly North American awareness of both the anguish and yet the release which arrive when being surges up without benefit of complementary beings. The kind of narcissistic joy which hovers in among the music, the suffering, and the flowers carries strong echoes and some of the weight Whitman gave us that time on Paumanok's shore when his boy, bare-headed, bare-footed, sent the bird of the body seeking after the lost bird of the soul. In their journeys west from varieties of Madtown our ocean-going Ishmaels, river-going Hucks and road-going Moriarities, seeking new Americas of love, are likely to come upon temporary Americas of self-love, no flesh so sweet as that clinging to Walt Whitman's self-honored bones or so rosy as Allen Ginsberg's himself his asphodel. But it is not the eros of heavy moon, drooping star in the west, or moody tearful night in which Ginsberg seeks the soul. So Ginsberg rushes up "enchanted" grabs the "unholy battered old thing" and swoops into "Sunflower Sutra" surely one of the most exuberant poems of our day, a perfect beauty of a comic, wistful, profound, goofy, touching North American poem. In the supermarket he felt absurd. Now he fixes upon that absurdity as insight and perception comes alive, unlocking Madtown. Swallow the keys, throw away the doors and sing a song of sunflowers. When the soul is repossessed its creditors become absurd, its old debts delirious, its hells handbooks on heaven. The flower becomes a flower again (just in time) rescued like Pauline of olden western epic from out the villainous clutch of "impotent dirty old locomotive." And locomotive is identified "forget me not" as true villain of those blues rising up from Kerouac's railroad earth, confessing from out its soulless soul that all those trains are tired. But dayflower, sunflower shakes off that "dress of dust, that veil of darkened railroad skin, that smog of cheek, that eyelid of black misery," and takes up once more a "perfect excellent sunflower existence," opens "a sweet natural eye to the new hip moon," and shines like Whitman and like Chaplin down on the "shadow of the mad locomotive riverbank." From yellow paper closet flower of near nonbeing, "only a hopeful little bit of hallucination," to solitary hopeful being among the flowers of the western cottage, "their leaves too have hope," to solitary stroll through supermarket counting up absurd correspondences to ward off the Lethean dark inside and outside, then on into the absurdity, into "Sunflower Sutra" where deepening consciousness of absurd being opens a way perception can follow and so provides Ginsberg with his best means by which to measure what he needs to know in order to be. And if you happen to be truly absurd in Madtown, what's to do, east side, west side, and all around North America, but sing a mad song. . . .[1]

2.

The resourcefulness of the phrasing in all of the San Francisco poems argues a resourceful, a supermarket sensibility and the impact of that phrasing, particularly of the images of burning, argues a hard-pressed one, almost run down by ten thousand unnatural shocks fresh in from the city street fields. Were this sum of Ginsberg's malimpressions the only active inner weather of perception he could summon up within the universe of himself, no stars at elbow and foot, he would surely be caught in that same undertow toward nonbeing which drags at his lambs. Strength to resist such a downdrift evidently traces to his early Blake vision as well as to the hallucinations and ecstacies which his sufferings have helped induce. It is his perception of these different transcendent objects from that "Heaven which exists and is everywhere about us" which enables him to summon up a different wind or weather to oppose the shuddering clouds which swirl from Moloch. And it is from the clashing of these opposed weathers that his vital perceptions of absurdity open out, poet aware of the incongruity of standing at a single corner as both "madman bum and angel," the circumstance which carries him in among these comic scenes of human tragedy into divine comedies. Chaucer putting Troilus on the wracks of an absurdity called love. Swift mocking Gulliver, Chaplin laughing at Chaplin. Were the transformations from tragedy to absurdity complete, "Howl" would fully convey Ginsberg's at once profound and absurd belief that the faces of all his chimney sweep lambs shine like the face of heaven in a single sunflower. But it seems to me that "Howl" is an incomplete sunflower, partial Chaplin rather than a work of unified single intelligence.

I do not think that the incompleteness traces to his spontaneous jazz measure since spontaneous improvisation at its best can be a motion of the whole man. It rather traces to abandonments of spontaneous measure as more calculated motives intrude. When for example he recounts the sexual misadventures of his lambs the length of the list argues more calculation than spontaneity. Some of the effects seem forced, maneuvred into place rather than riding on the swift current of the going moment. The side motive may be very laudable, possibly a desire to attack our Puritan sensibilities. But such motives are less important than the need to transform the lambs' sufferings into the absurdity which would release them from their thwarted and purgatorial sexual being in its downdrift toward complete nonbeing. Particularly when it is his perceptions of absurdity which convey—at least to this reader—truest tone and most complete Ginsberg. It may very well be that at a deeper level Ginsberg's visionary perceptions of the fields of Heaven, more sporadic and fleeting than Blake's, provide him with fewer heavenly objects and a lesser supply of the breathing winds, *angels* at elbow and foot, needed to accomplish transformations in among the misadventures he so courageously takes on. In consequence the sunflower dims in places leaving nightmare of Moloch in among the shadows. For me it is when Ginsberg's pace steadies on an underlying slowness that he most effectively produces a motion of the whole, as in "Transcription of Organ Music" and "Supermarket," solitude poems in which the suffering and the absurdity bear a weep/clown/laugh relationship. In going all out for his lamb friends he moves beyond an inner stillness even silence which may be the most integral feature of his universe, a well where love and grief lie mingled in a darkness inaccessible to all save himself alone.

Yet to call for perfect sunflower or complete Chaplin is, under the circumstances, itself absurd, something Chaplin didn't often and even sunflowers, even poets, only sometimes achieve. Nor do the imperfections cancel out the nobility and authenticity of the poem which reads like item one in a new Declaration of Independence holding that all men are born with certain inalienable rights, such as the right to be. It is only that in our time to be and yet walk through the Moloch-shadowed valleys of our cityside world is to be absurd, the angel who is also a bum, mad both ways. It is such a patriot who steps forward in "America" to sing "My Country 'Tis of Thee"—"America I've given you all and now I'm nothing." But just at the point that God is supposed to "crown thy good with brotherhood" the patriot begins to muff his lines: "America I used to be a communist when I was a kid I'm not sorry," and having lost his place in the text he wanders distractedly from song to mutter: "America its them, bad Russians. Them Russians them Russians and them Chinamen. And them Russians." Now a good poet and patriot never relinquishes his right of song, even when mixed up, so Ginsberg quickly regroups and begins to sing "Our Russia 'Tis of Her": "The Russia wants to eat us alive. The Russia's power mad. She wants to take our cars from out our garages. / Her wants to grab Chicago. Her needs a Red Reader's Digest. Her wants our auto plants in Siberia." Scratch a patriot and you offend his ancestors; Ginsberg now breaks out into pure cigar store Cherokee: "Him big bureaucracy running our fillingstations. / That no good. Ugh. Him make Indians learn read. Him need big black niggers. Hah."

Here, as is often the case in field of poetry, a relaxation of intensity—and this is by all odds the least intense of the San Francisco poems—brings the poet's characteristic tone to the surface. Wordsworth's "Daffodils" carries none of the force of his major poems but does convey the wonder of his delight in the phenomenal world. "America" is the nearest thing to a purely clown poem Ginsberg has, clown clowning around, ("I don't want to join the army or turn lathes in precision parts factories, I'm nearsighted and psychopathic anyway") and in the process bringing to the poem's surface that inner comic weather easily unified and enormously effective which is daffodil to the more ambitious sunflowers in which the Pilgrim takes pride.

But to be a pilgrim you must have suffered and to seek a complete sunflower you must go full circle from where you are to where you have been. If Ginsberg's San Francisco horses are set as Emily Dickinson's were, "Back home to eternity where the heart was left and farewell tears began," he must make his departure from "In The Baggage Room at Greyhound." I venture to guess that across the rather wide gap between her New England gentility and Ginsberg's San Francisco genitality Emily would nonetheless have appreciated the cryptic intensity which gives observation sharp edges and curious angles similar in places to her own because focused—as so many of her poems were—from inside an accepted suffering as this beat Pilgrim surveys the landscape of his human America where one last package "sits alone at midnight sticking up out of the Coast rack high as the dusty fluorescent light." A neon sun and a package mountain resting on the tough baggage racks of this world; contemplated by a tired clown in among the wracks, with one touch of Whitman—"sitting myself on top of them now as is my wont at lunchtime to rest my tired foot"—and one touch of bravado—"This is for poor shepherds. I am a communist"— prior to departure, "12:15 A.M., May 9, 1956." Pilgrim about to depart for still more open road valleys through the Moloch shadows of our time, speed slowed by pain into a curious calm. This calm, which flows from himself alone, dominates "Greyhound" and is the even breathing element unifying "Transcription of Organ Music" and "In a California Supermarket." Much like a steady, silent river moving under it bears up the antics which dance over in "Howl," "Sunflower Sutra" and "America." In a word, the clown is melancholy. And on this note makes his departure from San Francisco, "Farewell ye Greyhound where I suffered so much, hurt my knee and scraped my hand and built my pectoral muscles big as vagina." The vagina is the entrance to the womb and the pectoral muscles build up the breast; self-birth and self-nourishment for the departing Jacob among us who has struggled hardest with the bad angel shape of Moloch for possession of the lamb. And hurt his knee. And scraped his hand. And is gifted with poetry.

NOTE

1. The absurdity in question is not the European existentialist variety that poses a tragic universe. Ginsberg is looking from a heavenly vantage point.

GREGORY STEPHENSON

"Howl"
A Reading

> Where there is no vision,
> the people perish.
>
> —Proverbs 29:18

> Much Madness is divinest Sense—
> To a discerning Eye—
> Much Sense—the starkest Madness—
> 'Tis the Majority
> In this, as All, prevails—
> Assent—and you are sane—
> Demur—you're straightway dangerous—
> And handled with a Chain—
>
> —Emily Dickinson

The problem of transcendence, how to achieve it and where it leaves us afterward, is central to Romantic literature. Allen Ginsberg's "Howl" is a contemporary confrontation with this problem, an examination of its personal and social consequences.

The problem may be summarized in this way: the poet, for a visionary instant, transcends the realm of the actual into the realm of the ideal, and then, unable to sustain his vision, returns to the realm of the actual. Afterwards, he feels a sense of exile from the eternal, the numinous, the superconscious. The material world, the realm of the actual, seems empty and desolate. (Poe describes this sensation as "the bitter lapse into every-

---

From *Palantir* (London), April 1983. Reprinted with permission.

day life, the hideous dropping off of the veil.") The poet (like Keats's Knight-at-Arms) starves for heavenly manna. Beneath "Howl"'s description and resolution of this key Romantic dilemma lies, as a unifying image, the archetype of the Night-Sea Journey.

The Night-Sea Journey (or Night-Sea Crossing) is perhaps the earliest of the sun myths. It was the belief of ancient peoples who dwelt by the seashore that the sun, when it descended into the sea at nightfall, was being swallowed by a monster. All night the sun travelled in the belly of the monster, and then, in the morning, it was disgorged in the eastern sky. Carl Jung discusses the myth in his *Contributions to Analytical Psychology*,[1] and Maud Bodkin applies it to "The Rime of the Ancient Mariner" in her book *Archetypal Patterns in Poetry*. For Jung and Bodkin, the Night-Sea Journey is a descent into the Underworld, a necessary part of the path of the hero. As Circlot says in his *A Dictionary of Symbols*, it is "a plunge into the unconscious . . . darkness and watery depths. . . . The journey's end is expressive of resurrection and the overcoming of death."[2] The swallowing of Jonah by a great fish, *The Aeneid* of Virgil, and *The Inferno* of Dante are records of Night-Sea Journies.

The movement of "Howl" (including "Footnote to Howl") is from protest, pain, outrage, attack and lamentation to acceptance, affirmation, love and vision; from alienation to communion. The poet descends into an underworld of darkness, suffering and isolation, then ascends into spiritual knowledge, a sense of union with Man and God, blessedness and achieved vision. The poem is unified with and the movement carried forward by recurring images of falling and rising, destruction and regeneration, starvation and nourishment, sleeping and waking, darkness and illumination, blindness and sight, death and resurrection.

The first section of "Howl" describes the desperation, suffering and persecution of a group of outcast seekers-after-a-transcendent-reality, among whom the poet-speaker includes himself. They are "starving" and "looking for an angry fix" in a metaphorical more than a literal sense. Both metaphors suggest the intensity of the quest, the driving need. (William S. Burroughs uses the phrase "final fix" as the object of his quest at the end of his novel *Junkie*.) The metaphor of narcotics is extended by their search for "the ancient heavenly connection" (connection suggests not only a visionary experience in this context but was the 1940s and 1950s slang for a source of narcotics). These seekers are impoverished, alienated, arrested, driven to suicide both by the hostility of the society in which they pursue their quest and by the desperate nature of the quest itself.

Ginsberg's "angelheaded" seekers follow a sort of Rimbaudian "derangement of the senses" to arrive at spiritual clarity; they pursue a Blakean "path of excess to the Palace of Wisdom." They "purgatory" themselves in the manner of medieval flagellants with alcohol, sexual excess, peyote, marijuana, benzedrine and profligate and dissolute living. And through these means they achieve occasional epiphanous glimpses: angels on tenement roofs, "lightning in the mind," illuminations, brilliant insights, vibrations of the cosmos, gleamings of "supernatural ecstasy," visions, hallucinations; they are "crowned with flame," tantalized when "the soul illuminated its hair for a second," they "crash through their minds," receive "sudden flashes" and make incarnate "gaps in Time and Space," trap "the Archangel of the soul," and experience the consciousness of "Pater Omnipotens Aeterna Deus." And for such sensualized spirituality, for their frenzied pursuit of Ultimate Reality they are outcast, driven mad, suicided (as Artaud says) by society, driven into exile, despised, incarcerated.

What is at issue in the first section of the poem is, as Ginsberg has phrased it elsewhere: "The difficulties that nuts and poets and visionaries and seekers have. . . . The social disgrace—*dis*-grace—attached to certain states of soul. The confrontation with a society . . . which is going in a different direction . . . knowing how to feel human and holy and not like a madman in a world which is rigid and materialistic and all caught up in the immediate necessities. . . ."[3] The anguish of the visionary in exile from Ultimate Reality and desperately seeking reunion with it, is intensified by a society which refuses to recognize the validity of the visionary experience and maintains a monopoly on reality, imposing and enforcing a single, materialist-rationalist view.

388

A number of incidents in the first section are autobiographical, alluding to the poet's own experiences such as his expulsion from Columbia, his visions of Blake, his studies of mystical writers or of Cézanne's paintings, his travels, his time in jail and in the asylum. Ginsberg presents not only the personal tragedies and persecutions of his generation of seekers, but alludes back to an earlier generation with embedded references to Vachel Lindsay, "who ate fire in paint hotels," and to Hart Crane and other *poètes maudits* "who blew and were blown by those human seraphim, the sailors."[4] And for the poet the prototype of the persecuted and martyred visionary is his own mother, Naomi Ginsberg, who is twice mentioned in the poem, and whose spirit provides much of its impetus: " 'Howl' is really about my mother, in her last year at Pilgrim State Hospital—acceptance of her later inscribed in 'Kaddish' detail," wrote Ginsberg twenty years later.[5]

Several lines near the end of the first section (from "who demanded sanity trials" to "animal soup of time") describe the exploits and sufferings of the dedicatee of the poem, Carl Solomon, the victim in whom Ginsberg symbolizes his generation of oppressed celestial pilgrims. Ginsberg's statement of spiritual solidarity with Solomon, "ah Carl, while you are not safe I am not safe," presages the climactic third section of the poem. This compassionate identification with a fellow quester-victim is very similar to the Bodhisattva vow in Buddhism and anticipates the poet's later interest in Buddhist thought.

After a statement on the technique and intention of the poem, the section ends with strong images of ascent and rebirth and with a suggestion that the martyrs are redemptive, sacrificial figures whose sufferings can refine the present and the future.

The second section of the poem continues and expands the image of pagan sacrifice with which the first section concludes. To what merciless, cold, blind idol were the "angelheaded" of section one given in sacrifice, Ginsberg asks. And he answers: "Moloch!" Moloch, (or Molech) god of abominations, to whom children were sacrificed ("passed through the fire to Molech,") against whom the Bible warns repeatedly, is the ruling principle of our age. To him all violence, unkindness, alienation, guilt, ignorance, greed, repression and exploitation are attributable. The poet sees his face and body in buildings, factories and weapons, as Fritz Lang saw his devouring maw in the furnace of *Metropolis*.

Ginsberg presents a comprehensive nightmare image of contemporary society which is as penetrating as that of Blake's "London." And like Blake in "London," Ginsberg places the source of human woe within human consciousness and perception. Moloch is a condition of mind, a state of soul: "Mental Moloch!" . . . "Moloch whose name is the Mind!" We are born, according to Ginsberg, in a state of "natural ecstasy" but Moloch "enter[s] the soul early" (see Blake's "Infant Sorrow"). We can regain that celestial, ecstatic view of life, for "Heaven . . . exists and is everywhere about us," by emerging from the belly of Moloch, the monster that has devoured us, who "ate up our brains and imagination." We can "Wake up in Moloch!"

The remainder of the second section returns to a lament for the visionaries of section one. American society is seen as having consistently ignored, suppressed and destroyed any manifestation of the miraculous, the ecstatic, the sacred and epiphanous.

Section two is pivotal in "Howl." It names Moloch as the cause of the destruction of visionary consciousness and describes the manifestations of this antispirit. It also indicates that the "mind forg'd manacles" of Moloch can be broken and beatific vision regained. In this section the poet has also made clear that the problem of transcendence is not of concern only to poets and mystics but to every member of the social body. Ginsberg has shown the effects of a society without vision. Commercialism, militarism, sexual repression, technocracy and soulless industrialization, inhuman life and the death of the spirit are the consequences of Mental Moloch.

The third section of the poem reaffirms and develops the sympathetic, affectionate identification of Ginsberg with the man who for him epitomizes the rebellious visionary victim. The section is a celebration of the courage and endurance of Carl Solomon, a final paean to the martyrs of the spirit, and an affirmation of human love.

The piteous and brave cry of Solomon from the Rockland Mental Hospital is the essence of the poem's statement; it is the howl of anguished and desperate conviction: "the soul is innocent and immortal it should never die ungodly in an armed madhouse." The image of the "armed madhouse" may be understood at an individual or a social level of reference. Each human soul inhabits the defensive, fearful "armed madhouse" of the ego personality, the social self; and the American nation has also become "an armed madhouse." The psychic armor that confines and isolates the individual ego-selves and the nuclear armaments of the nation are mutually reflexive; they mirror and create each other. At both levels, the individual and the national, the innocent and immortal soul is starved, suffocated, murdered.

Imagery of crucifixion ("cross in the void," "fascist national Golgotha") reemphasizes Ginsberg's view of the visionary as sacrificial redeemer. Such images culminate in the poet's hope that Solomon "will split the heavens . . . and resurrect your living human Jesus from the superhuman tomb." I understand this to mean that Solomon will liberate himself from Mental Moloch "whose ear is a smoking tomb," and attain illumination and spiritual rebirth.

The final images are confident and expansive, a projected apocalypse of Moloch, the Great Awakening "out of the coma" of Life-in-Death. Confinement, repression, alienation and the Dark Night of the Soul are ended. The "imaginary walls collapse" (walls of egotism, competition, materialism, all the "woes and weaknesses" of Mental Moloch,) and the human spirit emerges in victory, virtue, mercy and freedom. The "sea-journey" of Solomon and of the soul is completed.

"Footnote to Howl," originally a section of the poem excised on the advice of Kenneth Rexroth,[6] extends Ginsberg's vision of how "the eye altering alters all." The poem is a rhapsodic Blakean, Whitmanian illumination of the realm of the actual, the material world. If we accept and observe attentively, if we *see,* Ginsberg tells us, then all is redeemed, reconciled and all is recognized for what it in essence is: holy.

The eye can become "discerning" in the deepest sense. Perceiving the "inscape" of each object and life, we can perceive the Divine Presence. We can see the "angel" in every human form, we can see "eternity in time," we can even see "the Angel in

Moloch." Perception is a reciprocal process. You are what you behold, what you behold is what you are ("Who digs Los Angeles IS Los Angeles"—that is, the dirty, lonely city of "woe and weakness" or the City of the Angels). The essence of everything is holy, only the form may be foul or corrupted. Therefore, "holy the visions . . . holy the eyeball." This is the fulfillment of Ginsberg's earlier assertion that "Heaven . . . exists and is everywhere about us." Waking up *in* Moloch, we may awake *out of* Moloch.

The acceptance of the body is essential for Ginsberg, for the senses can be a way to illumination. The body is where we must begin. Throughout "Howl" sexual repression or disgust with the body have been seen as Mental Moloch: "Moloch in whom I am consciousness without a body!" "where the faculties of the skull no longer admit the worms of the senses." That is why the "Footnote" proclaims: "The soul is holy! The skin is holy! The nose is holy! The tongue and cock and hand and asshole holy!" Body and spirit are affirmed and reconciled.

Heraclitus taught that "the way up and the way down are the same way." For Ginsberg in his Night-Sea Journey the path of descent described in the first two sections of "Howl," has become the path of ascent, the victory and vision of section three and of "Footnote to Howl." "Howl" records a solstice of the soul, a nadir point of darkness and then the growth again toward light. The poem exemplifies Jack Kerouac's understanding that to be Beat was "the root and soul of beatific."

For many of the Romantic writers the loss of vision, the return to the actual, was a permanent defeat. Their lives and their art became sorrowful and passive. They languished and mourned. Their behavior became self-destructive, even suicidal. Ginsberg transforms his "season in hell" into new resolve and purpose. Like Coleridge's Ancient Mariner, he has returned from a journey of wonders and suffering with a new vision of human community, a new reverence for life. Like Blake's Bard, his is a voice of prophetic anger, compassion and hope. Implicit in "Howl"'s vision of human solidarity and ultimate victory is the Blakean vow: "I shall not cease from mental fight . . . till we have built Jerusalem."

NOTES

1. Carl Jung, *Contributions to Analytical Psychology* (New York: Macmillan, 1928), p. 40.

2. J. E. Circlot, *A Dictionary of Symbols* (New York: Philosophical Society, 1962), p. 218.

3. Jane Kramer, *Allen Ginsberg in America* (New York: Random House, 1967), p. 101.

4. Allen Young, *Allen Ginsberg, Gay Sunshine Interview* (Bolinas: Grey Fox Press, 1974), p. 12.

5. Allen Ginsberg and Richard Eberhart, *To Eberhart from Ginsberg* (Lincoln, Mass.: Penmaen Press, 1976), p. 11.

6. Neeli Cherkovski, *Ferlinghetti* (New York: Doubleday, 1979), pp. 99–100.

GEOFFREY THURLEY

The Whole Man In

. . . In the volumes after "Howl" [Ginsberg's] poetry divides more and more decisively into two categories: there are "solid" poems of recollection, and rhetorical poems that tend to disintegrate into spiritual vapor. The poetry of the first sort can become excessively concrete, merely remembered: the remembrances are processed by juxtaposition, each suggesting the memory-trace next door. "Howl" itself perhaps tries to carry more luggage than the poet's rhythmic vitality can manage. By "Kaddish" and "To Aunt Rose" the recollective systems are clogged and overburdened. Toward the end of the 1960s (when Ginsberg's entire way of life had altered), even this act of recollection has gone, replaced only by a diaristic notation, the images mere tape-jottings. The poems of the second sort burn out into increasingly gaseous fulmination: the attitudes are peddled and, though sincere in the worldly sense, lack artistic compulsion. Between these two poles, of naturalism and spirituality, his poetry has always oscillated.

It seems reasonable to say that Ginsberg's most successful pieces occur close to the center of this spectrum, that is, when naturalist perceptions are shot through with spiritual emotion. In these poems—say, "Paterson," "Sunflower Sutra," "In Back of the Real," much of "Howl," "Transcription of Organ Music," "A Supermarket in California"—the image is considered unhurriedly, until under pressure of the contemplating mind it becomes symbolic. The symbolism accrues from the contemplation, it is not itself sought after. When the phenomenon resists

From *The American Moment: American Poetry in the Mid-Century* (London: Edward Arnold, 1977). Reprinted with permission.

the contemplation, and remains mere phenomenon, we get the opaque memory-collage of "Kaddish" or the diaristic notation of *Ankor Wat* or *Planet News*. At his best, that is, Ginsberg sees the thing in all its grubby essence, yet places it effortlessly in a spiritual dimension:

> . . . the gray Sunflower poised against the sunset, crackly bleak and
> dusty with the smut and smog and smoke of olden locomotives
> in its eye—
> corolla of bleary spikes pushed down and broken like a battered
> crown, seeds fallen out of its face, soon-to-be-toothless mouth
> of sunny air, sunrays obliterated on its hairy head like a dried
> wire spiderweb,
> leaves stuck out like arms out of the stem, gestures from the sawdust
> root, broke pieces of plaster fallen out of the black twigs, a dead
> fly in its ear,
> Unholy battered old thing you were, my sunflower O my soul, I,
> loved you then!
>
> ("Sunflower Sutra")

If we want to place the superiority of this over the poetic *lingua franca* current when it was written, we shall have to say simply that the last assertion in the extract quoted is fully meant: the flower hasn't been picked on and rifled of its symbolic possibilities, in spite of the literary precedents. On the contrary, Blake's flower is used intelligently, played off against the actual sunflower before the poet with wise and sufficient irony. This *mélange* of religious intensity and wry realism is, I think, Allen Ginsberg's most endearing and enduring gift. There is perhaps a suspicion that the sermon the poet delivers at the end of the poem, though "sincere," is cooked up in the literary consciousness ("we're all beautiful golden sunflowers inside") and this suspicion, aroused by the title of the poem, is partially confirmed by contrast with the beautiful lyric "In Back of the Real." This short piece, included in the "Howl" volume as an early poem, in a way shortcircuits its more famous sister-piece. The progression from "In Back of the Real" to "Sunflower Sutra" suggests the direction Ginsberg was later to take toward an ever-increasing religiosity. The situation in the early poem is the same as in "Sunflower Sutra": the poet discovers the flower at a tired moment on a sunset walk. But the flower is presented with an unaffected simplicity:

> A flower lay on the hay on
> the asphalt highway
> —the dread hay flower
> I thought—It had a
> brittle black stem and
> corolla of yellowish dirty
> spikes like Jesus' inchlong
> crown, and a soiled
> dry center cotton tuft
> like a used shaving brush
> that's been lying under
> the garage for a year.
>
> ("In Back of the Real")

In this sense of Beat futility and yet of persistent meaningfulness lies the essence of Allen Ginsberg. It is a quality seen also in the early poem "Paterson," a work which holds much the same relation to "Howl" as "In Back of the Real" holds to "Sunflower Sutra." "Paterson" handles the same material as "Howl," but with greater simplicity and candor, with none of the self-consciously high–powered religiosity that mars sections of the longer poem, bringing it occasionally closer to pastiche than to original poetry. Ginsberg's poetry testifies to strong religious experience, but his grasp upon it is insecure, his ability to communicate it fragmentary and vague. When he tries to address the absolute directly, a haze of literary verbiage sometimes obscures his spiritual eye—"Immense seas passing over the flow of time. . . ." Ginsberg is basically a Jewish reformer-moralist, trying desperately hard to be an Anglo-Saxon seer—a Blake, a Whitman, a Shelley. His shouting rant deafens truth, and the numinous end of the language spectrum is burned out by overuse. Language itself again needs purging and restoring:

> trailing variations made of the same Wood circles round itself
> in the same pattern as the original Appearance, [etc. etc.]

In the light of this, "Transcription of Organ Music" assumes special significance in Ginsberg's work. Ginsberg himself describes the poem as an attempt at "Absolute transcription of spontaneous material, transcription of sensual data (organ) at a moment of near Ecstasy . . . ," an attempt to "transcribe at such moments and try to bring back to the poor suffering world what rare moments exist."[1] The poem tries to transmit some of the sublime intensity, the exalted pathos of Bach (the natural world in the poem is experienced directly under the influence of the music); yet it never loses contact with the pitiable reality of the poet's own material existence—the flower in the peanut bottle, the lavatory door left open. There is a moving sense of the poet's own awareness of where he stands in relation not only to the religious universe, but to the art of the great masters. "Can I bring back the words?" he asks. "Will thought of transcription haze my mental open eye?" No; but what the poet has the power to relay back to the reader is not the experience itself, which is simply referred to—"I had a moment of clarity, saw the feeling in the heart of things, walked out to the garden crying." We believe that Ginsberg had a powerful religious emotion: the music of Bach lifted him up. But he lacks the power to hold onto the vision and to transmit its quality. And if the phrase in the extract just quoted suggests Wordsworth for comparison, I should say that it is not so much of Wordsworth that I am thinking in placing Ginsberg like this as of lesser poets—say, the Crane of "Cape Hatteras," the Francis Thompson of "The Hound of Heaven," and some of Ginsberg's own younger contemporaries.

For reasons of this sort, much of Ginsberg's finest poetry combines the religious and the political. His ability to grasp and embody exalted religious states is limited, it is true. Yet poems like "Death to Van Gogh's Ear!" and "America" are informed with a zestful humor that derives from a deep source of love and delight which reminds one of some Zen painting:[2] these poems do not attempt the absolute religious affirmation which usually defeats him. They are satirical, critical of organized society, yet qualitatively superior to merely political poetry. They are compact of intense political enthusiasm and deep religious disgust. "Death to Van Gogh's Ear!" is possibly Ginsberg's finest single poem, a politico-religious tract of manic yet deeply sane intensity, achieved with a natural brilliance and economy. Its mode is interesting, an aphoristically witty realization of spiritual perceptions of the sort first displayed by Smart in "Jubilate Agno" and Blake in "Auguries of Innocence."[3] In "Death to Van Gogh's Ear!" the Blakean wit is only intermittent—"Elephants of mercy murdered for the sake of an Elizabethan birdcage"—and there are glimpses still of the pasticheur, the witty undergraduate masquerading as great poet—"Owners! Owners! Owners! with obsession on property and vanishing Selfhood!" But the whole poem is irresistible, a truly revolutionary work. Like "America," its mode is satirical without being snide: its forcefulness springs from a basically affirmative attitude towards experience and even towards American society, rather than from the negativism which makes most radicalism slightly anemic and condescending. Nothing is more important in fact than to dispel the notion of Ginsberg and the Beats as fundamentally aligned with protest. Kerouac's novels and Ginsberg's finest poems are based upon acceptance, not rejection, upon affirmation, not negation. This is the primary difference between their work and that of writers like Saul Bellow and Robert Lowell.

In spite of this, however, in spite of the insistence on sexual release and the Blakean program, Allen Ginsberg's poetry really contains little joy. It is perhaps most alive when fiercely yet humorously attacking the evils of organized society in the capitalist and communist worlds, in poems like "America" and "Death to Van Gogh's Ear!." Otherwise, his most successful pieces are poems of exhaustion and Beat futility. How sad his world is emerges not only from poems like "Sunflower Sutra" and "Transcription of Organ Music," but from a passage in *Allen Ginsberg in America* in which he tells of his walks with Carlos Williams: "I'd show him where *my* epiphanous places were. Places like the river, under the bridge where I masturbated for the first time. Where I kissed that girl who moved away. Where I saw a gang fight. Where I always felt ashamed for some reason. The hedge where I was lonely."[4] This passive melancholy lies close to the heart of Ginsberg's life and writing. He takes up the hedonistic implication of Blake without apparently understanding how much pleasure Blake took in keeping himself spiritually collected, gathered together in one place, that place the center of the universe. Dignity and discipline, with their associations of ambassadors and headmasters, do not seem very relevant qualities today: yet spiritual dignity seems very radical to the thought, for instance, of D. H. Lawrence, and a discipline, zestfully renewed each morning, seems incalculably important in the life and work of Blake. Ginsberg takes up the unbridling implications of the later Lawrence—

> It is only immoral
> to be dead-alive—
>
> ("Immorality")

with no appreciation of the fact that this was indissolubly connected in Lawrence's work with ideas of order, sanity, inward peace, and above all a permanent vigilance, without which personal freedom and integrity could not be maintained. Lawrence advised us to

> keep still, and hold
> the tiny grain of something that no wave can wash away.
>
> ("Be Still!")

Ginsberg envisages a vast communal orgy:

> Tonite let's all make love in London as if it were 2001
> the year of thrilling God—
>
> ("Who Be Kind To")

Lawrence, on the other hand, knowing that as things are, the results would be something like a German beer festival or a Swedish mid-summernight orgy, in which only the pent-up nastiness is released, urges continuous continence—

> Let us contain ourselves
> and rally together
> to keep a sane core to life.

NOTES

1. Jane Kramer, *Allen Ginsberg in America* (New York: Random House, 1969), p. 169.

2. I am thinking principally of Sengai.

3. I am not sure the mode exists outside English. The essence of it really is a kind of paranoid prophecy, the poet striking through to truth by associating disparates with surreal acumen.

4. Kramer, pp. 134–35.

JAMES BRESLIN

The Origins of "Howl" and "Kaddish"

Most literary people have probably first become aware of Allen Ginsberg through the media, in his self-elected and controversial role as public figure and prophet of a new age. Ginsberg's public personality has changed over the years—from the defiant and histrionic angry young man of the fifties to the bearded and benign patriarch and political activist of the sixties and seventies—but the personality has remained one that most literary people find hard to take seriously. Compare Ginsberg's reception with that of Norman Mailer, another writer who is also a public figure and one who, like Ginsberg, wants to replace rational with magical thinking as the mode of public discourse. Mailer's public appearances and his confessional writings characteristically begin by humiliating but end by promoting himself, and they have been enormously successful: Mailer's talents have been widely exaggerated, especially by academic critics, who already have produced several studies of his work. Mailer has succeeded because his theorizing on all matters from the digestive to the political system, no matter how bizarre or brutal the content, are developed by a kind of intellectualizing most literary people respect, even when it is adopted (as in Mailer) half in the spirit of the put-on. Ginsberg is at least as intelligent, a lot less brutal, and often a lot more self-aware, but the man who took off his clothes at a Los Angeles poetry reading, who chanted "Om" during the gassings in Grant Park at the 1968 Democratic Convention in Chicago, and who has experimented with a wide variety of drugs, strikes those manning the literary

From the *Iowa Review* (Spring 1977). Reprinted with permission.

armchairs as at best a figure of fun or, more likely, a threat to Western civilization. Ginsberg's role as a public figure has been part of his attempt to reassert the romantic role of the poet as prophet; but one result of it has been that his genuine literary talents and more admirable personal qualities have been obscured.

It is true that, so far, the quality of Ginsberg's writing has been too inconsistent for him to rank as a major poet. Ginsberg writes often, quickly, and, as his career has advanced, apparently without too much revision; his cult of spontaneity results in unevenness, but it also generates some of the real strengths of his writing. A poet like Eliot, carefully turning a lifetime's experience into a single volume of highly finished work, helped to create the myth (dominant when Ginsberg began to write) of the modern artist who, a literary revolutionary in spite of himself, remained a hard-working, disciplined craftsman. Like many contemporary poets, Ginsberg, an avowed revolutionary, seems much more willing to risk imperfection, even failure; what he hopes to gain is an honesty and immediacy of feeling, rather than the finish of a well-wrought work of art. When he is least successful, Ginsberg has drifted into the solipsism of purely private associations, as he does in the drug poems in *Kaddish* and *Reality Sandwiches,* or he has fallen into the predictable patterns of thought and feeling characteristic of a polemicist, as he does in much of his political poetry. But the really exciting moments in reading Ginsberg come when he breaks through to new orders in the poem and in self-understanding. "Howl" (1956), "Kaddish" (1959), "The Change: Kyoto-Tokyo Express" (1963), and "Wales Visitation" (1967)—all poems of some length, all evolving from the pressures of some personal crisis—these poems seem to me to be the main such moments in Ginsberg's career.

Of these the most powerful—and influential—appear to be "Howl" and "Kaddish." Several poets have testified to the importance of Ginsberg's early poetry in establishing an alternative to the well-made symbolist poem that was fashionable in the fifties, and his early work does fuse two modes—the confessional and the visionary—that were to become important in the sixties.[1] Not that a case for Ginsberg can only be made on historical grounds; both poems, given the intense and concentrated energy of their surrealistic language, their vivid creation of a world of primitive terrors and hallucinatory brilliance, their striking shifts of voice and mood, have genuine literary merit. For a long time, their explosive *poetic* energy has been missed, partly because of the distractions of a "shocking" language and matter (drugs, madness, suicide, homosexuality, incest), but mainly because many readers, still not sympathetic to the *kind* of form found in these poems, have accused them of an *absence* of form. Moreover, while they achieve literary form and attain a public impact, these poems derive from deep, long-standing private conflicts in Ginsberg—conflicts that ultimately stem from his ambivalent attachment to his mother, his difficulties in asserting a separate, independent personality. While there is a progression of self-awareness from "Howl" (1956) to "Kaddish" (1959), both works seem to me to expose rather than to resolve these conflicts, though they make valiant efforts at such resolution. Nevertheless, it is Ginsberg's ability to probe these areas of conflict that largely explains their innovative energy and powerful appeal.

Allen Ginsberg is a mystical and messianic poet with intense suicidal wishes and persistent self-doubts, a would-be spontaneous artist whose most spontaneous thoughts characteristically turn toward feelings of being stifled and inhibited, walled and bounded in—and thus toward longings for some painful, apocalyptic deliverance—ultimately death itself. To read the notebooks and journals that Ginsberg has kept from adolescence onwards is to encounter a man with grandiose hopes for himself, but one who relentlessly flagellates himself for his failures and who tends to assume that all his undertakings will end, just as they have ended, in disaster.[2] Just the published *Indian Journals* (kept during 1962–63) amply reveal how this outwardly serene bard is intrigued with failure and death, spending much of his time contemplating the *ghats* where the Indian dead are cremated. Of the Ginsberg of the late fifties and early sixties, Lawrence Ferlinghetti remembers, "he is the flippy flesh made word / and he speaks the word he hears in his flesh / and the word is *Death*."[3] To say all this is not to say that Ginsberg's public manner is false but that, on the contrary, it has been hard-won. And poems like "Howl" and "Kaddish" have a key place in the evolution of his personality, developing out of a time in his life when his creative impulses came into something like a balance with his propensities for self-destruction. As Ginsberg himself tells it—a version of his life we should approach skeptically—the story of his literary career and in a way the real story of his life begin with his removal from New York to San Francisco in 1953.

"Howl" is not—contrary to popular impression—the work of an angry *young* man. When he wrote the poem, Ginsberg was thirty; in 1953, when he left family, friends and the established literary culture behind him in the East, he was twenty-seven—being, like his friend Jack Kerouac, a romantic wanderer who found it difficult to sever family ties. Ginsberg himself sees the 1953 journey west as a crucial and symbolic kind of act: "It was like a big prophecy, taking off for California. Like I had passed one season of my life and it was time to start all over again."[4] It was not quite this easy and final, as we shall see; but moving west was a dramatic attempt to loosen the parental grip—to free himself from pressures created by his mother's long history of psychotic illness as well as his frequently acrimonious relation with his father. Going west was, in short, a turn away from the threatening images of failure, disintegration, suffocation he associated with home—a gesture toward the future, toward life, an attempt to start all over again as *his own man*. Yet it is also true that Ginsberg made this journey half looking back over his shoulder—just as in "Howl" he would return to the experience and emotions of his life in New York in the late forties and in Part III of the poem ("Carl Solomon, I'm with you in Rockland.") deny that he had ever left. It is certainly mistaken to imagine a recreated Ginsberg floating into San Francisco on a magic carpet, dressed in long robes, with flowing hair, hand cymbals and a "San Francisco Poetry Renaissance" banner. The Ginsberg that emerged in "Howl"—Ginsberg the rancorous and somewhat gloomy mystic seer—must in some sense have been there, but he was apparently hidden at first beneath a deferential and conventional exterior. In fact, it would be more accurate to imagine him arriving in a three-button suit, striped tie, and an attaché case. Soon after his arrival in San Francisco,

Ginsberg was looking for a job in market research, and he quickly found one. There was no reason he shouldn't—since this was precisely the kind of work he had been doing back in New York.

Not long after he secured the job, Ginsberg became involved with a woman, with whom he eventually moved into an apartment in San Francisco's posh Nob Hill district. Life went along in this style for several months in the fall of 1953—until Ginsberg began seeing a therapist at Langley-Porter Institute, a Dr. Phillip Hicks, to find out why neither the job nor the woman seemed to satisfy him. According to Ginsberg, at one point in his treatment, the doctor asked,

"What would you like to do? What *is* your desire, really?" I said, "Doctor, I don't think you're going to find this very healthy and clear, but I really would like to stop working forever—never work again, never do anything like the kind of work I'm doing now—and do nothing but write poetry and have leisure to spend the day outdoors and go to museums and see friends. And I'd like to keep living with someone—maybe even a man—and explore relationships that way. And cultivate my perceptions, cultivate the visionary thing in me. Just a literary and quiet city-hermit existence." Then, *he* said, "Well, why don't you?"[5]

In several interviews Ginsberg discusses this encounter, mythologizing it into The Great Breakthrough that allowed him to start a new life. As Ginsberg tells it, the doctor's tolerant acceptance of Ginsberg's unconventional desires encouraged self-acceptance and the end of his misguided attempts to please his father—both of which, in turn, generated "Howl." So, the story goes, Ginsberg wrote a report showing how his firm could replace him with a computer; they fired him and he went on unemployment, free to enjoy a "quiet city-hermit existence." By this time he had already met Peter Orlovsky, then a student living with the painter Robert Lavigne in North Beach, and Ginsberg's increasing involvement with Orlovsky disturbed the woman he was living with. The eventual result—again not following too long after the episode with Dr. Hicks—was that Ginsberg left affluent Nob Hill for downtown Montgomery

Street, to live with Orlovsky. And soon after these dramatic shifts in his life he began writing "Howl."

Yet Ginsberg's account of these events sounds suspiciously like a fantasy of a magical cure, and a reading of the journals he kept at the time reveals that even chronology has been transformed a bit to promote the myth of the Breakthrough.[6] Actually, Ginsberg continued to work at his market research job for three or four months *after* he moved in with Orlovsky and insofar as his journals reveal his mood at the time, they suggest he felt depressed, not liberated, when he lost his job. Moreover, while Ginsberg strongly implies that his therapy (and even the need for it) ended with his doctor's laying on of hands, the journals indicate that he continued in treatment, perhaps for as long as several months, including the time in which "Howl" was written. Moreover, the lengthy and almost daily entries from late 1954, when he first met Orlovsky, show that Ginsberg entered into this relationship with the same expectations of salvation and the same premonitions of disaster with which he then launched all his activities. An entry for April 20, 1955—written four months after he had started living with Orlovsky—vividly conveys his mood at the time, and it was not one of emancipated self-acceptance:

> Not writing enough what can I say—rapid exchange of events, jobloss, peterloss,—isolation, no one I love loves me no contact, the isolation—facing loss of Jack [Kerouac] and Bill [Burroughs] as previous loss of contact with L—the myths held for the decade to fill time.[7]

"Howl" does affirm its author's capacity to survive an agonizing ordeal; yet the poem is charged with equally strong feelings of personal and literary failure, isolation and, most powerfully, loss, the feelings of this journal entry and many others like it. In fact, both "Howl" and "Kaddish" react to loss in precisely the way suggested in the journal—not by acceptance and working through the loss, but by idealizing, mythologizing, the lost object ("the myths held for the decade to fill time").

In addition, a more careful look at what Ginsberg tells of the transaction with his psychiatrist suggests a different interpreta-

406

tion from the one supplied by Ginsberg himself. In this encounter, he has clearly transferred onto the doctor, speaking to him as if he were speaking to his father, confessing his intimate feelings about work, about homosexuality, about "visionary" or hallucinatory experiences that he (like his mother) had experienced. He knows his father disapproves of all this, and he disapproves himself of these impulses, but projects such criticism onto the doctor: "I don't think you're going to find this very healthy and clear." He expects to be denounced, but what he hears is what he always wanted to hear from his father—permission. Permission is not, however, the only possible interpretation of the doctor's "Well, why don't you?"—a remark that could have led Ginsberg to examine his inhibitions and, ultimately, the origins of his wishes, all yearnings that, as we shall see, align him with the mother, against the father. The doctor, Ginsberg revealingly comments, gave him "the authority, so to speak, to be myself"—as if this authority were external to him.[8] In *Young Man Luther,* Erik Erickson points out that young men in a state of "identity diffusion," as Ginsberg clearly was at this time, often transform their therapy into "something like Jacob's struggle with the angel, a wrestling for a benediction which is to lead to the patient's conviction that he is an alive person, and, as such, has a life before him."[9] Ginsberg, seemingly satisfied with a "benediction" rather than a fuller exploration of his wishes and fears, temporarily wrestles himself "free" from guilt—but remains dependent upon the authority of the forgiving father for permission to be himself. In this exchange we can see some of the motives for Ginsberg's own later adoption of the role of the tolerant, benign patriarch toward younger people—while he himself continually turns toward older men (from Martin Buber to Swami Shivananada) in search for reassurance that he does indeed have the authority to be himself, a right to a life of his own.

It should come as no surprise that by virtue of moving across the country and acquiring an idealized father figure in his doctor, Ginsberg had accomplished a less than complete break with his past. Both the removal to a "safe" distance and the supportive context of therapy probably helped him more to explore, rather than shed, the past, and it was the very insistence of his private life as *the* material for his poetry that pushed Ginsberg away from the predominant idea of the poem as impersonal artifact and toward a sense of the poem as confessional outpouring. In reality the Ginsberg of the late fifties manifests a powerful wish to strike out on his own, along with an equally powerful fear of freedom. A poem like "Howl" angrily asserts the "real" self of its author, the "angel-headed hipster" persecuted by social and paternal authority, and the poem does so with a kind of tormented exhilaration that suggests the release of long-repressed feelings. More a cry of pain than of anger, "Kaddish," an elegy for Ginsberg's mother, also seeks to affirm a new and separate life for the poet. Yet for all of the rebelliousness of "Howl" and all the protestations of accepted loss in "Kaddish," both poems view independent life (in the language of the journal) as "isolation" and "loss." Independence and submission, struggling toward the future and being drawn back into the past: such are the conflicts that inform the best of Ginsberg's poetry—in ways that we can see even more clearly by examining the dynamics of his attachments to both his parents.

Anyone who has met Louis Ginsberg or heard him read his poems at one of the joint readings he's given with his son will have encountered a short, sturdy man well into his seventies, with large inquiring eyes and a slightly frowning, rather oppressed expression. At first glance he seems, in his poems as well as his person, a modest and mild man, a very likely candidate for just that kindly, forgiving father that Ginsberg wished for, a man whose weakness might be a reluctance to assert his authority rather than in withholding his sympathy. Yet the attitude of mutual respect which the two men now display toward each other has the quality of an uneasy truce which, if unlikely to break into open hostilities is still filled with critical sniping from both sides. At least this is the impression created by Jane Kramer in her *Allen Ginsberg in America,* especially in her report of a Sunday morning conversation in Paterson, prior to one of their father/son reading performances. Louis inquires if Allen has "some good clothes for the reading tonight," twits his son for not being home enough, scolds him for not writing enough when away, denounces the lack of discipline in Allen's life and poetry, and alludes uneasily to his son's greater fame. Allen himself, showing perhaps more discipline than his father credits him for, responds with gentle tolerance, even when the issues become a little more charged. At one point, after Allen's friend Maretta announces that her *sadhana* is hashish, Mr. Ginsberg asks,

"What's with this Maretta? Why can't you bring home a nice Jewish girl?"

Ginsberg, laughing, threw up his hands. "For the love of God, Louis," he said, "here for years you've been saying, 'Please, just bring home a *girl* for a change,' and now that I do, you want a *Jewish* one?"

"You're such an *experimenter,* Allen," Mr. Ginsberg said. "Tibetan Buddhist girl friends. Swamis, Drugs. All this talk from you about pot—'It's so elevating, Louis. So ecstatic. My soul is outside my body. I see ultimate reality.'" Mr. Ginsberg frowned. "You know what *I* say? I say, 'Allen, take it easy.'"[10]

With Louis in his seventies and Allen nearing forty, the father still does not accept the son's style of independence, while the son's experimental style itself seems arrived at as a direct challenge to the father's authority and a test of his love. In this exchange the most sensitive and persistent issues between the two are touched on—family loyalty, drugs, homosexuality, visions of ultimate reality—in a manner that suggests a mollifying (here through humor) of conflicts that were earlier expressed with much more acrimony. In John Clellon Holmes's novel of the Beat Generation, *Go*—a book he says he tried to make as factually accurate as possible—the conversations between David Stofsky (Ginsberg) and his father seem to represent the original clashes, ritualistically repeated on a much later Sunday morning in Paterson.

When [Stofsky] got home, he announced to his father that he had "visions," and when this brought forth little more than a pseudo-literary reaction, he appended, reckoning on its effect, that he was afraid he was going mad. His father rewarded him with the same sort of hysterical outburst that had seized him when, after several weeks of hesitant feelers, Stofsky had confessed his homosexuality. The two had an uneasy relationship anyway, at the bottom of which was mutual distrust, and when they were together they invariably squabbled over philosophical matters or Stofsky's "evil companions of the city" (as his father called them). [11]

The Allen Ginsberg Archives at Columbia contain an incomplete but still quite extensive correspondence between the father and son, dating from Allen's days at Columbia in the mid-1940s down to the early seventies. Much of the correspondence is given over to intricate and often heated political, moral, and literary debates. At a time when his son, still an undergraduate, was self-consciously identifying himself as a decadent and ardently reading such advanced modern thinkers as Gide, Spengler, Rimbaud, and Baudelaire, Louis advised: "A little of the Greek ideal of moderation would do you no harm, m'lad"; [12] and the father's perspective can be briefly characterized as a deliberate cultivation of a moderate, well-balanced, practical approach to life, though with a decided tilt toward the cautionary in his dealings with his son. Once in a while, the father explodes. As late as 1955, with Allen nearing thirty, Louis wrote: "All your vehement, vaporous, vituperations of rebellion move me not one jot. Your attitude is irresponsible—and it stinks." [13] In a much earlier letter, probably written during Ginsberg's second year at Columbia, the father proposes the safety of accommodation and warns against precisely those "deviant" routes his son was to take up.

Even if normal values are rationalizations as well as abnormal ones, the latter, as normal values *qua* normal ones, result in a better and safer adjustment to society and a greater integration of the person. According to your blanket statement, you would bracket the rationalizations of a homosexual or an insane person as satisfactory for society and for the person. The homosexual and the insane person is a menace to himself and to society. Danger and disaster lie that way! Your clever verbal solutions are incongruous with [the] reality of life. You are developed intellectually; but, emotionally, you lag.[14]

In his letters, as in his poetry, Louis Ginsberg's manner is characteristically sententious; but his timeless truths are often avowedly based either on the authority of his greater experience in the world or appeals to the "safety" of his position rather than its intrinsic value. The letters show a genuine concern for a troublesome son, but it is also easy to see how his son might get the impression that the father holds that truth can be arrived at by carefully examining both sides of every question, then coming down resoundingly in favor of the status quo. The trouble with Allen's undergraduate literary hero Rimbaud, his father tells him, is that the French poet sought "*absolute* moral values" rather than "*adequate* moral values."[15] At about the same time, just after reading Karl Shapiro's *Essay on Rime,* Louis asserted that, of course, modern poets reject the "superstitions in religious faith" and they detect the hypocrisies beneath the surface mores of contemporary society, BUT they should not leap to pessimistic conclusions: they must remain "clear-headed" enough (unlike Allen) to reject "decadence" as well and opt for "pragmatic values." "Concluding, I say, Allen, suspend your judgment; walk balanced between the seen world and the unseen one; and take care of your health!"[16] In fact, in the letter warning against Rimbaud, Louis had pronounced that one "must resign himself to pragmatic values or commit suicide."[17]

But the son, who later was to solve the problem of values by adopting a "religious faith," not only refused to suspend his judgment; he asserted radical views, declaring, for instance, all modern civilization corrupt and disintegrating. Such views the father dismisses, in a key term, as "off-balance."[18] It is clear that each, questioning the other's love, questions the other's sense of reality and demands that the other "see things as I do." A visionary poem sent to Louis in 1958 is judged as "brilliantly myopic."[19] In their long Cold War political debate beginning in the late fifties, Allen is accused of distorted *vision,* which makes him too harsh on the United States and too easy on Soviet Russia. And in their ongoing literary arguments, attitudes of parental caution again clash with adolescent egotism and rebellion. The older man conceives of poetry as a practical craft, generated by emotion and shaped by individual vision but designed to effect immediate communication with a fairly wide audience and hence comfortably drawing on traditional resources of technique and language. Louis Ginsberg, a steadfast traditionalist after forty years of modernist experiment, likes verse "neat, / Exact, / Compact— / To file / My style / And pare / It bare";[20] but the son who, as we shall see, feels he can only really identify himself in acts that shatter established boundaries (of self, of literary form), insists on poetic means that are more ample, more free—and more grandiose. In a follow-up letter on the Shapiro poem, Louis attacks modernist verse as "willfully obscure," unnecessarily creating a "gulf between the poet and the intelligent reader."[21] In his view, "the ideal of a poem is that it give a general meaning to the many and a deeper and more complex experience to the few," an ideal enacted in his own practice.[22] Moreover, the letters frequently offer comments on exchanged poems: Allen's earliest verses are often praised, but just as often criticized as too "knotty," "impacted," "inchoate"—in a word, obscure.[23] Again the message is that the son should quit his pretentious inaccessibility, his literary decadence, and accommodate himself to his audience. "Not bad advice," anyone who has read these poems might conclude, but it no doubt struck the young poet as philistine old fogeyism. Allen's poems are faulted, however, on deeper than stylistic grounds; their "false assumptions" about life are questioned as well.[24] A key instance is Louis Ginsberg's reaction to "Howl," a poem in which his son publicly admitted to the very hallucinations, drug use, and homosexuality his father had warned him against. Significantly, Ginsberg sent a copy of the poem to his father not too long after its completion, as if the poem, far from being simply a pure and naked confession of Ginsberg's inmost soul, made some kind of hostile reference, and perhaps an appeal, to the father, who responded with a characteristically balanced assessment. " 'Howl,' " he wrote, "is a wild, volcanic, troubled, extravagant, turbulent, boisterous, unbridled outpouring, intermingling gems and flashes of picturesque insight with slag and debris of scoriac matter. It has violence; it has life; it has *vitality*. In my opinion, it is a one-sided neurotic view of life; it has not enough glad, Whitmanian affirmations."[25] The poem does have emotional force, vitality, *but* its vision of life is, again, off-balance, sick—"one-sided" and "neurotic" in its angry disillusionment.

In view of the deep, persistent, and often acrimonious conflicts between the two men, it is tempting to read "Moloch," the wrathful child-devouring deity of "Howl," as an angry representation of the father. But to derive from the poem a picture of the author as the essentially innocent victim of sadistic, persecutory authorities is to derive exactly the picture the author would like us to carry from the poem. "Howl" may be an honest confession of Ginsberg's conscious feelings at the time he wrote it, but many of the poem's rebellious attitudes actually serve as a defense against feelings that he is less able or willing to admit. It is true that Louis Ginsberg became the focus for many of his son's resentments, and while many of these grievances really derived from other sources, the anger also had some genuine basis in reality, as did his criticisms of the social system. Even their correspondence, where conflicts might be more in abeyance than in personal encounters, reveals paternal vituperation and ultimatums—e.g., a letter sent to Allen in the summer of 1948 which consisted simply of the sentence "Exorcise Neal," a reference to Ginsberg's erotic attachment to Neal Cassady at the time[26]—and the father seems to have insisted upon the son's successful completion of college and his becoming, as Allen put it, "a fine upstanding completely virile son."[27] Moreover, the father often questions not just his son's judgments but his very mental balance, a sensitive issue given his mother's history of psychotic illness.

Yet if Allen feared his father as a severe judge and angry persecutor, it is also clear that he felt a deep attachment and admiration for Louis Ginsberg, the origin of the recurrent image of the idealized, tender father in his poetry. It was his father, after all, who introduced Ginsberg to poetry and literature, an area in which Louis himself seemed to display real mastery and which his son was to make his own life's work. Moreover,

Naomi Ginsberg was a mother who was often emotionally or even physically absent—or frighteningly present. As Louis Ginsberg remembers in a memoir called "My Son the Poet,"

> In the early years of my marriage, a shadow of sorrow fell on our family. My wife, Naomi, somehow developed a neurosis, which, as the years went on, thickened into a psychosis. She would spend two or three years in a sanitarium, then I'd take her out for half a year or a year. After that, ominous hints of her worsening condition made me take her back.

Once, when he had decided to take her back to the hospital, she threatened, then attempted suicide, slashing her wrists in the bathroom.

> She opened [the door] and came out with blood oozing at both wrists. They were surface cuts, so I bandaged them and got her to bed. The boys stood there, shivering in their night clothes, panic in their eyes. What traumas, I thought, might sink into them and burrow into their psyches.[28]

In view of Naomi Ginsberg's illness, apt to make her rigid in her expectations of her son's behavior and unpredictable in her own, it is likely that her son turned to his father as a refuge, hoping to find both a point of stability in the family and a benign protector. And it is in such yearnings for (and memories of) a tender attachment with a tolerant older male that we find the beginnings of Ginsberg's later search for a kind of maternal father, of the sort he felt he'd found in Dr. Hicks in San Francisco and in such literary mentors as Whitman and Blake. "The Father is merciful," Ginsberg ecstatically proclaims in "Transcription of Organ Music"; what he continually seeks is some mild, accepting, Christ-like saviour, who will protect him from the terrifying aspects of the mother and offer the tender acceptance that she does not. Seeking salvation from the father (rather than reconciliation with him) inevitably led to disappointment, but even during the bristly period of his adolescence, Ginsberg clearly courted the older man's love and approval by striving to perform "good works." If Allen could condemn his father's assessment of one of his short stories as "a symptom of the smug normalcy of the bourgeois intellectual attitude," he assured his father in the same letter that he was no longer cutting classes, indeed was dressing decorously (even wearing a conservative black tie) and had "started to really get an education, making the most of the College by returning unread to the library" all his volumes of Gide and Baudelaire.[29] Similarly, when he wrote a few years later that he was postponing his final term at Columbia, he explained that he was doing so in order to save enough money to start psychoanalysis, a course earlier suggested by the father himself. "Don't worry about me becoming a permanent wastrel just because I'm trying to 'save my soul' as scientifically as possible," he wrote.[30]

Such yearnings to yield to the father (or his surrogate, the psychiatrist) also threaten Ginsberg, however real his attachment and his desire to please. For Ginsberg's basic image of the father, during adolescence and early manhood, is neither that of the powerful foe nor that of the benign protector, but that of a timid, rather withdrawn man, one who, with his cult of practicality and normality, has himself surrendered to external pressures and is thus finally feared not because he is too powerful, but because he is not strong and certain enough to save his son. The picture of Louis Ginsberg we get in "Kaddish" is that of an introverted, neglectful man, frightened, worried, and humiliated by his wife's paranoid hallucinations but whose attention, it seems, can only be caught by such apocalyptic means. In this view, mother and son are linked as victims of the father's weakness and neglect; the final impression of the father is one of ineffectuality, inconsequence: Naomi Ginsberg, the psychotic mother rather than the poet-father, is celebrated as her son's muse. Moreover, Louis Ginsberg was a literary intellectual and writer who taught English in the high schools of Paterson and who published poems in places like the editorial pages of the New York *Times* and the *Herald-Tribune*. What may have seemed like impressive accomplishments to a very young boy must have come with the increasing sophistication (and grandiosity) of adolescence, to signify a singular lack of daring and ambition. It is not too surprising, therefore, to find in the introduction that Ginsberg wrote to the father's collection, *Morning in*

Spring (1970), that beneath the affectionate respect with which the now world-famous son writes of his father, we should hear persistent hints of disappointment. "Living a generation with lyrics wrought by my father, some stanzas settle in the memory as perfected," Ginsberg opens.[31] This (uncharacteristically) deliberate, well-formed sentence carefully defines an attitude of respectful but hardly enthusiastic admiration, a striking contrast to Ginsberg's frequently effusive praise of such of his contemporaries, like Jack Kerouac, who share his own ultimate assumptions. The son, remembering "some stanzas" but apparently no whole poems, is clearly not going out on any critical limbs for the old man, whose well-balanced views are now turned back on him. As soon as Louis Ginsberg is introduced, he is pitted (in a losing battle) against W. C. Williams. " 'In this mode perfection is basic', W. C. Williams wrote, excusing himself for rejecting my own idealised iambic rhymes sent him for inspection" (p. 11). Imitating Louis's idealized verses, Ginsberg went astray—until he was saved by a bolder, and more successful guide. In fact, in the first three pages of the introduction, Ginsberg mentions Williams and Pound four times each, every time making an invidious comparison between their boldness and his father's timidity. Says Ginsberg of his father's kind of poetry:

I have resisted this mode as an anachronism in my own time—the anachronism of my own father writing the outworn verse of previous century voices, reechoing the jaded music and faded effect or sentiment of that music in a dream-life of his own sidestreet under dying phantom elms of Paterson, New Jersey—at the very time that Paterson itself was (having been articulated to its very rock-strata foundations and aboriginal waterfall voice in W. C. Williams' epic) degenerating into a XX Century Mafia-Police-Bureaucracy-Race-War-Nightmare-TV-Squawk suburb. (P. 14)

While Williams dauntlessly combines primitive solidity with an awareness of contemporary social reality, Louis Ginsberg *neglects* the present, timidly withdrawing into the "dream-life" of his peaceful suburban street. It is not just that this establishes him as an irrelevant "anachronism," an unreliable guide for a

young man entering a bewildering world; the cost of such with-
drawal is finally the loss of real autonomy and even life. The
father's guiding voice is hollow, a mere echo, not *his own* voice:
Daddy is nobody. All the language associated with Louis
Ginsberg in this passage—"anachronism," "outworn," "jad-
ed," "faded," "dying phantom elms"—suggests death, as if the
life had been sapped out of him. The son may take a certain
satisfaction in such diminishing thoughts of that parental author-
ity whose judgments he feared. Yet disappointment with the
defeated actual father generates the "Pater Omnipotens Aeterna
Deus" of "Howl," the "Lord" of such poems as "Kaddish,"
"Laughing Gas" and "Magic Psalm"—all fantasies of an all-
powerful father whose strength *can* heal and direct the writer.
So, during the early phase of Ginsberg's career, the earthly fa-
ther, whose "failure" the son anxiously seeks to avoid for him-
self, becomes a negative model, ironic source for the bardic
grandiosity, literary experimentation and daring self-exposures
that characterize his son's poetry starting with "Howl." In fact,
what Ginsberg appears to have done in 1955 was to take up his
father's medium of communication (poetry) and, declaring it
hollow and dead, transformed it by infusing it with the halluci-
natory visions and human vulnerability of his mother.

"You still haven't finished with your mother."
(Elise Cowen to Allen Ginsberg, after typing the manuscript
to "Kaddish.")[32]

> "If only you knew
> How your poet son, Allen,
> Raves over the world,
> Crazed for love of you!"
> (Louis Ginsberg, "To a Mother Buried.")[33]

One reason for Ginsberg's disenchantment with his father is
that he often looked at the older man through the terrified—and
rancorous—eyes of his mother. In examining the kind of grip
Naomi Ginsberg had on her son's feelings the key document is
"Kaddish," a confessional/visionary/elegiac poem in five parts
in which Ginsberg (like Sylvia Plath in "Daddy") attempts to

transform literature into therapeutic magic: to exorcise the ghost of a parental influence. Neither of the two poems, for all their literary brilliance, succeeds in delivering the poet from the agonizing conflicts that generate the work in the first place, although Ginsberg comes closer. "Daddy" may heighten hatred into a form of hard eloquence, but the poem is pure anger and destruction, with the renounced father simply transformed from a godlike to a satanic figure: Plath, whose father died when she was just nine, was never able to make the crucial step of perceiving him as a human rather than a mythical figure. In "Kaddish" Ginsberg confronts his anger at his mother's abstraction from life, her abandonment of him in madness, his disgust with her careless physical habits, his fascination with her sexually seductive manner with him, his guilt about his treatment of her during her breakdowns—"Kaddish" lays bare all these feelings and then proceeds to a declaration of love for Naomi Ginsberg. In the poem there is, as Ginsberg announces at the start of Part II, a "release of particulars," and Naomi Ginsberg is encountered with elaborate and moving specificity, as a complex human figure.[34] Yet it is also true that by the end Ginsberg has not resolved his divided feelings about his "fatal Mama" (p. 27) as much as he claims; the poem tempts us to think, like certain forms of therapy, that to get feelings out is to resolve them. But in fact the poem, far from moving toward idealization of the mother, culminates with an apotheosis of death (as release from the agonizing conflicts of life) and a yearning for fusion with this lost parent.

Naomi Ginsberg, a member of the Communist Party from the time of her youth, believed her life was in danger from political authorities such as Hitler, Roosevelt, and the FBI, as well as family figures, notably her mother and her husband. Her fears characteristically concerned an invasion of her self by some external, invisible, and malevolent agency that could subtly creep inside and possess her: poison gas filtering its way under the door, the manipulation of her thoughts by means of three bars inserted in her back and wired to her brain by the FBI during one of her stays in the hospital. In "Kaddish" Ginsberg seems to understand these fantasies of political persecution as extensions of sexual fears and, though Ginsberg himself never says so, it would be natural for a young boy to equate these fears of violation with some assault by the father. In any case, Naomi Ginsberg's paranoia was the dark side of what her son calls her "mad idealism" (p. 24), her intense yearning for the Pure, the Beautiful, the Ideal evident in her nostalgia for the innocence of her girlhood, her political utopianism (which inspired her to write communist fairy tales—p. 16), her alternately dreamy and paranoid paintings ("Humans sitting on the grass in some Camp No-Worry summers yore—saints with droopy faces and long-ill-fitting pants"—p. 25), her romantic songs played on the mandoline ("Last night the nightingale woke me / Last night when all was still / it sang in the golden moonlight / from on the wintry hill"). As a boy Ginsberg must have admired her intensity, been awed by the loftiness of her idealism, and shared her fears of the father's "assaults."

Yet both the fears and the longings of Naomi Ginsberg dissociated her from immediate emotional realities; what made her admirable also made her distant, bewildering, even terrifying—and made her son angry. She, too, neglected Allen. "I will think nothing but beautiful thoughts," says Naomi in "Kaddish," and she tells her son of seeing God the day before: "I cooked supper for him. I made him a nice supper—lentil soup, vegetables, bread & butter—miltz. . . ." At that very moment she is serving Allen "a plate of cold fish—chopped raw cabbage dript with tapwater—smelly tomatoes—week-old health food . . . I can't eat it for nausea sometimes" (p. 2). "Kaddish" frequently refers to such nausea-inspiring meals. Naomi was not providing Allen with true sustenance: a son cannot live on beautiful thoughts alone. Moreover, not only did his mother fail to take care of him, Ginsberg was forced at crucial points in her illness to take care of *her*. In Allen's version at least, his father and older brother evaded the reality and responsibilities of Naomi's madness, thus leaving the youngest son with the excruciating practical problems of dealing with her illness. Both times she was hospitalized during Ginsberg's lifetime, he was the one who had to take her to a rest home or, worse, call the police for help. The first of these two episodes took place when Ginsberg was just twelve. At exactly that delicate point of transition between boyhood and manhood, between home and the world, independence and responsibility were thrust on him, leaving him frightened, resentful, uncertain, and tormented with guilt. At that time, when his mother started hallucinating "a mystical assassin from Newark" (p. 13), Ginsberg, who had stayed home from school because she seemed so nervous and distraught, called a doctor, who recommended a rest home. After a long, humiliating bus ride, after being thrown out of one rest home (because Naomi hid in the closet and demanded a blood transfusion), Allen finally left her alone in an attic room, got on the next bus home and "lay my head back in the last seat, depressed—the worst yet to come?—abandoning her, rode in torpor—I was only 12."

12 riding the bus at nite thru New Jersey, have left Naomi to Parcae in Lakewood's haunted house—left to my own fate bus—sunk in a seat—all violins broken—my heart sore in my ribs—mind was empty—Would she were safe in her coffin—

(P. 15)

The sequence of feeling here—from guilt at abandoning her, to pity for his own isolated fate, to exhaustion and apathy and finally to the wish that she would die—reveals Ginsberg's desire to be relieved of his mother and the conflicts she triggers in him. And the worst *was* yet to come; that night,

the telephone rang at 2AM—Emergency—she'd gone mad—Naomi hiding under the bed screaming bugs of Mussolini—Help! Louis! Buba! Fascists! Death!—the landlady frightened—old fag attendant screaming back at her.

(P. 17)

Ginsberg, who had already been criticized by his father for leaving her there, asks himself, "my fault, delivering her to solitude?" It's a possible question: Ginsberg nowhere says exactly why he left her, it was not something he *had* to do, he describes himself sitting on her bed "waiting to escape," and has wished her dead. The situation, filled with painful stresses even for an adult, must have seemed unbearably complex for a boy of twelve.

Later, visiting her in the hospital, Ginsberg was confronted with Naomi "begging my 13-year-old boy mercy," saying

"Take me home"—I went alone sometimes looking for the lost Naomi, taking Shock—and I'd say, "No, you're crazy Mama,—Trust the Drs."—

(P. 19)

and still later, just before her last hospitalization in the late forties, as Naomi imagines herself hounded by Louis and her own mother,

"—No wires in the room!"—I'm yelling at her—last ditch, Eugene listening on the bed—what can he do to escape that fatal Mama— "You've been away from Louis for years already—Grandma's too old to walk—"
We're all alive at once then—even me & Gene & Naomi in one mythological Cousinesque room—screaming at each other in the Forever—I in Columbia jacket, she half undressed.
I banging against her head which saw Radios, Sticks, Hitlers—the gamut of Hallucinations—for real—her own universe—no road that goes elsewhere—to my own—No America, not even a world—

(Pp. 26–27)

Even at this point much later in adolescence, Ginsberg emphasizes the way his mother's madness removed her into a private, hallucinatory world ("her own universe") where, beyond all hysterical screaming, she remained inaccessible ("no road that goes nowhere"). In her madness Naomi triumphantly transcended reality, but abandoned her son, who, similarly deserted by his father and brother, was left in the position of asserting reality, angrily denying the validity of her visions and delivering her over to those very authorities—doctors and police—she most feared. In a situation filled with exhausting stresses Ginsberg reacted with remarkable strength. In "Kaddish" he asks, "Louis what happened to your heart then?"—when he was confronted with his terrified wife shrieking that he had called out the "poison cops": "Have you been killed by Naomi's ecstacy?" Allen was not but he suspected a certain hardness in his strength, this intensifying the guilt already latent in the situation; "It's my fault," he must have felt, "if I had loved my mother more, this wouldn't have happened to her—and to me." As an adolescent, Ginsberg was left alone, searching for that "lost Naomi" who had nurtured him as a young boy, fearing those ecstatic hallucinations of the "fatal Mama" that seemed to kill all feeling between them, and yet longing to join her in the dramatic intensity and transcendence of her madness.

From the retrospective point of view of the adult poet, the ideal way to handle this excruciating situation would be to accept a certain amount of anger and vindictiveness as natural, to emphasize the positive strength and tenderness that Ginsberg did show and so to view a certain amount of "hardness" as a prerequisite for self-survival; but this is by no means what we find in "Kaddish," where unresolved feelings of guilt prompt the poet to exorcise her spirit and be rid of her at last—a maneuver that breaks down, however, in view of his even stronger desire to return and fuse with her in death. The deepest sources of this longing we can see in a crucial passage of "Kaddish":

> One time I thought she was trying to make me come lay her—flirting to herself at sink—lay back on huge bed that filled most of the room, dress up round her hips, big slash of hair, scars of operations, pancreas, belly wounds, abortions, appendix, stitching of incisions pulling down in the fat like hideous thick zippers—ragged long lips between her legs—What, even, smell of asshole? I was cold—later revolted a little, not much—seemed perhaps a good idea to try—know the Monster of the Beginning Womb—Perhaps—that way. Would she care? She needs a lover.
>
> (P. 24)

At first glance this passage seems a daring revelation of an incest wish and a shockingly realistic description of the mother's body. But what we really see here is how one post-Freudian writer, pretending to be open and at ease about incestuous desire, affects sophisticated awareness as a defense against intense longings and anxieties. The lines are charged with feelings that the poet, far from "confessing out," appears eager to deny. Ginsberg's tone of voice is noticeably more defensive than frank: he assumes an attitude of detached superiority toward the scene—idealizing the act into a mythical/psychological experiment ("know the Monster of the Beginning Womb") performed more for his mother's emotional gratification than his: "She needs a lover." All of the sexual initiative is attributed to Naomi, allowing her son, innocent in his sophistication, to view himself as a superior, liberated, and compassionate individual, beyond conventional moral restraints and thus willing and able to give a little help to one of his friends. Holding himself above this emotionally charged situation, Ginsberg seeks to deny both the powerful attraction he feels toward his mother—as well as the fears he experiences as soon as he imagines the possibility of acting on it. The persistent emphasis on scars, particularly on wounds made by cutting, suggests an association between the female body and mutilation, an association frequent among male homosexuals who, perceiving the woman's body as the castrated body of a man and frightened at the prospect of a similar fate for themselves, are more comfortable with sexual partners who also have penises. Immediately following the passage I have quoted, Ginsberg dramatically shifts the subject, inserting first the Hebrew words of the Kaddish (a mourning ritual) and then turning to the story of his father. It is as if the very thought of incestuous wishes immediately provoked thoughts of death and the presence of the father, who might administer just that punishment his son most fears. In fact, in Part I of "Kaddish" Naomi is lamented as a victim who "fought the knife—lost / Cut down" by a heartless father wielding a "sharp icicle" (pp. 10–11). Yet in his recollection of incestuous yearnings, Ginsberg's deepest fears seem inspired less by Louis than by Naomi herself. When he does turn to his father in the succeeding lines, he presents his most poignant picture of Louis: "hurt with 20 years Naomi's mad idealism"—father and son linked as victims of the all-powerful mother (p. 24). Moreover, Naomi's womb is imagined as "monster" and images throughout the poem reenforce our suspicion that it is a *devouring* monster. In Part IV Ginsberg speaks of his mother's pubic hair as a "beard" (a trite image of which he is inordinately fond)—as if her vagina were a mouth (p. 34); and in Part II, on his last visit to his mother in the hospital, he imagines the door

423

as a "crotch," on the other side of which lies death. The quotation of the Hebrew words of the Kaddish suggest, on the deepest level, Ginsberg's association of incest with death. It is as if, were he to get too close to his mother, she would swallow him up—though he can't finally separate himself from her either. In "Kaddish," as in all of Ginsberg's earlier poetry, the conflict is one of separation versus unity. Separation is never independence but always an absolute, sterile, and frustrating isolation, as in the passage where all members of the family are hysterically screaming at each other yet with each of them locked in a private world of his or her own, incommunicado. The separation is so radical that it cannot be resolved by mere verbal or emotional communication ("her own universe—no road that goes elsewhere"); so Ginsberg longs to be delivered from this agonizing isolation by a kind of self-annihilating fusion with the mother. From this point of view we can understand his incestuous desires as expressing Ginsberg's wish to get inside his mother and see things as she does. The progression of Ginsberg's early career, in fact, is toward a closer and closer identification with her paranoid politics, her hallucinatory visions, even her physical sloppiness and sexual "looseness."

In "Kaddish"—as in "Howl"—absolute isolation alternates with absolute fusion, each poem seeking "resolution" in spiritual transcendence, apocalyptic vision, a total fusion that could only be realized in the static perfection of death. As "Kaddish" proceeds, it comes less and less to accept the loss of Naomi, more and more to yearn for union with her in death or, while life remains, to incorporate her vision as the poet's own. "Die / If thou wouldst be with that which thou dost seek," says Shelley in the lines from "Adonais" that Ginsberg significantly chose for his epigraph. The poem not only celebrates death as deliverance from the frightening and frustrating separateness of human life; it also identifies Naomi as the source of that vision of death. In this rich sense Naomi is Allen's inspiration, his "muse."

> O glorious muse that bore me from the womb, gave suck
> first mystic life & taught me talk and music, from whose pained
> head I first took Vision—

Tortured and beaten in the skull—What mad hallucinations
of the damned that drive me out of my own skull to seek
Eternity till I find Peace for Thee, O Poetry—and for all
humankind call on the Origin
Death which is the mother of the universe!

(Pp. 29–30)

In just these few lines, Ginsberg characteristically moves from a
celebration of his mother as "glorious muse" to thoughts of her
suffocating hold on him, so that in the end she is conflated with
Death, at once feared and sought. At first Ginsberg asserts that
the *real* Naomi was not the overweight, scarred, lonely woman
locked in a room of a lunatic asylum—but the mother of his
earliest memories who fed him physically and spiritually: "gave
suck first mystic life & taught me talk and music"—creating an
intimacy so complete that he seemed to see with her eyes. Yet
such union of mother and son has its threatening aspect; her
vision of things is "pained," and her life suggests to her son that
the only way out of suffering is through a kind of immolation in
it—by being pained into "Vision." Such destructive-redemptive
gestures are repeated throughout Ginsberg's poetry, and they
derive not just from a self-punishing masochism, but from the
need to find experiences extreme enough, painful enough, to
shatter the boundaries of the separate self. In this passage the
modifying phrase "tortured and beaten in the skull" floats free
of any precise referent, allowing it to refer to both Naomi and
Allen, joined in suffering, in those moments when they "lose
their head." Her suffering, it appears, is his. Yet if such union is
hard to bear, so is separation: the curious phrase, "bore me from
the womb," makes it sound as if he were *cast out* from her
unwillingly at birth. And this kind of resistance to a life of his
own is yet another reason why Ginsberg himself is "tortured
and beaten in the skull"—i.e., tortured and defeated when
locked in the skull of private consciousness. Here, a sentence
that began as an apostrophe to Naomi as "glorious muse" and
which we expect to continue as some form of prayer to her
breaks off to frame a question ("What mad hallucinations,"
etc.), a question that in turn is never completed as it turns into an

agonized and helpless cry: what *drives* him to be like her, to lose his head in "mad hallucinations" like her own! The answer is that both her presence and her absence drive him out of his skull: when near, she absorbs him into her vision; but once separated, he is driven to return, and the only way he can return is by sharing her vision—by fusing with her. Either route ends in a kind of death for the separate personality, but Death itself (now his muse) is affirmed as a release from the frustrating boundaries of the self, and as allowing a peaceful and final merge with the mother.

During his mother's seizures the adolescent Ginsberg had tried to break through to her by asserting a realistic point of view (" 'No wires in the room!'—I'm yelling at her"), a line of approach that ended in rage, frustration, hysteria. But Ginsberg closes the long autobiographical Part II of "Kaddish" by recollecting a moment of communication with Naomi, one that came, "mystically," just after her death. While living in a cottage in Berkeley in 1957, having (he hoped) left familial strifes behind him in the East, Ginsberg dreamed of his mother's spirit—"that, thru life, in what form it stood in that body, ashen or manic, gone beyond joy— / near its death—with eyes—was my own love in its form, the Naomi, my mother on earth still" and wrote a "long letter" declaring this love "& wrote hymns to the mad." A few days later he received a telegram from his brother, informing him of his mother's death; and two days after *that,* he got a letter from his mother, the first he'd had from her in several years—a prophecy (seemingly) from beyond the grave. The letter wonderfully mixes conventional maternal advice with cryptic visionary utterances:

"The key is in the window, the key is in the sunlight at the window—I have the key—Get married Allen don't take drugs—the key is in the bars, in the sunlight in the window."

The key, according to the mother, is conventionality: "Get married Allen don't take drugs." But in Part III of the poem Ginsberg picks up on the letter's visionary metaphors, the image of the flash of light that frees the self from the locked room, the pained head—the prison of solitary consciousness.

"The key is in the sunlight at the window in the bars the key is in
    the sunlight,"
only to have come to that dark night on iron bed by stroke when the
    sun gone down on Long Island
and the vast Atlantic roars outside the great call of Being to its own
to come back out of the Nightmare—divided creation—with her
    head lain on a pillow of the hospital to die
—in one last glimpse—all Earth one everlasting Light in the familiar
    blackout—no tears for this vision—
But that the key should be left behind—at the window—the key in
    the sunlight—to the living—that can take
that slice of light in hand—and turn the door—and look back see
Creation glistening backwards to the same grave, size of universe,
size of the tick of the hospital's clock on the archway over the white
    door—

(P. 33)

Naomi Ginsberg, inmate of asylums for many years now, vic-
tim of shock treatments and strokes, locked alone in her room,
further isolated by her madness, lies in a "dark night" on an
"iron bed" like a prisoner, a kind of prisoner of life. As Ginsberg
makes clear, it is not just the harrowing experiences of her life
that make it nightmarish, it is the very condition of living in a
bounded, physical being—*divided* creation"—that creates the
"Nightmare." In the midst of all this, Naomi *is* pained into
vision, has her glimpse of "everlasting Light," finds the key to
the locked self. Yet the key, as Ginsberg interprets it, is to see
physical life, its ordeals, as unreal, a dream—as brief and insig-
nificant as the tick of the hospital clock. The vision does not
open, as in a Whitman or a Blake, a harmonizing of physical and
spiritual; rather it opts for the apocalyptic, the purely transcen-
dent. The moment of vision, here, is the moment of death; and
death is the key, releasing us from the nightmare of a fleshly (and
thus divided) existence.

In "Kaddish"'s last two sections, Ginsberg shifts from de-
tailed narrative in long "broken paragraphs" to shorter, more
intense liturgical chants which attempt to let go of the memory
of Naomi and accept her loss.[35] Yet the very means by which
Ginsberg comes to terms with her death is by identifying as his

own that very vision of life *as death* which she had imposed on him from his earliest years. Section IV utters "farewell" to Naomi Ginsberg by cataloguing parts of her body, aspects of her life, that are expressive of her ordeal—as if her life were passing before his mind in final review. As the list proceeds, Ginsberg focuses on her eyes: "with your eyes of shock / with your eyes of lobotomy / with your eyes of divorce / with your eyes of stroke / with your eyes alone / with your eyes / with your eyes" (p. 35). Her eyes convey a kind of mute, helpless suffering and to look into them is to become transfixed, paralyzed *by her vision;* in fact, the emotional force of this section is not toward a "farewell," but to show the poet mesmerized by the Medusa-like glance of his mother. The poem's final section, likewise liturgical in manner, similarly depicts Ginsberg as helplessly transfixed by the memory of his mother. Section V begins as a visit to Naomi's grave and proceeds by alternating the cries of crows in the cemetery ("caw caw caw") with a religious chant ("Lord Lord Lord"). The crows evoke decomposition, the inevitable fate of life in the flesh, while the "Lord" is intended to define an eternal perspective within which such cruel realities can be accepted. But the poem's final line—"Lord Lord Lord caw caw caw Lord Lord Lord caw caw caw Lord" (p. 36)—conflates crow and Lord, temporal and eternal, as devourers, and the effect of the line, which Ginsberg once described as "pure emotive sound," is that of a cry, or a "howl," of a suffering victim.[36] Life, with its impersonal physical processes, its movement through a divided and often indifferent world—that world into which Ginsberg was unwillingly cast—is intolerable. Hence, the only way it can be borne is by seeing it through Naomi's eyes—as a "vision":

> caw caw all years my birth a dream caw caw New York the bus the broken shoe the vast highschool caw caw *all Visions of the Lord.*
>
> (P. 36, my italics)

Whatever its agonies, life is merely a dream in the mind of an omnipotent Lord—a thought that, it seems, offers safety, if not selfhood. Yet it is the threatening qualities of this divinity which are stressed ("great Eye that stares on All," "Grinder of giant Beyonds"—p. 36) and it is clear that this "Lord," with his powerful glance and his threat to devour, is ominous in precisely those ways Naomi is. In fact, all the poem's deific figures—the glorious muse, omnipotent Lord—dissolve into a single figure, "the Naomi," who is the "Origin/Death"—the "fatal Mama."

A key result of the psychic conflict in the poem is a kind of formal tension. In seeking to link confessional and visionary modes, Ginsberg was advancing a poetic project that had begun with "Howl" and that would prove to be a generative one for contemporary poetry. Yet autobiographical and mystical motives are at odds with each other in "Kaddish." If Part II confronts us with a relentless "release of particulars" into powerful narrative, all remaining sections of the poem strive to chant those particulars into dream, Vision—a strategy that fails on at least two counts. In the first place, the need of the poet to get "out of his head" in many respects signals a *surrender to,* rather than coming to terms with, the memories of Part II. In addition, most readers will, I think, leave the work more impressed with the psychic conflicts of II than the sought resolutions of the closing sections. Moreover, Ginsberg's account of the poem's composition in "How 'Kaddish' Happened" implies the centrality of the second part and reveals that Ginsberg felt that he was in some sense "defeated" by the poem—i.e., by Naomi.[37] While individual sections of "Kaddish" were written spontaneously, some of them in drug-induced moments of "mad hallucination," long intervals separated the writing of these sections, the whole poem taking more than two years. Significantly, the order of composition went: first, part IV (the evocation of Naomi's mesmerizing stare), then a year later I and II, then some indefinite period after this, V; no mention is made of III. Most emphasis is given in the essay to the writing of II, which Ginsberg approached slowly, resistingly, yet felt he *had* to approach; Part II was written in twenty straight hours of effort after a night of no sleep, some mescaline and speed, listening to Ray Charles records and chanting aloud passages from Shelley's "Adonais" and the Hebrew Kaddish: Afterward,

I walked out in early blue dawn on to 7th Avenue & across town to my Lower East Side apartment—New York before sunrise has its own celebrated hallucinatory unreality. In the country getting up with the cows and birds hath Blakean charm, in the megalopolis the same nature's hour is a science-fiction hell vision, even if you're a milkman. Phantom factories, unpopulated streets out of Poe, familiar nightclubs bookstores groceries dead.[38]

The essay's title, "How 'Kaddish' Happened," implies that the poem *happened to* Ginsberg, surfacing from the depths of his buried self—a familiar claim of romantic poets but one that here carries the added suggestion that the poem was *thrust upon* a somewhat resistant poet. At the same time Ginsberg's account of the writing of the poem depicts the poet—via exhaustion, drugs, and careful selection of urban setting and suitably elegiac literary texts—deliberately flagellating himself into vision, into communing with his dead mother. Both versions, of course, are true—true to his divided fear of and longing for the woman who gave him "mystic life." What Ginsberg sees when he wanders down Seventh Avenue at dawn is the city seen through Naomi Ginsberg's terrified eyes; and it is also a landscape of loss—what life looks like to him without her: a hell vision of unbearable isolation in a cold, threatening environment.

After finally getting down a draft of the entire poem, Ginsberg tells us, he waited another year before even typing the manuscript, much less seeking publication. The poem seemed, he recalls, too massive, too messy and too private to reach an audience, suggesting that on an unconscious level the writing of the poem may have been an act of private communication between the poet and his "muse," like the letter he had received from her just after her death. In any case, "Kaddish," all too successfully recreating the overwhelming size, disorder, and inaccessibility of its subject, seemed to have "defeated" its author.

In these self-doubts we can hear the internalized voice of Louis Ginsberg, the side of Ginsberg that feared that identification with his mother's way of seeing things would leave him, like her, trapped in a private vision, with "no road that goes elsewhere." At this point, Ginsberg, showing that he may have derived more strength from the father than he liked to admit, sat down to the "patient scholar's task" of making the poem "shapely."[39] If he began by trying to bring the father's "dead" medium back to life by infusing it with the visions of his mother, it was his commitment to poetry that turned Ginsberg back toward the world, opened a road that did span the gap between private vision and external reality.

Of course, what Ginsberg himself stresses in his account of the composition of "Kaddish" is the need to go "all the way out" in order to capture a "continuous impulse," an emotional and creative thrust that would be stifled in a more orderly work.[40] In his view, poetic (and human) energy can only be generated by going out of one's skull—beyond the "dead forms" of reality and back to the Origin, the mother, who turns out to be Death. On a human level such regressive longings mark a kind of defeat, at least the defeat of the quest for independence, for a life of one's own. Yet "defeat like that is good for poetry," Ginsberg states.

> —you go so far out you don't know what you're doing, you lose touch with what's been done before by anyone, you wind up creating a new poetry-universe. "Make It New," saith Pound, "Invention," said W. C. Williams. That's the "Tradition"—a complete fuck-up so you're on your own.[41]

Such defeat does not guarantee good poetry; but in the literary atmosphere of the late 1950s—dominated by poetry that was self-consciously impersonal and traditionalistic—Ginsberg's breaking of established boundaries released a new life into contemporary American poetry.

NOTES

1. Robert Creeley cites the new sense of form in "Howl" in his "Introduction" to *The New Writing in the USA, A Quick Graph* (San Francisco, 1970), pp. 44–45 as do Galway Kinnell in "The Poetics of the Physical World," *Iowa Review* 2 (Summer 1971):115–16, and Adrienne Rich, "Talking with Adrienne Rich," *The Ohio Review* 13 (Fall 1971): 28–46.

2. All of these journals are part of the Allen Ginsberg Archives at Columbia University. Quotations from material in the collection are made with the kind permission of Allen Ginsberg and Columbia University.

3. *Starting from San Francisco* (New York, 1967), p. 27.

4. Jane Kramer, *Allen Ginsberg in America* (New York: Random House, 1970), pp. 39–40.

5. Ibid., p. 42.

6. See "Notebook, 1953–56" in the Allen Ginsberg Archives for information on this period in Ginsberg's life.

7. Entry for April 20, 1955 in "Notebook 1953–56."

8. *Allen Ginsberg in America,* p. 42.

9. *Young Man Luther* (New York, 1958), p. 103.

10. *Allen Ginsberg in America,* pp. 150–51.

11. *Go* (New York, 1952), p. 108. The statement about accuracy is made in Holmes's *Nothing More to Declare* (New York: Dutton, 1967), p. 56.

12. Louis Ginsberg to Allen Ginsberg, August 8, 1945, in the Allen Ginsberg Archives. All subsequent correspondence cited is also from the Archives.

13. Louis Ginsberg to Allen Ginsberg, December 12, 1955.

14. Louis Ginsberg to Allen Ginsberg, n.d.

15. Louis Ginsberg to Allen Ginsberg, November 2, 1945.

16. Louis Ginsberg to Allen Ginsberg, October 29, 1945.

17. Louis Ginsberg to Allen Ginsberg, November 2, 1945.

18. Ibid.

19. Louis Ginsberg to Allen Ginsberg, March 10, 1958.

20. "Terse," in *Morning in Spring and Other Poems* (New York, 1970), p. 119.

21. Louis Ginsberg to Allen Ginsberg, November 2, 1945.

22. Louis Ginsberg to Allen Ginsberg, n.d. (but probably sometime in 1948).

23. Ibid.

24. Louis Ginsberg to Allen Ginsberg, March 10, 1958.

25. Louis Ginsberg to Allen Ginsberg, May 27, 1956.

26. Louis Ginsberg to Allen Ginsberg, July 11, 1948.

27. Allen Ginsberg to Louis Ginsberg, September 3, 1947.

28. Paterson *News,* Monday, June 2, 1969, p. 4.

29. Allen Ginsberg to Louis Ginsberg, n.d. (but probably sometime in 1948).

30. Allen Ginsberg to Louis Ginsberg, September 3, 1947.

31. "Confrontation with Louis Ginsberg's Poems," in *Morning in Spring*, p. 11. Subsequent references are made in the text.

32. "How 'Kaddish' Happened," in *The Poetics of the New American Poetry*, ed. Donald Allen and Warren Tallman (New York: Grove Press, 1973), p. 347.

33. *Morning in Spring and Other Poems*, p. 93.

34. *Kaddish and Other Poems*, (San Francisco: City Lights Books, 1961), p. 13. Subsequent references are made in the text.

35. "How 'Kaddish' Happened," p. 345.

36. Ibid., p. 346.

37. Ibid.

38. Ibid., p. 345.

39. Ibid., p. 346.

40. Ibid.

41. Ibid.

EKBERT FAAS

Confronting the Horrific

> But at the far end of the universe the million eyed Spyder
>   that hath no name
> spinneth of itself endlessly
> the monster that is no monster approaches with apples,
>   perfume, railroads, television, skulls
> a universe that eats and drinks itself
> blood from my skull.[1]

This evocation of the horrific aspect of Nature or the "Great
Being" from Ginsberg's poem "Lysergic Acid" has many paral-
lels, not only in the poet's own work, but in contemporary
literature and art as a whole. Here, for instance, is a passage from
Burroughs's *Naked Lunch* describing a scene from the blue
movie shown at "A.J.'s Annual Party." What begins as a
straightforward pornographic film à la *Deep Throat* suddenly
turns into a surrealist orgy of sadism and murder, in which
Mary, the female participant, assumes the role of a bloodthirsty
Ogress:

> She bites away Johnny's lips and nose and sucks out his eyes
> with a pop . . . She tears off great hunks of cheek . . . Now
> she lunches on his prick . . . Mark walks over to her and she
> looks up from Johnny's half-eaten genitals, her face covered
> with blood, eyes phosphorescent. . . .

Among the passages charged as "brutal, obscene and disgust-
ing" in the Boston trial of 1962, this one is probably the most

From *Towards a New American Poetics: Essays and Interviews* (Santa Barbara,
Calif.: Black Sparrow Press, 1978). Reprinted with permission.

"offensive" in the entire novel.[2] Yet it is hardly more so than much that for millennia has been an accepted part of the artistic canon of many non-Western cultures. Tantric, Hindu or Taoist art provides examples of the almost total absence of sexual tabus in specific cultures of ancient Tibet, India or China, while a few quotes from Heinrich Zimmer's *Myths and Symbols in Indian Art and Civilization* could have easily convinced Burroughs's judges that a gruesomeness comparable to *Naked Lunch* is a common attribute of many Eastern divinities and, in the case of Black Kālī, of "the most cherished and widespread of the personalizations of Indian cult." "Innumerable representations of the devouring Black Kālī," Zimmer writes, "depict [the] wholly negative aspect of the Universal Mother." In a sculpture reproduced in the book, for instance,

> she appears as an emaciated, gruesome hag of bony fingers, protruding teeth, unquenchable hunger . . . [feeding] upon the entrails of her victim. And who among beings born is not her victim? She cleaves the belly and draws out and gobbles the intestines—that is what she is fond of—steaming with the last breath of expiring life.

Other representations show her "adorned with the blood-dripping hands and heads of her victims, treading on the prostrate, corpselike body" of Shiva, her spouse and lover.[3]

Moreover, such monstrosities are by no means a specific obsession of one particular religion. The Great Mother in her "negative elementary character"[4] is common to many of the world's mythologies and her archetypal attributes are clearly evident when we compare Black Kālī with, for instance, the Aztec Coatlicue whose monumental sculpture, now in the Anthropological Museum of Mexico City, miraculously survived the destruction of Montezuma's Holy City at the hands of the Christian conquerors. Like the Indian Goddess, Coatlicue is adorned with the blood-dripping hands and torn-out hearts of her victims. In this she also resembles Vishnu, supreme deity of the Hindu pantheon, as depicted in the celebrated eleventh chapter of the *Bhagavad Gita*. Like the latter's "Universal Form" as "Time," "the Destroyer of the worlds" equipped with many faces, eyes, arms, bellies, legs, terrible teeth and devouring mouths,[5] the Mexican Earth Mother and mother of all the Aztec divinities has myriad eyes, multiple serpent faces and devouring jaws, several bodies and claws as well as fearsome arrays of tusks.

Western culture proves to be different from most others in excluding such notions from the accepted part of its religious consciousness. Here, Heraclitus was both the first and last of the great philosopher prophets (before Blake or Nietzsche) who, in his famous proposition that "war is the father and king of all," affirmed the horrific as an intrinsic part of the divine. But such wisdom was obscured by the advent of Greek idealistic philosophy and Judæo-Christian eschatological thinking which reinforced each other in "the illusion that good may exist without evil,"—either in a Platonic realm of ideas or in a heavenly hereafter in which "there shall be no more death, neither sorrow, nor crying."[6] Evil was explained as an incomplete self-realization of the ideal or was relegated to the infernal region of the fallen angels, while on the level of secular religion the Great Mother was gradually replaced by "Frau Welt" whom Chaucer's contemporary, the preacher John Bromyard, describes as a beautiful lady with her back full of worms and festering sores.[7] By the late Middle Ages this image, which also adorns the outside of many cathedrals, had acquired the ubiquity of a literary *locus communis*.

What to most religions is an unalterable part of the divine is explained by Christianity as the result of man's sinfulness. Thus God assumes the role of a judge to whom the horrific, by a further twist of the same cosmological notion, becomes the justification for punishing man for the evil which is an inherent part of all creation. As if modelled on this scheme, the segregating, torturing and exterminating of large groups of people for their sinfulness, unorthodox beliefs, impure race or ideology has been one of the most obvious hallmarks of Western spiritual history. Ironically, the most frightening excesses of this kind have tended to occur in periods of enlightened ideologizing such as our own which, coincident with the breakdown of traditional values, has witnessed the total unleashing of the demonic forces ignored or suppressed by idealistic philosophy and Judæo-Christian religion. The concentration camps of this century may thus be seen as a secularized extension or psychological enactment of the horror world which Dante and others have portrayed with such zestful detail and ingenious precision.

The actual holocausts of recent decades were paralleled and often heralded by an unprecedented emergence of the horrific in art. It is the final irony of our tragic misconception of evil that such art was denounced as decadent and corrupt by the very ideologists who began to stage its imagined horrors in the barbed wire infernos of the German and Russian concentration camps. Of course, there were others who clearly recognized the function of this artistic phenomenon in the spiritual development of our time. Not long before the Nazi exhibition of decadent art in Munich opened its gates to innumerable visitors from Germany and abroad, a large Picasso retrospective in Zurich and the stir it had created caused C. G. Jung to write an essay about the artist (1932). To the psychiatrist it is a symptom of the general emergence of the "antichristian and Luciferian forces . . . in modern man" that Picasso follows "the demoniacal attraction of ugliness and evil," thereby dissolving the "accepted ideals of goodness and beauty" into "fragments, fractures . . . [and] disorganized units." Despite its obvious schizophrenic tinge, the painter's work (just like Joyce's *Ulysses*) complies to the fullest extent with the "social significance of art" in its time. For the latter, as Jung had written as early as 1922,

> is constantly at work educating the spirit of the age, conjuring up the forms in which the age is most lacking. The unsatisfied yearning of the artist reaches back to the primordial image in the unconscious which is best fitted to compensate the inadequacy and one-sidedness of the present.[8]

Eastern literature showed Jung that the images emerging in this process often resemble the symbols of various non-Western mythologies. As he found in 1938, the sequence of events described in *The Tibetan Book of the Dead,* for instance, "offers a close parallel to the phenomenology of the European unconscious when it is undergoing an 'initiation process,' that is to say, when it is being analysed."[9] Even Jung, however, might have been surprised to see how closely a description such as the following of the "blood-drinking wrathful deities" which the soul encounters on her journey after death comes to paralleling the horrific in the art and literature that began to emerge towards the end of his life (1875–1961):

> from the south-east, the Red Pukkase, holding intestines in the right [hand] and [with] the left putting them to her mouth . . . from the north-west, the Yellowish-White Tsandhalî, tearing asunder a head from a corpse, the right [hand] holding a heart, the left putting the corpse to the mouth and [she then] eating [thereof]; . . . from the north-west, the Black Crow-Headed One, the left [hand] holding a skull-bowl, the right holding a sword, and [she] eating heart and lungs.[10]

For although Jung's insights were preceded by artistic developments originating with "the Romantic Agony,"[11] it was only after World War II that the horrific began to dominate modern art. The full extent of this phenomenon and of its origins is as yet uncharted, but it is sufficient to mention names such as Francis Bacon or Edward Kienholz, Ted Hughes or William Burroughs to remind us that the horrific, far from being the subject matter of outsider visionaries such as Bosch, Goya or Blake, now holds center stage in the imaginative world of present-day art and literature. Among North American poets, Allen Ginsberg no doubt has had the strongest impact in this realm, and it may contribute to our understanding of modern art in general to follow the poet through his arduous struggle with the demons which loom so frighteningly in our contemporary consciousness.

The fourth book of *Paterson* reprints a letter which Ginsberg sent Williams, along with some poems, shortly after his release from a New York mental hospital. One of the poems, later published in *Empty Mirror* (1961), has the mysterious title "The Shrouded Stranger." As Ginsberg explained to Williams, it was based on a real dream about "a classic hooded figure" and "the void," a dream which had "become identified with [his] own abyss."[12] Thus inspired, the poem not only seems to prefigure a

438

more than fifteen-year-long search for the hidden divinity, but to anticipate some of its ultimate fulfillment:

> I dreamed I was dreaming again
> and decided to go down the years
> looking for the Shrouded Stranger.
> I knew the old bastard
> was hanging around somewhere.
>
> I couldn't find him for a while;
> went looking under beds,
> pulling mattresses off,
> and finally discovered him
> hiding under the springs
> crouched in the corner:
>
> met him face to face at last.
> I didn't even recognise him.
>
> "I'll bet you didn't think
> it was me after all," he said.[13]

Before Ginsberg, fulfilling his own dream prophecy, could face up to the "Shrouded Stranger" in real life, he had to subject himself to shamanistic rituals of self-destruction and learn to accept his bodily self in a "universe that eats and drinks itself."[14] What launched him on this fearsome journey was his 1948 Blake vision which Ginsberg, like a latter-day Ancient Mariner, has told and retold ever since. Even in this first of many hallucinatory experiences, the attainment of "cosmic consciousness," the exhilarating awareness that "existence itself was God," is overshadowed by dread and doom. As the poet recalled in 1965,

> I experienced "The Sick Rose," with the voice of Blake reading it, as something that applied to the whole universe, like hearing the doom of the whole universe, and at the same time the inevitable beauty of doom. I can't remember now, except it was very beautiful and very awesome. But a little of it slightly scary, having to do with the knowledge of death—

my death and also the death of being itself, and that was the great pain.

The experience left Ginsberg with no doubt that he "was born to realize . . . the spirit of the universe." But in his repeated attempts to fulfill this mission he more and more came to resemble Dr. Faustus who yearns to see God, yet only succeeds in conjuring up the devil. Shortly after the Blake vision, when once again he tried to invoke the "Great Spirit," it did indeed appear to him, but in the shape of "some really scary presence, it was almost as if I saw God again except God was the devil." And although Blake seemed to urge him on "To find a Western Path / Right through the Gates of Wrath," Ginsberg "got scared, and thought, I've gone too far."[15]

None of these early visions found direct expression in the poet's published verse, and to judge from their actual descriptions there was, in fact, little visual detail to record. Subsequent drug experiments, however, not only brought back the hallucinations, but filled them with an eerie phantasmagoria of archetypal images embodied in the concrete realities of modern life. Such a fusion is documented in Ginsberg's report of an experience which inspired the second part of "Howl":

I had an apt on Nob Hill [San Francisco], got high on Peyote, & saw an image of the robot skullface of Moloch in the upper stories of a big hotel glaring into my window; got high weeks later again, the Visage was still there in red smokey downtown Metropolis.[16]

. . . One of Ginsberg's most detailed and revealing self-interpretations explains how [in the Moloch section of "Howl"], for the first time, he succeeded in capturing one of the visions which ever since 1948 had been haunting his imagination with a sense of doom and destruction. To sum it up in terms of the poet's general concept of creativity, the vision is turned into poetry by a rhythmical articulation of the feelings it engenders in the body. By arranging themselves around this "definite rhythmic impulse" the words may, to the poet's own amazement, take their own illogical and unexpected course.

The poetry generally is like a rhythmic articulation of feeling . . . At best what happens, is there's a definite body rhythm that has no definite words, or may have one or two words attached to it . . . And then, in writing it down, it's simply by a process of association that I find what the rest of the statement is . . . [B]efore I wrote "Moloch whose eyes are a thousand blind windows," I had the word, "Moloch, Moloch, Moloch," and I also had the feeling DA de de DA de de DA de de DA DA. So it was just a question of looking up and seeing a lot of windows . . . So Moloch whose eyes— then probably the next thing I thought was "thousands." O.K., and then thousands *what?* "Thousands blind." And I had to finish it somehow. So I hadda say "windows." It looked good *afterward.*[17]

In his introduction to *Howl,* Williams expresses surprise at Ginsberg's "ability to survive," for literally, as he remarks, Ginsberg, "from all the evidence, [has] been through hell." Yet the worst was still to come. To assure his survival, the poet, only twenty-nine at the time he screamed out his "howl of defeat" (Williams), could either flee or accept the demons he had summoned from his subconscious. In this archetypal situation he resembled the soul in the *Bardo Thödol* who is advised not to fear or flee the Wrathful Deities it is about to encounter. Because met in the right spirit of self-abandonment, they are recognized to be no other than the Peaceful Deities in disguise, and like those, mere emanations of one's mind:

the fifty-eight flame-enhaloed, wrathful, blood-drinking deities come to dawn, who are only the former Peaceful Deities in changed aspect . . . the least of the least of the devotees of the mystic *mantrayāna* doctrines, as soon as he sees these blood-drinking deities, will recognize them to be his tutelary deities, and the meeting will be like that of human acquaintances. He will trust them; and becoming merged into them, in at-onement, will obtain Buddhahood.[18]

As if following such advice, Ginsberg decided to face the demons.

The crucial event in what followed was the death of the poet's mother. In and out of mental hospitals for most of Allen's childhood, she had turned into a living incarnation of the awesome divinity he later was to encounter in his vision—into the "fatal Mama," the "old woman of skulls,"[19] whose traumatic impact on the young boy finds expression in a ruthlessly realistic anecdote from "Kaddish," the elegy on Naomi's death:

One time I thought she was trying to make me come lay her— flirting to herself at sink—lay back on huge bed that filled most of the room, dress up round her hips, big slash of hair, scars of operations, pancreas, belly wounds, abortions, appendix, stitching of incisions pulling down in the fat like hideous thick zippers—ragged long lips between her legs—What, even, smell of asshole? I was cold—later revolted a little, not much—seemed perhaps a good idea to try—know the Monster of the Beginning Womb—[20]

The hold which this and similar experiences had on Ginsberg was all the stronger since he knew himself to be closer to his mother than any other member of his family. Her "mad idealism," her visions of God, her very insanity prefigure or even parallel ("I was in bughouse that year 8 months,"[21]) the poet's own experiences. Yet given his willingness to face evil and destruction, this "madness" now becomes the very means to redeem the media-perverted consciousness and Moloch-inspired violence which caused it and which, like many others who "suffered death and madness," had

>   murdered my mother
>   who died of the communist anticommunist psychosis
> . . . .
> complaining about wires of masscommunication in her head
>   and phantom political voices in the air
>   besmirching her girlish character.[22]

In this way "Kaddish" can celebrate "the Monster of the Beginning Womb" in her positive aspect of the "holy mother" whose "world is born anew" and thus becomes the source of the poet's inspiration:

O glorious muse that bore me from the womb, gave suck first mystic life & taught me talk and music, from whose pained head I first took Vision—

Yet such acceptance of suffering is still far from the abiding equanimity of the "devotee of the mystic doctrines," and in the very passage that follows, the redemptive power of the poet's visions is again called in doubt:

Tortured and beaten in the skull—What mad hallucinations of the damned that drive me out of my own skull to seek Eternity till I find Peace for Thee, O Poetry.[23]

So the search for the hidden divinity becomes ever more frantic and self-destructive. In the footsteps of William Burroughs, Ginsberg visits Peru to try the hallucinogenic ayahuasca in the company of the natives. His visions, recorded in the descriptions and drawings of the *Yage Letters* to his older friend, were the strongest and most frightening since his "Merry Visions of Blake" in Harlem. Still ruminating about his mother who died "in God knows what state of suffering," the poet experiences "the Great Being, or some sense of It, approaching [his] mind like a big wet vagina," and during a subsequent session

got nauseous, rushed out and began vomiting, all covered with snakes, like a Snake Seraph, colored serpents in aureole all around my body . . . like a snake vomiting out the universe—or a Jivaro in head-dress with fangs vomiting up in realization of the Murder of the Universe—my death to come—everyone's death to come—all unready—I unready.[24]

Ginsberg tried to preserve his sanity by somewhat artificially treating these hallucinations as a "temporary illusion," but the "fearful" and "almost schizophrenic alteration of consciousness," caused by the drug, proved to defy such psychological self-persuasion. "I don't know if I'm going mad," he reports to his friend. "I hardly have the nerve to go back, afraid of some real madness; a Changed Universe permanently changed." Bur-

443

roughs' reply to Ginsberg's plea for help ultimately turned out to be the right advice: "There is no thing to fear. Vaya adelante." Yet for Ginsberg such acceptance of the Wrathful Divinities was not to be achieved before several more years had gone by.[25]

The poems inspired by the Peruvian adventure read like one agonized howl of yearning, fright and despair. "[R]eady for [the] disintegration of [his] mind," the poet throws himself at the mercy of the "Creator and Eater of Mankind," imploring him to "devour [his] brain," to "attack [his] hairy heart with terror" and to "transfigure [him] to slimy worms."[26] Yet though the "Ever-Unknowable" fulfills the poet's longing for self-sacrifice, doom is his ultimate answer, and the shamanistic journey never penetrates beyond the valley of death and destruction:

No refuge in Myself, which is on fire
        or in the World which is His also to bomb & Devour!
                Recognise His might! Loose hold
        of my hands—my frightened skull
                        —for I had chose self-love—
    my eyes, my nose, my face, my cock, my soul—and now
                the faceless Destroyer!
        A billion doors to the same new Being!
    The universe turns inside out to devour me!
and the mighty burst of music comes from out the inhuman
                                door—[27]

Ginsberg's journey through India (1962–63), which he had hoped would prove to be his "promised land," only led him into the lowest region of this inferno. Though it was reassuring for him to note that the *Bhagavad Gita* representation of Vishnu in his negative aspect of "world-destroying Time" resembled what he had "seen often on LSD, etc.," he was only too well aware that "fearful Allen" had never lost his fear "in the face of that monster."

Because I am still clinging to my human known me, Allen Ginsberg—and to enter this thing means final, complete abandonment of all I know of my *I am* except for this outer-seeming otherness which requires my disappearance.[28]

Tantrism, a religion devoted to the worship of the Great Mother in her negative elementary character, teaches that this self-abandonment can only be achieved through a detached, though fully sensual, acceptance of one's physical passions and desires. "A whole series of India holy men" Ginsberg consulted on his journey gave similar advice, directing him "back to the body—getting *in* the body rather than getting out of the human form." Such words turned the tip of the scale. Years of shamanistic self-destruction led Ginsberg into an ever deepening despair in which, bereft of love, hope, even "sacred poetry," the meaningless suffering of himself and those around him seemed to provide the only sense of existence:

> Skin is sufficient to be skin, that's all
> it ever could be, tho screams of pain in the kidney
> make it sick of itself, a hollow dream
> dying to finish its all too famous misery
> —leave immortality for another to suffer like a fool,
> not get stuck in a corner of the Universe
> sticking morphine in the arm and eating meat.
>
> *Bankok—May 28, '63*
> Chinese meats hanging in shops— . . .

This is the state reached at the end of the Indian journey—a state of despondency so complete that it could transcend its proper bounds and reach out into a new realm beyond despair. This aloneness, as Ginsberg himself observed, "is like a returning home."[29]

It also marked the turning point in his quest of the "faceless Destroyer" who, elusive and threatening in his cosmic aloofness till then, is now forced to reveal himself in his own creation. This epiphany was recorded in "The Change: Kyoto-Tokyo Express," dated 7/18/63, on a subsequent journey through Japan.[30] "Seeking the Great Spirit of the / Universe in Terrible Godly / form," the poet still sees himself and the rest of mankind as the Destroyer's victim:

O suffering Jews
burned in the hopeless fire
O thin Bengali sadhus adoring
Kali mother hung with
nightmare skulls O Myself
under her pounding
feet!

Yet accepting his own body and suffering, the poet, like the enlightened soul of the *Bardo Thödol,* recognizes such phantoms as mere projections of his agonized self:

Who is, who cringes, perishes,
is reborn a red Screaming
baby? Who cringes before
that meaty shape in
Fear?

In this dream I am the Dreamer
and the Dreamed I am
that I am.[31]

And the "Destroyer of the World" who several years before had answered his "Magic Psalm" with a "Reply" of doom now appears as the "sweet lonely Spirit" who, eager to follow the poet's conjurations, seems ready to reveal himself in his own creation, forceful yet benign, with a gesture of "fear not" and ultimate peace:

Come, sweet lonely Spirit, back
to your bodies, come great God
back to your only image, come
to your many eyes & breasts,
come thru thought and
motion up all your
arms the great gesture of
Peace & acceptance Abhya
Mudra Mudra of fearlessness
Mudra of Elephant Calmed &
war-fear ended forever![32]

The epiphany on the Kyoto-Tokyo express left Ginsberg a man "in mid-age, finished with half desire / Tranquil in [his] hairy body"[33]:

> Joy, I am I
> the lone One singing to myself
> God come true—[34]

As if by miracle, all monster visions vanished from the poetry written after "The Change" and even failed to reappear when Ginsberg decided to resume his drug experiments. While in his 1965 *Paris Review* interview he claimed to have renounced all use of hallucinogenics, a footnote to this statement, added in 1966, reports that subsequent LSD experiments had produced no "monster vibration, no snake universe hallucinations."[35] Another such experiment inspired the "Wales Visitation" which Ginsberg describes as his "first great big Wordsworthian nature poem."[36] Here, the multiple million eyed "Monster of the Beginning Womb" has been replaced by the Great Mother of creativity and harmonious balance:

> O great Wetness, O Mother, No harm on thy body!
> Stare close, no imperfection in the grass,
> each flower Buddha-eye, repeating the story,
> the myriad-formed soul
> . . . .
> & look in the eyes of the branded lambs that stare
> breathing stockstill under dripping hawthorn—
> I lay down mixing my beard with the wet hair of the mountainside,
> smelling the brown vagina-moist ground, harmless,
> tasting the violet thistle-hair, sweetness—
> One being so balanced, so vast, that its softest breath
> moves every floweret in the stillness on the valley floor,
> trembles lamb-hair hung gossamer rain-beaded in the grass,
> lifts trees on their roots, birds in the great draught
> hiding their strength in the rain, bearing same weight.[37]

The lines, of course, bespeak an eagerness to proclaim the newly found happiness which belies the serenity they profess. But such exuberance is easily understood considering what preceded it, and nobody more than Ginsberg himself was aware of this self-defeating overassertiveness. So "Autumn Gold: New England Fall" from *The Fall of America* (1972) completely reverses our expectations of another "Wordsworthian nature poem" and, instead, gives a humorous self-portrait of the poet as the self-complacent saint and quester after "the spirit of the universe":

> I thought I was my body the last 4 years,
> and everytime I had a headache, God dealt me
> Ace of Spades—
> I thought I was mind-consciousness 10 yrs before that, and
> everytime I went to the Dentist the Kosmos disappeared,
> Now I don't know who I am—
> I wake up in the morning surrounded
> by meat and wires,
> pile drivers crashing thru the bedroom floor,
> War images rayed thru Television apartments,
> Machine chaos on Earth,
> Too many bodies, mouths bleeding on every Continent,
> my own wall plaster cracked,
> What kind of prophecy
> for this Nation.[38]

Ginsberg's recent development resembles Robert Bly's to the point where they could join hands in a common cause. Having come to terms with their psychoreligious problems, both began to devote more and more time to public issues, such as fighting the Vietnam war or the sociopolitical consciousness which caused it. The latter is the central theme of *The Fall of America,* in which the poet seems to refocus his concern with the horrific by directly analysing the destructive forces in our time. . . .

NOTES

1. Allen Ginsberg, *Kaddish and Other Poems* (San Francisco: City Lights Books, 1961), p. 86.

2. William Burroughs, *Naked Lunch* (New York: Grove Press, 1966), pp. viii, 97. Punctuation as in the novel.

3. Heinrich Zimmer, *Myths and Symbols in Indian Art and Civilization,* ed. Joseph Campbell. Bollingen Series, no. 6 (Princeton, N.J.: Princeton University Press, 1972), pp. 212–13, 215.

4. See Erich Neumann, *The Great Mother: An Analysis of the Archetype,* Bollingen Series, no. 47 (Princeton, N.J.: Princeton University Press, 1974), pp. 147–208.

5. *The Bhagavad Gita As It Is,* ed. A. C. Bhaktivedanta Swami (London: Collier-Macmillan, 1969), p. 229.

6. Alan Watts, *The Two Hands of God: The Myths of Polarity* (New York: Collier-Macmillan, 1969), p. 48.

7. *Summa Predicantium,* vol. 2 (Venice, 1586), 90v–91.

8. C. G. Jung, *The Spirit in Man, Art, and Literature.* Bollingen Series, no. 20 (Princeton, N.J.: Princeton University Press, 1972), pp. 82–83, 138–39.

9. *The Tibetan Book of the Dead,* ed. W. Y. Evans-Wentz, with a psychological commentary by C. G. Jung (London: Oxford University Press, 1960), p. xlix.

10. Ibid., pp. 142–43.

11. The title of the well-known study by Mario Praz.

12. William Carlos Williams, *Paterson* (New York: New Directions, 1963), p. 205.

13. Allen Ginsberg, *Empty Mirror* (New York: Totem Press-Corinth Books, 1961), pp. 46–47.

14. *Kaddish,* p. 86.

15. In *Writers at Work: Third Series,* ed. George Plimpton (New York: Viking Press, 1967), pp. 304–11.

16. D. M. Allen, *The New American Poetry* (New York: Grove Press, 1960), p. 416.

17. *Writers at Work,* pp. 289–90.

18. *Tibetan Book of the Dead,* pp. 131–32.

19. *Kaddish,* pp. 27, 31.

20. Ibid., p. 24.

21. Ibid., pp. 24, 25.

22. Allen Ginsberg, *Planet News* (San Francisco: City Lights Books, 1968), p. 132.

23. *Kaddish,* p. 29.

24. William Burroughs and Allen Ginsberg, *The Yage Letters* (San Francisco: City Lights Books, 1971), p. 52.

25. Ibid., pp. 53–64.

26. *Kaddish,* pp. 92–93.

27. Ibid., pp. 97–98.

28. Allen Ginsberg, *Indian Journals* (San Francisco: City Lights Books, 1970), pp. 28–29.

29. Ibid., pp. 208–10.

30. See Allen Ginsberg, "Mystery in the Universe," in *Rogue* 10, no. 3 (June 1965):6–7: "My poem 'The Change' is a renunciation of this first vision, as I'd got hung up on it abstractly, and it had become an obsession. So I'd had to remove it into my own body again. The realization that the whole visionary game was lost came to me on a train leaving Kyoto—at which point I started weeping and sobbing that I was still alive in a body that was going to die. Then I began looking around on the train and seeing all the other mortal faces, 'with their noses of weakness and woe,' and I saw how exquisitely dear they all were—we all were—so I pulled out my notebook, while the illumination was still glowing in my body, and, while my breath was still fitted to weeping, scribbled everything that came into my thought-stream—all the immediate perceptions of the moment in the order in which I could record them fastest. Later on, that becomes known as a poem. The mind supplies the language, if you don't interfere. That's something I learnt from Jack Kerouac,—how to let the mind supply the language."

31. *Planet News,* pp. 59–60.

32. Ibid., p. 61.

33. Ibid., p. 106.

34. Ibid., pp. 113–14.

35. *Writers at Work,* p. 312.

36. Jane Kramer, *Allen Ginsberg in America* (New York: Random House, 1969), p. 22.

37. *Planet News,* p. 141.

38. Allen Ginsberg, *The Fall of America: Poems of These States* (San Francisco: City Lights Books, 1972), pp. 50–51.

GEORGE DENNISON

Remarks from a "Symposium on the Writer's Situation"

The story of Ginsberg's development is the story of a great leap. I do not mean from one stage of mastery to another, but a leap of *being* which transforms life itself into a hazardous, yet brilliantly exciting, field of values. In this transformation deep subjects arise, and the act of sustaining them creates a universal relevance in the life itself. Ginsberg is loved by the young throughout the world.

> Nothing can make a man feel so much at home in the world as to realize that not only the role he has created for himself has value for his time, but that his very being, his whole underground, unconscious, instinctual life also belongs, in its most private aspect, without shame, to the universe of man. There is bound to be joy in this, and an end of the usual loneliness.

The words are Isaac Rosenfeld's. He is speaking of Gandhi. The thought applies remarkably to Ginsberg (whom Rosenfeld would surely praise were he alive today. Rosenfeld's own *An Age of Enormity*—now out of print—contains some of the finest literary criticism of the last thirty years).

Let me convert a few truisms into truths by giving them specific applications:

The formal structure of Ginsberg's poetry—the "nonlinear" accumulation of detail; the long breath of the rhapsodic voice— is identical with his attitude of compassion and his subject of the

From *New American Review* 9 (April 1970). Reprinted with permission.

natural sanctification of being. No amount of talent can achieve this kind of unity. I am saying, of course, that form and content are one; and that this unity, this syntax "is a function of the soul."

We know, too, that strong artists extend and transform the language. Both Ginsberg and [Paul] Goodman have done this. I am not aware, however, that their particular inventions have been mentioned yet by the critics, though it is precisely in these inventions that their stylistic brilliance resides.

The really dazzling quality of Goodman's style is the lucidity, accuracy, and downright *speed* of his thought—an unearthly speed that yet takes us along, and—if the word were usable—might deserve to be called *angelic*.

What does it consist of, this speed? In fact, it is a literary invention, i.e., a native quality of the author's. It consists of this: the original perception—far ahead of usage—that certain kinds of thoughts, certain presences of tradition, certain particular meanings, have begun to grow together, or will imminently grow together and take on, in our consciousness of them, the coherence of *forms*. He then treats them as forms, *new forms,* speeding us, as it were, into the future. Two remarkable things immediately happen: (1) *meaning* appears in its true colors as experience (for it is only as form that thought can deflect our lives—which, of course, is the underlying wisdom of psychotherapy); and (2) a value system springs into being, for we have suddenly been put into possession of the conclusions, the *therefore's,* the imperatives which were in fact imminent in the previously loose structure of experience and tested tradition. . . .

Where Goodman speeds us along—in what we must often experience as a shimmering arc—Ginsberg, yoga-style, creates a vortex that descends to stillness. He does not attempt to "expand our consciousness" (as many believe, equating his poetry with LSD), but copes instead with an already exacerbated, overburdened consciousness—for exactly this is the typical dilemma of modern man: that he is battered by mental forms he cannot act upon, or even join together: attitudes, pseudoevents, artifacts of culture, formulations of threat and anxiety, banal little myths of social cohesion—the swarming gnats of distraction. Ginsberg takes them upon himself (or finds them within himself), and then—often with hugely comic effect—proceeds to disentangle them, that is, *to name them*. His phrases are as compact and as crowded with presences as the totem poles of New Guinea—and many of the presences are, precisely, the totems of the berserk pseudoreligion of the Warfare State, now identified, named, and ranked. It is this naming, signifying quality of his language—it is associative, not analytical, and it is incredibly concentrated—that is such a striking invention. His use of it is beautiful: the distracting cloud is held in abeyance . . . we discover the still eye of the storm, separate sin from the sinner, and share a breath or two of the great breath of existence.

Bibliography

[Note: *For quick reference, a short-title bibliography of primary collections of poetry appears at the end of the Bibliography.*]

Collected Works
[Poetry, Lectures, Journals, Letters, etc.]

Airplane Dreams: Compositions from Journals. Toronto: Anansi, 1968; San Francisco: City Lights Books, 1969. [Thirty-five pages of text taken from journals kept between 1948 and 1968; "not exactly poems, nor not poems."]

Allen Verbatim: Lectures on Poetry, Politics, Consciousness. Edited by Gordon Ball. New York: McGraw-Hill, 1974.

Ankor Wat. London: Fulcrum Press, 1968. [Single poem; printed with photographs.]

As Ever: The Collected Correspondence of Allen Ginsberg and Neal Cassady. Berkeley: Creative Arts, 1977.

Bixby Canyon Ocean Path Word Breeze. New York: Gotham Book Mart, 1972. [Twenty-one pages; single poem, also printed in *The Fall of America*.]

Chicago Trial Testimony. San Francisco: City Lights Books, 1975.

Composed on the Tongue. Edited by Donald Allen. Bolinas, Calif.: Grey Fox Press, 1980). [Journal notes, lectures, conversations.]

Empty Mirror: Early Poems. With an introduction by William Carlos Williams. Corinth, N.Y.: Totem, 1961.

The Fall of America: Poems of These States, 1965–1971. San Francisco: City Lights Books, 1972.

First Blues, Rags, Ballads & Harmonium Songs, 1971–74. New York: Full Court Press, 1975. [Thirty-two improvised blues songs.]

The Gates of Wrath: Rhymed Poems, 1948–52. Bolinas, Calif.: Grey Fox Press, 1972.

Gay Sunshine Interview. With Allen Young. Bolinas, Calif.: Grey Fox Press, 1974.

Howl and Other Poems. San Francisco: City Lights Books, 1956.

Improvised Poetics. Berkeley: Anonym Press, 1972.

455

Indian Journals, March 1962–May 1963, Notebooks, Diary, Blank Pages, Writings. San Francisco: Dave Haselwood Books and City Lights Books, 1970.

Iron Horse. Toronto: The Coach House Press, 1972. [A long poem not printed elsewhere.]

Journals: Early Fifties Early Sixties. Edited by Gordon Ball. New York: Grove Press, 1977.

Kaddish and Other Poems, 1958–1960. San Francisco: City Lights Books, 1961.

Mind Breaths: Poems 1972–1977. San Francisco: City Lights Books, 1977.

Mostly Sitting Haiku. Paterson, N.J.: From Here Press, 1978. [Twenty-three-page pamphlet.]

Planet News, 1961–1967. San Francisco: City Lights Books, 1968.

Plutonian Ode: Poems 1977–1980. San Francisco: City Lights Books, 1982.

Poems All Over the Place, Mostly 70s. Cherry Valley, N.Y.: Cherry Valley Editions, 1978.

Reality Sandwiches, 1953–60. San Francisco: City Lights Books, 1963.

Sad Dust Glories: Poems During Work Summer in Woods. Berkeley: Workingmans Press, 1975. [Twenty-eight-page pamphlet.]

Scrap Leaves. Millbrook, N.Y.: Poet's Press, 1968.

Straight Hearts' Delight: Love Poems and Selected Letters 1947–1980. With Peter Orlovsky. Edited by Winston Leyland. San Francisco: Gay Sunshine Press, 1980.

T.V. Baby Poems. London: Cape Goliard Press, 1967; N.Y.: Grossman, 1968. [Seven poems later printed in *Planet News* and *The Fall of America*.]

To Eberhart from Ginsberg. Lincoln, Mass.: Penmaen Press, 1976.

The Visions of the Great Rememberer. With letters by Neal Cassady and drawings by Basil King. Amherst, Mass.: Mulch Press, 1974. [Reflections on Kerouac.]

The Yage Letters. With William S. Burroughs. San Francisco: City Lights Books, 1963. [Correspondence having to do with "Ayahuasca, an Amazon spiritual potion."]

Reference Collections

Dowden, George. *A Bibliography of Works by Allen Ginsberg, October, 1943 to July 1, 1967.* San Francisco: City Lights Books, 1971.

Kraus, Michelle P. *Allen Ginsberg, an Annotated Bibliography, 1969–1977.* Metuchen, N.J.: Scarecrow Press, 1980. [Includes much secondary material, concentrating on the underground press.]

Selected Secondary Material

[Note: *An asterisk indicates that the work, or a portion of it, is included in this volume.*]

Alexander, Floyce. "Allen Ginsberg's Metapolitics: From Moloch to the Millennium." *Research Studies of Washington State University*, June 1970.*

Allen, Donald and Warren Tallman. *The Poetics of the New American Poetry*. New York: Grove Press, 1973.

Alvarez, A. "Ginsberg and the Herd Instinct." *Observer* (London), 14 May 1961.*

Ammons, A. R. "Ginsberg's New Poems." *Poetry*, June 1964.*

Bartlett, Jeffrey. "*Howl* in High School" and "Allen Ginsberg Today." *North Dakota Quarterly*, Spring 1982.

Berkson, Bill. "Fourteen Books." *Poetry*, July 1969.

Berman, Paul. "Intimations of Mortality." *Parnassus: Poetry in Review*, Fall–Winter 1979.*

———. "Buddhagate: The Trashing of Allen Ginsberg." *Village Voice*, 23 July 1980.

———. Review of *Plutonian Ode*. *Village Voice*, 23 March 1982.*

Bliss, Shepherd. "Men, Poetry, and the Military: A Memoir."*

Bloom, Harold. "On Ginsberg's *Kaddish*," in *The Ringers in the Tower: Studies in Romantic Tradition* (Chicago: University of Chicago Press, 1971).

Bly, Robert. "The Other Night in Heaven." *The Fifties 3*, 1959.*

Borawski, Walta. "Curls Curses & Cum." *Boston Gay Review*, Fall 1978.

Bowering, George. "How I Hear 'Howl.'" *Beaver Kosmos Folio 1* (Montreal), 1969.*

Breslin, James. "Allen Ginsberg: The Origins of 'Howl' and 'Kaddish.'" *Iowa Review*, Spring 1977.*

Brinnin, John Malcolm. "The Theory and Practices of Poetry." *New York Times Book Review*, 2 March 1975.

Brownjohn, Alan. "Fblup!" *New Statesman*, 10 January 1969.*

Cargas, Henry J. *Daniel Berrigan and Contemporary Protest Poetry*. New Haven: College and University Press, 1972.

Carroll, Paul. "Death is a Letter that was Never Sent." *Evergreen Review*, July–August 1961.*

———. Interview with Allen Ginsberg. *Playboy*, April 1969.

———. *The Poem in Its Skin*. Chicago: Big Table, 1969.*

Carruth, Hayden. "Chants, Oracles, Body-Rhythms." *New York Times Book Review*, 19 March 1978.*

Ciardi, John. "Epitaph for the Dead Beats." *Saturday Review,* 6 February 1960.

Clark, Tom. Interview with Allen Ginsberg. *Writers at Work: The Paris Review Interviews.* 3d ser. New York: Viking, 1967.*

———. Interview with Allen Ginsberg. *Boulder Monthly,* March 1979.

———. *The Great Naropa Poetry Wars.* Santa Barbara: Cadmus, 1980.

Cohen, Mortimer J. "Is This Poetry?" *Jewish Exponent,* 10 November 1961.*

Cox, Harvey. "Open Letter to Allen Ginsberg." *Commonweal,* 21 April 1967.

"Craft Interview with Allen Ginsberg." *New York Quarterly,* Spring 1971.

Dennison, George. "Symposium: The Writer's Situation." *New American Review 9,* April 1970.

Dickey, James. "From Babel to Byzantium." *Sewanee Review,* Summer 1957.*

———. "Confession is Not Enough." *New York Times Book Review,* 9 July 1961.

"The Disorganization Man." *Time,* 9 June 1958.*

Eberhart, Richard. "West Coast Rhythms." *New York Times Book Review,* 2 September 1956.*

Eckman, Frederick. "Neither Tame Nor Fleecy." *Poetry,* September 1957.

Ehrlich, J. W., editor. *Howl of the Censor.* San Carlos, Calif.: Nourse, 1961.

Elman, Richard. "Beyond Self-Absorption." *Nation,* 12 November 1977.*

Faas, Ekbert. *Towards a New American Poetics: Essays and Interviews.* Santa Barbara: Black Sparrow, 1978.*

Ferlinghetti, Lawrence. "Horn on *Howl.*" *Evergreen Review,* Winter 1957.*

Géfin, Laszlo. *Ideogram, History of a Poetic Method.* Austin: University of Texas Press, 1982.*

Gertmenian, Donald. "Remembering and Rereading 'Howl.'" *Ploughshares,* Fall 1975.

Ginsberg, Louis. "To Allen Ginsberg." *Prairie Schooner,* Summer 1959.*

Grossman, Allen. "Allen Ginsberg: The Jew as an American Poet." *Judaism,* Fall 1962.*

Hazel, R. "Prefigures." *Nation,* 11 November 1961.

Heffernan, James. "Politics and Freedom: Refractions of Blake in Joyce Cary and Allen Ginsberg." *Romantic and Modern.* Ed. George Bornstein. Pittsburgh: University of Pittsburgh Press, 1977.*

Henry, William A., III. "In New York: *Howl* Becomes a Hoot." *Time,*
    7 December 1981.*

Hollander, John. "Poetry Chronicle." *Partisan Review,* Spring 1957.*

Howard, Richard. "Allen Ginsberg." *Alone With America: Essays on the
    Art of Poetry in the United States Since 1950.* New York: Atheneum,
    1980.

Hunsberger, Bruce. "Kit Smart's Howl." *Wisconsin Studies in Contem-
    porary Literature,* Winter–Spring 1965.*

Ignatow, David. "Accents of Death and Endurance." *New Leader,* 31
    July & 7 August 1961.

Justice, Donald. "San Francisco and Palo Alto." *Western Review* (Iowa
    City), Spring 1958.*

Klingenberg, E. "Ginsberg's Czech Expulsion." *Censorship* (London),
    Summer 1965.*

Kostelanetz, Richard. *New Republic,* 22 October 1977.

Kramer, Jane. *Allen Ginsberg in America.* New York: Random House,
    1969.

Leary, Timothy. "In the Beginning, Leary Turned on Ginsberg . . ."
    Esquire, July 1968.*

Lehman, David. "When the Sun Tries to Go On." *Poetry,* September
    1969.*

Lucie-Smith, Edward. *Mystery in the Universe, Notes on an Interview with
    Allen Ginsberg.* London: Turret Books, 1965.

Marin, Peter. "Spiritual Obedience." *Harpers,* February 1979.

Martin, Robert K. *The Homosexual Tradition in American Poetry.* Austin:
    University of Texas Press, 1979.

Merrill, Thomas F. *Allen Ginsberg.* New York: Twayne, 1969.

Mersmann, James F. *Out of the Vietnam Vortex:* Lawrence: University of
    Kansas Press, 1974.

Middlebrook, Diane. "Bound to Each Other." *Parnassus: Poetry in Re-
    view,* Spring–Summer 1974.

Miller, Brown. "Leaving Things Alone." *Small Press Review,* De-
    cember 1977.

Miller, James E. *The American Quest for a Supreme Fiction.* Chicago:
    University of Chicago Press, 1979.

Milosz, Czeslaw. "The Image of the Beast." *Visions from San Francisco
    Bay.* New York: Farrar, Straus & Giroux, 1982.*

Molesworth, Charles. "Republican Objects and Utopian Moments:
    The Poetry of Robert Lowell and Allen Ginsberg." In *The Fierce
    Embrace.* Columbia: University of Missouri Press, 1979.*

Moore, Marianne. Letter to Allen Ginsberg dated 4 July 1952.*

———. Letter to Louis Ginsberg dated 11 July 1952.*

Moramarco, Fred. "Moloch's Poet: A Retrospective Look at Allen

Ginsberg's Poetry." *American Poetry Review*, September–October 1982.*

Morse, Carl. "Reality Sandwiches." *Village Voice*, 14 November 1963.

Mottram, Eric. *Allen Ginsberg in the Sixties*. Seattle: Unicorn Bookshop, 1972.*

———. *The Wild Good and the Heart Ultimately: Ginsberg's Art of Persuasion*. London: Spanner Books, 1982.

Newberry, Mike. "'Kaddish' for Money Minded Madmen." *The Worker*, 7 November 1961.*

O'Neil, Paul. "The Only Rebellion Around." *Life*, 30 November 1959.

Oppen, George. "Three Poets." *Poetry*, August 1962.

Peters, Robert. *The Great American Poetry Bake-Off*. Metuchen, N.J.: Scarecrow Press, 1979.

Phillips, Robert. *The Confessional Poets*. Carbondale: Southern Illinois University Press, 1973.

Podhoretz, Norman. "A Howl of Protest in San Francisco." *New Republic*, 16 September 1957.*

———. "The Know-Nothing Bohemians." *Partisan Review*, Spring 1958.

Portugés, Paul. *The Visionary Poetics of Allen Ginsberg*. Santa Barbara: Ross-Erikson, 1978.*

———. "Allen Ginsberg's Paul Cézanne and the *Pater Omnipotens Aeterna Deus*." *Contemporary Literature*, Summer 1980.*

Rexroth, Kenneth. "San Francisco Letter." *Evergreen Review 2*, Summer 1957.*

Rodman, Selden. "Three Neurotics." *National Review*, 1 September 1978.*

Rosenberg, Harold. "Six American Poets." *Commentary*, October 1961.

Rosenthal, M. L. "Poet of the New Violence." *Nation*, 23 February 1957.*

———. *The New Poets: American and British Poetry Since World War II*. New York: Oxford University Press, 1967.*

Rosenthal M. L. and Sally M. Gall. *The Modern Poetic Sequence: The Genius of Modern Poetry*. New York: Oxford University Press, 1983.

Rumaker, Michael. "Allen Ginsberg's 'Howl.'" *Black Mountain Review*, Fall 1957.*

Sanders, Ed. *The Party, A Chronological Perspective on a Confrontation at a Buddhist Seminary*. Woodstock, N.Y.: Poetry, Crime & Culture Press, 1977.

Scully, James. "Search for Passion." *Nation*, 16 November 1963.*

Seelye, John. "The Sum of '48." *New Republic,* 12 October 1974.*

Shapiro, Harvey. "Exalted Lament." *Midstream,* Autumn 1961.*

Shechner, Mark. "The Survival of Allen Ginsberg." *Partisan Review,* Spring 1979.*

Shively, Charles. "Allen Ginsberg: A Prophet on the Electric Networks." *Gay Sunshine,* June–July 1973.*

———. "25 Rainbows on My Windowsill." *Gay Sunshine,* Autumn–Winter 1980.*

Simpson, Louis. *A Revolution in Taste: Studies of Dylan Thomas, Allen Ginsberg, Sylvia Plath, and Robert Lowell.* New York: Macmillan, 1978.*

Sorrentino, Gilbert. "Firing a Flare for the Avant-Garde." *San Francisco Examiner* ["Book Week" magazine], 3 January 1965.

Stepanchev, Stephen. *American Poetry Since 1945: A Critical Survey.* New York: Harper & Row, 1965.

Stephenson, Gregory. "*Howl:* A Reading." *Palantir* (London), April 1983.*

Stimpson, Catherine R. "The Beat Generation and the Trials of Homosexual Liberation." *Salmagundi,* Fall 1982–Winter 1983.

Symons, Julian. *New Statesman,* 3 November 1967.

Tallman, Warren. "Mad Song: Allen Ginsberg's San Francisco Poems." *Open Letter,* 3d ser. (Winter 1976–77).*

Thurley, Geoffrey. *The American Moment: American Poetry in the Mid-Century.* London: Edward Arnold, 1977.*

Trilling, Diana. "The Other Night at Columbia: A Report from the Academy." *Partisan Review,* Spring 1959.*

Tysh, Christine. *Allen Ginsberg: Étude, Choix de Poèmes.* Paris: Seghers, 1974.

Tytell, John. "Allen Ginsberg Howls Again." *Soho News,* 24 November 1981.

———. "Conversation with Allen Ginsberg." *Partisan Review,* Summer 1974.

———. *Naked Angels.* New York: McGraw-Hill, 1976.*

Vance, Thomas H. "American Poetry of Protest, from World War II to the Present." *Amerikanische Literatur im 20. Jahrhundert.* Ed. Alfred Weber and Dietmar Haack. Gottingen: Vandernhoek & Ruprecht, 1971.

Vendler, Helen. *New York Times Book Review,* 31 August 1969.

———. Review of *The Fall of America. New York Times Book Review,* 15 April 1973.*

———. "Poets." *New Yorker,* 18 September 1978.

Weinberger, Eliot. "Dharma Demogogy." *Nation,* 19 April 1980.

Whalen, Philip. *San Francisco Chronicle* ["This World" magazine], 4 August 1963.

White, C. "A Tortured Romanticism." *Manchester Guardian,* 1 August 1963.

Whittemore, Reed. "From 'Howl' to OM." *New Republic,* 25 July 1970.*

Williams, William Carlos. Letter to Marianne Moore dated 24 May 1952.*

Wilson, Robert Anton. "The Poet as Radar System." *Liberation,* November 1962.*

Zweig, Paul. "A Music of Angels." *Nation,* 10 March 1969.*

Short-Title Bibliography

[Primary collections of Allen Ginsberg's poetry, in chronological order]

Howl. San Francisco: City Lights Books, 1956.

Kaddish. San Francisco: City Lights Books, 1961.

Empty Mirror [early poems]. Corinth, N.Y.: Totem, 1961.

Reality Sandwiches. San Francisco: City Lights Books, 1963.

Planet News. San Francisco: City Lights Books, 1968.

The Fall of America. San Francisco: City Lights Books, 1972.

The Gates of Wrath [early poems]. Bolinas, Calif.: Grey Fox, 1972.

Mind Breaths. San Francisco: City Lights Books, 1977.

Plutonian Ode. San Francisco: City Lights Books, 1982.

POETS ON POETRY

David Lehman, General Editor
Donald Hall, Founding Editor

New titles

Thom Gunn, *The Occasions of Poetry*
Edward Hirsch, *Responsive Reading*
Philip Larkin, *Required Writing*
James Tate, *The Route as Briefed*

Recently published

John Hollander, *The Poetry of Everyday Life*
William Logan, *All the Rage*
Geoffrey O'Brien, *Bardic Deadlines*
Anne Stevenson, *Between the Iceberg and the Ship*
C. K. Williams, *Poetry and Consciousness*

Also available are collections by

A. R. Ammons, Robert Bly, Philip Booth, Marianne Boruch,
Hayden Carruth, Fred Chappell, Amy Clampitt, Tom Clark,
Douglas Crase, Robert Creeley, Donald Davie, Peter Davison,
Tess Gallagher, Suzanne Gardinier, Allen Grossman, Thom Gunn,
John Haines, Donald Hall, Joy Harjo, Robert Hayden,
Daniel Hoffman, Jonathan Holden, Andrew Hudgins,
Josephine Jacobsen, Weldon Kees, Galway Kinnell, Mary Kinzie,
Kenneth Koch, Richard Kostelanetz, Maxine Kumin,
Martin Lammon (editor), David Lehman, Philip Levine,
John Logan, William Matthews, William Meredith, Jane Miller,
Carol Muske, John Frederick Nims, Gregory Orr, Alicia Ostriker,
Marge Piercy, Anne Sexton, Charles Simic, Louis Simpson,
William Stafford, May Swenson, Richard Tillinghast,
Diane Wakoski, Alan Williamson, Charles Wright,
and James Wright